German Jewry

German Jewry

Its History and Sociology

Selected Essays by Werner J. Cahnman

Edited, with an introduction
by
Joseph B. Maier, Judith Marcus, and Zoltán Tarr

Transaction Publishers
New Brunswick (U.S.A.) and Oxford (U.K.)

Library of Congress Catalog Number: 88-20185
ISBN: 0-88738-253-3
Printed in the United States of America

Library of Congress Cataloging-in-Publication Data
Cahnman, Werner Jacob, 1902–
   German Jewry: its history and sociology: selected essays by Werner J. Cahnman; edited and with an introduction by Joseph B. Maier, Judith Marcus, and Zoltan Tarr.
      p.   cm.
   Bibliography: p.
   Includes index.
   ISBN 0-88738-253-3
   1. Jews—Germany—History.   2. Jews—Germany—Social conditions.
3. Jews—Germany (West)—Munich—History—20th century.
4. Germany—Ethnic relations.   5. Munich (Germany)—Ethnic relations.
I. Maier, Joseph, 1911–   .   II. Marcus, Judith, 1929–
III. Tarr, Zoltan.   IV. Title.
DS135.G3C34   1988   88-20185
943'.004924—dc19

Contents

Acknowledgments

This volume is dedicated to Dr. Gisella Levi Cahnman, who devotedly undertook the task of preserving and sorting her husband's literary estate. Without her devotion and generous support this collection could not have been.

We are fortunate in having found in Irving Louis Horowitz a knowledgeable and appreciative colleague and publisher.

Anita Stock's and Esther M. Luckett's careful attention to the editorial process at every stage was crucial in bringing the manuscript to its final form.

The Editors

Introduction:
Werner J. Cahnman on the Historical Sociology of the Jews

In 1935, two years into his self-exile from Nazi Germany and settled temporarily in Zurich before his permanent exile in America, Thomas Mann made the following entry in his diary:

> Had a visitor this afternoon, a Dr. Cahnman from Munich, young Jew, of delightful southern German disposition, and very smart to boot. We had some interesting but depressing discussions about the goings-on in Germany which lasted until almost 8 o'clock in the evening.[1]

The young Jew of Bavarian charm and keen intelligence who thus impressed the world-famous writer was Werner J. Cahnman. He went on to become a fellow refugee and sociologist in America, a proponent of comparative historical sociology, ethnicity, and intercultural relations, and a Tönnies scholar. After Hitler's ascent to power in 1933, Cahnman had undertaken several clandestine missions on behalf of his beleaguered people, especially the Jewish communities of the southern German region. It was probably on one such occasion that he payed a visit to Mann.

Werner Cahnman would have been the first to admit that such a friendly get-together and man-to-man talk would hardly have taken place under normal circumstances back in Munich. By 1935, though, things were anything but normal, and the same social rules applied no more. Albeit for different reasons, both Thomas Mann and Werner Cahnman found themselves excluded from the "New Order," and both, in turn, did what the order of the day demanded of them. All things considered, Cahnman was for Mann a source of reliable information about what was happening in Germany in general, and in Munich—erstwhile hometown of Thomas Mann—in particular.

The unfolding political and social crises in Germany led to young Cahnman's ever more intense absorption in Jewish learning and Jewish political and social activities. As *Syndikus* to the Centralverein deutscher Staatsbürger jüdischen Glaubens, teacher at the Jüdisches Lehrhaus, voluntary "social worker" (as he called himself at the time), and, after 1934, as "a leader of an illegal organization" who was briefly thrown into the Munich police prison, he gained first-hand experience with the "New Order," its ideologies and its

ix

praxis. Cahnman was, however, more than a social worker and man of intense community concern; he was also a shrewd participant-observer and astute analyst. What he said about himself some forty-odd years later may go a long way toward explaining and evaluating Werner Cahnman's concerns and writings from the 1930s on. In his review of Mario Cuomo's book *Forest Hills Diary—The Crisis of Low Income Housing* (1975), in which he figures as Cuomo's "sociologist friend from Forest Hills," Cahnman states:

> I am a Forest Hills [instead of Munich] resident, a sociologist who is a race and intercultural relations specialist, and I am active in Jewish life. It goes without saying that I am aware of the complexities of urban living. I believe I know of the needs [of the newcomers] as well as of the aspirations of the neighbors in the midst of whom I live.[2]

Indeed, Cahnman's essays, studies, and monographs—published and unpublished—dealing with Jewish history, community and family history, Jewish-Gentile relations, Jewish leaders and thinkers, and, last but not least, the once-existing German-Jewish symbiosis, attest to his awareness and deep understanding of the complexities and problems inherent in his chosen themes. As to why he devoted a great part of his life and scholarship to the examination of the various facets of Jewish Diaspora life, Cahnman's most likely answer would have been that it was the times and themes that chose him.

Scattered throughout his related writings we find the sense of urgency to record, to document, to tell, and to elevate to ideal-typical status the tribulations and ultimate fate of big-city and small-town Jewish communities, including his own family.

Werner Cahnman looked at the late 1920s of the Weimar Republic as the time when exciting things happened, full of "intellectual controversy," but also the time when "public affairs" took a discouraging turn. The 1920s also witnessed—at least in Germany—an abandonment of hope for meaningful political action and the collectivities' inward turn. As far as the Jewish communities were concerned, he noted that "Jewish themes pure and simple came to the fore," as the 1920s in general saw a revival of Jewish consciousness. For example, there was a large increase in the membership of the Central-verein, the principal Jewish civic defense organization; the Jewish Lehrhaus movement gained momentum, and there were many books on the essence of Judaism, the meaning of Jewish history, and Jewish philosophy and mysticism by Leo Baeck, Franz Rosenzweig, Martin Buber, and others.

All the while, there was in Bavaria a concoction of separatist, nationalist, clerical, and racial sentiments that put its stamp on post–World War I Munich life and made the city appear more antisemitic than ever before. It was only in the late 1920s that the Catholic Church and its party recognized that Hitler's movement stood against Christian values as well as against popular government and Bavarian autonomy, but by that time it was too late to halt the tide. Thus Cahnman felt a special urgency to collect data and describe Jewish life in order to preserve what otherwise would be irretrievably lost. His efforts were facilitated by his fatherly "inheritance," namely, a "historical enthusiasm" that made him collect family- and community-related data "since early youth, partly by consulting archives," interviewing older relatives, and so on.[3] It is safe to say that one of his last full-scale works, *Jews and Gentiles: The Historical Sociology of Their Relations* (unpublished manuscript), had been germinating ever since. Werner Cahnman's concise statement on the whys and hows of this study also describes his lifelong preoccupations:

> I have been working on a comprehensive, yet concentrated, account of Jewish-Gentile relations for a long time. I believe that a scholarly conceived yet fluidly written account of [these] relations is essential for the self-understanding of the present generation.
>
> The topic of the Jewish experience among the peoples in the midst of whom Jews live is not identical, although it is overlapping, with the usual histories of antisemitism. If the focus is on antisemitism, Jewish history is made to appear as if it were a record of unmitigated hostility against the Jewish people and of passivity on the part of the Jews. Jewish-Gentile relations refer to the mutuality of contacts, positive as well as antagonistic, even if conflict situations continue to require particular attention.
>
> [This account follows] a historical sequence, [but it] is sociological in conception. [It looks at the] patterns [that] are recognizable as common to all, or almost all, ages and places in which Jewish history has been enacted.[4]

Werner Cahnman's life came full circle in the 1970s, when he branched out from scholarship to promote intercultural relations and preservation of the Jewish past in a direct, practical way: Acting on his deeply felt conviction that after the obliteration of Jewish communities and institutions all around Europe, it was imperative that still-remaining, visible testimonies of the past be saved, he called upon his peers to establish the Rashi Association for the Preservation of Jewish Cultural Monuments in Europe. He designated Germany as the first and foremost place of activity because "the aim of Hitler to obliterate all traces of Jewish life from German soil must be frustrated."[5] Just as importantly, the sites which will be thus salvaged—places where Jews have lived and prayed and gone to school and buried their dead—will serve the future. As he wrote: "They must serve as pillars of the new Jewish consciousness which is to arise out of the memories of the past." Moreover, Cahnman thought that visible signs of Jewish continuity would have a significant psychological and educational impact: Gentiles in all these countries would be made to realize that Jewish history was part and parcel of their own, their country's history. Just as in his hometown back in the 1930s, with Werner Cahnman community concerns, scholarly endeavors, and Jewish activism always and everywhere went hand-in-hand.

The Man

Werner Jacob Cahnman was born in Munich on 30 September 1902 into an upper-middle-class Jewish family. His father, by then director of a chemical factory, was born in a small village, Rheinbischofsheim. He had come to Munich to get an education and finally settled there. The family of Cahnman's mother, on the other hand, belonged to the Munich haute bourgeoisie. His uncle, Anton Schülein, was a famous Munich painter; other members of the family were bankers, jurists, or industrialists. As recounted in an (unpublished) autobiographical essay,[6] Cahnman was exposed to two very different kinds of Judaism. His father's people held on to family and community values and displayed a somewhat rustic and folksy Judaism but no Jewish learning. The learned and highly cultured members of his mother's family were Jewish in a declaratory sense only; their free-thinking Judaism had a strong ethical bent. His mother was well-versed in Spinoza and Mendelssohn, but she had no use for dietary laws; nevertheless, she respected her husband's traditional values and helped to observe the Friday eve and Passover rituals. Cahnman's poignant summary of her fate shows the fragility of the position, and even the very existence, of the assimilated German-Jewish bourgeoisie: "The main idea of my mother was," said Cahnman, "that everybody, but especially the Jews, should promote justice in the world. She died in Piaski, Poland in unimaginably terrible circumstances and in a situation of utmost injustice."[7]

Werner Cahnman received his secondary education in the classical atmosphere of a Munich *Gymnasium*. He said he could recall no disagreeable experience in school; he thought his classmates liked him but were aware that he was Jewish, and he was "aware of their awareness." Cahnman grew up in an environment that put *Kultur* above everything else, where artists, intellectuals, professionals, and businessmen met and discussed the most diverse ideas, issues, and problems of the day, ranging from literature and the arts to socialism, Zionism, and women's issues. From a father, who was a traditionalist, a vice president and later president of the local chapter of B'nai B'rith, and an aunt, a well-known writer of stories about everyday Jewish life, Cahnman also learned to appreciate the feeling of belonging to a *Gemeinschaft*. Such diverse exposures put their indelible stamp on his views, scholarship, and preoccupations.

From 1921 to 1927, Cahnman studied economics, history, political science, and sociology at Berlin and at Munich universities. He wrote his dissertation, *Der ökonomische Pessimismus und das Ricardo'sche System* (1927; published in 1929), under the sponsorship of the noted exponent of *Sozialpolitik*, Professor Zwiedineck-Südenhorst. It may be of some historical interest that one of Cahnman's fellow students at the latter's seminars was Rudolf Hess. Cahnman's impressions of Hess, written up in an (unpublished) essay entitled "Rudolf Hess as a Symbol,"[8] portray the future deputy of the Führer as the prototype of a war-torn generation, now dipping into old-time romanticism and about to conceive an imperialist dream; Hess was a symbol of the forces that were operating and foreshadowing the catastrophe that was to follow.

Parallel with his university studies went Cahnman's abiding interest in the tribulations of the Jewish Diaspora in general, and in present-day concerns in particular. Still a teenager, he read widely and indiscriminately everything relating to things Jewish. The most profound influence on his thinking at the time was made by Arthur Ruppin's *Juden der Gegenwart* (English version: *The Jews in the Modern World*, London, 1934) and by Theodor Herzl's Zionist writings along with Davis Trietsch's *Palästina-Handbuch*. As a consequence, he developed a strong interest in demography and started to collect data on conversion, intermarriage, declining birthrates, and other matters relating to the continuity and vitality of the Jewish community; at the same time he made himself an expert of sorts on the early settlements in Palestine.

During his university years, his interests shifted increasingly towards Jewish learning, philosophy, and direct political activity. He thoroughly absorbed the writings of Leo Baeck, Franz Rosenzweig, Martin Buber, Graetz, Dubnow, Achad Haam, and Edmond Fleg, among others. He also mastered the antisemetic as well as the philo-Semitic literature of his time. His very first article, "Judentum und Volksgemeinschaft," published in *Der Morgen* in 1926, was a characteristic combination of elements: historiography, romantic philosophy, political democracy, and Jewish ethnicity. He met Buber in Munich and through his influence became first a student and later a lecturer at the Jüdisches Lehrhaus of Munich. After completing his university studies, Cahnman worked for a short time at his father's chemical factory but soon moved on to Berlin where he became a research associate of the Chamber of Industry and Commerce (1928–29). For 1929–30 he was offered a research position at the Institute of World Economics in Kiel.

The greatest challenge for Cahnman came when he was offered the position of *Syndikus* for Bavaria of the Centralverein deutscher Staatsbürger jüdischen Glaubens, the major defense organization for German Jewry. Considering the situation of German Jewry in the year 1930, such a position obviously demanded maturity, experience, and confidence, to say nothing of considerable cunning and political savvy. The fact that the elder statesmen of the organization chose the 28-year-old Werner Cahnman shows how apt Thomas Mann was in his appraisal of his young Jewish visitor. From day one, Cahnman was aware of the seriousness of the situation and the need for good defensive tactics on the part of the Centralverein. Soon enough, it was a matter of survival, first of the organization itself—its offices were first ransacked and ultimately closed in the wake of the 1933 *Machtergreifung*—and increasingly of the Munich Jewish community. Cahnman was imprisoned for having continued his Centralverein work illegally but was soon freed thanks to the intervention of his one-time fellow student, Rudolf Hess. He described and analyzed his work and the events leading up to and following the closing of the Centralverein in Munich in his essay, "The Jews in Munich: 1918–1943," published in this volume.

Until his escape from Germany in June 1939, Cahnman was working full-time for his beleaguered people in Munich and in the whole southern region. He often spoke of this period as his "social worker" years, although he was far more than that. These years saw several studies, beginning with the 1937 article, "Warum Hebräisch lernen?" in the *Frankfurter Israelitisches Gemeindeblatt*, and including "Village and Small-Town Jews of Germany," and "Role and Significance of the Jewish Artisan Class," published many years later in America.[9] But his main efforts, and most of his energies, were invested in saving records, keeping statistics, and doing battle with German officialdom to shore up Jewish community resources. Officially, he was the statistician of the Israelitische Kultusgemeinde of Munich, ostensibly a clerical position. The nature and scope of his activities, however, went far beyond that. He made common cause with, and sought to forge alliance among, the most diverse groups of people—Zionists, anti-Zionists, a variety of youth associations, and the *Ostjuden*—because he perceived the abiding need for strengthening bonds to face the advancing Nazi threat. In due course, he even became a severe critic of the Berlin leadership of the Centralverein because he considered its hyperpatriotic stance to be both unrealistic and undignified.

By then, Cahnman had considerable experience as a liaison man; already in 1932 he had been charged by the Centralverein with maintaining contact with Austrian sister organizations; in 1937, he visited Austria illegally in order to discuss the situation with religious leaders and scholars. In the spring of 1937, he went to Palestine where he met with—among others—Judah Magnes, president of the Hebrew University. But he abandoned plans for eventual settlement there, because he felt that his place was in Munich where help was badly needed. "I was a Jewish official, after all," he explained. In that capacity, he organized the *Berufsumschichtung* (retraining) of young Jews who had lost their jobs; he participated in securing the food supply to the Jewish community and in counseling those embarking on emigration. His activities, legal and illegal, came to an abrupt end when in November 1938 he was sent to the Dachau concentration camp. He was released two months later on the condition that he emigrate. On 20 June 1939 Cahnman left Germany[10] for England with a transit visa secured for him by the sponsorship of a distant relative and Bloomsbury House. In April 1940 Cahnman emigrated into the United States.

His Americanization began almost immediately with a summer seminar for foreign scholars and teachers at the Brewster Free Academy, the Quaker School in Wolfboro, New Hampshire. Herbert A. Miller, the resident scholar, had evaluated Cahnman's background and intellectual interests and declared him to be a "race and culture specialist in sociology." At Miller's recommendation he then went to study as a visiting Ph.D. in the Department of Sociology at the University of Chicago. His teachers—and later mentors—were Everett Hughes, Herbert Blumer, Robert Redfield, and, above all, Robert E. Park. With the latter, Cahnman established a long relationship and friendship. Things did not work out that well with Louis Wirth, another Chicago sociologist and Jewish sociologist to boot. This was probably due to Cahnman's survivalist perspective, projecting the survival of ethnic groups for both normative and empirical reasons. Wirth, on the other hand, held an assimilationist viewpoint. It was in Chicago, too, that Werner met and married Dr. Gisella Levi, a former Fermi student in Turin, Italy (and cousin of recent Nobel prize winner Dr. Rita Levi-Montalcini)[11] who taught physics at that time in Chicago.

In the years 1943–45, Cahnman was teaching sociology at Fisk and Vanderbilt universities in Nashville, Tennessee, followed by a short stretch at the University of Atlanta when Louis Wirth recommended him for the position of researcher at the National Jewish Welfare Board beginning in 1946. "In a way, I was thus relegated to an [academic] backwater," he wistfully remarked. It was the friendship and scholarly solidarity of such Jewish academics as Salo Baron or Mark Wischnitzer that sustained him in those trying years. There were others, such as Chaim Greenberg, editor of the (Labor Zionist) *Jewish Frontier*, who published many of his papers, or Henry Hurwitz, editor of the *Menorah Journal*, who did likewise.

In the mid-1950s, Rabbi Mordecai M. Kaplan and Eugen Kohn asked Cahnman to join the editorial board of *The Reconstructionist* magazine although he could not be considered a proper Reconstructionist. Thus, somewhat belatedly, Cahnman did find his home in American Jewish life. Until his death, he fulfilled his editorial duties faithfully and also published extensively in that magazine. At the same time he held other positions, which helped him to ease into American life, such as senior evaluation analyst at the International Broadcasting Division of the State Department, and executive secretary of the Conference on Jewish Social Studies.

No doubt the greatest satisfaction of the remaining two decades of his life was his finally making it in academia. First, he was a lecturer in sociology at

Hunter College (1956–59) and at Yeshiva University (1958–62). According to Cahnman, he was "finally rescued for sociology" when Joseph B. Maier, then chairman of the Department of Sociology at the Newark College of Arts & Sciences, brought him to Rutgers University in 1961. He retired from Rutgers as full professor in 1968. He had also lectured at the New School for Social Research in New York City and was a visiting professor at his old alma mater in Munich as well as at the University of Michigan.

Just as at the beginning of his career, the last years of Werner Cahnman's life were filled with varied scholarly, professional and political-social activities. At this time too he tried to do justice to all of them. For sociology, he charted a new way as a founding member of the (first) Historical Sociology Section of the American Sociological Association and by publishing (with Alvin Boskoff) the seminal volume, *Sociology and History* (1964). It signified the final emergence of his systematic concern with the historical perspective in sociology. At the same time, Cahnman garnered recognition as a leading Tönnies scholar. In fact, he was already terminally ill with cancer when he delivered the principal address at the Tönnies Symposium in Kiel, West Germany (1980). All along, he was preoccupied with the conceptual clarification of the term *stranger* as used by many German scholars from Brentano to Tönnies to Simmel. Passionately, and at times somewhat cantankerously, he argued for the validity of the term *Vermittler* (as against *pariah*, used sociologically by Max Weber and psychologically by Hannah Arendt) in the case of the Jews of Europe; like Simmel, another German Jew, Cahnman thought of himself as an "intermediary."

From a research trip to Israel, Cahnman brought back much archival data both for his ongoing project "Jews and Gentiles" (completed before his death and hitherto unpublished) and other historical accounts he planned to write on Jewish life in Germany and Austria. He prominently participated in the work of Columbia's "University Seminar on Content and Methods of the Social Sciences," and just as prominently organized and conducted the Conference on Intermarriage and Jewish Life, the proceedings of which were published under his editorship.[12] Much of his remaining time he devoted to the establishment and work of the above-mentioned Rashi Association, playing an important role in the restoration of the Rashi Lehrhaus in Worms, Germany.

Along with the four books he published in the last two decades of his life, Cahnman contributed dozens of articles in the field of general and Jewish sociology to journals in America and West Germany. His work on problems of ethnicity, and Jewish ethnicity in particular, were in some instances pathbreaking. When Jewish sociologists organized an Association for the Sociological Study of Jewry, Cahman served on the editorial board of its own organ, *Contemporary Jewry*. Shortly before his death, he published another significant contribution in the field, entitled "Nature and Varieties of Ethnicity" (1980).

Werner Jacob Cahnman died of cancer in Forest Hills, New York on 27 September 1980. He left behind two completed manuscripts, the above-mentioned "Jews and Gentiles: The Historical Sociology of Their Relation," and an even more ambitious work on "The History of Sociology," both still awaiting publication.[13]

The Theme

With the present volume, the editors present a representative anthology of Werner J. Cahnman's research papers and scholarly essays on Jews and Judaism. Though diverse in thought and style, they share a common theme. Indeed, whether he explores the stratification of pre-Emancipation German Jewry, the rise of the Jewish national movement in Austria, or such an esoteric issue as the influence of the kabbalistic tradition on German idealist philosophy, or whether he muses on the writing of Jewish history or reports on his firsthand experience in the Dachau concentration camp, the bulk of Cahnman's work reflects this central concern of his personal and scholarly existence. Because he often combines extensive empirical data with accounts drawing on his own background and personal experience, the result is a penetrating approach to the recent history of Jewish life in Central Europe.

Cahnman's concern and interest go beyond the descriptive analysis of the life and structure of the Jewish community he knew so intimately. He wanted to add one more piece to the large mosaic of Jewish Diaspora. He believed that the "writing of history is vital for the continued cultural identity of the human kind." The recorded story of its past, he thought, provides a people with that "consciousness of the self which links the present and future generations to the preceding." The importance of the writing of history becomes all the more obvious "when a people is in the process of estrangement from the heritage of beliefs and customs and ceremonies which once sustained its existence."[14]

Clearly, Cahnman believed that at certain historical junctures history can serve as a "lucid guide." Moreover, if the upheavals and changes in a dialectical process of disintegration and reintegration through many generations effect a state of affairs when "*instability* becomes . . . the only stable factor" in a people's experience, history must be reinterpreted to the new generation's needs and outlook. "In such times as ours," he said, "history must be rewritten in every generation," and this "applies with particular force to the Jewish people."[15]

As a scholar, eyewitness, and survivor, Cahnman felt a communal and intellectual responsibility, and a tragic one at that, to chronicle the "disintegration" of his own community. In due course, he recorded faithfully the assault on, the uprooting, the migrational moves, and the final destruction of his people, the first victims of Hitler's genocidal plans. At the same time, he never lost sight of what he considered the historian's duty: to provide an account of certain relations and configurations in terms that may help the self-understanding of future generations.[16]

At a more personal level, Cahnman experienced and then explored the relation of his immediate environment to Jewish reality here and now. Starting with his family, he discovered that it was one characterized by the acknowledgment of "being Jewish" and by generous contributions to Jewish charities. Reminiscing about what he and his generation believed, he noted they were aware of Judaism "as an idea, hovering . . . over the vastness of a bustling world" in which they were preoccupied with "striving for material success and social responsibility."[17] To be sure, decades before German-Jewish history drew to a violent close, several movements had sprung up—among them the Reform and Neo-Orthodoxy—but they did not have a wide appeal, and certainly not to Cahnman, who thought them to be individualistic and purely denominational. A far greater impact on him and his peers was effected by another movement of faith and devotion, the Freies Jüdisches Lehrhaus, founded by Franz Rosenzweig in Frankfurt in 1920. They responded to Rozenzweig's appeal for "a reintegrated Judaism, above parties and sections."[18] Decisive for Cahnman, however, was the towering figure of Martin Buber. When the "mighty socialist movement" on the one hand, and the escapist individualism of the artist and youth movements on the other, presented themselves as viable alternatives to a sizeable segment of post–World War I Jewish youth, Cahnman and many of his peers discovered Buber as "one of the greatest sages of all times." Anxious and disillusioned, they listened to Buber as he spoke about the "renewal of Jewish existence and the need for a new approach to human existence, as two aspects of one and the same thing." From that time dates Cahnman's firm belief in "openness to the world, confrontation, . . . activity, responsibility, mutuality," that is, a life "lived not in isolation of contemplation but in the togetherness of a common task." Buber at that moment in history had turned upside down the meaning and direction of the German-Jewish symbiosis: Moses Mendelssohn had introduced "the Jews of the Ghetto to the idiom of German culture," and Buber (and Rosenzweig) sought to "lead the heirs of the Emancipation back to the recognition of their Hebrew origin."[19] After 1933, Buber's direct role as teacher and comforter even reinforced the original impact; his Biblical exegeses, Cahnman recalled, compelled him and other young people to become "strong and of good courage." We have Cahnman's word for it that Martin Buber, the author of *I and Thou*, whom he considered an "inspired sociologist'' (and socialist of sorts), had colored his own sociological perception as well as his affinity to Tönnies's work, especially the latter's view of *Gemein-schaft*.

It was recently noted[20] that the history of post-Emancipation German Jewry and of the Holocaust aftermath has received considerable scholarly attention. The study of Jewish life in the 1930s and the subsequent migrational movements, on the other hand, has been somewhat neglected. Cahnman's studies and his research data, we believe, go a long way to fill this gap and will constitute an important element in any future large-scale historical account:

> I shall try to testify . . . in the belief that what I have to say will stand for the truth which, while it becomes manifest only in personal experience, nevertheless transcends it.[21]

Approach and Perspectives

The essays here assembled, whether written or published in Germany or America, all deal with the Jewish scene in Europe. During an interview on the occasion of his seventieth birthday, Werner Cahnman was asked about his approach to Jewish history.[22] His reply at the time is still the best summation of his approach to Jewish history, that is, from the vantage point of the historical sociologist, and as a scholar who is not chiefly concerned with ''isolated phenomena but with relations between phenomena.'' As he explained:

> Already as a young man I was dissatisfied with the manner in which a romantic nationalist such as the historian Heinrich Graetz would depict conflict, with the ''people of thinkers and sufferers'' as an innocent victim of malice and cruelty. This did not seem to me to be realistic. When I came to understand that [for example] the trader and the peasant live in symbiosis and conflict, I was relieved. . . . The Jewish people dwells among the nations, whether in Israel or in the Diaspora, and the tensions between intimate symbiosis and bitter conflict remains a guiding theme of Jewish history. In recognizing this fact, I would say, we are all post-Zionists.[23]

Cahnman was advocating not only a post-Zionist but also a post-liberal approach. What did he mean by that? He came from a straight liberal environment. But his more earthy and common sense inclinations, reinforced by Adolf Fischof's notion of cultural nationalism, made him increasingly adopt a view that, ''as you cannot occupy a country from the air, so you cannot come to grips with Jewish life without envisaging the Jewish people in the flesh. Consequently, post-liberal thought did not return to the Law, but moved forward to *peoplehood*.''[24] Indeed, Cahnman's early paper on ''Judentum und Volksgemeinschaft'' (1926) already revealed this post-liberal position.

Cahnman's examination of the "Jewish people that dwells among the nations" is focused on Germany because it was the country "where in modern times the symbiosis . . . has been most intimate and it also has been the country where the conflict degenerated into the monstrosity of the Holocaust."[25] The description of the cultural contours of Germany as the framework in which modern Jewish history takes place is of importance to Cahnman, for no other reason than that his views on some matters run counter to some commonly assumed positions.

Thus, the opening essay of the present volume *Part One*, "The Three Regions of German-Jewish History," elaborates on certain typological and historical differentiations in order to prove his point, namely, that there is no such thing as a "distinctive and unified German-Jewish history." Rather, it is divided into two major epochs, the German-French and the German-Polish, and into different geographical regions. The following essays attempt to view "the Jewish people in the flesh." "Pariahs, Strangers, and Court Jews: A Conceptual Clarification" scrutinizes the relation of Jews to governments in the changed circumstances of the post-emancipatory period by taking a closer look at some concepts introduced into the sociological vocabulary by Max Weber, but also used by Tönnies, Brentano, Simmel, and eventually taken up by Lewis Coser and Hannah Arendt. "The Role and Significance of the Jewish Artisan Class" and "Village and Small-Town Jews of Germany" again take issue with some commonly held views on the homogeneity and structural characteristics of post-Exilic Jewry. In a rather sweeping historical overview, yet not without basis in some hard data to prove the point, Cahnman demonstrates that the reality of Jewish artisanship and craft guilds is at complete variance with certain biased images of Jewish economic activities. He also establishes that, contrary to widely shared notions about the thoroughly urbanized Jewish communities of Central Europe, over 50 percent of the German Jews still resided in rural communities at the turn of the century, and according to the last census of Munich Jews (1938!), only 34 percent of the Jews were natives of the city. The typological study "Village and Small-Town Jews of Germany" is a sociological tour de force validating his proven method of merging historical overview with personal/family history and empirical research. "Socioeconomic Causes of Antisemitism" provides the elements of a sociological theory of antisemitism by examining the nature of Jewish-Gentile relations in the era of industrial society in the light of the fact that from the ninth to the nineteenth century Jews were members of an interstitial class—and as such were exposed to many more contact, and conflict, situations than other sectors of the population.

The three essays of *Part II* reflect in an extraordinarily direct way Cahnman's personal and professional experiences in the Munich of the 1930s. As the *Syndikus* for Bavaria of the Centralverein, and later as the social worker serving his own embattled and diminishing community, Cahnman conducted censuses, guarded files, and counseled emigrating Jews. "The Decline of the Munich Jewish Community, 1933–38" and "The Jews of Munich, 1918–43" amount to statistical reports on the effects of Nazi policy on the demographic structure of this group, and as such are important research documents. While the two essays constitute the sociological harvesting of Cahnman's years as a Jewish activist, the story of his two months in Dachau in the winter of 1938 is a moving document about Cahnman's trials and tribulations as a concentration camp inmate, and more striking at that because it shows how "the system was supposed to work."

Part III offers "Profiles in Jewish Courage and Vision," with essays on Theodor Herzl and Ludwig Gumplowicz; on Clementine Kraemer, the Jewish writer and Cahnman's favorite aunt; and on Martin Buber, the "great sage," and his idol. All these individuals are examined as representing ways of being Jewish at a certain historical juncture. In "Scholar and Visionary: The Correspondence between Ludwig Gumplowicz and Theodor Herzl," we first glimpse the ideas and (foolish?) optimism of a classical liberal, Gumplowicz, in contrast to the prophetic vision of the father of political Zionism and the Jewish state; then Cahnman highlights their diametrically opposing stance against their immediate environment, the multinational state of the Habsburg monarchy, to explain their respective positions. "The Life of Clementine Kraemer" portrays no star on the political stage. What that fine woman stands for, how she lived, and how she came to her end was of no mean importance to Cahnman, as she symbolized the thriving existence and savage destruction of the community of which they were both a part. To be sure, she was a public figure in Munich, one of the initiators of Jewish social work; she was well known as an author of children's books and short stories. But first and foremost, she was a repository of traditional Jewish values, a link between the warmth and folksiness of rural Jewish family life (an ideal *Gemeinschaft*) and the urbanizing and intellectualizing liberal bourgeois Jewish life of the city. And just as her way of life was representative of her people, so was her death in Theresienstadt in 1942. In "Martin Buber: A Reminiscence," Cahnman tells of how and why Buber brought home a different meaning of Jewish existence. It was a "new interpretation not so much of Judaism as of Jewish existence, and not of Jewish existence of and by itself, but as a call to all men." It was when the "enemy was at the gate" that Buber spoke to a whole generation "about the renewal" of this very Jewish existence and "about the need for a new approach to human existence, as the two aspects of one and the same thing."

The last, most elaborate, and most philosophical of Cahnman's writings is devoted to the "old" theme: the German-Jewish symbiosis. "Friedrich Wilhelm Schelling and the New Thinking of Judaism" addresses the problem of the "elective affinity" or the state of affairs when "the Jews achieved some sort of synthesis between Judaism and European culture," as Selma Stern put it.[26] As the title indicates, Cahnman goes back to the early nineteenth century and traces the line of development up to the early twentieth century. Cahnman's reconstruction involves close textual reading and exegesis: After kabbalistic beliefs fell into disrepute in the German-speaking areas of Central Europe during the eighteenth century with the collapse of the carriers, the Sabbatian and Frankist movements, the subterranean continuation of these beliefs commenced in Germany. It came to the fore in the "garb of romantic philosophy," as the combination of that Jewish tradition with "national-cultural" ideas, meaning that it continued but in a new language. Cahnman identifies Schelling as the catalyst of this new trend in Jewish thought and illustrates his point with Schelling's 1815 lectures on the "Philosophy of Mythology" and the "Philosophy of Revelation." The Schellingian influence on the thinking of the representatives of the second Emancipation in Germany is known to have emanated from kabbalistic sources. The line, in fact, stretches up to the twentieth century, to Franz Rosenzweig and the neo-Kantian Hermann Cohen, according to Cahnman—and, we may add, to the writings of Max Horkheimer and his Frankfurt School, where Schelling's *Naturphilosophie* shows through their critique of science and technology.[27]

All of the papers here collected were preserved by Dr. Gisella Cahnman, widow of Werner, who shares the literary executorship with Joseph B. Maier. The editors wish to express their thanks to Dr. Gisella Levi Cahnman for her all-out help with this volume.

Joseph B. Maier, Judith Marcus, and
Zoltán Tarr
November 1987

Notes

1. Peter de Mendelssohn, ed., *Thomas Mann: Tagebücher, 1935–36.* (Frankfurt am Main, 1978), p. 167. The exact date of Werner Cahnman's visit was 31 August 1935. As is well known, Mann had been recording his daily activities, from the significant to the most trivial, since his youth.
2. The reference is to Cahnman's role in the Forest Hills housing controversy as the "social scientist" consulted by Mario Cuomo, then mediator between warring parties. See Werner J. Cahnman, "The Forest Hills Experience," in *The Reconstructionist*, 12, no. 2 (March 1975): 25.
3. Cahnman, "Methodological Note," in the *Year Book XIX of the Leo Baeck Institute* (London, 1974), pp. 128–30.
4. See Cahnman's notes published in the *Newsletter* of the Association for the Sociological Study of Jewry (1975), pp. 20–21.

5. See "Program and Purpose" of the Rashi Association for the Preservation of Jewish Cultural Monuments in Europe, drawn up by Cahnman as the founder of this organization.
6. Reference is to Cahnman's unpublished manuscript, "My Relation to Jews and Judaism," written in 1979.
7. See "The Jews of Munich: 1918–43," in this volume.
8. Reference is to Cahnman's unpublished manuscript, "Rudolf Hess as a Symbol," written in the 1940s. Intended as a contribution to the "understanding of German geopolitics," the essay recounts how fellow student Rudolf Hess "tried seriously to complete his education . . . after the Bierkeller putsch of 1923," and in due course became an assistant to Karl Haushofer in planning for world conquest. Haushofer sought to base imperialist dreams on solid geographic knowledge. Hess's move toward Haushofer, Cahnman suggests, symbolized the circuitous route from a "vitalistic blood-and-soil philosophy to an intercontinental and interoceanic plot years before the National Socialist movement came to power in 1933."
9. "Village and Small-Town Jews in Germany: A Typological Study" was first published in the *Year Book XIX of the Leo Baeck Institute*, pp. 107–30; the essay "Role and Significance of the Jewish Artisan Class" appeared in *The Jewish Journal of Sociology*, 7, no. 2 (December 1965): 207–20.
10. For an account of Cahnman's Dachau experience, see "In the Dachau Concentration Camp," in this volume.
11. Rita Levi-Montalcini is regarded as one of the world's most prominent scientific investigators of the nervous system and her recently published memoirs give a vivid description of the non-orthodox family environment in Turin which was the same as that of Gisella Levi-Cahnman. See: Rita Levi-Montalcini, *In Praise of Imperfection. My Life and Work* (New York, 1988).
12. W. J. Cahnman, ed., *Intermarriage and Jewish Life: A Symposium* (New York: 1963). The book presents the proceedings of a conference of the same title held in 1960 with the participation of rabbis and Jewish educators as well as social scientists.
13. For accurate and extensive biographical data see Herbert A. Strauss and Werner Röder, eds., *International Biographical Dictionary of Central Europe Emigrés 1933–1945.* (München/New York/London/Paris, 1983), vol. 2, pt. 1: A–K, *The Arts, Sciences and Literature*, 178.
14. Cahnman, "On the Writing of Jewish History," *The Menorah Journal*, 36, no. 1 (Winter 1948): 103.
15. Ibid.
16. This is a recurrent theme in many of Cahnman's essays on the subject of Jewish histories and peoplehood, as well as intercultural relations.
17. See "Martin Buber: A Reminiscence," in this volume; first published in *The Reconstructionist*, 31, no. 12 (15 October 1965): 7.
18. Ibid.
19. Ibid., 8.
20. See, For example, Herbert A. Strauss, *Jewish Immigrants of the Nazi Period in the U.S.A.* (New York/München/London/Paris: 1987).
21. "Martin Buber," 7.
22. Ira Eisenstein, "Werner Cahnman at Seventy," *The Reconstructionist* (June 1973): 24–33.
23. Ibid., 26–27.

24. Ibid., 31.
25. Ibid., 28.
26. Judith Marcus and Zoltán Tar, "The Judaic Element in the Teachings of the Frankfurt School," in the *Year Book XXXI of the Leo Baeck Institute* (London: Secker & Warburg, 1986), p. 351. The *Year Book* is devoted to the topic "From the Wilhelminian Era to the Third Reich." Selma Stern's statement comes from her book *The Court Jew*, translated by Ralph Weiman (Philadelphia: 1950), p. 241.
27. For a discussion of *Naturphilosophie*, see Zoltán Tar, *The Frankfurt School. The Critical Theories of Max Horkheimer and Theodor W. Adorno* (New York, 1985), pp. 95–97. See also Joseph Maier, "Jüdisches Erbe aus deutschem Geist," in *Max Horkheimer heute. Werk und Wirkung*, edited by Alfred Schmidt and Norbert Altwicker (Frankfurt am Main, 1986), 156–61.

Part I

A New Approach to German-Jewish History

1

The Three Regions of German–Jewish History

It is commonly assumed that the history of the Jews in Germany is the continuous story of a single homogeneous community living within the confines of Bismarck's German Empire. Each period of this history is regarded as issuing naturally from its predecessor, the modern Jewish population of the country is seen as the lineal and spiritual descendant of its medieval Jewry, and the House of Rothschild an outgrowth of the Mendelssohn era. No types, regional or otherwise, are delineated. It is the thesis of this paper that such an approach is erroneous and that there is no such thing as a distinctive and unified German-Jewish history.[1] What is usually so described is actually a series of disparate chapters belonging properly to the Jewish history of such contiguous areas as (in chronological order) France and the Rhineland, Bohemia and Austria, Hungary and Galicia, Poland and Lithuania. Interwoven with the story of Germany in a variety of ways, among all these different chapters there has been neither uniformity nor conformity until recently; while both the German and the Jewish elements have undergone significant mutations and transformations, fusing and blending into the most complex and diversified patterns.

To sustain this point of view, it will be advisable to consider first what may be described as the cultural contours of Germany. The pivotal point of all German history—perhaps, indeed, of all European history—is the fact that Roman penetration stopped short at a line extending from the middle Rhine, north of Mayence, to the upper Danube, west of Regensburg. This line, the *limes Romanus*, bisected the country into two distinct culture areas. West of the wall, where a number of new, territorially conceived nations were born, Roman influence prevailed, symbolized especially by the introduction of a *jus soli* and of Latinized forms of speech. East of this line the ancient tribal societies survived, preserving their traditional *jus sanguinis* and continuing to speak their native tongues. Until the time of the Hohenstaufen dynasty, in the

3

twelfth century, all of the leading centers of Germany lay to the west of the wall. Only later did they shift to the South-East, and, still later, to the North-East.[2] Berlin emerged very late as a capital city in Germany.

But the *limes* was not the only cultural frontier in Germany. Scarcely less significant was the line which marked the western-most limit of Slavic penetration. This line ran transversally through Bavaria and Thuringia and crossed the lower Elbe in the vicinity of Hamburg, dividing the area of large estates from one of peasant holdings. Again, if we adopt the distinction between *oceanic* and *continental* areas suggested by such political geographers as Friedrich Ratzel[3] and Sir Halford Mackinder,[4] the drainage basin of the Elbe will constitute another important line of demarcation between the West and the North-East, while the Danube valley will form the connecting link between Southern Germany and the countries to its South-East.

Jewish history follows along strikingly similar lines. From Palestine and Egypt a western wing of migration proceeded along the shores of the Mediterranean, first to Italy and Spain and thence to France and the Rhine valley, while an eastern wing moved partly through Byzantium to the Russian steppes, and partly along the Danube valley as far as Prague.[5] In the early Middle Ages, these two widely separated worlds were represented, respectively, by Hasdai ibn Shaprut (915-75) in Spain and the Judaized King of the Chazars on the banks of the Volga. Central Europe was an interstitial area between the two. It originated as the Eastern terminal of the Western drive but derived its significance from the fact that, in the course of time, East and West met and merged there and contended for supremacy.

In the heart of this area lies Germany. Its Jewish history is therefore neither eastern nor western, nor, indeed, uniform or independent. Its character is different in each epoch and is conditioned by the particular cultural currents which happened to sweep across it, now from the one direction and now from the other. It divides into two major epochs separated by what is, really, no more than a breathing-spell. Each can be correlated with one of the contiguous areas.

The German-French Epoch

The first epoch was a German-French epoch. Its characteristic figure is Rashi (1040–1105). Its center was located at the Rhine, the highroad of the medieval empire.[6] This is shown by the fact that the liturgical rite (*minhag*) current in the Rhenish communities of Speyer, Worms and Mayence (SHUM) was recognized as the official German rite. The rite obtaining east of the Elbe and Saale was regarded as foreign and termed, by contrast, the rite of Poland-Bohemia-Hungary, while in Bavaria and Franconia the German rite fused with the Italian rite. The Jewish population of this area was neither Sephardic nor Ashkenazic, but existed before this classic division originated. It went back to the days of the late Roman Empire, the third and fourth centuries. The ultimate origin of the first settlers may be established through the ancestral traditions followed by their more illustrious descendants. Thus, the family of Kalonymus, prominent communal leaders in Mayence, is said to have come from Lucca, Italy; Gershom ben Judah (960–1040), one of the foremost scholars of the Middle Ages, who established his academy in the same city, hailed from Metz. Rashi, who is reputed to have taught at Worms, was a native of Troyes, deep in the heart of France. Conversely, it was the German-born Meir of Rothenburg (1215–93) who composed the famous poem *Shaali Serufah*, commemorating the burning of the Talmud in Paris in 1242.

Not until the time of the First Crusade did an unmixed German idiom gain currency in the settlement. Earlier rabbinic records and responses are full of French expressions and idioms, regardless of whether their authors lived in France proper, in the Rhineland, or as far east as Regensburg.[7]

The tragic events of the twelfth and thirteenth centuries and the persecutions of 1348, the year of the Black Death, all but destroyed this early settlement between the Rhine and the Elbe, while the expulsion of the Jews from France, in 1394, added the crowning touch to this period of tribulation. The cultural tradition embodied in the so-called *hassidei Ashkenaz*, or "pious men of Germany," thereupon shifted eastward, with Austria, Bohemia, Moravia, and Silesia as stepping stones.[8] Its influence survived for many centuries. Indeed, the mystical and moral teachings of Isaiah Horowitz of Moravia (ca. 1555–1630) and the Hassidic pietist, Israel Baal Shem Tov of Podolia (ca. 1700–1760), may be regarded as in direct line of succession to those expounded some three or four hundred years earlier, in the *Sefer Hassidim* of Judah ben Samuel of Regensburg.

The German-Polish Epoch

Not until 1648, exactly three centuries after the close of the Jewish medieval period, did the second epoch of German-Jewish history begin. This was to be the German-Polish epoch, characterized by a mass migration back to the West. In the wake of the Chmielnicki massacres, thousands of Polish Jews whose ancestors had previously moved eastwards, there to mix with the Tartaric brethren and to develop the Yiddish language, now retraced their steps—forerunners of the large-scale exodus from the same quarter in the nineteenth and twentieth centuries. Indigent Polish Jews thronged the highways and flooded the hospices, but with them there came to the West a marked regeneration of Hebrew and rabbinical scholarship. Indeed, since the middle of the seventeenth century, a large proportion of rabbis throughout the German-speaking areas of Middle Europe has been of Eastern European provenance,[9] while many of the lay leaders of modern Jewry have been their descendants. Thus, both Jonathan Eybeschütz (1690–1767) and Jacob Emden (1697–1776), the two great controversialists, were of eastern origin, the former a native of Cracow and the latter a son of the famous Hakham Zevi of Amsterdam, who was born in Moravia as the son of a refugee from the Chmielnicki pograms. Likewise of eastern European origin, to cite but a single typical example, was Gabriel Riesser (1806–63), vice president of both the Hamburg *Bürgerschaft* and the National Assembly at Frankfort in 1848. His maternal grandfather was Rabbi Raphael ben Yekuthiel Cohen, who had come to Hamburg from Lithuania, while his father, Lazarus Riesser (alias Eliezer Katzenellenbogen) was the son of Rabbi Jacob Katzenellenbogen of Oettingen, Bavaria, himself of Polish descent.[10]

Around 1800, the overwhelming majority of Ashkenazic Jews lived in the East, beyond the borders of the Reich, at the fringes of the German culture area, and among Slavic-speaking populations. Hungary and the Bohemian-Moravian-Silesian region formed interstitial areas. Only a small remnant of medieval German Jewry remained in the West. They clustered around the Rhine and Main, separated from their brethren by wide areas which at that time were still almost *judenrein*. Regions like East Prussia, Mecklenburg, Saxony, and Old-Bavaria had no Jewish settlement prior to the eighteenth century, while Berlin and Vienna, which lay right between the Western outposts and the Eastern centers, had but recently begun to assume major importance, Berlin already during the eighteenth century, Vienna only around the year 1800.

The Modern Period

Out of this original configuration developed the three main regions which characterize German-Jewish history in the nineteenth century, the North-East, the old West and South, and the South-East, with Berlin, Frankfurt, and Vienna as their respective centers. Even a century later, on the eve of the Hitler regime, these areas had still preserved their sharp differences, although migration and intermarriage had begun to blur the lines of demarcation.

The modern history of German Jewry begins in the North-East. Moses Mendelssohn's translation of the Hebrew Bible (1780–83) divided Ashkenazic Jewry into German-speaking and Yiddish-speaking wings, but their social and cultural relations became even more pronounced than before. Both the Emancipation and the Haskalah movements started in Berlin, at the time the capital of a semi-Polish territory exposed to the influences of both West and East; and the movement linked with Mendelssohn made itself felt in that city and in Koenigsberg long before a similar development took place elsewhere in Central and Eastern Europe. Many of the philosopher's friends and disciples were immigrants from the East, as were his ancestors. Through his mother's family, he was related to Rabbi Moses Isserles of Cracow (1510–72), a commentator of the Shulhan Arukh. His father's family was likewise of Polish origin.[11]

With the conquests of Frederick II and the successive partitions of Poland (in 1772, 1793, and 1795) the Jews in Eastern Germany gained preponderance over the older groups of their brethren in the West and South. As a consequence of the king's successful campaigns, there had emerged a single large territorial unit, unifying the Jews with their Gentile neighbors, stimulating contacts between communities previously separated and generally broadening their outlook. At the same time, the partition of Poland had resulted in the incorporation into the Prussian state of the provinces of Poznan and West Prussia, each of which harbored a considerable Jewish population. The significance of the new influx can scarcely be exaggerated. Even in 1816, after the annexation of the Rhineland had brought an additional group of West-German Jews under Prussian domination, almost 54 percent of Jews in Prussia and more than 25 percent of Jews in all Germany (excluding Austria) lived in previously Polish or semi-Polish provinces or districts of Poznan, East and West Prussia.[12] The addition of such a substantial minority effected a profound change in the composition of German Jewry,[13] though intermarriages between the older and newer strata, or between West and East, were rare before the close of the nineteenth century.

The Jews of the East were not only more numerous, they were different. At the time of the incorporation, those of Poznan had formed an economically poor but socially well-integrated Yiddish-speaking community in the midst of a larger and predominantly Polish-speaking peasantry. As late as 1873, more than 84 percent of all the Jews in the eastern districts of Posen, Bromberg, Marienwerder, and Oppeln lived in townships, as against only 9 percent in the western provinces of the Rhineland and Westphalia. Further, in the above-named eastern districts, there were 20 Jewish communities with over 1,000 inhabitants each, and 33 with over 500 inhabitants, whereas in the Rhineland and Westphalia not a single Jewish community counted more than 500 members.[14]

As might be expected, rabbinic culture was more at home in the semi-urban communities of the East than among the scattered villages of the West, Jews of the former region being imbued with the time-honored tradition of Talmudic learning. Moritz Lazarus's father, who made the small boy listen to learned discussions early in the morning, was as typical of the sophisticated eastern Jew as Berthold Auerbach's mother—who endowed her émigré nephew with a sacred amulet—was of the unlearned village Jews in the South and West.[15]

The intellectual proclivities of eastern Jewry were channelled later on into more secular departments of life. In the German-Polish cultural conflicts of the nineteenth century, the newly assimilated Jews of Posen, with the zeal of neophytes, rushed to the support of German-language schools and other German institutions. Their descendants formed the core of the Berlin Jewish community, gained positions of influence in commercial and professional life, in the sciences and in journalism, and provided the leadership of local and national organizations. Representative examples are: Moritz Lazarus (1824–1903) of the Deutsch-Israelitischer Gemeindebund; Marcus Horowitz (1844–1910) and Paul Nathan (1857–1927) of the Hilfsverein der Deutschen Juden; and Eugen Fuchs (1856–1923) and Julius Brodnitz (1866–1936) of the Centralverein Deutscher Staatsbürger Jüdischen Glaubens.

Thus Prussia, the paramount power of Protestant Germany during the eighteenth and nineteenth centuries, at the same time became the power center of Germany's modern Jewish communities. Their cultural complexion was influenced from the outset by the authoritarian rationalism of Frederick II, the tolerant optimism of Lessing, and the critical philosophy of Kant. A typical offspring of this atmosphere was the philosopher Hermann Cohen (1842–1918), whose presentation of Judaism as a "religion of reason" completed the attempt of the Lithuanian immigrant Solomon Maimon (1754–1800) to interpret his traditional faith through the medium of Kantian ethics and metaphysics. Cohen was the son of a cantor in Coswig-Anhalt and was married to a daughter of the composer Louis Lewandowski (1823–94), who hailed from Wreschen in Posen. Cohen had a distinguished university career as a philosophic expounder of Judaism.

Rationalism, however, was not the only trend which characterized the Jewry of the North-East. In the same area rose also the Romantic movement,[16] which found its Jewish expression in the "Science of Judaism" of Leopold Zunz (1794–1886),[17] the "Historic Judaism" of Zacharias Frankel (1801–75), and the sentimental and nationalistic approach to Jewish history which marked the work of Heinrich Graetz (1819–91). All of these men were of eastern origin; Zunz (who lived in Berlin) came from Detmold, Frankel from Prague, and Graetz from Xions, in Posen. Characteristic of the cultural atmosphere which pervaded the area is the fact that in the three German rabbinical seminaries, located in Berlin and Breslau, the curriculum took equal account of both the romantic and the rationalistic schools of Jewish scholarship.[18]

Quite different was the situation in the South and West. There, in compact family groups, lived the descendants of those Jews who had not migrated eastwards in the late Middle Ages, but who, when driven from the cities by commercial envy, had sought refuge in smaller towns and villages controlled by petty princes. Thoroughly integrated into the rural communities where their ancestors had appeared as "wandering Jews," they were an inseparable, though segregated, part of the environment, and did not constitute a distinctive society. Socially hidebound and slow to change, they were at the same time determined individualists. From humble peddler to court Jew, they professed no other group loyalties than those to their own families or immediate neighbors. The court Jews and their successors, the great capitalists and *shtadlanim* of the past two-and-a-half centuries, such as the Oppenheimers, Wertheimers, Rothschilds, Hirsches, Bischofsheims, Guggenheims, Schiffs, Kahns, Lehmans, Monds, Morgenthaus, and Warburgs, were the most significant contribution of the region to the gallery of Jewish types. Their influence was felt not only in Europe but also in America.

Both culturally and commercially, the Jews of South and West Germany were closer to Paris than to Berlin or the despised "colonial" regions of the East. Unlike their "enlightened" brethren across the Elbe, they had been emancipated by France, when the armies of Napoleon split the old Reich asunder. Consequently, it was not philosophical reason but political liberty that became the watchword of an entire generation of Jewish writers from the Rhineland. For more than a century Paris served as a secondary center of South-West German Jewry and as a haven for its refugee artists and authors, of whom Boerne, Heine, Offenbach, Hess, Marx, and Bamberger may be regarded as typical. Similarly, Alsace and Lorraine, because of their political ties with France, became favored centers of emigration, developing, as it were, into the equivalents of Posen and Silesia, for Paris.

Nevertheless, despite these Francophile tendencies, the main center of South-Western Jewry remained Frankfurt. Here, its peculiar character and temper, a combination of individualism and emotionality, received full expression. Every intellectual approach to Jewish problems and every nationalistic program for concerted action was foreign to the Jews of that area. In the seventeenth and eighteenth centuries, they distrusted rabbinical casuistry and educational techniques; in the nineteenth, the radical Reform movement; and, in the twentieth, political Zionism.[19] It is not without significance that, while many North-German congregations supported the religious liberalism of Abraham Geiger (1810–74), Frankfurt am Main became the seat of the Neo-Orthodox movement founded by Samson Raphael Hirsch (1808–88).[20] The most tragic representative of West- and South-German Jewry, apart from Heinrich Heine, was the novelist Jacob Wassermann., The conflict between Jewish "blood" and German "soil" tore him, and others, asunder.

A third center of Jewish life in Middle Europe grew in the Danube basin. Here were revealed all the traits and characteristics of an interstitial area. The Austrian Alpine countries contained only a tiny Jewish population. The Jews in Bohemia and Moravia were distributed in the same way as those of North-Western and South-Western Germany, village and small-town settlements being grouped around a time-honored central community—in the one case Frankfurt, in the other Prague. Further East, in Slovakia, however, 5 percent of the total population was Jewish, as against 1 percent in Bohemia; while in Carpatho-Russia (which later belonged to the Republic of Czechoslovakia, and was incorporated into the Soviet Union in 1946) the percentage of Jews was as high as 14 percent, thus indicating the unmistakable pattern of the East.

The character and temperament of these Jewries was well expressed in Czechoslovak census returns. Given the choice of declaring themselves of Jewish rather than German, Czech, or Hungarian nationality, only 20 percent of the Jews of Bohemia availed themselves of this opportunity, whereas over 50 percent did so in Moravia and as many as 95 percent in Carpatho-Russia. Seeing that in the two former areas (where Yiddish culture played a minor role) this declaration entailed endorsement of Czech-language schools, and in the latter of Yiddish and Hebrew schools, these figures would tend to suggest that a nationalistic conception of Judaism was more congenial to the spirit of the East and a religio-cultural conception to that of the West. Nevertheless, throughout the Danubian area, clear-cut lines of demarcation were lacking. In fact, almost every type of nineteenth-century Jew was represented there in extreme forms. Thus, while the wave of baptism and escapism rose to phenomenal heights in Vienna, that city was also the center of an intransigent nationalism, both among Jews and Gentiles. Similarly, while Jews nowhere participated as freely in the life of the community as in the Austrian capital, it is equally true that antisemitism was nowhere more malicious and more militant.

The Jewish mass settlements in Hungary and Galicia poured an inexhaustable stream of immigrants from the East into Vienna, where they met with a highly sophisticated community of longer standing. The Jewish "Forty-eighter" Adolf Fischhof (1816–93), born in Budapest, became the protagonist of democratic cooperation between the entangled nationalities of the Habsburg monarchy. A little later, a follower of Fischhof, Rabbi Joseph S. Bloch of Floridsdorf (1850–1923), of Galician origin, admonished his fellow Jews to be neither Germans nor Czechs nor Poles, but simply Jews and Austrian patriots. To establish a nationality of their own seemed natural to many Jews in an area where every problem developed into a nationality conflict.[21]

The general atmosphere in Germany led to an advocacy among Jews of institutionalized religion within the framework of a unified nation, while the political temper in Austria was bound to become increasingly nationalistic as soon as the dream of unconditional assimilation was shattered. This, more than any other factor, accounts for the similarity of attitude with which Austrian Jews of seemingly diverse outlook approached the problem of their environment. Thus, at the same time as Joseph Samuel Bloch was busy establishing the *Oesterreichisch-Israelitische Union* as a bulwark against the rising tide of antisemitism, Nathan Birnbaum (1864–1937) and his friends were founding the first fraternity of Zionist students in the West, Kadimah, a still more pronounced answer to antisemitism.[22] In retrospect, the difference between the two organizations appears negligible, a matter of degree rather than kind. Intellectuals of Hungarian, Galician, and Russian origin preached the doctrine of national independence as missionaries to an unbelieving Jewish West. They conceived of the Jewish people as an ancient "folk" which was to be transformed into a militant nationality. In later years, their faithful disciples spread these tenets throughout the entire German-speaking area, but, according to the different environment, the stimulation turned cultural where originally it had been political. The standard-bearers were not Herzl and Nordau (both born in Budapest, Hungary) but the Bohemian writers Brod, Weltsch, Beer-Hofmann and, above all, Martin Buber,[23] the magician who combined East and West in his work and whose personality left its imprint upon two generations of German-Jewish intellectuals and the entire German-Jewish youth movement. The influence of Sigmund Freud reached still further: He translated Viennese frustrations into universal anxieties.

Conclusions

The three regional groups crossed and blended in several ways and in varied degrees. Nevertheless, typological and historical differentiations should be recognized. Typologically, the North-Eastern and South-Eastern groups, being somewhat in the order of compact societies, belong together, as against the more isolated sector to the South and West. Each represents, although in different degrees, the Western frontier of Eastern Jewry gradually moving from Slavic and Magyar soil into the environment of German culture and, during the nineteenth century, in turn, transmitting German classical literature to the settlements of the Russian pale. Berlin and Vienna and, to a lesser degree, Koenigsberg and Breslau shared in that task. Jews from Poznan penetrated Silesia and flooded Berlin and Hamburg. East Prussia was settled largely by early Russian arrivals, Saxonia by recent immigrants from Poland. Bohemia and Moravia remained a meeting-ground. Vienna was dominated by Bohemian, Moravian, Hungarian, and, finally, Galician strains, in that order. On the other hand, the West- and South-German sections preserved much of their old-established peculiarities. Traditions there were more deeply rooted, and, by virtue of the isolation and numerical weakness of the communities, had already become petrified by the time emancipation dawned.

Historically, commercial and organizational relations and, finally, intermarriages, developed between North-East and South-West during the late nineteenth and early twentieth centuries, while the separation of the Habsburg monarchy from the Prussianized Reich cast the Jews of the former region upon a life of their own, although they were destined to exert a marked influence over their brethren in Germany proper through literature and music. The Jews of Alsace-Lorraine underwent a development which led them far away from their previous affiliations. So, too, did those numerous German, and especially South-German, Jews who migrated to the United States. Among the Jews in the Reich, however, a common middle-of-the-road type of Judaism, equally removed from Orthodoxy and Reform, gradually emerged. This type was fostered by common institutions and was reinforced rather than shattered in the first years of the Hitler regime. By 1938, however, at the latest, the work of separation from the larger society and of atomization to the point of dissolution which had begun even prior to 1933 had been completed, and physical extinction was imminent.[24]

The second epoch of German-Jewish history has ended as catastrophically as the first. Yet its seeds are scattered over the face of the earth and will surely blossom in God's good time. And a third epoch is about to begin.

1943; 1969

Notes

1. The conclusions here advanced are based principally on genealogies, biographies, and autobiographies, and especially on a list of birthplaces of several hundred outstanding German and Austrian Jews. The author is indebted, as regards methodology, to Friedrich Ratzel's *Anthropogeographie*, 4th ed. (Stuttgart, 1921–22) and Joseph Nadler's *Literaturgeschichte der deutschen Stämme und Landschaften*. 2d ed. (Regensburg, 1922–28). An earlier version of this paper was published in *Jewish Social Studies*, 5, no. 3 (1943) under the title "A Regional Approach to German-Jewish History." For complementation, compare "Two Maps on German-Jewish History" in *Chicago Jewish Forum*, 2, no. 1 (Fall 1943).
2. In the sixteenth and seventeenth centuries, this line marked a further important division: areas west and south of it remained largely Catholic, or adhered to the Western, Calvinistic branch of Protestantism, while those to the east and north became overwhelmingly Lutheran. It should also be observed that the northern and eastern frontiers of vine cultivation coincide largely with the same line.
3. Friedrich Ratzel, *Politische Geographie* (Berlin and Leipzig, 1903), pp. 184-753.
4. Sir Halford Mackinder, *Democratic Ideals and Reality* (New York, 1919), pp. 38-141.
5. *Germania Judaica* (Breslau, 1934), vols. 18–19, pp. 28, 164, 270.
6. Ibid., vol. 18, pp. 175ff, 303, 307, 380, 499. See also Moritz Güdemann, *Geschichte des Erziehungswesens und der Cultur der Juden in Frankreich und Deutschland* (Vienna, 1880), appendix 3, pp. 273, 288; Salfeld, ed., *Das Martyrologium des Nürnberger Memorbuches* (Berlin, 1898), pp. 181, 423.
7. Characteristically, the *Sefer Hassidim* recommend the French benediction *Soit beneit et soit louez* (Hebrew: *yissborakh ve-yishtabakh*) and renders the name of God as *Notre Sire*.
8. *Germania Judaica*, pp. 275, 400; Güdemann, pp. 25, 27, 40, 55, 295. The transition from West to East is foreshadowed in the person of Isaac ben Moses of

Vienna (1180–1250), author of the celebrated *Or Zarua*, a pupil of Jacob ha-Lavan, the French Tosafist, who had migrated to Bohemia, and of other distinguished Franco-German refugees.

9. Among the four rabbis of Kleve during the eighteenth century, three (Meier Raudnitz, Loeb Holleschau, and Israel Lipschutz) were of Moravian or Galician descent; the descent of the fourth, Moses Saul, is uncertain, but it is probably Galician. See Fritz Baer, *Das Protokollbuch der Landjudenschaft des Herzogtums Kleve* (Berlin, 1922). Shmarya Levin, in his *Jugend im Aufruhr* (Berlin, 1937), relates that in his own day most of the students at the Berlin Hochschule für die Wissenschaft des Judentums were of Galician and Hungarian provenance.

10. The pedigree of the Katzenellenbogens is given in Loewenstein, *Beiträge zur Geschichte der Juden in Deutschland* (Berlin, 1895), vol. 1, pp. 322–23.

11. Max Freudenthal, *Zum 200 jährigen Geburtstag Moses Mendelssohns* (Berlin, 1929).

12. Jacob Lestchinsky, *Das wirtschaftliche Schicksal des deutschen Judentums* (Berlin, 1932), pp. 50–58.

13. Gerhard Kessler, *Die Familiennamen der Juden in Deutschland. Mitteilungen der Zentralstelle für deutsche Personen- und Familiengeschichte*, fasc. 1111 (Leipzig, 1935), pp. 44, 63. Prussia counted only 32,000 members of protected Jewish families in 1787, whereas the second division of Poland in 1793 brought 53,000 Jews under Prussian jurisdiction. Not all of them, however, remained in Prussia after 1815.

14. Georg Davidsohn, "Die Juden im Preussischen Staate von 1837," in *Zeitschrift für die Geschichte der Juden in Deutschland* (1937), pp. 114–16; Kessler, pp. 32, 44.

15. L. W. Schwartz, ed., *Memoirs of My People* (Philadelphia, 1945), pp. 376–77.

16. Josef Nadler, *Die Berliner Romantik* (Berlin, 1921), pp. 1–46; Koppel S. Pinson, *Pietism and the Rise of German Nationalism* (New York, 1934).

17. On Zunz's indebtedness to Herder, see Luitpold Wallach, "The Scientific and Philosophic Background of Zunz's Science of Judaism," in *Historia Judaica*, vol. 4 (1942), pp. 51–70.

18. Ismar Elbogen, *Ein Jahrhundert Wissenschaft des Judentums* (Berlin, 1922).

19. See Jacob Wassermann, *My Life as German and Jew* (New York, 1923), and also the author's article, "Munich and the First Zionist Congress," in *Historia Judaica*, vol. 3 (1941), pp. 7–23.

20. It should be noted, however, that Geiger was himself a native of Frankfurt am Main. Actually, his and Hirsch's movement exhibit more similarities than partisans from either side are ready to admit. Hirsch's definition of Israel as a *Religionsfolk* seems strikingly akin to Geiger's notion of Jewish survival as due to Israel's supposed "genius for religion." Both movements used different techniques against the background of related philosophies. The Reform movement attempted to reduce Judaism to the semblance of a modernistic sect, while Neo-Orthodoxy tried to ossify it as a rigidly defined religious code in compensation for the loss of a total and political conception of Jewish life. Yet both movements were strictly individualistic and purely denominational and, for that reason, both seem somewhat out of place in a growingly collectivist environment. Nevertheless, both sprang up naturally out of their place and time. So much, indeed, was this the case, that it was not before German-Jewish history drew to a close that another movement of faith and devotion arose in the same region: the Freie Jüdische Lehrhaus was founded in Frankfurt in 1920. The leading spirit of the Lehrhaus

was Franz Rosenzweig, a philosopher who later devoted his attention to Jewish studies and proclaimed a reintegrated Judaism, above parties and sections. Shall we regard it as symbolic that Franz Rosenzweig's Jewish teachers had been the Liberal Herman Cohen and the Orthodox Jeremiah Nobel? Liberal or Orthodox, both came from the East.

21. Refer to my paper, "Adolf Fischhof and his Jewish Followers," in the *Leo Baeck Yearbook*, 4 (1959): 111–42.

22. Bloch came from Dukla, in Galicia, while Birnbaum, though born in Vienna, was the child of Eastern European parents who spoke Yiddish as their mother tongue. Moreover, not only Birnbaum but all of the founders of Kadimah (Bierer, Kokesch, Schnirer, and Smolenski) were of Galician, Romanian, or Russian origin. See *Festschrift zum 25 jährigen Jubiläum der Oesterreichisch-Israelitischen Union* (Vienna, 1910) and L. Rosenheck, ed., *Kadimah Festschrift* (Moedling, 1933); also my article, "The Fighting Kadimah," in *Chicago Jewish Forum*, 17, no. 1 (Fall 1958): 24–27.

23. Martin Buber lived in Heppenheim, near Frankfurt am Main, but was born in Vienna. His grandfather, Salomon Buber, was a noted rabbinical scholar in Lemberg, Galicia. See Buber's autobiography, *Begegnung* (Stuttgart, 1961).

24. See the author's article, "Jewish Morale in Our Time," in *Social Forces*, 20 (1942): 491–96, for an analysis of the process and relevant literature; also numerous articles in the *Leo Baeck Yearbook*.

2

Pariahs, Strangers, and Court Jews

In a sociological investigation of the relations between Jews and Christians over the centuries, the concepts of the *pariah*, the *stranger* and related concepts need to be reviewed and evaluated. In this context, the relations between Jews and sovereigns are of particular importance. At the same time, the question is raised as to how and to what extent sociological concepts are applicable to historical reality. It will be shown that it is the nature of historical phenomena that they have another side. A comparative analysis serves this multiple purpose.

A further reason for engaging in the evaluation is a 1972 paper by Professor Lewis A. Coser. In his paper, Coser elaborates on the topic of "The Alien as a Servant of Power,"[1] using as examples the court Jews of the seventeenth and eighteenth centuries and the Christian boys that were pressed in the corps of the Janissaries in the Ottoman Empire. Coser considers the Jews of the Middle Ages as well as those of the absolutistic era as "wholly unprotected . . . communities of pariahs" and characterizes them simultaneously as "prototypical strangers." About the court Jews he says further that they had been "raised from the depths" by the ruling princes of the time and, in an analogous passus, that they had been "lifted by the princes from their status as pariahs." Regarding the ex-Christian boys in the corps of the Jannissaries, Coser uses the term *renegade*; for the totality of the phenomena under investigation he uses the term *alien* which he does not distinguish from the commonly used sociological concept of the stranger. The ex-Christian boys and the Court-Jews are then subsumed under the concept of aliens. Equipped with a vaguely indicated conceptual instrumentarium of this kind, Coser engages in "sociology with the hard work left out." Concrete phenomena are not critically investigated because they are not endowed with intrinsic interest: they are used to verify a hypothesis. In such a manner, Coser, while emphasizing superficial similarities, overlooks essential dissimilarities and is likely to spread confusion among his readers. The relations between Jewish subjects and Gentile sovereigns are part of the entire complex of Jewish-Gentile relations and must be pursued throughout the length and breadth of European history. If one intends to grasp their significance, he must analyze the concepts of the pariah and the stranger, as well as a number of related concepts, and scrutinize them regarding their applicability to such phenomena as the *shtadlan*, the court Jew, and the state banker.

The Concepts of the Pariah, the Millet, and the Stranger

I am starting with Max Weber's concept of the pariah which, not unlike other so-called ideal types of Weberian coinage, has been widely quoted and used without much deliberation as to its significance or its applicability. As one looks at the pertinent passages more closely, he will find that the concept is by no means unambiguous, namely:

1. The concept has been interpreted by Max Weber differently in different passages of his writings;
2. The concept has not been sufficiently clarified by Max Weber as far as the initial Indian context is concerned;
3. The applicability of the concept to the Jewish situation and possibly to other extra-Indian situations is open to doubt.

The third point is decisive in the present context, but the two preceding points cannot be entirely disregarded either.

Weber's position is most clearly expressed in *Ancient Judaism*, where he says that a *Pariavolk* is "a guest people that is ritually, formally or factually, separated from its environment."[2] In *The Religion of India*, he adds that pariah peoples are "migratory peoples that are 'excluded from connubium and commensality' and considered as 'ritually unclean.'"[3] Not only the "separateness" but also the "uncleanness" is emphasized at this point. In *Economy and Society* Weber designates a *Pariavolk* as "a distinctive hereditary social group lacking autonomous political organization and characterized by internal prohibitions against commensality and intermarriage originally founded upon magical, tabooistic, and ritual functioning on the one hand, and political and social disprivilege on the other hand."[4] In the same volume he speaks of "specific occupational traditions," "belief in the ethnic community," "strict segregation from any avoidable personal intercourse" and a "legally precarious situation"; Weber continues that, by virtue of their economic indispensability, pariah peoples are tolerated, indeed "frequently privileged," and that they live "interspersed" in political communities. The Jews, he says, "are the most impressive historical example."[5] The last quotation indicates the nature of Weber's interest because one can hardly maintain that the Indian pariahs are "privileged."

Sigrist[6] has pointed out that Weber does not restrict his attention to a few attributes and that he seems to consider an attribute at one time as necessary, at another time as dispensable. One might add that Weber is not even sure as to whether he wishes to use the term pariah "in the usual European sense"[7] or with reference to "what we know from India."[8] It appears that he leans toward the former interpretation because he designates the Jews as a pariah people, with the further comment that the designation "has little to do with the particular situation of the pariah caste in India."[9] Nevertheless, the comparison with the Indian pariah caste can hardly be avoided, or else, the term should not have been chosen. I agree with Sigrist that it is hardly admissible to say that what we have here before us is an "ideal type" which rests on the imagined summation of attributes that need not be present in their totality in a concrete case. The concepts of pariah and *Pariavolk* obviously are not so much an "ideal-type" concept but a "historical totality concept" or a "relatively historical concept" in Schelling's sense. One might even go further and agree with Hempel when he says that impure ideal types of his kind are not concepts, properly speaking, but theories.[10]

It is not within my intention or competence to analyze the place of the pariahs, or Parayan, within the social structure of India. However, the older as well as the newer literature which I have consulted[11] agrees that the Parayan are a low and despised caste within the Hinduistic social system—not necessarily the lowest caste, as Weber already observed. They engage in low and menial tasks against a puny compensation, live from hand to mouth and in dirt and misery, and their character and living conditions are believed to be immutably fixed. One can say that the designation of these people as ritually unclean is a mirror and consequence of the actual situation; the actual situation is subsequently sanctioned by ritual segregation. Fuchs considers it unlikely, for anthropological and anthropometric reasons, that the Parayan are the remnant of a subjected aboriginal population. That amounts to saying that the Parayan are not ethnic or religious strangers; they are included in the ethno-religious universe of Hinduism. Strangers in India are the Parsis. One gains the impression that the Parayan are a degraded proletariat, possibly representing a prototype of what Oscar Lewis has called "the culture of poverty." I must leave further elaboration at this point to the Indologists. I would, however, complement the diffuse formulations of Max Weber by the following definition: The pariahs are: 1) a low, despised and exploited caste, 2) which is considered unclean factually and ritually and 3) which therefore is excluded from connubium, commensality, and each and every kind of personal contact, and 4) whose members accept the exclusion as legitimate. What we have before us, then, is not an ideal type, but a relatively historical real type.

It would seem more appropriate to refer to a mideastern model rather than to apply a phenomenon which is indigenous to India when it comes to the social history of the Jews of Europe. At the same time, such a model will serve to evaluate Coser's attempt to use the ex-Christian boys that were pressed into military service in the Ottoman Empire as a prime example for what may be meant by "aliens as servants of power." I am referring here to the concept of the *Millet*, as I have elaborated in the paper "Religion and Nationality."

> The Millet may be defined as the peculiar political organization which gave to non-Moslem subjects of the Ottoman Empire the right to organize into communities possessing delegated political power under their own ecclesiastical chiefs. The head of the Millet was directly responsible to the state for the administration of all its subjects. Although the Millet lacked territorial cohesion and military power and had therefore to be protected by the ruling warrior caste, it formed in many respects an autonomous unit within the state. Yet, the members of the Millet were limited in their general citizenship by the fact that the laws of personal stature were based on religious sanctions.[12]

Thus, the Greek Patriarch of Constantinople was the political head of the Greek Millet—the most important of them all because it represented the continuity with the Byzantine Empire that was now under Turkish sovereignty. The Greeks were not only indispensable commercially; the Phanaroite families of Constantinople were the administrators and diplomats of the Ottoman Empire, while military positions, to be sure, were closed to them. That hits closer to home than the example of the ex-Christian boys in the corps of the Janissaries. Things go further back as far as the Jews are concerned. The Rosh-Galuta (Prince of the Exile) was recognized as the legitimate head of the Jewish community by the Sassanid rulers and Arab caliphs in Babylonia and Persia, and the basic idea that religion and ethnicity are merely two sides of the same thing harks back to models of the ancient Orient and to Biblical documentation. This model was congenial to the Jews, it was accepted (if ever so reluctantly) by the emperors of Rome, and it provided the underlying principle for the legal construction of Jewish existence in the Middle Ages.

Included in the concept of the Millet is the concept of the stranger. The concept of the stranger has been elaborated upon repeatedly in the classic sociological literature, especially in Germany. It is to be found by Ludwig Gumplowicz, by Lujo Brentano, by Ferdinand Tönnies, and by Georg Simmel.[13] I am referring here chiefly to Tönnies and Simmel. According to Tönnies, the trader is always a stranger; he adds that even if he is not a stranger, strictly speaking, he will be considered as one. The trader who leaves his own clan-community because he is prevented from trading among brothers, Tönnies continues, is "the first thinking and free human being to appear in the normal development of human life";[14] he is the protagonist of *Gesellschaft*, weighing advantage and disadvantage, separating means and ends. Simmel has added a psychological dimension to the sociological concept of the stranger when he says that in him "distance becomes proximity"; the stranger is not so much "the wanderer who comes today and leaves tomorrow." The stranger who, as Tönnies indicates[15] does not need to be a recent migrant, lives in the midst of the native population but belongs to another class and serves another God. He becomes a neighbor but one who maintains his extended relations, so that proximity is indeed merged with distance: he turns out to be the *intermediary*. I am using the term *intermediary* not exclusively microsociologically in Simmel's sense—he refers to a third person as intermediary between two others— but rather macrosociologically in the sense of Tönnies, that is, as a commercial and cultural intermediary within a social structure. To be sure, others have also fulfilled these functions, but none as exclusively as the Jew, who without support from a political homeland has lived always and everywhere on the periphery and consequently in mediation. The function of mediation has its two sides: on the one hand, the intermediary as an outsider is looked upon with suspicion; on the other hand, because he is an outsider, he is welcomed as a friend, a counsellor, and an impartial judge. He is a neighbor, but he has the advantage of remoteness.

The Pariavolk in Antiquity and in the Middle Ages

We must now return to the simplest of Max Weber's definitions of a *Pariavolk*, namely that of "a guest people that is ritually formally or factually separated from its environment." In this restricted sense, the concept may be applicable to the Jewish situation, but it does not carry our understanding very far. To speak, as Max Weber does, of a "*Pariavolk* that lives in a casteless environment,"[16] would be equivalent to talking of pariahs who are no pariahs; historically speaking, the pariah situation remains suspended in midair without the matrix of a caste society. Consequently, Max Weber admits that ritual separation, as distinguished from physical segregation, that is, exclusion from connubium and commensality, was at no time imposed on the Jews from the outside, as it was on the pariahs in India. Rather the Jews enjoyed the status of an autonomous community, or a *politeuma*, in the Roman Empire. Theodor Mommsen[17] sees in this fact the main reason for the aversion against them. Max Weber sees the main reason in Jewish exclusivity, that is, in their self-segregation: the Jews refused to participate in the meals of the Gentiles as they refused to participate in the cult of the divine emperor. That earned them the reputation of indulging in *odium generis humani*. But the Gentiles participated in the meals of the Jews and many joined Judaism as proselytes. What one can say is that the pagan authors whose diatribes have been preserved were "viewing with alarm" what was going on, namely, the attraction which Judaism held to many a searching mind among their contemporaries. The spectacle was irritating for a variety of reasons, not least, as Seneca put it, because it seemed that "the vanquished [had] given laws to the victors."

Moreover, if one disregards ad hoc definitions and adopts a more common understanding of the term *pariah* which, by the way, is subtly implied in Max Weber's own argument, namely, that of a population of low position and prestige that is shunned and held in contempt by the remainder of the population, the name antedates the reality to which it refers by about a millennium. Far from considering themselves, or being considered by others, as persons of low caste, the Jews of late antiquity called themselves "the People of God," and this all the more so as the Church proclaimed itself as "the true Israel." If a Jewish trait bothered the Gentiles, it was overweening pride rather than impotent resentment of servile submissiveness. One must agree with Julius Guttman when he says that a "plebeian or *Pariavolk* ethic vis-á-vis native or foreign potentates can be observed neither among the prophets nor among the pharisees."[18] Hans Gerth feels that Weber's terminology is "unfortunately lending itself to misconceptions";[19] Guttman considers the designation of the Jews as a *Pariavolk* as factually incorrect. I happen to agree with both critics.

The degradation of the Jews—not in ritual but in socioeconomic terms—to the lowly occupations of small-scale moneylending, pawnbroking, and to the trade in used goods is a phenomenon of the high Middle Ages and was deepened in more recent centuries. The occupational structure of the Jewish communities remained diversified in the countries of the first Diaspora, that is, in the Mediterranean area, until the late fifteenth century.[20] The occupational structure was more lopsided in the countries of the second Diaspora, that is, in western and northern Europe, yet the function which the Jews served in commerce and finance was highly appreciated until the period of the Crusades. In the core area of emerging Europe, the Carolingian Empire, the social position of the Jews was so elevated that the aggressive anti-Jewish campaign of Bishop Agobard of Lyon came to naught on account of the influence which the Jews wielded at the court of Emperor Louis the Pious. The bishop objected that the faithful accepted invitations to Jewish homes, that they preferred rabbinic sermons to those of their own clergy, that they celebrated the Jewish Sabbath rather than the Christian Sunday, and that they accepted employment with Jews, especially in Jewish homes and vineyards. Agobard's Church looked upon the Jews not as despised pariahs but as dangerous competitors.[21] The situation was slow to change. The Gothic statue of the Synagogue over the portal of the southern transept of the Münster at Strasbourg is veiled with blindness and her power is broken, but her bearing is noble, in stark contrast to the Judas Iscariot of the baroque passion plays, who haggles for his silver coins.

It is dubious whether the concept of the *Pariavolk* can be applied even to the period from the twelfth century onward. The term refers to untouchables and in a certain sense to unredeemables; redemption by means of an anticipated migration of souls in the hereafter can be disregarded in the present context. The Jews were in contact with all strata of the population; Jewish hospitality was eagerly sought and finally made impossible only by strict ecclesiastical ordinances. In the Jewish view, the Jews were ready for the coming of the redeemer at any time; in the Christian view, they were redeemable by conversion. However, conversion was a long way off; individual Jews converted by their own choice, others were converted under duress, but the bulk of the Jews preferred death at their own hands or the hands of killers to surrendering to what in their eyes was an inferior faith. The conclusion from our deliberations thus far is that the concept of the pariah, outside of its Indian context, has little explanatory value.

What one can say, following Robert E. Park and Howard Becker, is that the Jews are a "marginal trading people."[22] Surely Park's is a "more fortunate and less ambiguous terminology" than Weber's.[23] However, here, too, caution is called for, if one compares Jews, as Howard Becker does, with Scots, Greeks, Armenians, and similar ethnic groups, because all that the Jews have in common with these groups is marginality. In addition, the Jews must be considered as prototypical strangers especially if the concept of the neighbor and the intermediary is included in the concept of the stranger. The quality of strangeness was recognized by Jews and Gentiles alike. The Jews understood themselves as living in the *Galut*, that is, in exile or in captivity; they attributed the condition in which they found themselves to the sins they had committed. The people in whose midst the Jews dwelled agreed: they considered the Jews as captives of the Roman emperor and dependent on his protection or, to use the language of medieval law—spelled out in the privilegium to the Jews of Worms, 1236, and the Charter of Vienna, 1237, both issued by Emperor Frederick II—as *servi camerae imperatoris* (serfs of the Imperial Chamber). The Jews were free in private law, even if they stood in need of special protection, while they were subject to the emperor and eventually to other sovereigns in public law.[24] The protection of the sovereign, which was granted against payment, was the guarantee of their survival. But the paramount power of the Emperor declined and the rapaciousness of the minor sovereigns, including ecclesiastical rulers and municipalities, impoverished the Jews to the extent that the authorities lost interest in them and expelled them from their territories. All the larger territories were affected.

Coser, Weber, and Court Jews

The situation changed in the seventeenth and eighteenth centuries, gaining momentum toward the end of the eighteenth century and in the first half of the nineteenth century, and ultimately leading to the emancipation of the Jews and the granting of civic rights to them. It is incorrect and even misleading to talk as Coser does about the court Jews, purveyors and agents of the baroque period, as if they had been pariahs and in the context to confuse the concepts of the pariah and the stranger.[25] These self-assured and even haughty men were not "raised from the depths"; they were independent entrepreneurs with widely ramified contacts, who knew how to recognize and utilize new opportunities. Of Jost Liebmann, according to Glueckel of Hameln,[26] "the richest man in Germany," it is said that he was a man of reckless energy and "imperious, self-assertive, always demanding, never asking" in his dealing with the Prussian court, including the king.[27] A prime example of independence is the great Samuel Oppenheimer, who did not move from Frankfurt to Vienna as a supplicant: his services were commissioned.[28] It was he who financed the central administration and diplomatic services of Austria, cared for the logistics of the imperial armies, and made the campaigns of Prince Eugene possible. Surely, to use an expression of Max Weber, his legal status was "precarious": he had no political backing and he had to contend single-handedly with cabals and intrigues. His heirs were compelled to go into bankruptcy because the imperial treasury refused to honor its obligations. A similar fate befell other court Jews. They were unable to collect what their princely debtors owed them; some were imprisoned, many died in poverty.[29] But the heirs of Samuel Oppenheimer met with no different fate than the firm of Fugger, which two centuries earlier had earned the proverbial "gratitude of the House of Austria."

An example of the assertiveness of the Jewish money magnates is provided by the case of the Alsatian agent Cerfberr. He pointed out to the royal representative that without him the armies of the King of France could not take to the field, and that he therefore should receive a lettre-patent which would guarantee to him the right to take up residence in the city of Strassburg — a right which had been denied him by the city of Strassburg until that time. The request was granted immediately.[30] Cerfberr's legal status in the litigation which ensued, and which lasted from 1775 until 1789 (when the Revolution disposed of quarrels of that kind), was not more "precarious" than the status of the city. It is interesting to note that it was at the request of Cerfberr and the instigation of Moses Mendelssohn that Christian Wilhelm Dohm wrote his famous treatise "The Civil Improvement of the Jews,"[31] with a special appendix "*sur la condition des Juifs en Alsace.*" Thus, the connection between the ideas and the de facto socio-economic position of the new elite becomes thoroughly translucent.

The representatives of the new elite were *shtadlanim*, that is, well-to-do men who were in regular contact with the potentates, and who could use their close relations in case of emergency, such as the threat of confiscation or a decree of expulsion, in order to intervene for their endangered coreligionists. One encounters such interlocutors in Spain during the thirteenth, fourteenth, and fifteenth centuries, and in Poland during the sixteenth, seventeenth, and eighteenth centuries. What distinguished the court Jews is that they mark the emergence of an entire class of *shtadlanim* who may have been exposed individually but whose collective importance could not be overlooked. Hannah Arendt is correct in saying that the court Jews were "overprivileged" in comparison with the Christian merchants and craftsmen, and certainly in comparison with the peasants, while the poor Jewish peddlers and occasion-hunters were "underprivileged" inasmuch as they had to bear patiently with a demeaning and discriminatory treatment.[32] The court Jews enjoyed special privileges, were exempted from tolls and custom duties, and had access to high places.[33] Two consequences follow from this situation. It was the court Jews who were "in the vanguard of Jewish upward mobility," not, as Coser assumes, their descendants and followers, who merely collected the fruits. The conversion of some of the grandsons and granddaughters of court Jews and state bankers was a consequence of their being established at the top of the social pyramid, not a cause. It follows further from a privileged situation that the court Jews as *shtadlanim* were by no means "despised" and "rejected" by their poorer fellow Jews, as Coser asserts but fails to document. The court Jews, with hardly an exception, were strictly observant men; it was the ignorant village Jews who permitted themselves occasional laxities. Quite a few among the court Jews were learned in rabbinic law and lore, such as the imperial court agent Samson Wertheimer, who bore the title of chief rabbi of Bohemia and Hungary. Others endowed religious schools and supported sacred scholarship. As a rule, they dominated the Jewish communities—some of which they even initiated—and influenced despotically in line with the lifestyle of the period.[34] The antagonism often mounting to bitter hostility encountered by the court Jews originated not so much with the princes but with the established estates, as in the case of Joseph Suess Oppenheimer in Stuttgart,[35] or with plotting Jewish competitors, as in the case of Elkan Fraenkel in Ansbach.[36] The court Jew was indeed a servant and ally of the absolutistic state without, however, being a puppet or even a pariah in the sight of the ruler.

The degree to which the lifestyle of the baroque was the common property of the courtly and the Jewish elite is illuminated by the story of the marriage of one of the daughters of Glueckel of Hameln and the son of the wealthy Elia Cleve, a subject of the elector of Brandenburg.[37] Prince Moritz von Nassau and Prince Frederick, later King Frederick I of Prussia, the latter then but thirteen years of age, requested to be invited to the sumptuous celebration. Glueckel relates with a Jewish mother's prideful satisfaction that the princely guest held the hand of her five-year-old son in an admiring and caressing manner throughout the proceedings. The gathering at Cleve was a meeting of almost equals, foreshadowing a juridically more formalized equality.

In this context, more precisely in the course of the discussion about the origin of modern capitalism, we are to meet with the Weberian pariah concept for the last time. As is well-known, Max Weber[38] contrasts the continuing and rationally conducted "bourgeois" enterprise with the politically secured commercial and financial operations of the Jews, which he terms "pariah-capitalism." The factuality of the observation need not be doubted, but the following must be added: 1) A statement of this kind comes suspiciously near to the protonazistic contradistinction of *schaffendes* (creative) and *raffendes* (rapacious) capital, of which one is supposedly "Aryan" and the other "Semitic" in origin; 2) the disparaging term "pariah-capitalism" fails to do justice to the economic role of the Jews. Max Weber himself has pointed to the development of modern bureaucracy, especially an orderly financial management, as the prerequisite for, and accompaniment of, the development of modern capitalism. The Jewish contribution to that development through the court Jews and the state bankers, who are their successors, cannot be gainsaid. Beyond that, one must think of the emergence of joint-stock banks in Europe, especially in Berlin, Paris, Brussels, Vienna, and Munich, institutions which in all those places owe their existence to the initiative and capital investment of private Jewish bankers. The Jewish contribution to that development throws into proper relief the somewhat too generalizing, quasi-ideal-typical contention that Jewish merchants have failed to participate in the buildup of "continuing enterprises." To be sure, Jewish participation was delayed, for reasons that cannot be elaborated at this point. What can be said is that the *Bayerische Hypotheken-und Wechselbank* which was founded in 1835 with 65 percent of the capital investment coming from Jewish sources, continues until this very day.[39]

The Pariah as a State of Mind

Hannah Arendt's conception of the pariah[40] is a different matter altogether. She touches only slightly on the question of whether or not, or to what degree, the Jews are a *Pariavolk*, although she seems to agree with the eighteenth-century writer Johann Jacob Schudt that individual Jews might attain "happiness" and exert considerable influence on account of their wealth, but that the Jews considered as a *corpo* are disregarded because they are "strangers everywhere" and lack sovereignty.[41] The important consideration at this point is that Hannah Arendt's pariahs emerge only in the nineteenth century and that they are a particular class of Jews. From the Middle Ages up to the period of the emancipation, the leadership of the Jewish community had shifted from rabbinical scholars to pious men of wealth, but Jews had taken themselves for granted throughout the shifting constellations. However, in the nineteenth century two rival elites appeared in sharp contrast, the parvenus and the pariahs. The *parvenus* were the financial magnates, the monied upstarts, who in the benign climate of the liberal era continued to be concerned with public finance and speculative venture; the pariahs were the new class—or anticlass—of intellectuals, journalists, critics, and free-lance writers. The parvenus were upstarts in the eyes of onlookers, while the pariahs were outcasts in their own eyes. To be a pariah in this sense was a state of mind. The monied aristocrats knew how to help themselves, and the average Jew never intended to leave the fold. But those intellectuals who separated themselves from the community of Israel but were not accepted in the larger community as anything else but Jews presented a problem. Indeed, some of them, like Michael Beer, author of a dramatic play entitled *The Pariah*, saw themselves as similar to the Indian Untouchables.[42] Ludwig Boerne (1786-1837) explained the emotional state of these men and women perceptively when he confessed about himself that "some accuse me of being a Jew, others forgive me for being a Jew, still others praise me for it, but all of them reflect on it."[43] Surely his desire to be considered a human being pure and simple could not be granted. Hence he and those like him were floating between the camps as true outcasts, that is, as belonging to no caste or class. Theirs was marginality with a vengeance. Under the conditions created by the Emancipation, the stranger had become a "marginal man." A more accurate discription of the marginal intellectuals would be the one of "frustrated escapists."[44] They were unable to escape yet unwilling to return. A statement of this kind is a melancholy postscript to the perennial accusation of Jewish "self-segregation."

Conclusion: Jews and Governments

The foregoing deliberations are preliminary to the understanding of the relations between Jews and government. The medieval theory and practice of servitus Judaeorum relates the Jews primarily to the central power of the imperium and secondarily to the delegated power of the territorial sovereigns. The nineteenth century retained that relationship but modified it in essential points. The Millet-like autonomy of the Jewish communities was abolished and replaced by the principle of citizenship, that is, by unified law with equal rights and obligations for all. The conception which the Jews had of themselves as living in *Galut* had to be abandoned. To Napoleon's incisive question to the Jewish delegates assembled in the Paris Sanhedrin, whether the Jews of France considered France as their fatherland and Frenchmen as their brothers, the delegates replied: "*La France est notre patrie, les Francais sont nos frères.*"[45] In the "Notes" to his question, Napoleon referred to the consequences of Titus's capture of Jerusalem as a thing of the past and he ended with the significant assurance that he wanted the Jews "to find in France a new Jerusalem".[46]

These sentences mark profound alterations in the status of the Jews, but in another view they hardly affected the relations between the Jews and the state. The Jewish state bankers, with the House of Rothschild as protagonist, became the mainstay of the inter-European system of governments, so much so that Prince Metternich could indicate to the Viennese Rothschilds: "If I should go to the dogs, you would go with me."[47] Jews everywhere became fervent patriots, attached more to the state than to the nation, because they knew that they owed their emancipation to governmental fiat in the face of popular reluctance. When, later in the nineteenth century, the Jews were confronted with antisemitic movements, they referred to their quality as citizens, as they had formerly referred to their special privileges, and to the obligation of governments to protect them in their constitutional rights. However, when in the aftermath of World War I the state was taken over by a totalitarian party, and especially by the NSDAP as a racist party, the state had been reduced to being the executor of racist policies. Herewith the point was reached where the very fact that the Jews were patriotic citizens came to count against them. They continued to rely on a protector who turned out to be a prostrate image of his former self. The state had ceased to be the arbiter of social forces and the guarantor of internal peace. If the party-state as a racial agent was to crush the challengers of the "master race," the Jews, who were considered the archchallengers and the very incarnation of the counter race, were faced with an implacable foe. Even with the deadly racial component removed, it remains likely that any party-state will have to consider the organized Jewish community as a community of strangers. The concept of the stranger includes the concept of marginality which has been developed from it and to which the concept of the pariah in Hannah Arendt's (but not in Max Weber's) sense can be reduced. To be sure, the stranger is an outsider who may become a foe. However, if he is permitted to be an intermediary, he can be a neighbor, friend, helper, and healer.

1974

Notes

1. Lewis A. Coser, "The Alien as a Servant of Power," *American Sociological Review*, 37, no. 5 (1972), pp. 574-581.
2. Max Weber, *Ancient Judaism*, Tr. and ed. by Hans H. Gerth and Don Martindale (Glencoe, Ill., 1952).

3. Max Weber, *The Religion of India*, Tr. and ed. by Hans H. Gerth and Don Martindale (New York, 1958), pp. 12-13.
4. Max Weber, *Economy and Society*, Ed. by Guenther Roth and Claus Wittich (New York, 1968), vol. 2, p. 493.
5. Weber, *Economy and Society*, v. 2, pp. 933-34.
6. Christian Sigrist, "The Problem of 'Pariahs,'" in Otto Stammer, Ed., *Max Weber and Sociology Today* (New York, 1972); see also Joseph Maier, "A Comment on Weber's *Ancient Judaism*", Ibid., pp. 192-6.
7. Weber, *The Religion of India*, p. 13.
8. Weber, *Ancient Judiasm*, p. 3
9. Weber, *Economy and Society*, vol. 2, p. 493.
10. Carl G. Hempel, "Problems of Concept and Theory Formation in the Social Sciences," in *Science, Language and Human Rights* (Philadelphia, Pa., 1952), pp. 71ff.
11. J.A. Dubois and Henry K. Beauchamp, *Hindu Manners, Customs and Ceremonies* (Oxford, 1897), Stephen Fuchs, *The Children of Hari* (Vienna, 1950), Edgar Thurston and K. Rangachari, *Castes and Tribes of Southern India* (Madras, 1909), vol. VI.
12. Werner J. Cahnman, "Religion and Nationality," in Werner J. Cahnman and Alvin Boskoff, eds., *Sociology and History*, (New York, 1964), pp. 271-80.
13. Lujo Brentano, *Der wirtschaftende Mensch in der Geschichte* (Leipzig, 1923), pp. 21, 214-5, 369 et passim; Ferdinand Tönnies, *Community and Society*, Tr. and ed. Charles P. Loomis (New York, 1957), p. 53, 75f., 168f.; Ferdinand Tönnies, *On Sociology: Pure, Applied and Empirical*, Tr. and ed. by Werner J. Cahnman and Rudolf Heberle (Chicago, 1971), pp. 288-317; *The Sociology of Georg Simmel*, Tr. and ed. Kurt Wolff (Glencoe, Ill., 1950), pp. 402-408.
14. Tönnies, *Community and Society*, p. 81.
15. Ibid., p. 15.
16. Weber, *Ancient Judaism*, p. 5.
17. Theodor Mommsen, *Römische Geschichte* (Berlin, 1885), vol. V, pp. 487-552.
18. Julius Guttman, "Max Webers Soziologie des Judentums," *Monatschrift für Geschichte und Wissenschaft des Judentums*, 69, 7/8, (1925), pp. 195-223.
19. Weber, *Ancient Judaism*, "Preface," p. XXIII.
20. Werner J. Cahnman, "Role and Significance of the Jewish Artisan Class," *The Jewish Journal of Sociology*, VII, 2, (1965), pp. 207-212.
21. Arthur J. Zuckerman, "The Political Uses of Theology: The Conflict of Agobard and the Jews of Lyon," Western Michigan University Studies of Medieval Culture, III (1970), pp. 23-51.
22. Robert Park, "Human Migration and the Marginal Man," *American Journal of Sociology*, 33, 6 (1928), pp. 881-893.
23. Weber, *Ancient Judaism*, "Preface."
24. Guido Kisch, *The Jews of Medieval Germany. A Study of Their Legal and Social Status* (Chicago, 1949), pp. 131-135, 145-153; Salo W. Baron, *A Social and Religious History of the Jews* (New York, 1962-65), vol. IX, pp. 136-146.
25. Coser, "The Alien . . ."
26. Glueckel of Hameln, *The Life of Glueckel of Hameln, 1646-1724*, Tr. and ed. by Beth Zion Abrahams, (London, 1962).
27. Selma Stern, *Der Preussische Staat und die Juden*, Part I, (Tübingen, 1962).
28. Selma Stern, *The Court Jew* (Philadelphia, Pa., 1950), pp. 19f., 25f.
29. Stern, *The Court Jew*, Chap. X.

30. Zosa Szajkowski, *Jews and the French Revolution of 1789, 1830 and 1848* (New York, 1970), pp. 298f.
31. Christian Wilhelm Dohm, *Über die bürgerliche Verbesserung der Juden* (Berlin and Stettin, 1781)
32. Hannah Arendt, *The Origins of Totalitarianism* (New York, 1966), p. 14.
33. Stern, *Der Preussische Staat . . .*, p. 129.
34. Stern, *The Court Jew*, pp. 208f.
35. Stern, *Jud Suess*, pp. 81, 144.
36. Stern, *The Court Jew*, p. 256.
37. Glueckel of Hameln, pp. 77-80.
38. Max Weber, *General Economic History*, Tr. by Frank H. Knight (New York, 1961), p. 264; see also Weber, *Economy and Society*, vol. 2, pp. 611-617.
39. Jakob Lestschinsky, *Das wirtschaftliche Schicksal des deutschen Judentums* (Berlin, 1932), pp. 27-28.
40. Arendt, *The Origins . . .*, pp. 56-58.
41. Ibid., pp. 24-25; see also, Johann Jacob Schudt, *Jüdische Merkwürdigkeiten* (Frankfurt am Main, 1715-17), p. 19.
42. Lothar Kahn, "Michael Beer (1800-1833)," *Yearbook of the Leo Baeck Institute*, vol. XII (1967), pp. 149-160.
43. Arendt, *The Origins . . .*, p. 64; quoted acc. to L. Boerne's *Briefe aus Paris*, 74th letter, Feb. 1832).
44. Werner J. Cahnman, "The Frustrated Escapist," *Reconstructionist*, vol. XXIV, no. 2, pp. 15-20.
45. Robert Anchel, *Napoleon et les Juifs; essai sur les rapports de l'état français et du culte israelite de 1806 à 1815* (Paris, 1928), p. 173.
46. James M. Thomson (Tr. and ed.), *Napoleon Self-Revealed in Three Hundred Letters* (Boston and New York, 1934), p. 158.
47. Arendt, *The Origins . . .*, p. 25.

3

The Role and Significance of the Jewish Artisan Class

The economic activities of the Jews in the post-Exilic period are usually considered as having been primarily, and even exclusively, commercial in nature. Whether the Jews are seen as international bankers of the Rothschild type or as miserable peddlers in the image of the "old clo'es Jews," whether they are described as a *Pariavolk* by Max Weber,[1] or as the epitome of a "marginal trading people" by Howard Becker,[2] the near-unanimity of proverbial saying and fairy tale, of political pamphlet and scholarly treatise, remains impressive. Jewish authors, perhaps because they have been preoccupied with ideological and political matters, have not challenged, or even scrutinized, this view seriously—to the extent that, a great many valuable monographs notwithstanding, a comprehensive economic history of the Jews, written by a Jewish scholar, is still lacking. Professor Wischnitzer's *A History of Jewish Crafts and Guilds*,[3] therefore, fills a gap in our knowledge and affords a welcome opportunity to test the thesis of the essentially commercial character of Jewish economic activities.

The task is complicated by the fact that the aims of the historian and the sociologist, in approaching the same topic, are not the same. The historian, once he has chosen his subject matter, aims at telling a story that may range from the earliest to the latest manifestations of a phenomenon, without much consideration for related phenomena the recording of which is left for another story. The sociologist, on the other hand, is interested not so much in the story itself as in the categories which it contains. In addition, he is not concerned with phenomena but with relations between phenomena. Where the historian records and interprets what he is recording, the sociologist compares the recorded data with other recorded data and attempts to arrive at a systematic view of their interrelationships. In the present case, Mark Wischnitzer tells the story of Jewish artisanship from its beginning until the late eighteenth century and up to the threshold of the industrial era. Within the time covered, he has recorded the activities of Jewish artisans and the structure of their guilds in many lands. He has shed light on the question of what position Jewish artisans have occupied in the Jewish community and in the larger society. He has followed up the struggles of the Jewish artisan against the dominant Christian guilds and the struggles of the journeymen within the Jewish guild system. But it was not his intention to relate Jewish artisanship to the concept of the Jews as a "marginal trading people" or to any other concept. Nevertheless, he has ordered his data in such a way as to enable us to check previously held notions with newly ascertained facts and to confirm or modify them according to the findings.

What conclusions do the data permit? Historically speaking, we discern two periods in Wischnitzer's story. The earlier period covers the formation of Jewish artisanship and the establishment of craft guilds in ancient Palestine and extends into the oriental and Mediterranean Diaspora. The later period fills the modern centuries and has its locale chiefly in northern and eastern Europe. In the earlier period, the ancestors of the Jewish people grew from a wandering tribe into a settled community in their own land, where they developed agricultural skills and the traditions of craftmanship. These skills and traditions were carried over into the neighboring Middle Eastern and Mediterranean territories to which the Jews of Palestine migrated. These territories may be called the countries of the first migratory settlement, or the first Diaspora. In them the social structure of the Palestinian Jewish community was largely preserved. The transfer of craftsmanship was most immediate in regard to Babylonia into which country Nebuchadnezzar had transported especially those artisans who, he feared, might have created an independent armaments industry if they had stayed behind in Palestine. However, agriculture remained for a long time as important as artisanship among the descendants of the exiles.

The situation continued under Persian overlordship and came to an end only after the Moslem conquest of the Sassanian empire. In Christian lands, a similar situation lasted well up to the period in which the Roman Church established its hold on the society of the Mediterranean area. Concerning Mesopotamia, then the center of the Diaspora, Wischnitzer reports that the Jews abandoned farming only from the end of the eighth century.[4] The reason was not, as Max Weber assumed, that agriculture was incompatible with the growing religious orthodoxy, but rather that agricultural pursuits by Jews were incompatible with feudal obligations. The land taxes imposed by the caliphs were onerous, and Jewish owners were more heavily taxed than others. In addition, political unrest and brigandage, the brunt of which was borne by the minority populations, made the countryside insecure and drove farmers into the cities. The Jewish artisan class in the urban centers therefore increased considerably, swelling the established groups of artisans with masses of newcomers. In Christian countries, ecclesiastical obligations and frequently-outright bigotry exerted the same kind of pressure. Such was the case in early medieval Sicily and in Visigothic Spain.[5] As a result, Jewish farmers either accepted baptism and stayed on the land or they remained Jews and migrated to the cities.

In the area of first settlement, the Jews were part and parcel of an indigenous population. Such was the heritage of the Roman and Sassanian empires and the consequences of the intermingling of populations in the rapidly growing urban centers. In this area, the Jewish artisan class continued to be an important segment of the total artisan class and, at the same time, a conspicuous element within the Jewish community. This was true in Mesopotamia, Egypt, the Byzantine lands, Italy, Provence, Spain, and North Africa. Even in Salonica and other Jewish communities which grew into prominence after the Expulsion from Spain, that is, in a period when Jews everywhere were footloose and humiliated, this character indelibilis of Mediterranean Jewry was maintained. Jews either had their own guilds or, among Moslem populations, were admitted into Moslem guilds.[6] In some places, as in Thebes in Greece, in Lucena in Spain, and in Salonica under the Turks, they held a virtual monopoly of guild membership.

Quite different was the situation as it evolved in the area of second settlement, or the second Diaspora. The Jews became estranged from handicrafts during the Middle Ages and in northern Europe, where they appeared as latecomers, outsiders, and strangers. There, Church ideology and the interests of the native middle classes worked hand-in-hand to exclude the Jews from the Christian guilds, to prevent the formation of their own guilds, and to relegate them to the position of petty traders and moneylenders. The image of the Jews as an economically restricted and socially depressed caste of hucksters and usurers is of northern and central European coinage. This image was not modified until much later, when a new Jewish artisan class arose in what may be called an area of third settlement in eastern Europe. This further development culminates in the modern Jewish Labor movement and in the colonization in Palestine.

The historical considerations are borne out by statistical analysis. To be sure, the scarce statistical data which the sources yield are merely illustrative in nature.[7] The important thing is whether a Jewish settlement constituted a small minority or a large minority within a total territorial society. By a small minority, we mean a community amounting to only a few percent (occasionally less than 1 percent) of the entire population of a country and rarely more than between ten and fifty families in any particular locality. Such was the proportion in the territories of northern and western Europe. The Jews of England, France, Germany, and northern Italy played a more or less important role in the economic life of their respective countries, but their numbers remained small. It will be observed that these are the countries where the Jews were excluded from the guilds and where permission for them to establish a "holy congregation" was predicated upon their being relegated to purely commercial activities, especially in connection with pawnbroking and the extension of consumption credit. In such countries, Jewish artisans were chiefly confined to crafts of a ritual nature, such as bookbinding and illuminating, printing, *tallith* (prayer scarf) weaving, barbering, butchering, and the like. They catered to a predominantly, even exclusively, Jewish clientele, and consequently there were very few of them. Only where larger Jewish communities existed do we find a Jewish artisan class of considerable size and diversity working for a wider market. This was the case in many oriental and Mediterranean communities, from Babylonia to Spain and from Yemen to Salonica, and likewise in eastern Europe from the fifteenth century onward. Especially where economic conditions deteriorated within the Jewish community even as its numbers were swelling did a large Jewish artisan class come into existence. In other words, the size of a Jewish artisan class stands in direct proportion to the size of a Jewish community, but in inverse proportion to its prosperity.

A sociology of the Jewish artisan class would have to consider the position of the Jewish artisan within the Jewish community as well as the role which he plays within the larger community. Contrary to Max Weber's assumption about the preference of rabbinical Judaism for the money trade, talmudic literature, as quoted by Wischnitzer, abounds in admonitions to learn a craft and in the praise of craftsmanship. Since scholarship was considered a sacred service rather than a profession, many of the sages of Palestine and Babylonia were humble craftsmen who lived by the work of their hands and sat in the houses of study after their work was done. Their learned piety was appreciated, but this does not mean that craftsmen as such enjoyed high prestige. More often than not, the opposite was the case. Apart from crafts that were capable of producing for wider markets (such as the brewing of date wine and goldsmithing in Babylonia), and apart from learned crafts that attained professional status (such as cartography, pharmacy, and medicine in medieval Spain), manual labor and artisanship retained the marks of low status.

The reasons are not far to seek. In Babylonia, as in other countries of the Near and Middle East, the number of craftsmen increased through the migration into the cities of dispossessed villagers, causing a surplus of hands seeking employment. At other times and places, the influx was caused by restriction in commercial activities and by outright expulsion from neighboring localities or distant countries. Whenever the influx was of considerable magnitude, as in Salonica in the sixteenth century, the moneyed aristocrats of the Jewish communities had to set up employment opportunties for their poorer brethren or provide relief. These social problems are reflected in rabbinic writing. Juridical opinions and decisions form an impressive body of social legislation in favor of the working man. To be sure, the craftsman or laborer had to render an honest day's work, repair damages he caused, provide for a substitute in case of absence from work, and so forth, but it is a distinguishing feature of Jewish legislation, as compared with similar legislation elsewhere, that the laborer's interests were no less protected than those of his employer. For instance, the working man's right to insist upon immediate payment, which is established in the Mishnah,[8] is unique. On the other hand, it must not be overlooked that some of the privileges of a religious nature accorded to working men, such as the permission to shorten the prayer of grace after meals in order to save time, or the permission to work until noon on the day before Passover, are negative privileges, denoting a lowered status. Wealthy men, having more leisure to learn, could accumulate more *mizvoth* (meritorious deeds). In this regard, Max Weber is vindicated. However, whether the merchants and financiers availed themselves of the opportunity for pious learning which their affluence afforded them, is another question. In times of stress, especially when confronted with the threat of confiscation of their earthly goods, the rich were prone to desert their faith in order to preserve their status. Salomon Alami, a Spanish scholar who witnessed the pogroms of 1391, blamed the rich for "the ruin of their people," while he expressed high regard for the steadfastness of the artisans.[9]

The antagonism between the upper and the lower classes, a continuing theme in Jewish history, has never been adequately described. A history of Jewish artisanship, while not primarily centered on that theme, affords an opportunity to discern the internal class struggle at many points. As a rule, the Jewish communities in the Diaspora were dominated by commercial interests. But the heritage of nomadic equality in ancient times and the fervent message of social justice propounded by the prophets were elaborated by the sages of pharisaic and talmudic Judaism to such a degree that the welfare of the laboring man was sufficiently protected. Accordingly, Babylonian Jewry in the period of the great academies achieved a considerable measure of social equilibrium; the task of formulating the rules of Jewish living after the loss of political independence overshadowed everything else. But the more the Jews migrated westward and northward from the Palestinian and Babylonian centers, and the more they became exposed to peripheral pressures, the more firmly established became the predominance of the men of means. We know of Jewish communities which were preponderantly communities of artisans, but their status was either depressed, as in Yemen, or they failed to stand up to the vicissitudes of fortune, as in Greece and Sicily. The Jewries of southern Italy and Sicily are a case in point.[10] In the reign of Emperor Frederick II of Swabia, the silkweavers and dyers of these territories were fashioned into a state monopoly; but when that organizational device crumbled, the artisans were left without effective leadership. At the time of the Spanish Expulsion, the Jews of Sicily, by then almost exclusively a community of craftsmen, were too impoverished to maintain intellectual activities and a vigorous community life.

The prime examples of heightened class antagonism are found in medieval Spain and in eastern Europe, especially in the old Kingdom of Poland. Before the Emancipation movement of the nineteenth century, Spain had been the country in which individual Jews climbed highest on the ladder of socioeconomic success. The court and the Jews were in firm alliance, and the Jewish courtiers participated in the splendor of their noble connections. Spanish Jewry also comprised a broad middle class of traders, artisans, and their apprentices, who depended, as did all of Spain, on the king and enjoyed patronage, protection, and autonomous status; but in the Jewish community councils, or *aljamas*, the influence of wealthy financiers and entrepreneurs predominated. This changed to some degree after the pogroms and antisemitic campaigns of 1391 and 1412–14. So many frightened men of means deserted the Jewish faith that the *aljamas* lost the majority of their administrative and juridical officers, and artisans had to replace them. However, as documentary evidence from the city of Saragossa shows, the baptized ex-Jewish gentlemen retained sufficient contact with Jewish affairs to sneer at the ignorant "taylors and strapmakers" and to remain at the disposal of the king when he called upon them to restore a competent conduct of affairs.[11] The contrary testimony of Salomon Alami was mentioned above.

The story of class antagonism within the Jewish community can be illustrated by examples from many lands. In Italy, in the seventeenth century, two different sorts of "Jewry-Law" existed, one for the privileged loan bankers, and one for the *università degli ebrei*, a miserable proletariat of peddlers, secondhand dealers, woolcarders, and ragpickers.[12] In the Bohemian registration of the eighteenth century, artisans ('wretched taylors') figured at the very bottom of the list, following merchants, lessees, and traders.[13] But it is only in Poland, likewise in the eighteenth century, that we find instances of actual class struggle. Contrary to the situation in Spain, the Jewish craft guilds in eastern Europe were not autonomous but depended on the elders of the Jewish communities for confirmation. Wischnitzer reports controversies and violent clashes between the Kahals (*Kehillot*), the official Jewish communities, and the Jewish craft guilds.[14] The Kahals of Minsk, Vitebsk, and other cities, which were dominated by businessmen, were accused by the representatives of the artisans of arbitrary taxation and other abusive practices, even of floggings and capricious arrests. The offices of the Kahals were physically attacked by the artisans, but the wealthy householders retained the reins of power. Even more depressed than the status of the masters was that of the journeymen, who grew increasingly restless as they failed to gain representation, even within the Jewish guilds. Wischnitzer's story grows dramatic at this point, which is a turning point in Jewish history. We are here witnessing the first stirrings of the Jewish labor movement. Jewish villagers fleeing before Ukrainian pogromists and Jewish traders succumbing to competition swelled the ranks of the artisan class to such an extent that it grew into a proletariat. Subsequently, in the socialist and Zionist movements of the nineteenth century, the impoverished masses, under secular-intellectual leadership, fashioned for themselves new ideologies.

In terms of Jewish-Gentile relations, a number of statements can be made. Wherever a sizable Jewish artisan class existed, the typical antisemitic image of the Jew as an idle exploiter and a money-monster could not arise. To be sure, this did not prevent discrimination, persecution, and expulsions, but it forestalled their congealment into a devil-ideology of Jewish existence. This devil-ideology grew into predominance in Germanic lands where it corresponded to the actual anomaly of Jewish status. In this regard, then, the Jewish artisan appears as the antagonist of the Jewish moneylender. In a structural view, however, the existence of a Jewish artisan class is not contradictory to the theory which characterizes the Jews as a "marginal trading people." The Jewish artisan, as a rule, is not a merchant or trader, but he shares the intermediary character of the trader's social position and role.

In order to substantiate this thesis, we shall have to review the list of Jewish crafts that can be drawn from Wischnitzer's text. One group of crafts and craftsmen however has to be excluded, namely, those that serve exclusively the internal needs of a Jewish community. Among these are butchers, bakers, winemakers, soapmakers, barbers, embroiderers, *tallith* and *tzizit* weavers, papermakers, scribes, bookbinders, printers, and similar tradesmen. Occasionally, engravers and gold- and silversmiths may be added to that list. All these trades have one thing in common, namely, that they are more or less ritualistic in nature; they are necessary for the conduct of a "holy congregation." Consequently, these are the trades which were represented even in countries where powerful Christian guilds excluded Jews from membership. Some of the trades mentioned were carried on in Jewish homes as a sideline; some, like the scribe's or the *shochet*'s (ritual slaughterer) trade, were regarded as holy vocations. None of them was part of the power structure of a Jewish community, and none was in any but the most superficial communication with the outside world. However, the borderline is hard to draw, as in the case of the butchers, who, at any rate, have to dispose of the ritually unclean hindparts of animals, and who have usually enjoyed a reputation for quality meats among the Gentiles.

Turning to the crafts that work for a wider market, one encounters those that are connected with the position of the Jews in the fields of monetary and cultural exchange. To the monetary group belong minters, jewelers, gold- and silversmiths, and medal engravers; to the cultural group belong bookbinders, illuminators, papermakers, printers, cartographers, designers of nautical instruments, pharmacists, and medical practitioners. These are the privileged crafts that come closest to banking and the international trade in metals and precious stones on the one hand, and to artistic and professional activities on the other. The Jews at all times dealt in gold and precious stones, because of the easy transferability of this kind of capital investment. Throughout the Mediterranean region and the countries of the Near East, they traded in these and related commodities. This brought them in contact with the courts, the nobility, and even the monasteries, either as providers of luxury articles and utensils or as creditors who took such articles in pawn. The artisans who worked on the material of precious stones and metals were closely connected with that trade. They brought techniques from afar, worked to specification, and refashioned according to local taste. Spanish Jews excelled in this field, and some oriental Jewish communities, such as those of Lybia and Yemen, specialized in it. Even in Central Europe, otherwise an area of stunted Jewish craftsmanship, the court Jews of the seventeenth and eighteenth centuries supplied Jewish jewelers and engravers, who then worked for their high-born clients. The connection of Jewish minters with monetary activities is obvious.

The Jews were intermediaries in the cultural field as well as in the world of finance. The foremost example is provided by the Jews of Spain who, along with the Moors, brought to Christian Spain the scientific knowledge of the Greeks in Arabic garb and many of the techniques of the older civilizations of the East. The Jews had a tradition of learning and utilized it for making a living in fields where scholarship and manual skill had to be combined. Linguistic and mathematical knowledge was utilized in calligraphy, cartography, the making of astronomical and nautical instruments, and linguistic and naturalistic knowledge in such highly professional skills as pharmacy and medicine. The Cresques family in Majorca gained fame as mapmakers. The Jewish printing enterprises which were established in Italy, Bohemia, and the Netherlands in the sixteenth and seventeeth centuries served, along with internal Jewish purposes, the needs of Christian Hebraists, and thus contributed to the spread of intercultural contacts. Similarly, Jewish musicians in eastern Europe entertained both at Jewish weddings and at parties of the Bohemian and Polish nobility.

Mentioning the symbiosis of Jews and nobles does not exhaust the topic of privileged Jewish crafts. The insecurity of the social position of the Jews, which made them dependent on the protection of Moslem and Christian rulers, lent itself to fiscal exploitation and the promotion of monopolistic industries. The fact that the Jews of southern Italy and Sicily held an important position in the various branches of the silk industry made the Norman and Swabian rulers of these regions intent on using their skills as a source of income. Roger II of Sicily, during his raids on Byzantium, went so far as to carry away as captives Jewish silkworkers of Thebes and other Greek cities in order to employ them in his royal factory in Palermo.[15] As the industry took root, the Hohenstaufen emperor Frederick II transformed it into a state monopoly, with Jews as administrators, buyers, supervisors, and workers. The profit flowed into the emperor's treasury. In the sixteenth and seventeenth centuries, the armies of the Turkish Sultans were clad in uniforms produced by the Jewish woolen manufacturers in Salonica.[16] At the same time, Jewish armourers provided the Turkish army with weapons.[17] Similarly, in early capitalistic Europe, Jewish capital and skill were used in the establishment of state monopolies and new industries. The capital employed was venture capital in enterprises in which the guild merchants were disinclined to invest, such as the Austrian tobacco monopoly. By the same token, Jewish manual skill found an outlet in these industries, which were not organized as guilds. This is true with regard to diamond cutting and tobacco dressing in Holland and such fine arts as seal engraving, gold and silver embroidery, and the like in eighteenth-century Prussia. In the nineteenth century, such new industries as the manufacture of cotton fabrics, ready-made garments, and tobacco products employed considerable numbers of Jewish workers in Russia.

Numerically more important than the privileged crafts, and sociologically as significant, are the depressed crafts. Since Jewish economic activities were frequently interstitial in nature, Jewish craftsmen found themselves often relegated to despised, dirty, and unhealthy work, repair work, and finishing work. In numerous instances, various of these characteristics were combined. For example, the tanning and dyeing trades formed a Jewish monopoly in many Mediterranean countries because the Gentile population did not care for the dirty work. In Greek cities, tanners were isolated and shunned. In Morocco, where the degradation of the Jews reached its nadir, Jews were occupied as scavengers and as cleaners of latrines, and they were charged with disposing of the corpses of executed criminals.[18] Tailoring, which has remained a Jewish occupation through the centuries, would likely be unhealthy work, carried on in cramped quarters and associated with cramped postures. A typical Jewish occupation in the Italian ghettos was the sewing and mending of old clothes and the remaking of used mattresses, activities which led to diseases of the eye and skin, to headaches, coughs, and consumption.[19] Also detrimental to health were the glassblower's craft, which was plied in the countries of the Near East, and the work of housepainters and furriers, in which many Jews in eastern Europe were employed.

Repair work means employment in auxiliary and subservient occupations. Italy was not the only country in which Jewish craftsmen were thus employed. Jewish men in Yemen used to spend the week in specified Arab villages where they tinkered and hammered and fused and mended until they returned to their homes and families on Friday. This is reminiscent of the Jewish peddler's role among the peasants in central Europe. Tradesmen or craftsmen—the functions are identical. But the analogy goes even further. Wischnitzer reports that in the sixteenth and seventeenth centuries Jewish pawnbrokers and secondhand dealers in Bohemia began to patch up old shoes, bags, trousers, furs, and other damaged articles which they had acquired and to sell them at reduced prices to their clientele.[20] The process seems to be best documented for Prague, but it assumed historical importance in the Kingdom of Poland. The secondhand trade and the repair business were the soil out of which the emerging Jewish artisan class in Poland drew a large part of its sustenance.

Generally, it must not be thought that the occupation of a Jewish craftsman and the historical function of the Jew as creditor are contradictory. True, Jewish artisans were frequently engaged in manual occupations, which did not entail selling of the product and delayed payment for services rendered. The Jewish silk weavers, dyers, potters, and leather and metal workers in the Mediterranean countries and, in later centuries, the woolen and clothing workers, the armorers, porters, and longshoremen of Salonica are examples. But the Jewish workingmen were employed exclusively by Jewish employers, and these, in turn, stayed in contact with the non-Jewish community to whom the products of their industries were sold. The same applies to the Jewish working classes in eastern Europe in the nineteenth and twentieth centuries and to the New York garment industry. We do not know a historical example of a Jewish working class being employed by non-Jewish employers. Hence, the image of the Jewish workingman remained remote to the Gentiles.

However, the above-cited examples notwithstanding, Jewish artisans in the majority of instances were individual entrepreneurs, selling their products in their own booths, stalls, and shops, and extending credit to their customers. Indeed, in the pawnbroking business, which had become the mainstay of Jewish economic activities in many parts of central and eastern Europe by the close of the Middle Ages, credit operations were of the essence, and the repair crafts that grew out of them were secondary in nature until, by the end of the eighteenth century, the roles appeared reversed. By then, the Jewish artisan class, soon to emerge into a modern working class, had become a factor in its own right. However, a particularly potent example for what we have in mind is provided by one of the most typically Jewish crafts in eastern Europe, namely, distillery, combined with inn keeping. Polish noblemen leased to Jews the right to distill brandy on their estates and the liquor was then sold to the estate's peasants on credit. Here, the craftsman and the creditor are fused in one and the same image, and the intermediate and interstitial nature of this kind of Jewish craftsmanship is clearly evident.[21]

A last point remains to be clarified. We have seen that Jewish crafts were widespread and their exercise uncontested in the area of first settlement—in the Near East and the countries around the Mediterranean—and that they were stunted in the area of second settlement—northern and western Europe. How, then, did the growth of Jewish artisanship in eastern Europe, the area of the third settlement, come about? If powerful Christian guilds succeeded in excluding Jewish artisans from membership and consequently from the exercise of their crafts in England, France, Germany, and northern Italy, and if they further succeeded in stifling or utterly cutting down the growth of Jewish guilds, as in Spain, how is it that effective Jewish guilds and a Jewish artisan class were capable of a new and independent development in eastern Europe? The answer is that Poland, Lithuania, and large parts of the Ottoman Empire in Europe and Asia had no native middle classes and that the Jews were called upon to fill a void in the social structure of these countries.

The rulers of Poland, Lithuania, and Turkey welcomed Jewish immigrants to promote trade and the useful crafts and to provide much-needed revenue. The Jews were all the more welcome because there were competitors on the scene. The Turks, having swallowed Byzantium, had become dependent in commerce and in the crafts, as well as in administration, on the ever-present but unreliable Greeks; they used their new Jewish subjects as a politically innocuous counterpoise. The situation in Poland and Lithuania was not dissimilar. The Jews who settled in the cities and towns of these countries alongside German burghers were considered indispensable for purposes of economic development but also feared as political antagonists. Hence, the sultans and the grand dukes and the kings fostered Jewish economic activities and protected the Jewish guilds. In the Ukrainian and Byelo-Russian parts of Poland, again, Jewish artisans along with Jewish traders were useful as revenue producers and economic auxiliaries to the crown and the nobles. When the power of the crown declined and the by-then Polonized Christian urban middle classes asserted themselves, the nobles continued to encourage Jewish artisans to settle in the localities (streets, districts, private towns) which remained under their control. These localities were exempt from the jurisdiction of the municipal councils.[22] The Jews and their guilds profited from a doubly and triply interstitial position. This was the reverse side of the coin whose obverse was political powerlessness and exposure to violence.

Additional circumstances furthered the growth of a Jewish artisan class and its guilds. The growing numbers of the Jewish population in Poland and Lithuania constituted an internal market of considerable magnitude. In this respect, conditions had never been so favorable for Jewish artisanship since the days of the Sassanian empire. The Jewish community in Poland and Lithuania grew away from the caste-like aspect of Jewish existence and assumed the character of a society. By and large, Jewish customers sustained many Jewish artisans. On this basis, some of them, like the lacemakers of Cracow and the furriers of Lvov along with Jewish carpenters, glaziers, and housepainters, gained clientele among the Polish nobility.[23] But their decisive advantage was that Jewish artisans could undersell the guild-monopolists and thus serve a mass clientele of Christians as well as Jews. The Jews were forced into this revolutionary avenue by a variety of circumstances. Fiscal discrimination in the field of commercial activities and the general impoverishment of the Jewish community in the wake of the Ukrainian pogroms in the seventeenth century drove the Jewish masses into manual occupations, sometimes in connection with petty trade. These marginal craftsmen had to earn a living by hook or by crook. Having learned their craft by trial and error, frequently with the assistance of runaway Christian journeymen, their work was likely to be of a shoddy quality and had to be sold at a reduced price. Wherever a craft grew out of the pawnbroking business and the trade in used goods, the refurbishing of worn and damaged merchandise added another incentive in favor of doing business by price-cutting. That the Jew at any rate was expected to grant credit added the final touch to the mechanism which had been set in motion. The modern economic role of the Jews in catering to needs of the growing mass market is thus adumbrated in the history of the Jewish artisan class in eastern Europe.

To summarize, the history of Jewish artisanship and craft guilds disposes of the prejudicial image of Jewish economic activities as chiefly those of hucksters and usurers—with an upper layer of bankers—which had grown out of the earlier fixation of social historians on the history of the Jews in central Europe. If the history of the Jews in the Mediterranean countries, on the one hand, and in eastern Europe, on the other, is taken into proper consideration, the importance of Jewish artisanship, besides commercial activities, becomes obvious. Lack of documentary evidence prevented Wischnitzer from consideration of the history of Jewish artisanship in the Maghreb (Morocco, Algeria, Tunisia), Lybia, and Yemen, and his untimely death prevented him from carrying the story of eastern Europe farther into the nineteenth century. Nevertheless, the picture that emerges is one of a remarkably widespread utilization of manual skills and craft activities. The textile and clothing crafts, especially tailoring, but also leather work and the food and beverage trades, predominate, but hardly any activity of the human hand is unrepresented. There is no such thing as a "racial" disinclination of the Jews to engage in manual labor. However, the general characterization of Jewish economic activities and of their role in the larger society as intermediate and interstitial is not invalidated by that statement. Invariably, the Jews form a middle layer in the societies in which they live, between the aristocracy and the laboring classes, with Jewish artisans as a part of that middle layer. There is one proviso, however: when the middle layer is numerically small, the Jewish artisan class is also small. When the middle layer, that is, the Jewish population, grows in numbers, the Jewish artisan class tends to grow into a broad working class. In this sense, the existence of a large Jewish artisan class appears as the prerequisite for the emergence of Jewish peoplehood and national consciousness.

1965

Notes

1. Max Weber, *Gesammelte Aufsaetze zur Religionssoziologie*, (Tübingen, 1923): vol. 1, p. 181; vol. 2, pp. 11–13; vol. 3, pp. 2, 351–79, 392, 434; *The Protestant Ethic and the Spirit of Capitalism*, trans. Talcott Parsons (London, 1930), p. 115; *The Religion of India*, trans. Hans H. Gerth and Don Martindale (Glencoe, Ill., 1958), pp. 11–13; *Ancient Judaism*, trans. and eds., Hans H. Gerth and Don Martindale (Glencoe, Ill., 1952), pp. 3, 336–43, 375, 417; *Wirtschaft und Gesellschaft* (Tübingen, 1922), pp. 282–83; *The Sociology of Religion*, trans. Ephraim Fischoff (Boston, 1963), pp. 108–10; *Wirtschaftsgeschichte* (Munich and Leipzig, 1923), pp. 175–76, 305–7; *General Economic History*, trans. Frank H. Knight (New York, 1961), pp. 151–52, 362–65.
2. Howard Becker, *Through Values to Social Interpretation* (Durham, N.C., 1950), pp. 109–13.
3. Mark Wischnitzer, *A History of Jewish Crafts and Guilds* (New York: Jonathan David for Yeshiva University, 1965).
4. Wischnitzer, chap. 5; see also J. Mann, "The Responsa of the Babylonian Geonim as a Source of Jewish History," *Jewish Quarterly Review*, N.S., 10 (1919–1920): 310ff.
5. Georg Caro, *Sozial—und Wirtschaftsgeschichte der Juden in Mittelalter und der Neuzeit*, vol. I: *Das frühe und das hohe Mittelalter* (Frankfurt am Main, 1924), p. 35.
6. The non-Moslem members of the Moslem guilds were in an anomalous position because of the religious character of the guilds, but they were not excluded from membership; apparently the intention was to facilitate the peaceful conversion of the artisan class to Islam. See Hamilton A. R. Gibb and Harold Bowen, *Islamic Society and the West; a Study of the Impact of Western Civilization on Moslem Culture in the Near East*, pt. 1 (London and New York, 1957), p. 294.
7. For instance, the census of the population of Rome (1526) and the census of one thousand Jewish men, women, and children in Prague (1546); see Wischnitzer, chaps. 14 and 15.
8. *Baba Meziah*, IX. 12; for other pertinent passages, see Wischnitzer, chap. 3.
9. Salomon Alami, *Iggeret Mussar* (Letter of Moral Instruction), quoted by Wischnitzer, chap. 12.
10. Julius Guttman, "Die wirtschaftliche und soziale Bedeutung der Juden in Mittelalter," *Monatschrift zur Geschichte und Wissenschaft des Judentums*, vol. 51, (1907), pp. 288–89; and Cecil Roth, *The History of the Jews in Italy* (Philadelphia, 1946), pp. 228–61.
11. Baer, Yizhak F. ed., *Die Juden im Christlichen Spanien, Urkunden und Regesten*, part 1: *Aragonien und Navarra*, (Berlin, 1929–36), p. 318; see Wischnitzer, chap. 12.
12. Cecil Roth, p. 340 et passim.
13. Koestenherg, "Mifkad 1724," *Zion* (1944), 23, and "Toledot ha Kalkalah shel

Yehudei Behm Shemechuz i Prag Bamea ha 17 weha 18,'' *Zion*, no. 64 (1947), quoted by Wischnitzer, chap. 16: "Expansion of Jewish Artisanship in Bohemia and Moravia, 1650–1780.''

14. Wischnitzer, chap. 23: "Relationship between Jewish Guilds and Jewish Community Councils in Poland-Lithuania, 1600–1800.''

15. Joshua Starr, *The Jews in the Byzantine Empire, 641–1204* (Athens: Verlag der Bysantinisch Neugriechischen Jahrbuecher, 1939), p. 223.

16. Isaac Samuel Emmanuel, *Histoire des Israelites de Salonique; histoire sociale, economique et litteraire de la ville mere en Israel*, vol. 1, (Thomon, 1936), p. 111; Evliya Efendi, *Narrative of Travels in Europe, Asia and Africa*, trans. Joseph Ritter von Hammer-Purgstall, vol. 2 (London, 1834), p. 166.

17. Nicolas de Nicolay, *Les Navigations, peregrinations et voyages, faits en la Turquie* (Antwerp, 1577), p. 245; Wischnitzer, chap. 13: "Jewish Crafts in the Ottoman Empire, 1500–1800.''

18. Jose Benesch, *Essai d'explication d'un mellah* (Paris, 1940).

19. Cecil Roth, pp. 371–72, 374.

20. Wischnitzer, chap. 15: "Jewish Artisans in Bohemia and Moravia from the early Middle Ages to the end of the Thirty Years' War.''

21. In Islamic countries, the fact that the Jews had a monopoly on liquor-making carried a particular meaning. For while Moslem law forbids the consumption of alcoholic beverages, a number of individual Moslems, some of them high-placed, could not do without wine and spirits, which they obtained only from Jews. Alcoholic beverages thus became a means of bargaining and of blackmail, almost the functional equivalent of an insurance policy. See Carleton Coon, *Measuring Ethiopia and Flight into Arabia* (Boston, 1935), p. 235.

22. Wischnitzer, chap. 19: "Jewish Artisans in Poland and Lithuania, 1350–1650.''

23. Ibid.

4

Village and Small-Town Jews in Germany

At first glance it would seem that village and small-town Jews comprise only a small segment of the total Jewish community in Germany on the eve of its destruction. Only 77,168 (15.5 percent) of the 499,682 Jews that were counted in the official census in 1933 lived in communities with less than 10,000 inhabitants, and an additional 17,172 (3.4 percent) in communities with 10,000-20,000 inhabitants. The comparable percentage figures for 1925 are 17.2 percent and 3.6 percent respectively.[1] But in a typological view, these figures represent an underestimate of the actual situation because a large percentage of the Jews living in communities of over 20,000 inhabitants had been born in villages and small towns from which they had migrated to larger cities. For instance, in 1895 almost one half (44.8 percent) of all Bavarian Jews still resided in rural communities.[2] As late as 1938, when the Statistical Bureau of the Jewish Community in Munich undertook a special census, only 34 percent of the Jews then residing in Munich were natives of the city, while 25 percent were born in other—mostly small—places in Bavaria; an undetermined number of the remaining 25.4 percent, who were born in Germany outside Bavaria, must be added to this group.[3] In my own family, my father and his sister—and practically all their relatives—were born and raised in a village (Rheinbischofsheim in Baden and Mühringen in Württemberg, respectively). My mother and grandmother and most of their relatives were natives of Munich, but my maternal grandfather and his brothers had come to Munich from Thalmässing (in Mittelfranken) in their younger years. I believe that the case of my family is not atypical. Barely more than one hundred years prior to the catastrophe of German Jewry, at the beginning of the nineteenth century, about 90 percent of the Jews living in the German-speaking countries of Central Europe resided in villages and tiny country towns. The figures for Württemberg are 93.04 percent for 1832 against 21.52 percent for 1933.[4] In the southern and western regions of Germany, only the Jewish communities

43

of Frankfurt am Main, Fürth, and Mannheim could be considered urban when the Holy Roman Empire was finally dissolved in 1806. A likewise limited number of other urban Jewish communities, namely, Prague, Metz, Hamburg-Altona-Wandsbeck, and Berlin were adjacent to, but outside, the area that is being scrutinized in this essay.

In earlier essays I have put forward the thesis that three separate regions of what later was to become German Jewry must be discerned, namely, South- and West-German Jewry, East-German Jewry, and the Jews of the Bohemian-Moravian-Silesian area.[5] Of these, only South- and West-German Jewry is the subject of the present treatise, not only because the author knows this partic-ular region well, but also because the phenomenon which we wish to inves-tigate is localized there. The Jews of Poznan and the neighboring territories that were incorporated into Prussia as a consequence of the division of Poland in the late eigthteenth century had a different pattern of settlement and a different outlook on life. The Jews of the Sudeten countries, outside of Prague, and even those of the Burgenland, on the one hand, are more nearly comparable to those of southern Germany than the Jews of Poznan but, on the other hand, they show features that reveal the transitory character of their settlement between east and west. The Bohemian *Dorfgeher* is a relative of the Franconian peddler, but other aspects of the life of the rural Jew in these parts, for instance those that are depicted in Leopold Kompert's story "The Children of the Randar," are reminiscent of Galicia.[6] There were no lessees of estates among the Jews of southern Germany. However, the Jews of Alsace must be included in the present investigation, at least as far as its historical dimension is concerned. Their socioeconomic status and their attitudes ini-tially were not different from the status and attitudes of other Jewish com-munities along the upper Rhine. The literary testimony for a statement to this effect is found in the *Erzählungen des Rheinischen Hausfreundes* by Johann Peter Hebel.[7]

I

In a historical view, the importance of the village and small-town Jews of southern and western Germany can hardly be overrated. The rise of modern Jewries in central Europe out of the degradation of the late Middle Ages originates in the villages of the Imperial Knights and Counts into which the Jews that had been expelled from the cities had retreated. As is well known, by the beginning of the sixteenth century the Jews had been reduced to petty moneylending combined with pawnbroking and the trade in used goods, and these activities had aroused the bitter hostility of the guilds. This closing chapter of the preceding period is superbly documented in Raphael Straus's study *Die Judengemeinde Regensburg im ausgehenden Mittelalter*.[8] In the villages, however, the guilds meant little, and the protection of the territorial sovereigns was more effective. In the villages, the Jews perceived an opportunity to re-enter merchandising by opening up markets for the agricultural products of the villages, such as cattle, wine, grain, and hides.[9] In addition, they provided credit for the acquisition of parcels of land which the peasants initially had merely leased from the nobles. Loans were also needed by peasants to pay taxes and to tide them over the lean period before harvest time. To be sure, it frequently occurred that the peasants fell into debt, so that their land was sold through the courts or otherwise alienated, but peasants as well as Jews knew that they needed each other. The city merchants were not inclined to grant small-scale and often risky loans to unknown debtors or to accept produce in lieu of cash. Towards the end of the eighteenth century, the prince of Birkenfeld, one of the more enlightened *Seigneurs* of Alsace, wrote that the Jews were useful to the inhabitants of the villages (for instance Bergheim near Ribeauville, from where one branch of my paternal family originates), because the peasants could purchase what they needed from the Jews without having to travel great distances and at prohibitive cost.[10] A few decades later, an Alsatian ex-peddler related in his memoirs that the Jewish peddler was a newsbearer, an intermediary, a connoisseur of coins; he bought and sold cattle and helped to sell the crop.[11] As time went on, many a Jew grew into the role of family adviser—a role that is immortalized in the figure of Rabbi Sichel in Erckmann-Chatrian's sentimental story, *L'Ami Fritz*.[12]

The village Jews suffered along with the rest of the population in the terrible ravages of the Thirty Years' War and the Wars of the Spanish Succession. In Alsace alone, according to Zosa Szajkowski, over 550 villages and towns had disappeared when the peace of Westphalia was concluded in 1648, and only 20 percent of the prewar population, including a remnant of the Jewish population, had survived.[13] But for some Jews, the wars offered new opportunities. We learn from Grimmelshausen's *Simplicissimus* that Jewish traders not only bought booty from soldiers and sold it in the opposing camp, but also that Jewish dealers were entrusted with the task of providing horses for the army.[14] Again, this significant trade seems to have been most pronounced in Alsace. While a petty German prince, like the Markgraf of Ansbach, merely obliged his Jews to sell the worn-out horses in his stables, the kings of France availed themselves of their Jews more contructively.[15] Even the emperor in Vienna was hard put to compete with them.[16] The armies in the field needed vast quantities of grain, wine, horses, and meat on the hoof, and only "the Jewish nation" knew where to get what was desired. It was sufficient to commission one Jew who was more aggressive and somewhat more affluent than others of his kind: he would engage ad hoc poorer relatives and business acquaintances as subcontractors, agents, helpers, and go-betweens, and extend credit on delivery. The intendant Turgot (1728) could say in acknowledgement of the services of the Jews of Metz that *"ils se mêlent de tout."*[17] The single historically most significant case in this context is the one of an agent Cerfberr, a native of Medelsheim near Zweibrücken (in what later was to be the Bavarian Palatinate). In 1756, he moved to Bischheim in Alsace and became the chief supply agent of the French army units that were stationed in that area.[18] His protracted litigation with the city of Strasbourg (1775-1789), whose town council declined to recognize a royal lettre patent granting him the right of domicile in the city, caused Cerfberr to turn for support—among other things—to Moses Mendelssohn in Berlin, who in turn asked his Gentile friend, Christian Wilhelm Dohm, to write the desired brief.[19] The outcome was Dohm's celebrated pamphlet *Über die bürgerliche Verbesserung der Juden.*[20] Thus, one of the most influential documents of the Enlightenment is unmistakably connected with the rise to affluence of an enterprising village Jew. As is well known, the burden of Dohm's argument (especially the appendix containing the *Mémoire sur l'État des Juifs en Alsace*) was that the Jews of Alsace, then in ill-repute because of their practice of usury, could be made into "useful citizens" if the cruel restrictions were removed and legal equality established.

The social stratification of village Jews on the eve of the emancipation was threefold: out of the multitude of ordinary cattle and horse dealers, cattle and horse dealers' sales agents (*shmoosers*), dealers in hides, produce, and used goods, and, most importantly, occasional dealers (*Gelegenheitshändler, Nothändler*) who eked out a miserable existence following Gluckel von Hameln's maxim that a *Jud nascht von a jeder Sach*, rose a thin upper crust of provision agents, purveyors, contractors, and bankers; but underneath them was to be found a kind of *Lumpenproletariat* of vagrants and *Betteljuden* who lacked even the precarious right of residence (*Schutzbrief*) of the average member of a Jewish village community. This group was in itself stratified in a variety of ways. Some of these people, as Lestschinsky assumes, may have been peddlers who mingled with the vagrants because they lacked a *Schutzbrief*;[21] others may have peddled stolen goods; still others may have been members of loosely organized bands of robbers and thieves; not a few converted to Christianity, either singly or as members of Christian bands, and made clever use of the chance which they thus acquired of having a foot in both the Christian and Jewish camps; many were average *Schnorrers* who appealed to the charity of one Jewish community after another.[22] The charity consisted in the establishment of beggars' hostels and the issuing of scripts (*Zettel*) which entitled the holder to receive a free meal at the home of a Jewish householder in the community: hence the expression *Gascht*, which in Judendeutsch parlance designates not a welcome guest at the table, but a nuisance of a guest, an unavoidable nuisance at that, and frequently a pretentious nuisance.[23] According to the meritorious researches of Rudolf Glanz, Jewish beggars and vagrants were already an intrinsic part of the Jewish scene in the fourteenth century,[24] but became a veritable plague in the seventeenth and eighteenth centuries, in the wake of the Chmielnitcky pogroms and the general deterioration of Jewish life in the old Kingdom of Poland. They even appeared on the agenda of the German Diet of Regensburg in 1736.[25] They gradually disappeared in the nineteenth century, but I know of no study which would enlighten us as to how they were absorbed—in the Jewish and Christian communities, and through overseas migration.

The Emancipation opened new avenues for stratification, by means of the freedom of trade. As a matter of fact, the Christian advocates of emancipation had two major goals in mind: first, to induce the Jews to abandon their "separateness," either by converting to a more tolerant, yet decidedly Germanic, Christianity, or by embracing a general citizenship in the manner of a moderate Jacobinism; and second, to diversify their lopsided economic structure. On both counts, the Emancipation failed, as far as the village Jews are concerned. On the religious side, the village Jews, and the peasants likewise, considered conversion and intermarriage an inconceivable and unforgivable sin, with the result that converts and young people contemplating intermarriage had to remove themselves to the city; these cases were rare enough, in any event.[26] Neither did the village Jews (in Württemberg, in this case) agree with Rabbi (Kirchenrat) Josef Maier that Stuttgart was "our Jerusalem."[27] We will return to the matter of religious attitudes later. On the occupational side, the village Jews were more than willing to avail themselves of new opportunities, but the obstacles were formidable. Jews could acquire land, and many village Jews owned or leased pieces of land throughout the nineteenth and twentieth centuries for use as meadows, vineyards, fruit and vegetable gardens, and the like. My great–grandfather Moses Kahnmann in Rheinbischofsheim was registered as "Ackersmann."[28] But as the potato field, pear tree, goats, and chickens, which was all he owned, did not suffice to make a living, he peddled ribbons, buttons, aprons, and accessories in a neighboring village and occasionally traveled up into a Black Forest valley to exchange his wares for the peasants' *Kirschwasser*.[29] It was only late in life, and at the urgings of his son (my grandfather), that he gave up the goat stable and opened a drygoods store. In other places, for instance in Rexingen/Württemberg and Alsdorf/Hessen, practically all Jewish families, especially the cattle dealers, owned larger and smaller pieces of land (mostly between two and four hectares) planted with wheat, rye, barley, and oats, in addition to meadows and gardens, and they held cattle in their own stables.[30] This does not mean, however, that these landowners worked their fields themselves. Some did, chiefly those who owned only small patches of land; others employed Christian fieldhands. Occasionally, one could even find a full-time Jewish peasant-landowner, with sixty to eighty hectares of property, as was the case in the neighborhood of Alsdorf; but that was an exception. By and large those Jews who owned land did so on the side, chiefly in support of the cattle trade. By the end of the nineteenth century, this had become the accepted state of affairs, but in the first half of the century, when the authorities, especially in Bavaria and Württemberg, frantically tried to compel the Jewish traders and dealers into "productive" activities, the official files are replete with complaints that the Jews merely ostensibly performed agricultural labor, while in reality they concerned themselves with the buying and selling of cattle and horses.[31] In retrospect, one is inclined to say that this behavior was nothing to be amazed about at a period in history when markets expanded all around, and a freewheeling, capitalistic cast of mind carried the day.

However, there were obstacles other than the Zeitgeist. Rabbi Adler in Kissingen, in his emotional "open letter" to the clerical and antisemitic representatives to the Bavarian Diet—Ruland, Sepp, Allioli and others—first published in the *Neue Fränkische Zeitung* in 1849, draws attention to the fact that free land was not available in sufficient quantity in the overpopulated Franconian villages where many Jews resided while the so-called Matrikel-legislation, whose declared and achieved purpose was to decrease the Jewish population, impeded the free movement of Jews to places where they might have acquired landed property.[32] A different, yet comparable, situation existed with regard to the manual crafts. The enlightened, paternalistic liberalism of the bureaucracy clashed with the narrow interests of the guild-masters who were intent on keeping potential Jewish competitors at bay; if and when a master might have been persuaded to accept a Jewish apprentice, the insistence of the youngster on observing the rules of Kashrut operated against his taking up room and board with him; and to place the boy in a nearby Jewish home was beyond the means of most Jewish parents in the villages. Besides, an arrangement of this sort was inconvenient for master and apprentice alike. Nevertheless, a Württemberg census of 1852 counted 412 butchers, 274 weavers, 121 shoemakers, 86 tailors, 74 bakers, and 50 soapmakers.[33] But apart from the butchers, who always had been present in a Kehilla Kedosha, most of these craftsmen never exercised their craft and instead went into a related branch of business. I have myself known a number of dry goods store owners and textile salesmen who told me that they had been tailor's apprentices in their youth, and I venture to guess that others of these ex-apprentices were among the early emigrants to America. Serious research on these matters is still in its infancy. Again, one must return to a consideration of the general trend of affairs. The Jewish peddlers had been trying for a long time to enter the regular retail trade against the resistance of the shopkeepers' guild, but had been only partially successful—for instance in Landau (Palatinate) in 1713 and in the territories of the counts of Hanau and Birkenfeld in Alsace.[34] When Count Reinhard II of Hanau-Lichtenberg, after the Thirty Years' War, moved his residence to Rheinbischofsheim (Bischofsheim am Steg) on the right bank of the Rhine, he permitted Jews to open stores over the protests of the merchants of Strasbourg;[35] one branch of my maternal family, who resided in Ichenhausen (between Augsburg and Ulm), adopted the name Kraemer in the eighteenth century. These were but straws in the wind, but they serve to illuminate that one of the most solid achievements of the Emancipation, from the village and small town Jew's point of view, was the permission to open retail stores. The Jewish dry goods and hardware store soon became ubiquitous in central Europe. One can almost hear a restless Jewish youngster say to his peddler father: "Papa, you don't have to run about anymore to the peasants in all weathers; open a store and let them come to you." As late as the first decades of this century, many a Jewish storeowner, who had inherited the business from his father, proudly would show me around in his well-stocked magazine, a testimony to his hard-won but solid respectability.

It might be worthwhile to follow the developments of the Jewish occupational structure in the nineteenth century by means of one example which is readily available, namely, the one of Landau in the Palatinate.[36] Landau is a small town with an agricultural hinterland which grew from about 5,000 inhabitants in 1816 to 16,736 in 1933; the Jewish population increased from about 150 to 596 in the same period. Landau was transferred from French to Austrian sovereignty in 1815 and to the crown of Bavaria in 1816. In 1808, under French rule, 13 dealers in secondhand goods (*Trödler*) were listed, along with 7 peddlers, 5 traders (most likely cattle and horse dealers), 3 innkeepers, 1 tailor, 1 baker, and 1 butcher. A listing of the Jewish families from the year 1833 already shows almost twice as many retail and wholesale merchants and craftsmen as peddlers and dealers in secondhand goods, plus several landowners, teachers, religious functionaries, and even one lawyer, plus a number of persons without occupations. It is further estimated that about 10 percent of the Jewish population in the Palatinate consisted of beggars who had no fixed residence—until this category practically disappeared with the end of the economic depression in the 1850s.[37] In 1857, there were already 11 Jews among the highest taxpayers in the town. From the 1850s until the 1920s some Jews migrated from Landau to larger cities, chiefly Frankfurt, Mannheim, and Paris, while others moved to Landau from neighboring villages, especially Albersweiler, Böchingen, Essingen, Niederhochstadt, Henchelheim, and Ingelheim. A listing from 1912 includes 41 merchants (including 1 banker), 47 wine dealers and wine commissars, 22 dealers in agricultural products other than wine (cattle, hides and leather, grain, fruit, tobacco, lumber, and real estate), 18 other dealers and traders (textiles, shoes, hardware, etc.), 4 craftsmen, 10 manufacturers (cigars, confectionary, basketry, matches), 6 academicians (lawyers, doctors, dentists), and some pensioners, religious functionaries, and other residual persons.[38]

The percentage of Jews in the wine trade was almost 70 percent, in the textile and food trades about 30 percent (with a higher percentage in the tobacco trade and the manufacture of tobacco products). The occupational structure was now solidly middle class in character, but the continuing importance of Jewish economic activities in the agricultural sector becomes especially obvious if one considers that the district of Landau was, and still is, the district with the greatest percentage of the total acreage devoted to viticulture in Germany.

Space does not permit a systematic analysis of the occupational structure in the villages and country towns on the eve of the Nazi advent to power (which could be done at least for Baden and Württemberg/Hohenzollern, thanks to the painstakingly comprehensive listing undertaken by the Archivdirektion in Stuttgart).[39] However, for the purposes of this paper, and in a very preliminary way, I have collected the data for Rheinbischofsheim and Freistadt in Baden and Baisingen, Mühringen, and Rexingen in Württemberg because of my family's connection with these places, and for Ichenhausen, Gunzenhausen, and Straubing in Bavaria because of my knowledge of these places from my activities as executive secretary of the Centralverein in Bavaria in the years 1930-34. Further, I have some data from Alsdorf, Kirchheim, and Gau–Odernheim in Hesse. Ichenhausen (where likewise I have family connections) is well documented by the researches of the late Dekan Heinrich Sinz.[40] In Ichenhausen, the initial picture differs somewhat from the one obtained in Landau, since according to the registration of 1811, there were 22 dealers in used goods and 79 peddlers in textiles and accessories, against 23 horse and cattle dealers, 17 butchers and produce dealers, and 7 small shopkeepers, among others. By 1930, the dealers in used goods and the peddlers and hucksters disappeared. While there were many cattle and horse dealers who either kept their own stables (a minority) or stationed animals with peasants in neighboring villages, the most esteemed members of the community including the *parnassim* were garment manufacturers, wool, cotton, linen, hide, and leather wholesalers, and some of the larger textile retailers. The situation was different again in Rexingen, where the wealthier cattle dealers dominated the local scene. Generally, however, I believe one cay say that the stratification pyramid had been flattened to a large degree during the nineteenth century. The two "lower-lower" classes, the beggars and the occasional (hand-to-mouth) dealers were gone, either to more profitable pursuits or to America, and the wealthiest Jews, like the Kaullas in Hechingen or the Hirsches in Königshofen, had become residents of the larger cities. A comfortable style of living prevailed. In some places the highest taxpayer was a manufacturer or a banker (two manufacturers of spirits in Rheinbischofsheim, a garment manufacturer both in Ichenhausen and in Mühringen, a banker in Gunzenhausen), but in other places (Straubing, Kirchheim) it was a large retailer, and in still others (Rexingen, Baisingen, Alsdorf, Gau-Odernheim), the more affluent cattle dealers.[41] There was an income differential between the largest cattle dealers (''a *Thaler* business'') and those cattle and produce dealers who merely got along (''a *Pfennig* business'').[42] But the prestige difference between retailers and wholesalers, on the one hand, and cattle dealers, on the other, was of greater importance. As already indicated for Ichenhausen, the retailer and wholesaler (of frequently a combination of a local store with a *Reisegeschäft*, that is, the sale of merchandise—mostly textiles—in distant localties) was almost always a highly respected citizen, while those wealthy cattle dealers that were at the same time, and sometimes prominently, engaged in real estate dealings did not always enjoy the most salubrious reputation among Jews or Christians. This was especially true when they were concerned with the division of larger peasant holdings into single lots (*Güterschlächterei*). Even J. Rülf, who refuses to admit (in his treatise about antisemitism in Hesse) that deals of this sort were unjust or usurious, regards them as ''unfortunate'' (*unselig*) for Jewish-Christian relations.[43]

A word remains to be said at this point about the Jewish teacher. By the end of the nineteenth century, more than sixty rabbis in southern and western Germany still served communities with less than one hundred families. Up to that time, the teacher had been a *quantité negligeable*, but after 1900 he became leader of the congregation.[44] He taught the dwindling number of children, saw to it that kosher meat was available and a *minjan* assembled on the Sabbath, officiated as Chazzan, was an expert on *minhagim*, and was arbitrator of communal animosities and an ambassador to the Gentiles. He had to supplement his teacher's salary in a variety of ways, be it through rewards for *misheberach* (marriage brokerage), help with petitions and archival enquiries, or as the representative of an insurance agency. I preserve a high regard for these men, some of whom were the strongest pillars of Jewish civic defense activities in the trying years prior to 1933. Many remained at their post even after Hitler's assumption of power.

II

In the round of life and the attitudes of the village Jew, the principles of *Gemeinschaft* and *Gesellschaft* are inextricably intermingled, and so are the corresponding, but not identical, categories of time and space. The temporal aspect, which is older, is given in kinship. Kin relations connect the generations of man, the ancestors that once have been and the offspring not yet born. The spatial aspect derives from neighborliness, which initially is identical with kinship inasmuch as kinsmen settle in proximity, but grow apart as soon as commercial relations develop among strangers in kin who dwell alongside each other in the same locality. However, in the old villages, neighborly and commercial relations are not yet categorically separated—they interpenetrate each other in a variety of ways. The Jews in the village, even in the entire region, are like an extended clan, yet they are often commercial rivals. The Jews and the peasants belong to different kin and are economic antagonists, yet they help each other on the strength of their neighborliness, inadvertently and deliberately, in a variety of ways. But the initially and essentially significant fact is the linkage of time and space in the consciousness of the village Jew. The symbol of that linkage is the cemetery. There, the temporal cohesion "has its invisible metaphysical roots, underground, as it were, and derived from common ancestors," precisely as Ferdinand Tönnies developed the idea in the last pages of *Gemeinschaft und Gesellschaft*.[45] At the same time, however, the cemetery is part of the visible soil of the *Heimat*, the physical here and now. In the cemetery rest one's forebears, at least those who died in the general neighborhood; but contrary to peasants, who do not know whence their families came in times beyond memory, the Jews know, or believe they know—and the peasants know it with them—that they are the descendants of Abraham, Isaac, and Jacob. Whenever possible, a clump of earth from the land of Israel is buried with the Jewish dead, so that they may rest on it forever, associating space and time over the distance of both. Yet, the sacred clump of earth mingles with the soil of the *Heimat* in such a manner that the two become indistinguishable, exchangeable in sentiment, one and the same thing.

The cemetery is the focal point, where the mentality of the village Jew can be grasped. Wherever Jews came, the first thing they negotiated, after the terms of settlement had been fixed, was the acquisition of a burial ground. What distinguishes the Jewish cemeteries in southern and western Germany, including those in Alsace and Bohemia, from Jewish cemeteries in many other places is the location in the open country. The Jews were strangers among the peasants, but at home amidst the fields, on the grassy hillsides, at the edge of the woods. The "old" Jewish cemetery at the Thalkirchner Street in Munich, once outside the city limits, has preserved that at-home-like quality, and surely even more so have the cemeteries of Ichenhausen, Schopfloch, Thalmässing, Rheinbischofsheim-Freistedt, Rexingen, Nordstetten (where Berthold Auerbach rests), and especially the cemetery in the Talwald near Mühringen. When Clementine Kraemer, a sentimental writer, speaks of the tomb of her grandfather Joel Levi as "*umrauscht von Schwarzwaldtannen*," she has the two ingredients, Jewish "blood" and German "soil," ideally combine.[46] But even a shrewd and successful industrialist, like my grand-uncle Joseph Schülein, lavished infinite care on the tombs of his father and his grandparents in Thalmässing, a place which he had left at an early age.[47] It is therefore superficial of Utz Jeggle to say that "woods and meadows were relegated to the background'' in the *Heimat*-consciousness of the village Jews, when compared with the family and the Jewish community.[48] They are part and parcel of one and the same thing. The merger of temporal and spatial aspects, that is, of the Jewish family and the surrounding natural environment, is impressively documented by Jacob Picard and Berthold Auerbach.[49] What fell by the wayside in 1933 was the feeling of nationality, which was city-bred in any case.[50] Even the participation of the Jews in the *Kriegerverein* was meant to be more a local than a national affair, until the *Reichsbund jüdischer Frontsoldaten* turned a different corner. After all, it was the Jewish dead that were honored along with the rest. They were supposed to have died for the vindication of the Jewish name more than for anything else. In this regard the Jews differed from their peasant and craftsmen neighbors chiefly on account of their greater self-consciousness.

Whatever else one might say about the religiosity of the village and small-town Jews follows from the initial statement. The religiosity of the village Jew was matter-of-fact, without embellishment and the display of fancy cantorial singing, not so much a thing of devotion but a fulfilment of duty. As a young man upon reaching a certain age was supposed to enter the army, so a Jewish adult above the age of thirteen should not be missed from a service. If only nine men were assembled and the tenth man was tardy, he was fetched from his home; only his presence was required, not his enthusiasm. The service was to be conducted literally, with not a word omitted, and heated arguments would arise over small infractions. Even more acrimonious controversies would break out over questions of prestige, for instance, who would be permitted to do the *oren* (lead in prayer), who would get the first *alijah* (in case there were several Kohanim present, as in Rheinbischofsheim), who had offered a higher bid earlier when the *alijot* were auctioned off, who could occupy a coveted seat, and so forth.[51] One can say that internally Jewish life was suspended between the emotional poles of prestige (*kavod*) and food (*achila*), but only the prestige angle was of concern at the service; food, although endowed with intense religious meaning, was a domestic affair. The *tertium comparationis*, quite obviously, was economic in nature: the highest honors in *shul* would go to the highest bidder, and the wealthiest cattle dealer could praise the Lord over the most opulent meal. The matter is beautifully handled in reverse, as it were, in Jacob Picard's short story about the *parness* who learned a lesson from the mayor of the village. The mayor, in a surprise visit to the synagogue on Sim'hat Torah, put in a bid for Moishele, the poor barber, to be called up for the third *alijah*—an honor that had been denied him up to that moment.[52] Picard relates that from that time on every year on Sim'hat Torah, the poorest man in the community was called up for the third *alijah*, but he omits to say that this was done more in honor of the mayor than of the poor congregant. However, the main point in the present context is that the *minhag* (usage) was created by the mayor's intervention. Never mind the meaning—one did it this way or that way, and that was all. In that regard, the Jews and the peasants differed not very much.

I am aware of the fact that I have presented a picture of but one type-image of a village as it existed in the first decades of this century, with approximately twenty to forty Jewish families in it. The canvas should be enlarged to encompass both the development that occurred during the two centuries from 1730 to 1930 and the situation prevailing in small country towns, especially those that were the seat of a rabbinate. Erich Rosenthal, in his sensitive reportage about a small-town Jewish community in Hesse in 1933, points out that what had been a divine commandment for the grandfathers tended to become a hallowed usage for the fathers and finally was performed merely perfunctorily because public opinion still seemed to insist on it.[53] In this context, a story comes to mind that is told about the Jewish shopkeeper who closes the front entrance to his store on the Sabbath but serves his customers at the rear entrance. When asked whether he believed that the Lord-on-High could not observe what happened at the rear entrance as well as what was not happening at the front entrance, he is supposed to have replied: ''The *olam-hashalom* knows that I am a *ganef* [thief], but is it necessary that the people know about it?'' This is about as far as one can go in a small community. However, Rosenthal's sequence is stylized and stands in need of historical complementation. A careful perusal of Herman Pollack's *Jewish Folkways in Germanic Lands (1648–1806)* leaves the reader with the impression that a creeping disintegration, as evidenced by complaints about disregard of intensive Jewish study among adults, scant attendance or inattentiveness at services, negligence in the observance of the Sabbath and the like, was setting in already in the wake of the dismal failure of the *Shabbatai Zwi* movement.[54] On the other hand, usages connected with the life cycle, observances in the home, and education of the young, that is, usages that had a family connotation, continued to be strictly upheld. To be sure, Pollack's sources chiefly refer to larger communities, but what was observed with laxity in Frankfurt and Fürth must be presumed to have been further relaxed in the villages—long before a breath of modernity could have reached them. Pollack does refer occasionally to the difference in knowledge between urban and rural Jews, but there is also a difference in the quality of social contacts. A story shedding light on this phenomenon is reported by Johann Jacob Schudt.[55] In order to illustrate what he means by Jewish ''indulgence and insolence,'' he relates that a Jew must rinse a cup from which a Christian has drunk before he can drink from it himself, but he comments that in the villages (and also in Italy!) one does not adhere to these usages as uncompromisingly as one does in Frankfurt and that the village Jews even drink wine that comes from Christian winepresses. A village Jew and a peasant were not as far apart, physically as well as socially, as an urban Jew and a Christian burgher.

An equally telling story about rural disregard of *halakhic* requirements that may have stood in the way of practicality has come down from my grandfather's grandfather in Rheinbischofsheim. When one of his sons showed up too late at potato harvest time with the excuse that he had to lay *tefilim* (phylacteries), the father is supposed to have replied that it would have been better had he laid eggs! That ancestor, surely not a stickler after the Frankfurt fashion, was renowned for his practical jokes (and his physical prowess) in the Hanauerland.[56] A further difference must be made between localities where the Jews subsisted on the level of peasants, even if they may have roamed far and wide in search of a livelihood and thus acquired a more restless outlook on life, and others, like Mühringen, where they were equally poor but more thoroughly steeped in Jewish lore and learning; Mühringen was the seat of a rabbinate, and it was already a Jewish centre in the eighteenth century and had an academic rabbi, Dr. Moses Wassermann (1835–1872), early in the nineteenth century.[57] Finally, one can lay down the rule that a householder's orthodoxy was more pronounced the higher he was positioned on the social scale. Berthold Auerbach's paternal grandfather was so comfortable and at the same time so learned that he could afford to officiate as a rabbi and *shtadlan* (spokesman for Jewish interests) without remuneration.[58] A still more striking example for the correlation between orthodoxy and affluence is provided by Hänlein Salomon Kohn of Wassertrüdingen in Bavaria, a distant relative of my maternal grandmother's family.[59] In his youth, he learned the sievemaker's craft in order to acquire the right to settle in Wassertrüdingen (under the provisions of the Bavarian *Matrikelordnung*), but he never needed to practice that skill. Having acquired a fortune in real estate from his father and a dowry when he married, he became a dealer in real estate himself, as well as an owner and manager of widely scattered agricultural property. He used to inspect his holdings in a horse-drawn carriage. He was a latter-day court Jew in that he conducted himself as a rigid authoritarian and a generous dispenser of charity. He had the means to maintain a resident rabbinic scholar for the instruction of his children and the leisure to engage in a daily Talmudic lesson. These few examples may serve to show how difficult it is to generalize about village and small-town Jews without envisaging a variety of regional, local, and occupational sub-types. However, what all these sub-types have in common is fairly obvious: a solid rootedness in time and space.

Religion and the family are closely connected at all times because the core of religion is ancestor worship. Literally, religion—in the Latin meaning of the term—is the tie that binds us to those that came before us. The cemetery is the *gute Ort* because there we communicate with the spirits of the deceased.

The Kaddish is the most popular prayer of the synagogue. Yizkor is the service that is most universally attended. In Judaism, one prays to the God of Abraham, Isaac, and Jacob, but when Yizkor was said in the village *shul*, the more immediate ancestors were more immediately present. At home, in the flicker of the Yahrzeit candle, the soul of the dear one became peculiarly alive. By the same token, the Jewish festivals are dedicated to the family, so that around the table the ties to the living should be as strong and enduring as the ties to the dead.

The importance of food and food symbolism in the life of the village Jew cannot be exaggerated. An oppressed people takes refuge in the joys of eating because they cannot be contested, a rural people appreciates the daily bread that has been earned by the sweat of one's brow; but the Jewish festivals, that are almost all agricultural festivals, not only bestow a blessing on what has been harvested here and now, but they carry the participants back in time, when they eat the "bread of affliction" on Passover, when the devour a crisply baked *haman* with a cup of coffee on Purim, when they assemble in a gaily decorated *succah*, and when they indulge in orgies of gratification on Sim'hat Torah. Still more important for the old-time village Jews was the Friday evening meal which reunited the family after the husband and father had been away during the week. In his wanderings all over the countryside, the Jew occasionally might find in a village inn or with a friendly peasant a pan especially marked with the sign of *kashrut*, for the exclusive use of Jewish guests, but otherwise the peddler subsisted on what he could carry: hard bread, smoked meat, dried fruit, and the like, in addition to a cup of black coffee or a *gläsle kirsch* that he could accept from an old customer. When he arrived back home, worn-out and tired, he might bring along a live chicken for the wife and nuts for the children, but after he had washed and dressed, he was indeed king at a royally bedecked table, and his wife could bask in glory when he praised the "virtuous woman" above all the goods of this earth.[60] At a later period, when I visited Rheinbischofsheim, the uncle, now a comfortably placed storeowner, would take me along to the Friday evening service, but on the way home he would admonish me not to forget to say a word of praise about his elderly sister's potato salad which she used to bring from the kitchen immediately after the soup had been eaten. Indeed, the salad glistened in a beautiful yellow, it was cool but not cold, soft but not mushy, moist but not greasy—a veritable piece of art about which the old lady was as proud as Michelangelo might have been about his *David* or *Moses*. The same ahs and ohs that had to be exclaimed over the potato salad were repeated over the *Grünkern* soup, the sweet-sour carp, the boiled beef in the parsley sauce, the tomato salad, the pickled cucumbers, the wine, the coffee, the cookies, the apple compote with raisins, the beautifully preserved candied fruit—all prepared by the aunt as the very stuff of family cohesion.[61] Possibly, the uncle would good-naturedly comment about the daughter of the house getting a little too well-rounded, but this, too, was meant to contribute to the sense of shelter and loving care. This world has been destroyed very thoroughly.

There has always been much jealousy, arguments, and competitive striving in the Jewish family, for instance among brothers or cousins who trespassed on a peddler's or dealer's trading territory (*medina*), among sisters-in-law who fought about the prerogatives of their sons and husbands, among the children in the house that got in each other's way.[62] But after the din of battle had died down, the Jewish family stood unimpaired. The religious quality of family cohesion is best illustrated by the story which Berthold Auerbach's mother used to tell (to quell her children's controversies) about how the Holy Temple on Mount Zion was erected on the ground and soil of brotherly love. When King Solomon, wandering about on a sleepless night, observed two brothers who owned in common a field on the mount, each of them unseen by the other removing the dividing stones so that the brother's half would be enlarged, he knew that this hallowed ground was the long-sought place upon which the santuary should be built.[63] But the impact of the story reaches beyond the relations between brothers and sisters, to embrace their spouses, their children and children's children, grand-uncles and grand-aunts, first and second cousins and their offspring — an entire clan. When a son or daughter married, the in-laws and their relations were accepted into the family, just as the son or daughter was accepted into theirs. Thus it came to pass that after a few generations of continued settlement practically all the Jewish families in a particular region were somehow related. Indeed, quite a few families were related several times over, without this necessarily implying inbreeding in the narrower sense. What happened was that in small- and medium-sized communities not enough prospects for a suitable marriage existed, so that deliberate efforts had to be made to establish contacts over a wider area. An aunt or a grandmother had a bright idea, or else the cattle market served as a news exchange and a marriage market.[64] Once the first liaison was consummated, a brother or a cousin might find access to the new family eased and further efforts by third parties could be dispensed with. For instance, to refer only to my own family, Daniel Cahnmann of Rheinbischofsheim, then residing in Karlsruhe, married Mina Marx of Nördlingen, whereupon Mina Marx Cahnmann saw to it that my grandfather's younger brother-in-law, Louis Levi, got married to Sophie Kraemer, a daughter of one of her cousins, Regina Kraemer, née Marx. A son of Regina Kraemer, Max, then came to know and married my grandfather's daughter, Clementine Cahnmann, and my father got engaged to Hedwig Schülein, a daughter of Regina Kraemer's oldest daughter, Johanna. I found similar multiple relationships among the Levi-Kahn families in Mühringen-Baisingen, among the Schülein-Gunzenhäuser families in Thalmässing-Feuchtwangen, and among the Kraemer-Affhauser families in

Ichenhausen. These early contacts indicate a narrower regional radius than those mentioned above, but they are all of the same kind, the idea being that multiple linking guaranteed the solidarity of family cohesion.[65] The knowledge of relationship ramifications (*mishpochology*) has now lost much of its importance in an enormously enlarged marriage market, but inasmuch as the preservation of the Jewish people is a prime *mizvah* in Judaism, one is impelled to conclude that the decline of the art of marriage brokerage is one of the indications of the loosening of the ties of religion.

In contrast to the relations between Jew and Jew, which are decidely *Gemeinschaft*-like in origin, although they increasingly shade over into *Gesellschaft*-like contacts, the relations betweeen Jew and peasant or Jew and local craftsman are predominantly *gesellschaftlich* in character. No love is lost between them. Jews and craftsmen were hostile to each other over long centuries. Jews and peasants needed each other as buyers and sellers, lenders and borrowers, creditors and debtors, with each participant soberly calculating advantage and disadvantage in the deal that was under consideration.[66] To sell a sick cow as healthy, an old horse as young, required consummate skill in sales strategy, in which peasant and Jew were every bit each other's equal. If one lost out in one deal he would try to come back in another, as is illustrated in Johann Peter Hebel's anecdote "Gleiches mit Gleichem."[67] Sometimes, as in Clementine Kraemer's story "Vom Grossvater und vom Hofbauer," the coming back might have been delayed for years, but it finally came.[68] Per saldo, there were neither victors nor vanquished, or else the relationship would not have been continued. I believe this is a fairer way of putting it than to depict the peasant as the innocent country yokel and the Jew as the exploiter. Also, in credit operations the risk was mutual: the peasant could lose his farm, and the Jew could lose his money. But Jew and peasant were neighbors besides being traders; the neighborly relations, even if they are not kin relations, always carry an element of helpfulness. As John K. Dickinson explains in his intimate portrait of a Hessian village in the early 1900s, for a Jewish trader "to put a cow in a poor man's stable" means that the peasant feeds the cow for him, so that he can take her out in good condition at the end of the growing season and sell her.[69] But it also meant that the peasant, who otherwise would be at a loss how to get along, can avail himself of the cow's services as a draught animal and at the same time use her to provide milk for his family. Conversely, Jewish women could not do without domestic servants, but peasant girls would be most eager to enter service with them because it meant that they got the best possible home economics course in preparation for their own marriages, with free room and board and occasional gifts into the bargain. Many of these girls became closely attached to a Jewish family; some of them remained faithful during the Hitler years when neighbors and business friends succumbed to social ostracism, and those who are still around indulge in glowing reminiscences about the former glory.[70] In addition, Jewish housewives were sources of folk medicine and solicitous providers of chicken soup for sick neighbors.[71] In Rheinbischofsheim, there even developed a friendly trading partnership between the Cahnmann dry goods and groceries[72] store and the *Bärenwirt* across the street. The peasants and their womenfolk waiting to be served at the counter in the meantime would move to the inn for a glass of wine or a cup of coffee. Thus, both merchant and innkeeper increased their clientele. The daughter of the innkeeper and the only surviving granddaughter of my great-uncle are now intimate friends, long after the former trade relationship has been dissolved. J. Rülf is very right when he says that "the sharp division of the nationalities, of speech, custom, way of life, behavior, and demeanor" between Jews and peasants stood not in the way of friendship.[73] In the exchange of *mazzoth* and painted eggs at Easter time, which is reported from a number of places, the relationship even overcame the religious barrier, if only for a brief moment.[74] For it must be said that the teaching of the Church, particularly around Easter, did not provide for a friendly atmosphere. John K. Dickinson observes that "the relative harmony between the two religions in rural Hesse (and elsewhere) was a remarkable demonstration of how intimate daily contact can obscure religious differences without defusing them."[75] In this regard, Berthold Auerbach's reminiscence about a happening in his youth is of symbolic significance. On his way home he was ambushed by three boys from a neighboring village and bound in the shape of a cross, when he refused to say: "Christ is risen." But Auerbach also reports that Jewish and Christian friends from his own village took physical revenge on his tormentors afterwards.[76] The Jews in the villages knew how to help themselves, either physically or by some clever device. For the latter method, Johann Peter Hebel's *anecdote* "Glimpf geht über Schimpf" is as good an example as any.[77] Hebel relates that a Jewish peddler, upon entering a village in the Alsatian Sundgau, was molested by boys who threw pebbles at him and insulted him with cries of "*Judenmauschel.*" He decided not to meet the challenge head-on but to bring along small coins which he distributed among the yelling children. After he had done this several times, he changed his tune. He told the youngsters that he could not afford to continue the game, whereupon they retaliated by discontinuing to call him *Judenmauschel*! By this device, which would delight social psychologists, peace was restored.

These stories, as well as others which could be told, should lay to rest the widely held notion that has received scholarly approbation from Max Weber, namely, that the Jews were a pariah people in anything like the Indian prototype of the term.[78] To be sure, tension was unavoidable in the first half of the nineteenth century, when the Jews surged ahead economically, encroached on established interests, and aroused jealousies, while the image of the lowly peddler remained on everybody's mind.[79] But towards the turn of the century, when economic antagonisms lessened, the "neighbor" had become a more pervasive reality than any pariah-related reminiscence. It should be added that the Jews, unlike the Indian *Parayan*, never looked upon themselves as pariahs. In this regard, Jeggle's comment that the Jews were "pariahs who did not react like pariahs" is not unjustified.[80] There was a discrepancy between the conviction of the Jews in the Franconian villages that they were "the favorites of God" (*die Lieblinge Gottes*) and the opinion of Judaeophobes that this conviction denoted a "ridiculous boast of lineage";[81] the discrepancy may have caused irritation. It is nevertheless questionable whether the simple Christian folk in the countryside ever accepted the pariah designation. It is not expected of pariahs that they hire domestic servants, travel in horsedrawn carriages, and engage in tests of physical strength.[82] The peasants respected the Jews, often physically—as Picard also suggests—but certainly on account of their alertness of mind. They appreciated the sacred usages of the Jews, partly because obeisance to custom is inbred in country folk, partly because the Jews were presumed to be conversant with magic forces. Annette von Droste-Hülshoff's short story *Die Judenbuche* preserves the Westphalian peasant's belief in the Jews' command of magic.[83] At that point the actual Jew and the mythical Jew coalesced. For the peasants, the Jews remained the "chosen people," even if they had strayed from the right path, and the Jews concurred wholeheartedly with at least the first part of that sentiment. Even the lowliest village Jew never depreciated his Jewishness. It remained for the scion of an assimilated Berlin family, Michael Beer, to write a thinly disguised dramatic play about the Jewish condition, entitled *The Pariah*.[84] Marginality, in the Parkian sense, is an urban phenomenon.[85]

III

In conclusion, it ought to be said that the village Jews were not peasants of a different ethnicity. They were urbanites transmuted into rural folk. This follows from their origin in the late Middle Ages, when the expellees from the cities took refuge in the territories of the Imperial Knights. To mention but one example, the Jews of Augsburg went to Kriegshaber and Pfersee, just outside of Augsburg but under a different sovereignty, and continued to trade in the city. The process was repeated in many places. In the nineteenth century, the village Jews moved back to the country towns and from there to the larger urban centers or to America. For instance, Jews moved to Ichenhausen from Bernheim, Binswangen, Fellheim, Hürben, Neuburg, Steppach, and Wettenhausen, places that were empty of Jewish inhabitants by the early 1900s. Their mobility is further attested to by such typical family names of Ichenhauser Jews as Erlanger, Harburger, Heilbronner, Öttinger, Regensburger, and Weimersheimer and others. Miserable as the country Jews may have been in the eighteenth century, they became the leaders in modernity in the places where they resided in the nineteenth century. They awakened new needs and desires, promoted voluntary associations and cultural activities. Utz Jeggle reports about the Jewish villages in Württemberg that local Jews frequently took the initiative in suggesting better means of communication and advanced schools, that they supported social institutions such as orphan asylums and hospitals, that their houses were larger and more solidly built, their furniture more representative of the newest taste, their meals more opulent, and their wives and daughters better groomed and dressed after the newest fashion.[86] The younger generation were avid readers of the German classics, and even an old tradesman, like my great-grandfather Moses Kahnmann in Rheinbischofsheim, used to entertain his neighbors with the recitation of the sermon of the Capuchin monk from Schiller's *Wallensteins Lager*. Not a few of the ladies, and also some of the men, spoke French. According to Dickinson, the only Jewish woman in a Hessian village was the only woman in the village who knew French.[87] The father of my great-grandmother Schülein, David Gunzenhäuser in Feuchtwangen, put his knowledge of French to good use during the occupation of the town in the Napoleonic wars. His services were rewarded by the municipality with a permit to open a distillery.

The fact that the village Jews were transplanted urbanites notwithstanding, they carried rural attitudes back to the city when they transferred their businesses and families to the larger urban centres. In the villages their mood had been Hasidic rather than *mitnagdic*, but the intensity and inventiveness of the Hasidim of the East had been lacking—although exceptions like the Baalshem of Michelstadt must not be overlooked. In the cities, their religiosity did not embrace Jewish learning; it remained sentimental, family-centered, and fixed by custom and habit. Even Berthold Auerbach, steeped as he was in Jewish lore, could not comprehend, let alone master, the rabbinic casuistry with which he was confronted at the yeshiva in Hechingen. His Judaism had a poetic quality, and even his holiday reminiscences are at one with his impression of woods and meadows, because the boys were sent out in the open on Friday afternoons so that they could not interfere with preparations in the house.[88] Consequently, many an ex-village Jew in the city felt that the accustomed practices of Judaism had been rendered meaningless by the physical separation from the former habitat. These practices, they thought, had become old-fashioned. They were maintained as long as aged parents were alive, out of filial consideration for their feelings, and then abandoned. By the same token, neither the radical liberalism of the reformers, nor the generalized patriotism of the Centralverein, nor the highstrung Jewish nationalism of the Herzlian type found many adherents. The opposition to Zionism was informed by the unwillingness to jeapordize solid achievements and material comforts.

The Centralverein had many members, in the city as well as in the country-side, but their interest lay in civic defense, not in ideology. The *Hauptsyna-gogen* were "liberal," but without being imbued with reformist zeal; they resembled Conservative congregations in America. Orthodoxy remained entrenched in smaller centers, such as Regensburg, Ansbach, Fulda, and Mergentheim, but the Orthodox congregations in the larger cities failed to attract the bulk of the ex-village Jews. The top-hatted worshippers that flocked to the *Hauptsynagogue* on the High Holidays intended to be "good Jews," but moderately so. The one movement that succeeded in attracting large numbers of ex-village Jews was B'nai B'rith. The fact that the warring political and religious factions were to be reconciled in B'nai B'rith appealed to the sense for Klal Jissrael. The feeling of Jewish solidarity, that is, that all Jews are responsible for one another, proved to be ineradicable, and philanthropy (*gemilut chassadim*) began to assume the place that formal piety had occupied at an earlier period. It is not without interest to note that the members of the München Loge in B'nai B'rith (1893–1938), where my father and grandfather were active in committees and in the presidency, were chiefly middle-class businessmen who had moved to Munich from smaller communities in the Franconian and Swabian districts of Bavaria and the neighboring areas of southern Germany, while the city-born and city-bred haute volée, apart from the Orthodox Fränkel and Feuchtwanger families, were conspicuous in their absence. Some of their spokesmen were actively opposed to what they considered voluntary segregation and a return to the dreaded ghetto. Their conception of the *Kultusgemeinde* was precisely what the word indicated, an association for the promotion of worship, and nothing else. Social policies in a Jewish context were entirely beyond the horizon of these men. As a result, philanthropies such as the Israelitische Jugendhilfe, the *Toynbeehalle*, Kinderheim, Lehrlingsheim, Schwesternheim, and the Jüdische Haushaltsschule had to be promoted by the München Loge and by organizations sponsored by the München Loge.[89] In retrospect, therefore, the difference between the charitable activities of *B'nai B'rith* and the Zionist demand for a *Volksgemeinde* rather than *Kultusgemeinde*, which loomed large at the time, shrinks to insignificance. I do not know to what extent the Munich experience can be generalized. But if further research is going to prove that such generalization is warranted, which I suspect will be the case, a statement which now has merely tentative validity could be confirmed: the ex-village Jews in the city had remained true to themselves in preserving and reviving Jewish ethnicity.

1974

Notes

1. *Statistik des Deutschen Reiches, 1925*, vol. 101, pt. 2, p. 603; *Statistik des Deutschen Reiches, 1933*, vol. 101, pt. 5, p. 9; see Erich Rosenthal, "Jewish Population in Germany 1910–1939," *Jewish Social Studies*, 6, no. 3 (1944): 232–74.

2. Stefen Schwarz, *Die Juden in Bayern im Wandel der Zeiten* (Munich and Vienna, 1963), p. 302.

3. Cahnman, "The Decline of the Munich Jewish Community 1933–38," *Jewish Social Studies*, 3, no. 3 (1941): 285–300.

4. Utz Jeggle, *Judendörfer in Württemberg* (Tübingen, 1969), p. 198; A. Tänzer, *Die Geschichte der Juden in Württemberg* (Frankfurt am Main, 1937), p. 68.

5. Cahnman, "A Regional Approach to German-Jewish History," *Jewish Social Studies*, 5, no. 3 (1943): 212–24; Cahnman, "Two Maps on German-Jewish History," in *Chicago Jewish Forum, Jubilee Volume dedicated to Curt C. Silberman*, eds. Herbert A. Strauss and Hanns G. Reissner (New York, 1969), pp. 1–14; see "Juden in den deutschen Landschaften," *Der Morgen*, 10 (1934–35): 410–14; "Ost und West," *Der Morgen*, 12 (1936): 533–36.

6. Leopold Kompert, *Scenes from the Ghetto* (London, 1882), pp. 79f.

7. Johann Peter Hebel, *Sämtliche Werke*, vol. 3 (Karlsruhe, 1832); see particularly pp. 17–22, 73–74, 114–18, 144–46, 190–91, 261–62, 310–11; three of these seven stories are set in Alsace.

8. Raphael Straus, *Die Judengemeinde Regensburg im ausgehenden Mittelalter* (Heidelberger Abhandlungen Heft 61, Heidelberg, 1932).

9. For a most informative account of this development, see Zosa Szajkowski, *The Economic Status of the Jews in Alsace, Metz and Lorraine (1648–1789)* (New York, 1954), particularly, pp. 5–8, 18, 50–54, 74, 95 and appendixes. One finds complementary evidence in such works as Fritz Bär, *Das Protokollbuch der Landjudenschaft des Herzogtums Kleve* (Berlin, 1922); A Eckstein, *Geschichte der Juden im ehemaligen Fürstbistum Bamberg* (Bamberg, 1899); S. Hänle, *Geschichte der Juden im ehemaligen Fürstentum Ansbach* (Ansbach, 1867); L. Müller, "Aus fünf Jahrhunderten-Beiträge zur Geschichte der jüdischen Gemeinden im Ries," *Zeitschrift des Historischen Vereins für Schwaben-Neuburg*, 26, (1899–1900); Berthold Rosenthal, *Heimatgeschichte der Badischen Juden von ihrem geschichtlichen Auftreten bis zur Gegenwart*, (Bühl/Baden, 1927). B. Rosenthal quotes significant passages from Grimmelshausen, *Simplicissimus*. Similar indications are dispersed in the literature, including folk tales, but have never been combined. However, the standard publications of the Archivdirection Stuttgart — Paul Sauer, *Die jüdischen Gemeinden in Württemberg und Hohenzollern* (Stuttgart, 1966); Franz Hundsnurscher and Gerhard Taddey, *Die jüdischen Gemeinden in Baden* (Stuttgart, 1968); tracing the settlement of all Jewish communities in these regions — make it clear that the majority were founded immediately preceding or shortly after the Thirty Years' War. Even in such places as Gunzenhausen in Franconia, where Jews were already documented in the fourteenth century, the settlement was interrupted, so that the more recent settlement dates from 1593, when a Jew from the neighboring village of Bechofen, with two married and two unmarried sons, a son-in-law, a teacher, and their children and servants were permitted to reside in the place; see Wilhelm Lux, "Beiträge zur Geschichte der Gunzenhäuser Judengemeinde bis zum 19. Jahrhundert" and "Die Juden im Gunzenhäuser Bürgerbuch," in *Alt-Gunzenhausen, Beiträge zur Geschichte der*

Stadt und des Kreises (Gunzenhausen, 1959/60 and 1962). Finally, one might consult the standard works about the court Jews, especially: Heinrich Schnee, *Die Hoffinanz und der moderne Staat—Geschichte und System der Hoffaktoren and deutschen Fürstenhöfen im Zeitalter des Absolutismus*, 3 vols. (Berlin, 1953–55); and Selma Stern, *The Court Jew* (Philadelphia, 1950).

10. Szajkowski, p. 62.
11. Ben Levi, *Memoires d'un colporteur Juif, ecrits par lui'meme*; quoted by Szajkowski, p. 63.
12. Erckmann-Chatrian, *L'Ami Fritz*, 2d ed. (Paris, 1865).
13. Szajkowski, pp. 5f., 18f., 57.
14. B. Rosenthal, pp. 56, 84.
15. S. Hänle, p. 28; Szajkowski, p. 76.
16. Jeggle, p. 57.
17. Robert Anchel, "La vie economique des Juifs de Metz aux XVIIe et XVIIIe siecles," *Les Juifs de France* (Paris, 1946), p. 176 et passim.
18. M. Ginsburger, *Cerfberr et son epoque* (Gübwiller: Publications de la Societe pour l'Histoire des Israelites d'Alsace et de Lorraine, 1908); M. Ginsburger, *Histoire de la Communaute israelite de Bischeim au Saum* (Strasbourg: Publications de la Societe . . . , 1937).
19. Zosa Szajkowski, *Jews and the French Revolutions of 1789, 1830 and 1848* (New York, 1970), pp. 298f.
20. Christian Wilhelm Dohm, *Über die bürgerliche Verbesserung der Juden* (Berlin & Stettin: 2nd ed., 1783); first ed. 1781; Heinrich Graetz, *History of the Jews* vol. 5 (Philadelphia, 1895), pp. 351–57.
21. Jacob Lestschinsky, *Das wirtschaftliche Schicksal des deutschen Judentums* (Schriften der Zentralwohlfahrtstelle der deutschen Juden no. 7; Berlin, 1932), p. 17.
22. B. Rosenthal, p. 159; S. Hänle, p. 91; Jeggle, pp. 47–49; and most extensively, Rudolf Glanz, *Geschichte des niederen jüdischen Volkes in Deutschland—Eine Studie über historisches Gaunertum, Bettelwesen und Vagabundentum* (New York, 1968), pp. 74, 102, 112 et passim.
23. Abraham Tendlau, *Sprichwörter und Redensarten deutsch-jüdischer Vorzeit (Frankfurt am Main, 1860), p.* 79.
24. R. Glanz, p. 7; reports that Rabbi Meir Rothenburg held about some Jewish converts to Christianity in the fourteenth century that "the reason why they did not want to be considered Jews was that they desired to have a chance to eat, to steal and to satisfy their lusts."
25. Moses Schulvass, *From East to West—The Westward Migration of Jews from Eastern Europe during the Seventeenth and Eighteenth Centuries* (Detroit, 1971), p. 14.
26. Jeggle, pp. 60–62.
27. Jeggle, p. 132. Jeggle quotes from L. Stern (Gabiah ben Psisa), *Wohin kommen wir? Ein Wort an die gesetzestreuen Juden Württembergs* (Mainz, 1863). The sentence "Stuttgart ist unser Jerusalem" was the conclusion of Maier's sermon at the opening ceremonies of the synagogue in Stuttgart in 1861.
28. Documentation to be found at the Akten des Evangelischen Pfarramts, Rheinbischofsheim, Baden.
29. This was my great-grandfather's case, but a more general statement to the same effect is found in A. Sartorius von Waltershausen, *Deutsche Wirtschaftsgeschichte 1815–1914* (Jena, 1920), p. 29.

30. Personal information. Compare Jacob Picard's statement about "Ownership of fields, meadows, orchards, gardens and even vineyards" in Wangen am Bodensee in "Childhood in the Village," in *Leo Baeck Year Book*, 4 (1959): 277; and "Erinnerungen eigenen Lebens," *Der Morgen*, 14 (1938): 14–20; also Bruno Stern, *Meine Jugenderinnerungen an eine württembergische Kleinstadt und ihre jüdische Gemeinde* (Stuttgart, 1968), pp. 66, 72.

31. See the documented analysis in Jeggle ("Veränderungsversuche im wirtschaftlichen Leben"), pp. 144–62.

32. Dr. Adler, *Offener Brief an die Herren Landtagsabgeordneten Ruland, Sepp, Allioli und Konsorten* (Abdruck from *Fränkische Zeitung* Munich, 1850).

33. Jeggle, p. 146; regarding legislation about crafts and trades in Bavaria, see Stefan Schwarz, pp. 190–205.

34. Hans Hess, *Die Landauer Judengemeinde—Ein Abriss ihrer Geschichte* (Landau, 1969), p. 14; Szajkowski, *Economic Status*, p. 51.

35. Hundsnurscher and Taddey, p. 24.

36. The Landau community study is one of the most informative small community studies that are available. Throughout the nineteenth century, the majority of the members of the Jewish community of Landau originated in the surrounding villages. See Hess, pp. 16, 20 et passim.

37. Hess, p. 22.

38. Ibid., p. 42.

39. Hundsnurscher and Taddey see n. 9; Sauer.

40. Heinrich Sinz, *Geschichtliches vom ehemaligen Markt und der nunmehrigen Stadt Ichenhausen* (Ichenhausen, 1926), chaps. 12, 13; *Ergänzungen zur Ortsgeschichte Ichenhausen* (Ichenhausen, 1928), chap. 5; *Ergänzungen zur Ortsgeschichte Ichenhausen und Umgebung*, pp. 89f. et passim.

41. I am greatly obliged to Richard Hellman, Alfred Kahn, Julius Katten, Leopold Künstler, Erika Lebell, Thea Löwengart, Alice Maier, Lore Meier, and Heinrich Neuburger for personal communications.

42. Hermann Schwab, *Jewish Rural Communities in Germany* (London, 1955), pp. 34–37.

43. J. Rülf, *Entstehung und Bedeutung des Antisemitismus in Hessen* (Mainz, 1980).

44. Schwab, pp. 42–46.

45. Ferdinand Tönnies, *Gemeinschaft und Gesellschaft* (Darmstadt, 1970; 1st ed., 1887), pp. 252–54; English ed.: Charles P. Loomis, ed., *Community and Society* (New York, 1963), pp. 232–34; see also Cahnman, *Ferdinand Tönnies—A New Evaluation* (Leiden, 1973), p. 118.

46. Clementine Kraemer, "Erinnerungen," *Jüdisch-Liberale Zeitung* [1922]; "Vom Grossvater und vom Hofbauer," *Hannoverscher Kurier* (17 April 1915). Clementine Kraemer, who was my father's sister, refers both to Rheinbischofsheim (Amt Kehl) and to Mühringen (Neckar kreis); the story of the grandfather is about Joel Levi in Mühringen. See Stefan Schlatter, "Der jüdische Friedhof im Mühringer Talwald," (Isr. Religionsgemeinschaft Württembergs: Rosch Haschana 5732/September 1971 and 5733/September 1972) pp. 35f., 45f.

47. Joseph Schülein, a brother of my maternal grandfather, was the founder of the Unionsbrauerei Schülein & Co. in Munich; the enterprise, then the second largest brewery in Bavaria, was fused with the Löwenbrauerei in 1921.

48. Jeggle, p. 212.

49. Jacob Picard's statement in "Childhood in the Village," p. 293 that "the happy course of the first ten years of my life cannot have been very different from the

lives of Jewish children in many villages in Southern Germany'' is very true, even if it refers only to the period prior to the 1920s. Picard's sentence is quoted by Jeggle only two pages away (p. 210) from the previously quoted statement. Equally telling is the testimony of Berthold Auerbach who dreamed "von Nordstetter Feld- und Waldgängen" when far away, visited "das Nordstetter Witwenstubchen seiner Mutter" on his honeymoon, and finally was laid to rest in the Jewish hillside cemetery in Nordstetten. See Anton Bettelheim, *Berthold Auerbach— Der Mann, sein Werk, sein Nachlass* (Stuttgart and Berlin, 1907), pp. 1–2.

50. Jeggle, p. 207; quotes a patriotic poem by Alexander Elsässer, which fuses Germanic and Semitic sentimentality. To be sure, Jeggle finds Elsässer "ridiculous,'' but he adds that "one must overcome a strong reluctance against laughing"— the reason being that a sense of *Heimatverbundenheit* is merged here with a forced nationalism.

51. Herman Pollack, *Jewish Folkways in Germanic Lands (1648–1806)* (Cambridge, Mass.: 1971), p. 150; he reports on the behavior patterns of this kind from rural communities in the Frankfurt and Düsseldorf areas in the eighteenth century. I observed the same attitudes in a number of instances in Baden and Franconia in the 1920s; see also Bruno Stern, p. 94.

52. Jacob Picard, *Der Gezeichnete* (Berlin, 1936), pp. 87–100; Picard, *The Marked One* (Philadelphia, 1956), pp. 73–84.

53. Erich Rosenthal, "Eine jüdische Kleinstadtgemeinde," *Der Morgen*, 9 (1933): 372–78.

54. Pollack, pp. 69, 150 et passim.

55. Johann Jacob Schudt, *Jüdische Merkwürdigkeiten* (Frankfurt am Main: 1727), pp. 359f.

56. I have the story about Shimshon Kahnmannn from my father who has heard it from his grandfather, and also Louise Levy in Bischwiller, Alsace.

57. Paul Sauer, pp. 129–31.

58. Anton Bettelheim, p. 10.

59. Jean Kohn, *Die Familie Kohn aus Wassertrüdigen* (mimeo; Paris, 1948).

60. Personal experience, interviews, family reminscences, and a number of biographical and literary sources must be combined to arrive at a composite picture such as the one outlined here. For the area and period here under review, Anton Bettelheim's opening chapter ("Im Heimatdorf Nordstetten") about the life and work of Berthold Auerbach is outstanding. Jacob Picard's sensitive stories as well as Bruno Stern's and Clementine Kraemer's reminiscences, as quoted above, may serve as complementary. Of particular interest is the way in which Jewish traders dealt with the weekday problem of balancing their obligation to observe *Kashrut* and the need to remain on tolerable terms with the peasants. Hans Bach, "Zur Geschichte einer schwäbisch-jüdischen Familie," (Stuttgart: Rosch Haschana 5732/ September 1971), relates (p. 26) that the peddlers stayed overnight with peasant acquaintances with whom they left their own kosher crockery for repeated use; Hermann Schwab (pp. 34–37) reports that some country inns were in the habit of keeping a saucepan with the word *kosher* written on the reverse side, for Jewish guests; the peddler carried with him bread, eggs, and spirits. Berthold Auerbach tells about a peddler who lived with a Gentile friend during the week, where he subsisted on bread, coffee, and an occasional egg or pancake; see Berthold Auerbach, *Eine Auswahl aus seinen Schriften* (Berlin, 1935). After these make-do arrangements the Sabbath was an all-the-more glorious experience.

61. I owe the account of the Friday evening dinner in Rheinbischofsheim to Lore Meier of Strassburg, the only surviving daughter of Moritz Cahnmann. Compare Bruno Stern's account of Friday and Saturday dinners in Niederstetten, Württemberg, op. cit., pp. 93f. and the note about "Jüdische Speisen im Elsass" in Arthur Zivy, *Elsässer Jiddisch* (Basel, n.d.), p. 87.

62. A *medina* is the trading territory of a peddler into which no competitor is supposed to intrude; see the comment in Schwab, pp. 34–37.

63. Anton Bettelheim, pp. 13–14.

64. Erich Rosenthal, "Der Viehmarkt," *Der Morgen*, 10 (1934–35), pp. 356–59.

65. Comparative genealogical research about multiple-family relationships is lacking; for one more example, see Jacob Picard, "Childhood in the Village," p. 189.

66. Zosa Szajkowski, *The Economic Status*, pp. 5, 58, 63 et passim.

67. Johann Peter Hebel, pp. 362–64.

68. Kraemer, see note 46.

69. John K. Dickinson, *German and Jew* (Chicago, 1967), pp. 3–26.

70. Dickinson, pp. 15–16; see also Utz Jeggle's splendidly conducted interviews in Württemberg villages, op. cit., pp. 224–26; also Picard, "Childhood in the Village," p. 286.

71. Dickinson, p. 17; Picard, "Childhood," p. 281; Hermann Fechenbach, *Die letzten Mergentheimer Juden* (Stuttgart, 1971), p. 158; also Kraemer, "Erinnerungen"; these are only a few of many possible quotations.

72. The term *dry goods and groceries* includes a large assortment of merchandise, according to an old business announcement, namely, "hemp, seagrass, cloth, fabrics, buckskin, feathers, groceries, liquors, cigars and tobacco."

73. J. Rülf.

74. Kraemer, "Vom Grossvater," Bruno Stern, p. 102; Dickinson, p. 20.

75. Dickinson, p. 12.

76. Bettelheim, pp. 29–30.

77. Hebel, pp. 261–62.

78. I have analyzed the contradictions in Max Weber's concept of the "pariah people" in the essay "Pariahs, Strangers, and Court Jews—A Conceptual Clarification," in this volume.

79. The pervasive anti-Jewishness in the first half of the nineteenth century is amply documented in Eleonore Sterling, *Er ist wie Du. Aus der Frühgeschichte des Antisemitismus in Deutschland (1815–1850)* (Munich, 1956), and complemented in Reinhard Rürup's detailed analysis in "Die Judenemanzipation in Baden," *Zeitschrift für die Geschichte des Oberrheins*, vol. 114, (1966), pp. 241–300. I am obliged to Professor Rürup for his comments at Arden House.

80. Jeggle's comments, op. cit., pp. 21–28 are penetrating, yet do not seem to justify the use of the term "Pariah."

81. Elkan Henle, *Über die Verfassung der Juden im Königreiche Baiern und die Verbesserung derselben zum Nutzen des Staates* (Munich, 1811).

82. My paternal great-great–grandfather Shimshon Kahnmann of Rheinbischofsheim and my maternal great-grandfather Joel Schülein of Thalmässing, both tall men, were renowned for their physical strength. Picard, "Childhood" (p. 276), confirms that the Jews were respected by their Christian neighbors "not least because they knew we were not physically inferior—an important consideration among simple people."

83. Inselbücherei, No. 271.

84. Lothar Kahn, "Michael Beer 1800–1833," in *Leo Baeck Year Book*, 12 (1967): 149–60.
85. Robert E. Park, "Human Migration and the Marginal Man," *American Journal of Sociology*, 33, no. 6 (May 1928).
86. Jeggle, pp. 165, 183, 219 et passim.
87. Dickinson, p. 15.
88. Bettleheim, pp. 17f., 41f.
89. I have referred to the importance of the München Loge (B'nai B'rith) regarding the initiation of Jewish social services in my paper "The Life of Clementine Kraemer," in this volume. Reference to the rural and small-town derivation of many Munich Jews is found in Ludwig Feuchtwanger, "Neuere Geschichte, Verwandlungen 1817–1887–1937," in *Festgabe-Fünfzig Jahre Hauptsynagoge München* (Munchen, 1937), pp. 30–42.

5

Socioeconomic Causes of Antisemitism

I

The aim of this essay, in discussing the socioeconomic causes of anti-semitism, is to arrive at a sociological theory of antisemitism. We exclude, therefore, causes that refer to the frailty of individual human nature and that are more properly dealt with in psychology and personality theory. Representatives of the psychological approach have themselves admitted that the emotional factors in antisemitism remain merely latent as long as the socioeconomic environment is not conducive to bringing them to the fore.[1] Recent personality research has gone a step further and come up with the statement that concern with status is more closely related to antisemitism than is, for instance, authoritarianism, and that the relationship between authoritarianism and antisemitism may be largely explained by their mutual relationship to concern with status.[2] All the structural theorist has to add to this is that the solid facts of class and status antedate concern with them and that, consequently, clarification of the position of the Jews in a system of social stratification will go a long way in predicting the behavior of individuals within that system.

A further qualification should be added. The "Jewish problem" is the oldest, the most persistent, and in many ways the most perplexing problem in occidental civilization, and it would, therefore, be presumptuous to study it as if it had arisen yesterday and could be expected to disappear tomorrow. Such a problem has a history and can only be studied by the historical method. No other approach will yield the variety of cases on which a generalized theoretical formulation of any problem depends. Moreover, if a patterned arrangement of social forces repeats itself generation after generation, an image is formed in the minds of men which in continued cultural transmission becomes itself a factor of structural potency. The image of the Jew in the minds of the occidental peoples has served to justify his position in the social structure and his position, in turn, has served to illuminate the image. In such a way, socioeconomic causations are interwoven with religious, moral, juridical, and other causations, and the interaction of these causations amounts to more than a summation of facts: history becomes the seedbed of that collective consciousness which gives to facts their meaning and direction. Consequently, since socioeconomic and social-psychological factors condition each other within the social structure, a purely materialistic interpretation of social processes becomes impossible to sustain. In this respect, we differ from the otherwise brilliant analysis of A. Leon.[3] We may isolate socioeconomic factors for the purpose of analysis, but we must never separate them from the total social reality of which they are a part.

II

In order to place Jewish-Gentile relations and their propensity to produce conflict situations in proper perspective, one must take one's departure from the observation that the Jews have never been in the low-class position of downtrodden peasants, menial laborers, dependent serfs, and slaves; they were never oppressed and exploited by an upper class of employers, especially large landholders, in the way subjected low-class populations usually are. Surely, there existed at all times numbers of miserably poor Jews, ragpickers, repairmen, peddlers, beggars, and tramps, but they were considered a burden on Jewish charity, not on society at large; many of them rarely left the Jewish quarters. The poor Jew always was of profound disconcern to the Gentiles. Not even the Jewish agricultural settlements that were scattered throughout the Mediterranean world in late antiquity and in the early Middle Ages had their image engraved on historical memory; not a trace of them is left. Considering the influence which the Church of Rome exerted at the time, it stands to reason that the Jewish sharecroppers of that period in the long run must have disappeared either as tenants or as Jews. These Jews either made their peace with the Church and stayed on the land, or they gave up agriculture and migrated to the city.[4] Only in independent economic positions could they maintain their nonconformist cultural heritage. Such independence was possible for the Jewish artisan class, which was numerous at times, but the leadership in the Jewish communities necessarily fell to those who were able to sustain the communal institutions, namely, the merchants. Besides, in the relations of the Jews with the outside world, it was not so much "prayer, repentence, and charity" which prevented evil decrees, but the lure of hard coin: that was the language which convinced the rulers. In other words, the Jews had their poor and their artisans, but their representatives were men of means. In the eyes of the world, the Jews were conceptualized as merchants and traders, with a host of subcontractors, agents, interpreters, translators, even medical practitioners surrounding them. What all these occupational categories have in common is that they refer not so much to substance but to relations. Those engaged in them do not aim at the transformation of matter but at the management of minds. They are members of an intermediary class. This can be said about the ninth as well as the nineteenth century.

A number of important consequences flow from this initial observation. In intergroup relations, conflict arises on the periphery where contacts are made; widely dispersed trading communities are exposed to many more contact situations than large, compact settlements of agriculturalists; and peripheral tension increases, therefore, wherever such minorities of traders and specialized artisans are found. This structural marginality, which has been formulated by Perez Bernstein and Adolf Leschnitzer, antedates the psychological marginality introduced into sociological discussion by Robert E. Park and Everett Stonequist.[5] The Jews are a marginal people; their marginal individuals, namely the men of means and all others who are continually in contact with outsiders, are doubly exposed.[6] In some cases, marginality is carried to the point where the conflict is being fought among the exposed individuals themselves and even, tantalizingly, within the minds of individuals. The periphery is thereby extended into the core and the tension immeasurably multiplied. In the extreme case, when the center collapses completely and the periphery, as it were, is the only reality that is left, the antisemitic tension must be expected to be at a fever pitch. The verification is provided by the example of Spain after the terrifying pogroms of 1391, and especially after the final expulsion of 1492, when the remaining *conversos*, their religious disabilities removed, surged high in society but experienced all the more the murderous hostility of the populace and of the Inquisition.[7] Surely, when the opponent is no longer clearly discernible, his assumed ubiquitous presence would seem most threatening. We have a situation approximating, but not quite equaling, the one of the Spain of the Inquisition in nineteenth- and twentieth-century Vienna, with its large numbers of illustrious converts and near-converts and its virulent racism.

Another elaboration, in historical analysis, of our stated observation leads to the recognition of the identity of the merchant and the stranger. The wholesale merchant especially, who offers his wares in services in faraway places and receives other wares and services in return, is a man whom one needs badly and awaits anxiously, but with whom, because he does not belong to one's clan, one never feels entirely at ease. One must be on guard with him: what the neighbor, as kinsman, would have to offer free of charge, if he only had it, can indeed be had from the merchant; but he does not offer it free of charge, he sells; and since he sells, he stands under the assumption that he takes his advantage. The Jew, the merchant, the stranger, the wanderer, the magician from the East, the man who is everywhere and belongs nowhere—this picture begins, at the beginning of the Middle Ages, to take shape and form. It has grown to mythical proportions since. In Georg Simmel's words, it is the picture not so much of the man who comes today and goes tomorrow, but rather of the man who comes today and stays tomorrow.[8] We prefer to call the latter not the stranger but the *intermediary*. By intermediary we mean the outsider who settles among the in-group yet remains sufficiently remote from it to be looked upon with mistrust, on the one hand, and to be appreciated for his impartiality, on the other. Next to the Jew as the agent and the trader stands the Jew as the healer, the counsellor, the judge.

Periods of appreciation and periods of mistrust succeeded each other. The Jew was welcome whenever he was a trailblazer of urbanism in rural surroundings. This was true in late antiquity and in the early Middle Ages, when he brought the wares of the East to the underdeveloped West. It was true of Christian Spain, when he brought the wisdom of the Greeks in Arabic garb. Later, it was true in the old Kingdom of Poland, when German Jews along with German Gentiles were called in from the land to populate the cities. It would be fascinating to trace elements of that appreciation in America, whether the reference is to the mail order catalogue or to Albert Einstein. But these periods of appreciation did not dispel the mistrust that was always latent and in times of crisis insuperable. How do we account for this recurrence? To say that competitive jealousies are easily stirred up seems not enough. In introducing at this point what may be called the historical image of the Jew, it must be kept in mind that in a preindustrial society, class conflicts are centered around the conflicts between creditors and debtors, and that such conflicts become intensified whenever the socioeconomic antagonism coincides with an ethnoreligious differentiation.[9] For instance, the Armenians, a Christian creditor people, were left essentially unmolested among Christian peasant populations in Russia and in the Balkans while, at a moment of political crisis, they were massacred among Moslems. The Jews of the Middle Ages were everywhere creditors *and* everywhere an ethnoreligious minority. In the course of time, the two antagonisms reinforced each other until they became indistinguishable. Although there was never such a thing as a monopoly on interest taking on the part of the Jews, the terms "Jew" and "usurer" came to be used interchangeably by the thirteenth century.[10]

The reason for this development is that the Jews were considered more than "different"; they were considered the enemies of Christ. There is an element of self-fulfilling prophecy in this most-involved story. The destruction by the Roman emperor of the Temple of Jerusalem was seen as a punishment for the rejection of Christ, and the curse that was laid upon the Jewish people by this double event was subsequently used as a rationale for discriminatory treatment. The depressed status that was brought about was then taken as further proof of the curse. The usury legislation of the medieval Church must be understood in that light. In an attempt to reconcile the Church's strict interdict on interest taking as a cardinal sin with the undeniable need for commercial credit and for distress loans, the Church conceded that the Jews might as well adhere to the evil practice; they lived anyway *in statu reprobationis*. To put it bluntly, it was assumed that the Christians, in taking interest, were acting against their better nature, but that the Jews, being sons of the devil, were acting in conformity with theirs. This must not be taken as mere symbolism. To the high Middle Ages, Satan personally was a Jew, a monstrous creature with a hooked nose and a goatee who prayed in the synagogue and plotted in the marketplace.[11] In the meantime, other devils have appeared on the screen of the human mind, but we know that they could be made to seem all the more threatening when they resembled the archimage of the Jew.

The Jews were, and still are, the people of the twilight, the strangers, the intermediaries. Perhaps one can say that appreciation and mistrust are mingled in the belief that everything can be expected from them. But to define the typical position of the Jew in a system of social stratification, a further qualification is necessary. Never in their post-biblical history were the Jews as a group relegated to the status of slaves of masters in private law, but they were considered the servants of kings and emperors in public law. This was the meaning of the expression *servi camerae imperatoris speciales* which appeared first in the decree of Emperor Frederic II in 1236.[12] In other words, the Jews were considered subjects of the imperial treasury.[13] Special legislation attempted to protect Jews against footloose mobs, discontented debtors, and sheer superstitition, but as time went on, protection degenerated into exploitation—as it frequently does. Sociologically speaking, no more significant statement can be made about the role which the Jews played in occidental history from this point on, if not earlier, than to say that they were the allies and the tools of the crown and the nobles and, as such, one of the constituent elements in the development of the modern state. The admonition of the Jewish sages "Don't put your trust in princes" notwithstanding, the choice was inescapable. The Jews would only be admitted to a territory by the ruler of that territory, and it was he who promised protection against considerable and frequently renewed payment. The ability of the Jews to pay depended on the permission which was granted them to lend money against interest. The ruler was the silent partner in Jewish business. For instance, in the middle of the fourteenth century, the Jews of Nuremberg, no more than 8 to 10 percent of the inhabitants, provided more than 50 percent of the city's tax income; part of that income went to the emperor.[14] At times, as in Spain in the thirteenth, fourteenth, and fifteenth centuries, in Austria and other German states in the seventeenth and eighteenth centuries, a bolder step was taken: the most prominent Jews were appointed councillors of the crown and served as tax gatherers and commercial monopolists. Theirs was the task to transform the natural wealth of the kingdom into the cash on the strength of which the crusades of the kings of Aragon and Castile against the Moors and the wars of Prince Eugene against the Turks were predicated. The activities of these court Jews, so-called, mark the beginnings of a modern financial administration in large parts of central Europe.[15]

The symbiosis of the Jews and the nobles antedates and accompanies that of the Jews and the state. In western Europe in the early Middle Ages, Jewish merchants brought luxury goods to palaces and manor houses; in more recent centuries, Jewish agents disposed of the surplus products of the landed estates of the Polish gentry. The Jews fulfilled the functions of a middle class where no native middle class existed. The nineteenth-century German economist Wilhelm Roscher must be credited with establishing the theory that anti-semitism became a potent force whenever a competing national middle class arose.[16] From the high Middle Ages onward, Jews were excluded from the guilds, and consequently from the trades and crafts, and relegated to the distasteful credit operations connected with pawnbroking. However, in the way that undesired consequences sometimes flow from seemingly well-aimed actions, this established the Jewish trade in secondhand goods, which catered to the needs of the lower classes and later led to Jewish prominence in the finishing industries, especially in the manufacture of garments.[17]

Again, a clamor arose for special legislation, even expulsion. The Jews and the middle classes remained locked in a bitter competitive struggle.[18] It was in the course of this struggle that the Jews ceased to be free agents and became agents of their protectors, the territorial lords. They found themselves in the status of social outcasts; but, far from being removed from class conflict, they were put right in the path of it; and in the larger struggle of the mercantile and laboring classes, they served as lightning rod and whipping boy at the same time.

Without ever constituting a ruling class, or part of a ruling class, the Jews found their interest linked to those of the ruling class. This was the condition for their admission and the reason for their downfall. It is likewise the reason for the wrong perspective in which they have been placed so often. From above, they looked quite insignificant, mere figures on the political chess-board, while from below they assumed the proportions of dangerous monsters because they appeared as the representatives of an exploitative system. Of this situation, we have examples so numerous, from all ages and societies, including our own, that we must abstain from mentioning a single one. What ought to be added, however, is an elaboration on the creditor-debtor relation that was indicated earlier: if the socioeconomic antagonism is interlocked with an ethnic one, that is, if the ruling classes are of one people and the laboring classes of another, then one tension reinforces the other, and a revolutionary explosion, of which the wedged-in Jews are likely to be the foremost victims, becomes inevitable. The classic example is provided by the revolts of the

Ukrainian cossacks against their Polish overlords in the seventeenth century.[19] This outbreak led to the wholesale massacre of the Jewish estate agents, innkeepers, suppliers, and merchants, who had acted as the representatives of the absentee gentry. The gentry, on their part, panicked into belated agreement with the rebels, attempting to save their skin by abandoning the Jewish population. In precarious situations of this type, the exposed intermediary position of the Jews is patently evident and these situations are everpresent. In the nineteenth and twentieth centuries, the Jews of Greece were caught in the struggle between the Greeks and the Ottoman Empire; the Jews of Bohemia and Moravia found themselves in a trap between the rival aspirations of the German and the Czechs; the Jews of Hungary between Magyar nationalism and the stirrings of the slavic peoples; and I tremble to predict what the fate of the Jews of Algeria and those of the Union of South Africa will eventually be.

III

In conclusion, the survey of the history of Jewish-Gentile relations, in which we have been engaged, reveals a structural relationship, the pattern of which appears firmly established long before the period in which we now live, namely the one of industrial society, is reached. The role of the Jews among the peoples of Europe and the Near East has been defined and redefined in ages past; we cannot escape it. If we study Jewish-Gentile relations in the modern world in as many places as pleases us and by whatever means, be it occupational statistics, personality tests, or qualitative or quantitative analysis, we may expect to find modifications, combinations, cross-fertilizations, even one line of causation occasionally counteracted by another line of causation; but the pattern will stand. For instance, the era of liberalism, in establishing freedom of conscience, freedom of press and assembly, and freedom of trade, changed the position of the Church and revolutionized the life of the middle classes as well as of the laboring classes everywhere, but it merely unleashed the energies of the Jews and gave them a free rein.[20] The Jews had been conditioned to competitive risk taking for a long time. Now, the rules which had governed their conduct under specific circumstances found wide application. A French antisemitic writer of the time put it succinctly when he said that the Jews should be considered "the kings of the epoch."[21] Yet, one of the outstanding events of the liberal era, as far as the Jews are concerned, the spectacular rise of the house of Rothschild, has added no new facet or aspect either to the social status or to the image of the Jew, except the hysterically enhanced fear that, with legal barriers removed, the Jews might be swept into a position where they could utilize their association with rulers and nobles to attain world domination;[22] this fear has carried us to

Auschwitz and Treblinka. But they were not swept into a position of power; otherwise Auschwitz and Treblinka, and the entire horrid genocide for which these names stand, could not have occurred. It is fascinating to observe how in country after country, the Soviet Union and the United States included, the social body resisted the inclusion of the Jews in the commanding positions in industry, the armed forces, and institutionalized intellectual life. The liberal era was concerned with ''rights'' and has done much about them; but in terms of social stucture, nothing that is essential has been changed.

Is America different? Does Israel mark a break? We may have a particular look at these two societies, with the models in mind which structural theory offers. As far as America is concerned, the balance sheet would open hopefully: the medieval attitude towards money plays no role, as Uncle Sam himself is a keen trader; wealth, in the Puritan tradition, is considered a blessing, and even a gambler's fortune is now surrounded by a halo; the ethnic and religious diversity of America has guaranteed freedom of worship; the Negro problem holds first mortgage on the conscience of the nation; and a dynamic economy stifles ordinary jealousies. But in the decisive area, namely in social stratification, the familar picture emerges.[23] The Jews of America, typically, are agents, consultants, interpreters, finishers, middle-men; they are prominent in those kinds of enterprise that are near to the consumer, such as the garment, tobacco, and liquor industries, movie making, real estate, retailing, and a host of auxiliary services, but they are excluded, or almost excluded, from power positions in the heavy industries, such as steel and oil, in banking, insurance, and corporation law.[24] There are a thousand and one devices, subtle and not so subtle, for keeping Jews out of key positions in a variety of fields. Jews, all over the country, are found participating in the activities of community chests, but not in the membership of country clubs.[25] It is rare indeed for the name of a wealthy and renowned Jewish family to appear in the social register, and almost unheard of for the daughter of such a family to come out at a debutante ball.[26] In brief, while human relations, under the circumstances, may run the full gamut from repressed hostility to open friendliness, one must be afraid that in terms of structural analysis America is not turning a new leaf in the book of Jewish-Gentile relations.

How about Israel? Will the spectacular reconstruction of the Jewish state remove the socioeconomic causes of antisemitism, as we have known them? Will it do away with the image of the Jew as it has been fixed in the memory of Western man? Such founders of modern Zionism as Leon Pinsker and Theodor Herzl were impressed by the argument that antisemitism was thriving on the disconcerting concept of the Jewish people as an everlasting, everpresent minority.[27] We Jews suffer, said Herzl, from an overproduction of middle-strata intellectuals who offer sharp competition to the Gentile middle classes; tension, he thought, would be relieved, if some of the com-

petitors were removed. Herzl revealed considerable insight when he emphasized that only in a Jewish state could Jews expect to recapture a hold on
agricultural and industrial production, blot out the image of the Jew as a
spectre and parasite, and take their place as equals among equals in the society
of nations.[28] Indeed, the Jewish Middle Ages were entombed only in 1948,
when, for the first time since the days of the Maccabees, the symbol of the
wandering Jew was replaced in the sight of the peoples of the world by the
symbol of the Jewish worker and soldier. This was not the least revolutionary
event among the many revolutionary events of our time. If one considers the
host of disparaging remarks, prior to the establishment of the Jewish state,
about the presumed inability of the "old clothes Jew" to work productively
and to act heroically, the magnitude of the change appears impressive. Nevertheless, the question marks which accompanied the Zionist movement from
its inception remain: Will the concentrated enmity of the Arab rulers, which
is nourished on a fear complex, be preferable to the jealousy of commercial
competitors in many lands? Will sovereignty over a small territory offer
effective protection? Will the power inherent in geography and economic
resources, or the lack of it, not carry the same weight internationally as within
a society? In short, will the position of the state of Israel not be strikingly
similar to the position which the Jews have always held? These considerations
must arrest our thoughts before we arrive at a final judgment.

1957

Notes

This paper was delivered before the Twenty-seventh Annual Meeting of the Eastern
Sociological Society, 14 April 1957. The research on which it is based has been made
possible by a grant from the Cultural Division of the Conference on Jewish Material
Claims against Germany.

1. Else Frenkel-Brunswick and R. Nevitt Sanford, "The Antisemitic Personality: A
   Research Report," in Ernst Simmel, ed., *Antisemitism—A Social Disease* (New
   York, 1946), p. 123.
2. Walter C. Kaufman, "Status, Authoritarianism, and Antisemitism," *The American Journal of Sociology*, 62 (January 1957): 379–82.
3. Abram Leon, *The Jewish Question. A Marxist Interpretation* (New York, 1970).
4. Georg Caro, *Sozial- und Wirtschaftsgeschichte der Juden im Mittelalter und in
   der Neuzeit*, vol. 1: *Das frühe und das hohe Mittelalter* (2d ed., Frankfurt am
   Main, 1924), pp. 35–44.
5. P. Bernstein, *Der Antisemitismus als Gruppenerscheinung. Versuch einer Soziologie des Judenhasses* (Berlin, 1926), pp. 163–65; Adolph Leschnitzer, "Antisemitismus," in *Woarterbuch der Soziologie*, eds. Wilhelm Bernsdorf and Friedrich
   Buelow (Stuttgart, 1955), pp. 16–20. See also Everett V. Stonequist, *The Marginal Man* (New York, 1937), noting particularly Robert E. Park's introduction.

6. Kurt Lewin, "Self-Hatred Among Jews," in *Resolving Social Conflicts: Selected Papers on Group Dynamics, 1935–1946* (New York, 1948), pp. 186–200.

7. Americo Castro, *The Structure of Spanish History* (Princeton, 1954), pp. 466–589, noting the literature mentioned there. See also Cecil Roth, *A History of the Marranos* (Philadelphia, 1941), pp. 11–54 et passim.

8. Kurt H. Wolff, ed., *The Sociology of Georg Simmel* (Glencoe, Ill., 1950), pp. 402–8.

9. Max Weber, *Wirtschaft und Gesellschaft* (Tuebingen, 1922); vol. 2, pp. 583–84; vol. 3, pp. 632–34.

10. J. Aronius, *Register zur Geschichte der Juden im fränkischen und deutschen Reiche bis zum Jahre 1273* (Berlin, 1902), p. 319.

11. Joshua Trachtenberg, *The Devil and the Jews. The Medieval Conception of the Jews and its Relation to Modern Antisemitism* (New Haven, 1943).

12. Guido Kisch, *The Jews in Medieval Germany—A Study of Their Legal and Social Status* (Chicago, 1949), pp. 145–53.

13. It should be observed that the theory of the subjection of the Jews to the imperial chamber, in referring to the Passion of the Lord and the subsequent conquest of Jerusalem, merely served to clothe day-by-day injustice with the mantle of ancient law. It should further not be overlooked that the emperor had to assert his title as a "protector" of the Jews against similar claims of the Holy See. The Jew was hit, but the political adversary was meant. This sort of substitution is so frequent that it amounts to a sociological law. We hesitate to call this "scapegoatism," though, because the idea of expiation of sin does not operate on the political chessboard.

14. Otto Stobbe, *Die Juden Deutschlands während des Mittelalters in politischer, sozialer and rechtlicher Beziehung* (3rd ed., Berlin, 1923), p. 53 et passim. Stobbe's small volume, which first appeared in 1866, has remained an unsurpassed source for the social history of the Jews in central Europe. Among English works, compare Kisch, op. cit., and James Parkes *The Jew in the Medieval Community. A Study of his Political and Economic Situation* (London, 1938).

15. Selma Stern, *The Court Jew. A Contribution to the History of the Period of Absolutism in Central Europe* (Philadelphia, 1950), pp. 15–37, 60–136.

16. Wilhelm Roscher, "Die Stellung der Juden im Mittelalter, betrachtet vom Standpunkte der allgemeinen Handelspolitik," *Zeitschrift für die gesamte Staatswissenschaft* 31 (1857): 503–26.

17. Raphael Mahler, "Antisemitism in Poland," in *Essays on Antisemitism*, ed. Kopple S. Pinson, (New York, 1946), pp. 145–72. See also Trachtenberg, *The Devil and the Jews* and Mark Wischnitzer, "Origin of the Jewish Artisan Class in Bohemia and Moravia 1500–1648," *Jewish Social Studies* 16 (October 1954): 335–50.

18. This struggle lasted throughout the nineteenth and extended into the twentieth century, especially in such countries as Austria, Hungary, Poland, and Rumania, where capitalistic behavior patterns were late in spreading. A good analysis by a social scientist is contained in a work by Heinrich Waenting, *Gewerbliche Mittelstandspolitik. Eine rechtshistorisch-wirtschaftspolitische Studie auf Grund oesterreichischer Quellen* (Leipzig, 1898), pp. 136–68.

19. Simon M. Dubnow, *History of the Jews in Russia and Poland from the Earliest Times until the Present Day*, 3 vols. (Philadelphia, 1916): vol. 1, p. 139 et passim.

20. Eva G. Reichmann *Hostages of Civilization—The Social Sources of National Socialist Antisemitism* (Boston, 1951), p. 65 et passim.

21. Alphonse Toussenel, *Les juifs, rois de l'epoque; histoire de la feodalite nanciere* (Paris, 1846).
22. Conte Egon Caesar Corti, *Der Aufstieg des Hauses Rotschild 1770–1830* (Leipzig,1927) and *Das Haus Rotschild in der Zeit seiner Blüte 1830–1871* (Leipzig,1928).
23. Jacob Lestchinsky, "The Position of the Jews in the Economic Life of America," in *Jews in a Gentile World—The Problem of Antisemitism*, eds., Isaaque Graeber and Stewart H. Britt (New York, 1942), pp. 402–16.
24. The publication *Jews in America* (by the editors of *Fortune*, New York, 1936), which contains some of the data for the 1920s and 1940s, must be read with a great deal of caution. The facts presented are not incorrect, but the interpretation reveals the subconscious antisemitism of the authors.
25. John P. Dean. "Patterns of Socialization and Association Between Jews and non-Jews," *Jewish Social Studies* 17 (Paper and Proceedings of the Tercentenary Conference on American Jewish Sociology, July 1955): 247–68.
26. According to the *New York Times* (4 February 1957), the top carnival balls in New Orleans cannot be attended by Jews. As a result, Mr. and Mrs. Edgar B. Stern, Sr., who previously made a record $300,000 gift to the New Orleans Philharmonic Symphony Orchestra, were out of town for the entire carnival period. Mrs. Stern is a daughter of the late philanthropist Julius Rosenwald of Chicago; she surely would have loved to participate in socialite activities. Reminders such as this one are necessary because of the frequently heard assertions that Jews "exclude themselves."
27. Theodor Herzl, *A Jewish State—An Attempt at a Modern Solution of the Jewish Question* (3rd ed., New York, 1917); see also Leo S. Pinsker, *Auto-emancipation* (New York, 1944).
28. Herzl, *A Jewish State*.

Part II

Community and Family History

6

The Decline of the Munich Jewish
Community, 1933–38

Thanks to the census of the Jewish population of Munich and vicinity, taken 16 May 1938 by the statistical bureau of the local Jewish community, it is possible to study the statistical effects of the Nazi policy on the demographic structure of this group. The decline of the Munich Jewish community is typical for the Jews of southern Germany in general. The availability of data regarding the emigration during the first five years of the Hitler regime, as well as the structure of the population remaining at the end of that period, makes it possible to measure the decline of this community in some detail.

Population Census

The 1938 census enumerated a total of 6,392 persons under the jurisdiction of the Jewish community of Munich, some of whom resided outside the city in nearby localities. Not included in this total were 171 youths, almost all under 20, who had come from other communities to receive vocational training and who were not classed as members of the local Jewish community. The 6,392 Jews constituted less than 1 percent of the total population of Munich (830,892 on 17 May 1939). To what extent had the Jewish population declined since 1933? According to the general consensus at the beginning of that year, the professing Jews in Munich numbered 9,005 (1.2 percent of the total of 735,388), and about 200 in the vicinity.[1] Inasmuch as some of the Jews did not identify themselves as adherents of the Jewish religion, the official figure should be compared with other data. On the basis of calculations to be presented below in the section dealing with emigration, it is estimated that in 1933 there were some 10,000 Jews in Munich and vicinity. Hence, in the course of the ensuing five years the area lost about one-third of its Jewish population. According to the general census of May 1939, the number of Jews in the city had further declined to 5,050.[2]

TABLE 6.1
Family Status of Jews in Greater Munich, 1938

Status	Number		Percent	
	Male	Female	Male	Female
Married	1,586	1,426	54.9	40.7
Widows and widowers	177	744	6.1	21.3
Separated and divorced	58	90	2.0	2.6
Unmarried	649	796	22.4	22.7
Minors (under 20)	421	445	14.6	12.7
Total	2,891	3,501	100.0	100.0

There were in 1938 considerably more females than males in the Munich Jewish population, 3,501 and 2,891, respectively, or a ratio of 121 to 100. This is typical for a community the emigrés from which were chiefly men and youths. If one adds the 1,983 male and 1,591 female Jews who emigrated between 1933 and 1938, the ratio is reduced to 104 to 100, or approximately the same as that found in the general central European population. As shown by Table 6.1, the widows greatly outnumbered the widowers. Likewise, among separated, divorced, and single persons there were more women than men. Among the minors, the girls were somewhat more numerous than the boys. The fact that among the married persons men outnumbered the women finds its explanation in the statistics regarding intermarriage. There were 82 "Aryans" who had Jewish wives as compared with 242 Jews married to "Aryan" women. If one includes these mixed couples there were 1,668 married couples in the Jewish community and of these 324 (19.4 percent) were cases of intermarriage. These figures refer only to those cases in which the partner had remained a professing Jew. These mixed couples reported a total of 168 "half-Aryan" children growing up on the periphery of the Jewish community.[3]

In its unnatural age composition, Munich Jewry showed the effects of both the declining birth rate and of emigration (Table 6.2). Almost half (47.4 percent) of the Jews were over 50 years old. The large proportion of widows (about 8 percent) suggests that the percentage of women over 50 must have been very high. The oldest age-group had the greatest, and the youngest one the lowest, number of persons. It should be noted that persons born in the decade 1918–27 (11–20 years of age) outnumbered those born in the preceding or subsequent one. This should not be attributed to the fact that the birthrate normally drops in war-time and rises in the postwar years. In the case

TABLE 6.2
Age Distribution of the Munich Jewish population, 1938

Age	Number	Percent
10 years and under	305	4.8
11 to 20 years	622	9.7
21 to 30 years	494	7.7
31 to 40 years	796	12.4
41 to 50 years	1,093	17.1
51 to 60 years	1,251	19.6
Over 60 years	1,780	27.8
Unknown	51	0.9
All ages	6,392	100.0

of Munich Jewry, the relative size of the population between the ages of 11 and 20 was due to the loss of persons between 21 and 40 through emigration (Table 6.6).

Most of the Jews living in Munich in 1938 were not born there, a situation which is typical of the population of all large cities (Table 6.3). The greatest influx occurred during the economically favorable period of fifteen years preceding the World War. For many Jews who arrived after 1933 Munich was only a temporary residence; it was easier to make arrangements for emigration in Munich than in the provincial towns. Nevertheless, emigration from Munich exceeded immigration after 1932.

Almost 60 percent of the Jews were born either in Munich or in other parts of Bavaria, while 25 percent were born in other parts of Germany, including the Rhine Palatinate (Table 6.4). Poland was the place of birth of a large number of those born outside of Germany. In this group the Galician Jews

TABLE 6.3
Munich Jewish Population, 1938, by Period of Arrival in the City

Period	Number	Percent
Born in Munich	2,169	34.0
Before 1900	779	12.1
1900-17	1,439	22.6
1918-32	927	14.5
1933-38	700	10.9
Unknown	378	5.9
Total	6,392	100.0

TABLE 6.4
Nativity and Nationality of Munich Jewish Population, 1938

Country	Number		Percent	
	Natives	Nationals	Natives	Nationals
Germany	5,393	4,936	84.4	77.2
Munich	2,169	----	34.0	----
Other places in Bavaria	1,599	----	25.0	----
Austria	115	94	1.8	1.5
Poland	531	804	8.3	12.5
Czechoslovakia	91	158	1.4	2.5
Hungary	44	56	0.7	0.9
Russia, Lithuania, Latvia, Estonia, Finland and Rumania	84	24	1.3	0.4
British Empire, France and colonies, Luxembourg and Switzerland	50	18	0.8	0.3
United States	20	3	0.3	0.04
Stateless	----	236	----	3.7
Other countries and unknown	64	63	1.0	1.0
All countries		6,392	100.0	100.0

predominated in Munich, whereas in northern Germany the Polish-born Jews had migrated from the area once under Tsarist Russia. Those of French origin came from Alsace, while many born in Czechoslovakia came from former Hungarian and Carpatho-Russian districts. Most of the fifty persons whose place of birth could not be ascertained were probably foreign-born.

The ratios for each country of birth did not correspond as closely with the respective citizenship ratios as might have been expected. Although 84.4 percent of the Munich Jewish population were born in Germany, only 77.2 percent were German citizens. On the other hand, the ratio of Polish and Czechoslovak nationals (12.5 and 2.5 percent) was about one-third larger than that of those born in those states (8.3 and 1.7 percent). This shows that about one-third of the Jews of Polish and Czechoslovak citizenship living in Munich were native-born Germans; most of this group were born in Munich. There was practically no influx of Jews from Galicia after the World War. On the other hand, a larger proportion of Munich Jewry were born in eastern Europe (not including Hungary), especially in Russia, and in other parts of Western Europe than the figures regarding citizenship suggest. As far as western Europe is concerned, the ratios refer chiefly to women born there who married German Jews. The number of stateless Russian-born Jews was relatively high, and most of these were classified by nativity in former Polish territories, which accounts for the excess of Polish citizens over those born in Poland. One must also bear in mind the fact that Poland was the birthplace of some Jews holding German citizenship, especially those born in the provinces of Posen and Upper Silesia, which were part of Germany before the World War. On the whole, 21.5 percent of the Jews were nationals of eastern European countries (including Austria), although only 13.5 percent were born in those states.

In sum the census of 16 May 1938 shows that the Jewish community of Greater Munich had a large percentage of aged persons and an excess of women. It was not, however, very heterogeneous in composition. Most of the members of the community were born either in Munich or in the Franconian and Swabian sections of Bavaria. Those who came from eastern Europe had larger families than the other Jews.

Emigration of Jews from Munich

As part of the same census a study was made of Jews who had emigrated or moved away from Munich since 1 March 1933. This enumeration was made by means of a questionnaire which was supplemented by information secured from communities and trustworthy persons in Germany and abroad. To be sure, complete data for the five-year period was not always obtainable. In some cases, only the year of emigration was ascertained but not the destination or vice versa; in others, the date and place of birth, citizenship, family status, or other data were not available; in certain instances no information at all was forthcoming. This was inevitable considering that the census was an unofficial undertaking. To a large extent the missing details were recovered from information supplied by residents and from organizational records. It is possible, on the other hand, that there were included some persons who had left Munich before 1933.

The statistical material thus obtained may be accepted as accurate and fairly complete. Altogether 3,574 Jews emigrated or moved away between 1 March 1933 and 16 May 1938 from the capital of Bavaria and from places in Upper Bavaria under the jurisdiction of the Jewish community of Munich. It follows, if one adds the 6,392 Jews returned by the 1938 census, that the Jews of Munich and vicinity at the beginning of 1933 numbered 9,966. One has to take into account, however, that 1,616 new members (comprising 118 newly born and 43 newcomers) were admitted and that 940 were stricken off (803 deceased and 137 others) during the period under consideration. This makes a decrease of 779 which must be added to the 1933 total. On the other hand, the 700 persons who settled in Munich during 1933–38 have to be deducted; hence, on 1 March 1933 the Greater Munich Jewish community had an estimated 10,045 members.

TABLE 6.5
Sex Ration of Jews Emigrating from Munich, 1933–38

Year	Male		Female	
	Number	Percent	Number	Percent
1933 (March 1 to December 31)	389	57.5	277	42.5
1934	228	51.5	215	48.5
1935	190	53.5	167	46.5
1936	327	57.8	240	42.2
1937	313	53.2	276	46.8
1938 (January 1 to May 16)	142	54.9	117	45.1
Unknown	394	57.5	299	42.5
Total	1,983	55.8	1,591	44.2

This estimate is corroborated by another group of data. At the time of the general census of 1933 Greater Munich had about 9,200 professing Jews. It is recorded that 666 Jews emigrated from Munich during 1933, and it is safe to assume that many of the 693 Jewish emigrants, the exact year of whose departure is not known, likewise departed in 1933, and in the majority of cases during the first half of that year. There is thus reason to believe that 700 to 800 left between March and June 1933. Hence, if one adds this figure to the 9,200 Jews living in Greater Munich in 1933, there were about 10,000 Jews in the city and vicinity at the beginning of that year. This corresponds closely to the estimate given above on the basis of the 1938 emigration inquiry, indicating that the deficiencies of the Jewish community's data do not invalidate the results.

The emigration from this typical Jewish community of southern Germany to the United States was relatively greater than from northern Germany and relatively smaller to other overseas countries because of family connections. The period covered, from the advent of the Nazi regime to the annexation of Austria, was marked by a carefully organized system of emigration, as distinguished from the later months of panic.

Of the 3,574 Jews who emigrated or moved away from Munich between 1 March 1933 and 16 May 1938, the males comprised 55.8 percent (1,983), although, as shown above, females outnumbered males in the local Jewish population in 1938. This situation is typical of the ratio among emigrants in general (Table 6.5). Persons between 30 and 40 years of age contributed a larger proportion (20.7 percent) than those between 30 and 40 (18.9 percent);

TABLE 6.6
Age Distribution of Jews Emigrating from Munich, 1933–38

Age	Number	Percent
10 years and under	190	5.3
11 to 20 years	459	12.9
21 to 30 years	677	18.9
31 to 40 years	742	20.7
41 to 50 years	492	13.8
51 to 60 years	377	10.5
Over 60 years	310	8.7
Unknown	327	9.3
All ages	3,574	100.0

TABLE 6.7
Family Status of Jews Emigrating from Munich, 1933–38

Year	Persons in Families		Single Persons	
	Number	Percent	Number	Percent
1933 (March 1 to December 31)	436	65.5	230	34.5
1934	294	66.4	149	33.6
1935	199	55.7	158	44.3
1936	291	51.3	276	48.7
1937	272	46.5	317	53.5
1938 (January 1 to May 16)	138	53.3	121	46.7
Unknown	350	50.5	343	49.5
Total	1,980	55.5	1,594	44.5

the other age groups had considerably lower ratios (Table 6.6). There were among these emigrants 658 families comprising a total of 1,980 persons, as compared with 1,594 single persons (Table 6.7). The number of recently married couples among the emigrants must have been considerable.

About one-eighth (435) of the emigrants moved from Munich to other parts of Germany, and of the 3,139 who sought refuge in other countries, 701 (about 20 percent) were reported living in Palestine on 16 May 1938, more than in any other country, and 637 in the United States;[4] 207 persons went to Italy, 199 to France, 176 to England and more than 100 each to Switzerland,

TABLE 6.8
Jewish Migration from Munich, 1933–38, by Destination

Destination	Number	Percent
Other parts of Germany and Danzig	444	12.4
Western Europe	728	20.3
Switzerland and Liechtenstein	135	
Italy	207	
Spain and Portugal	16	
France and colonies, Belgium and Luxembourg	244	
Holland and colonies	116	
Denmark, Sweden, Norway	10	
Eastern Europe	322	8.9
Austria	112	
Czechoslovakia	113	
Poland	58	
Southeastern Europe (Yugoslavia, Hungary, Rumania, Bulgaria, Turkey)	39	
Great Britain and Ireland	176	4.9
Union of South Africa and South-West Africa	71	2.1
Australia and New Zealand	21	0.6
United States of America	637	17.9
Latin America	182	5.0
Argentina	84	
Brazil	63	
Uruguay	20	
Others (Colombia, Equador, Chile, Peru, Mexico)	15	
Palestine	701	19.7
Other countries (Canada, Philippines, Japan, India, Egypt) and unknown	292	8.0
All destinations	3,574	100.0

TABLE 6.9
Nativity and Nationality of Jews Emigrating from Munich, 1933–38

Country	Number		Percent	
	Natives	Nationals	Natives	Nationals
Germany	2,685	2,394	75.2	67.0
Bavaria, excluding Munich	521		14.6	
Munich	1,479		41.2	
Austria	89	122	2.5	3.4
Poland	285	499	8.0	14.0
Czechoslovakia	48	97	1.3	2.7
Hungary	15	45	0.4	1.3
Russia, Lithuania, Latvia, Estonia, Finland and Rumania	57	46	1.6	1.3
British Empire, France and colonies, Luxembourg and Switzerland	45	18	1.2	0.4
United States	11	16	0.3	0.4
Stateless	....	101	....	2.8
Other countries and unknown	339	236	9.5	6.7
All countries	3,574	3,574	100.0	100.0

Czechoslovakia and Austria respectively (Table 6.8). It goes without saying that this shows only the countries of first settlement, often only temporary asylums. It was impossible to ascertain how many had subsequently departed to overseas countries or to other parts of Europe. Outside of the United States, a relatively small proportion went to such places as South America and the British dominions. Argentina admitted 84, the Union of South Africa 70, and Brazil 63; Australia and Uruguay received an insignificant number, and the other countries practically none.

A relatively larger percentage of non-German, especially Polish, Jews than of German citizens emigrated during the period under consideration (Table

TABLE 6.10
Jewish Emigration from Munich, 1933–38, by Year of Departure

Year	Number	Percent
1933 (March 1 to December 31)	666	18.6
1934	443	12.4
1935	357	9.9
1936	567	15.9
1937	589	16.5
1938 (January 1 to May 16)	259	7.3
Unknown	693	19.4
Total	3,574	100.0

6.9). Among the emigrants 14 percent were not German citizens, as compared with 12.5 percent among those remaining in Munich. Thus the German nationals constituted 67 percent of the Jews who left the city, as compared with 77.2 percent of those remaining in Munich. The reasons for this lie in the differences among the groups holding German citizenship and the other Jews as to economic and family status, possibility of returning to the native country, and expulsion. Of the 3,268 emigrants regarding whom data was available, 2,685 or 81 percent were born in Germany and 41 percent in Munich, as compared with 34 percent of those remaining. This must have been due to the fact that the younger emigrants, most of whom were born in Munich, outnumbered the others.

It appears that more Jews emigrated from Munich in 1933 than in any of the subsequent four years, particularly when one takes into consideration the large number of Jews the date of whose emigration could not be ascertained and the majority of whom probably left in 1933 (Table 6.10). It may be estimated that one-fourth to one-third of all Jews who left during these five years emigrated in 1933. This was primarily due to the more favorable opportunities rather than to the more urgent necessity for emigration in the first year. The number of emigrants was relatively small in 1935 but rose in 1936 and 1937. There is reason to believe that emigration was more intensive, as well as more chaotic, in 1938 than in 1934–37.

As for the ratio of the sexes among each year's emigrants, it appears that the excess of males was greater in 1933 than in any of the subsequent years, when the number was about the same for both. The ratio varied from country to country, but in the principal havens, Palestine, the United States, Italy, France, and England, it was about the same as for the total number of immigrants. The excess of males was, however, smaller in Italy and Palestine than elsewhere. The older immigrants generally went to countries which received relatively few of the younger ones. For instance, 37.1 percent of those who went to Switzerland[5] were in the two oldest age-groups, as compared with only 10.9 percent of those settled in the United States.

The ratio of family-unit emigrants to single persons was approximately the same ratio as the ratio of male to female emigrants. The average family consisted of three persons, largely due to the large proportion of newlywed and other childless couples. During 1933 and 1934 the percentages of family-unit emigrants were 65.5 and 64.4 of the total, respectively. Thereafter, however, the proportion of single persons increased. In 1937 and the first four-and-a-half months of 1938, only 46.5 and 53.3 percent, respectively, were family-unit emigrants. Among those who sought refuge in South Africa, single persons constituted 74.7 percent, as compared with 52.3 percent of those who went to England (young girls) and 51.2 percent of those admitted to the United States. A larger percentage of family-unit emigrants than single persons was found, however, among those who settled in European countries, with the exception of England. The percentages of family-unit emigrants admitted to France, Holland and Czechoslovakia were 63.9, 78.4 and 66.4, respectively. In Brazil they constituted 68.2 percent and in Palestine 66.6 percent. The latter figure deserves some attention because the general impression is that most of those who went to Palestine were young people sent by the Youth Aliyah and Hechaluz organizations. The discrepancy between impression and fact is, however, more apparent than real. There were numerous young married couples among the Haluzim.

According to Table 6.8, the percentage distribution of the emigrants by countries of immigration was as follows: European countries, 34.1; Palestine, 19.7; United States, 17.9; other parts of Germany, 12.4; other overseas countries, 8.3; place of destination unknown, 7.6. One reason why the European countries seem to have received such a large share of these refugees is undoubtedly the fact that data regarding persons who had subsequently emigrated to overseas countries was not available at the time of the study. Furthermore, it may be assumed that in 1938 more of them probably went to the United States than to Palestine. The small number of those who found refuge in the other overseas countries is truly remarkable. Especially instructive are the results of the analysis of the annual immigration to each of the several countries. Thus, whereas 16.2 percent of the total went to France in 1933, only 2.5 percent were admitted to that country in 1937. The percentage of those who reached Palestine fluctuated each year as follows: 27.9, 28.4, 32.3, 24.0, 8.5, and 8.9. The percentage of those who went to the United States, on the other hand, increased each year, namely, 5.7, 8.8, 11.8, 25.6, 33.8, and 27.3. England's share increased from 3.6 percent in 1933 to 6.6 in 1937 and 6.9 in 1938. The peak year for South Africa was 1936, for Brazil, 1937, and for Argentina and Australia, 1938.

As for the citizenship of the emigrants, it has already been remarked that Polish citizens formed a rather large proportion (14 percent) of the total. The assumption that this was due to differences in economic status and family connections between German and other Jews is corroborated by the fact that 24.4 percent of all the Polish Jews, 46.6 percent of the Russian, 54.4 percent of the Rumanian, and 22.7 percent of the Czechoslovak Jews who emigrated left in 1933, as compared with 10.7 percent of the German Jews. Moreover, the countries of refuge found by these groups varied. Only 19.5 percent of the German citizens migrated to Palestine, as compared with 31.3 percent of the Polish and 46.4 percent of the Russian citizens. On the other hand, 21.4 percent of the German Jews found refuge in the United States, as compared with 9.4 percent of the Polish Jews. These figures undoubtedly reflect differences both in ideology and family connnections between these two groups.

Munich was the place of birth of 41.2 percent of the Jewish emigrants, while among the Jewish inhabitants remaining, 34 percent were born there. The larger proportion among the emigrants was due to the fact that there were relatively more young people among them than those who remained. Many of the parents of those born in Munich hailed from rural places in Bavaria, from other parts of Germany, and from foreign countries. A larger percentage of those born outside of Germany were among the emigrants during the later years. Furthermore, the differences in place of destination between German and foreign-born Jews were similar to those between German citizens and others: 23.1 percent of those born in Munich, 16.5 percent of those born in Bavaria, and 13.7 percent of those born in other parts of Germany went to Palestine, as compared with 27.6 percent of the Polish-born and 39.6 percent of the Russian-born. The corresponding percentages for those who went to the United States were: 21.3, 20.7, and 18.2, as compared with 9.5 and 11.6.[6]

Summary

On 16 May 1938 the number of Jews in Greater Munich was 6,392, as compared with about 10,000 five years earlier. This population consisted of 60 percent females, and almost half of the Jews were past 50. About 85 percent of the total had been born either in or around Munich or elsewhere in Germany. During the 5 years of the Nazi regime the recorded number of Jews who left Munich and of those who had migrated was 3,574, of whom about 40 percent were between 21 and 40 years of age. Outside of more or less temporary asylums in European lands, the most important havens of refuge were Palestine (20 percent) and the United States (18 percent). The latter ratio is typical for southern Germany but higher than that among refugees from the northern part of the country. The ratio of persons migrating to the United States increased while the ratio of those who migrated to Palestine decreased from year to year. More Jews emigrated in 1933 then emigrated each year from 1934 to 1937. But, as may been seen from the official census of 17 May 1939, there must have been a large Jewish emigration in the second half of 1938 and the first half of 1939; most of these refugees are known to have immigrated to England and the United States.

1941

Notes

1. *Statistik des Deutschen Reiches*, vol. 151, no. 5 ccccli/5; *Die Glaubens juden im Deutschen Reich* (Berlin, 1935), pp. 14–15; *Zeitschrift des Bayrischen Statistischen Landesamts*, vol. 66 (1934), appendix: "Bayr. Gemeindeverzeichnis nach der Volkszählung vom 16. Juni 1933."
2. "Die Juden und die jüdischen Mischlinge in Deutschen Reich. Vorläufiges Ergebnis der Volkszählung vom 17. Mai 1939," in *Wirtschaft und Statistik*, vol. 20, nos. 5, 6 (March 1940), p. 85. The half-Jews numbered 1,345 and the quarter-Jews 624.
3. Probably incomplete.
4. During and after 1938, however, changes in the selection of a destination undoubtedly occurred, and it is safe to assume that the United States gained the lead over Palestine. At the same time, the number received by Great Britain increased.
5. Persons retired from active life for the most part.
6. It should be noted that the preparation of the material and the analysis were conducted under unusually unfavorable conditions. In its final stages, when the work required particular care and attention, the study was carried on in noisy rooms while the synagogue was being demolished and the evacuation of the community buildings located on Herzog Maxstrasse had begun. That the work was nevertheless successfully completed was due to the untiring collaboration and cooperation of Frau Paula Hirsch and Dr. Hugo Jacob.

7

The Jews in Munich: 1918-43

[handwritten margin notes: support Gilman's idea of anti-semitism anti-semitism had to change nothing is funny thing is it was Germans who were responsible for new change law in 1861.]

The Structure of the Jewish Community

The Jewish community in Munich revealed a historical stratification that was clearly recognizable in the decade following World War I.[1] This very community began as a community of Court Jews during the end of the eighteenth and the beginning of the nineteenth century. From the time of their official recognition in 1810 until the end of the Bavarian System of Registration (*Matrikelordnung*) in 1861, only a select group of Jews were allowed to settle in Munich: bankers and financiers, army- and court-appointed merchants, and, in exceptional cases, some factory owners and retailers with outstanding reputations. There were no more than 1,206 Jews counted in a city population of 92,000 in 1859, two years before the abolition of the System of Registration. All that changed after 1861 when the Jewish community became a civic one. Industrious men came to Munich in large numbers from the villages and little towns of the Swabian and Franconian countryside, further from the Upper and Rhine Palatinates, from Württemberg, and many other parts of Germany. First it was the skilled craftsmen, art dealers, antiquarians, real estate dealers, agricultural merchants, and all those working in the credit banks, textile industry, wholesale and retail businesses who first achieved respectable status; soon they were followed by those in the judiciary, medical, and legal professions. Jews came from everywhere to study at the University of Munich; upon completion of their studies, many of them settled in the city. In addition, there were the artists and scholars, the latter group consisting mainly of converts to Christianity; a few exceptions aside, an academic career remained outside the reach of professing Jews. After 1881, and even more so after 1904, there was a heavy influx of east European Jews, who sought refuge from the pogroms in Russia or were driven by extreme poverty from Galicia. From very modest beginnings as welfare recipients, tobacco workers, or peddlers, these immigrants soon developed a flourishing trade, mostly in the shoe and fur business. In 1910, the Jewish community numbered 11,083, only 52 percent of which were born in Munich or adjoining communities in Bavaria; 21 percent were born in other parts of Germany, and 27 percent were of foreign origin, born in Austria, Hungary, or Russia.[2]

After World War I, the total number of Jews in Munich declined by 9 percent, partly due to losses suffered in the war (the memorial for the fallen in the Garchinger Street cemetery lists 175 names—by no means a total), partly because of changing demographic trends: among old-established families it became fashionable to have one or, at most, two children; many families remained childless, and remaining single became acceptable. Last but not least, a slow but steady emigration flow after Hitler's 1923 coup further depleted the community. At this time, however, the losses could not be made up through immigration from the countryside. Parallel with this, the number of foreign-born Jews decreased, partly due to the fact that no permits were issued for settling in the city, and partly due to the arbitrary and capricious expulsions during the Kahr regime.[3] It is thus safe to say that even if the Nazis had not instituted their bloody butchery of Jews, the Jewish population of Munich would still have experienced a sharp decline.

In sociological terms, the stratification picture is much more complex than what shows up in the demographic statistics. In 1895, for example, the first official census was taken of all religious denominations relating to age and place of birth. It turned out that there were only 372 Jews over thirty years of age who were Munich-born. In 1910, 11,000 Jews were already living in Munich, 3,000 of whom were born there; of these, only 176 were born in Munich before the System of Registration was abolished (1861). Obviously, there were not too many older, more exclusive, well-established Jewish families in Munich; in fact, the phrase "older, more exclusive, well-established Jewish families" makes little sense as far as Munich, not Bavaria as a whole, is concerned. One can, however, distinguish an elite group of Jews who were born in Munich before 1895 or went to school there—or were born in the other urban Jewish community of Bavaria, Nuremberg–Fürth and did not belong to any Orthodox congregation. They prospered and attained prominence as owners of art galleries, antique shops, and retail businesses, especially banking institutions related to real estate ventures, and in the legal profession. Their social life took place within their own intimate circle, but they also had the opportunity to do business with and meet the leaders of local government. They sent their children, especially their daughters, to schools where they were able to fraternize with the children of the upper government bureaucracy. Both Jews and Christians were keen to keep out the children of the Jewish nouveau riche. Philip Löwenfeld relates, for example, that he could not quite understand why his parents wanted him to attend a posh social dancing circle frequented by the sons and daughters of the local haute bourgeoisie as well as the offspring of the leading Jewish businessmen, lawyers, and doctors, when his best friend who came from a less prominent Jewish family was not acceptable (see note 2). His father, Professor Theodore Löwenfeld, was a well-known Social Democrat and champion of working class rights, who would not abandon his Judaism, if for no other reason than because "one does not flee from a beleaguered fortress." The men of this group were interested in the affairs of the Jewish community (mainly religious education and cemetery arrangements, in addition to ritual and worship), not only for reasons of defense but also for reasons of status and prestige. The official leaders of the *Kultusgemeinde* did not necessarily belong to that elite but were mainly members of the merchant class or the legal profession, whose liberal Jewish piety was mostly serious and genuine. These men gathered around the Rabbinate and Cantorate of Munich (represented by excellent men). During my time, chief Cantor Emanuel Kirschner, a beloved teacher and prominent composer of synagogal music, was one of the most outstanding persons of the community.[4] The elite was the nucleus of a steadily growing group, recruiting its members from a periphery of decent and industrious people engaged in their respective occupations and remaining Jews out of parental loyalty. On the margin of that periphery, then, there were those who paid their dues to the *Kultusgemeinde*, but whose interest in Judaism was limited to wishing to be buried in the Jewish cemetery.

Members of the Munich branch of B'nai B'rith and of the Orthodox Congregation Ohel Jakob constituted special groups. They may be defined in more clearly ideological and sociological terms. Congregation Ohel Jakob, although remaining part of the general Jewish community, was from the very beginning (1886) a private association that was established against the strong opposition of liberals in the community. From its start to the very end in the Hitler era, this congregation was led and ruled by two families, the Fränkels and the Feuchtwangers, who formed extensive clans that produced many prominent lawyers, scholars, artists, and businessmen and may be regarded as the Orthodox wing of the Jewish elite. To be sure, there were others less elite and even poor families among the members of Congregation Ohel Jakob. Somewhat later, there appeared on the scene *Agudah* (anti–Zionist) as well as *Misrachi* (Zionist) wings that joined in perfect solidarity when voting in general Jewish community elections.

Modeled after its American counterpart, the Munich branch of B'nai B'rith was established on 21 March 1897 and counted among its members both liberal and Orthodox Jews. Its purpose was to bring together Jews of diverse orientations in social or charitable activities under the motto: "Charity, Brotherly Love, and Concord." The beginnings of Jewish social work in Munich date back to the founding of B'nai B'rith. Youth counselling, the building of Toynbee-Hall, a foster home for children, and another for youth in vocational training, the establishment of the Jewish Health Care System (that later became the Jewish Nursing Home and Hospital) —all would have been impossible without the support of B'nai B'rith. In sponsoring these projects, B'nai B'rith had to ward off attacks by the old liberals who feared a reghettoization of Jewish community life. While it is true that many prominent members of the elite joined B'nai B'rith (after 1929, even the Isaah-Loge), the majority of its members were merchants and academics who had moved to the city from the countryside.

The foreign-born, mostly Russian and Galician, Jews, who from 1900 onward constituted about one-fourth of the Munich Jewish community, constituted a special group with its own marked subdivisions (see note 2). There was the ultra-Orthodox group Shomre Schabbos, and several religious and charitable associations, such as Linas Hazedek and Agudath Achim, with their own little prayer rooms. The latter two joined in 1931 to build the synagogue in Reichenbach Strasse that became the main house of worship for the newly emerging Jewish community after World War II. This is not to say that the majority of the *Ostjuden* were Orthodox Jews; most of them were simply more interested in business and social contacts. They were either outright Zionists or sympathized with Zionism. There were wealthy *Ostjuden* and very poor ones. Initially, the social barrier between eastern and western Jews was marked, but essentially the two grew friendlier toward each other, especially after the shock of expulsions under the Kahr regime had worn off. Intermarriages became more frequent as time went by; and the Orthodox and Zionist youth groups, such as Blau-Weiss, Bar Kochba, and Esra, recruited their membership from among both groups. This means that an integration of the community on the basis of Jewish peoplehood had begun.

There is another group whose existence first became known after a census based on the Jewish community records of 15, May 1938 was made under my direction. In my article, "The Decline of the Munich Jewish Community: 1933-38," I provide a detailed account of the figures and their significance. In addition, I consulted a wide range of statistical data from the 1920s, 1930s, and 1940s.[5] As is well known, the Nazi laws established new categories of Jewish people: *Volljuden* (pure Jews) and *Mischlinge* (Jews of mixed parentage). The former were subdivided into *Glaubensjuden* (Jews by faith, and who so regarded themselves) and *Rassejuden* (Jews by race, that is, persons whose parents were Jews but who did not belong to the Jewish community themselves). Jews of mixed parentage could be *Mischlinge* of first grade (i.e., having two Jewish grandparents) or of second grade (having only one Jewish grandparent). Here we must rely on guesstimates. Based on my own counting and on other census takings, I would venture to estimate that, in addition to the 9,000 to 10,000 Jews living in Munich in 1933, there were approximately 3,000 who could be called either *Rassejuden* or *Mischlinge*. This is the formerly unrecognized group I referred to above. It was by no means a homogeneous group. There were *Volljuden* who paid no church taxes but were connected to the Jewish community by family ties or social contacts. And then there were those living in mixed marriages who preferred Jewish to Christian social contacts or formed special cliques with other such couples. There were quite a few converts to Christianity, among them many prominent scientists who had severed all contacts with the Jewish community and many artists, from the most famous to the relatively unknown, who did not want to have anything to do with any religious or church group but kept company mainly with their fellow artists.[6] Regardless of their preferred lifestyle, all of them were profoundly affected by the Nazi ascent to power in 1933. Their ultimate fate showed variations, but that was not because of any reasons of Nazi ideology.

Munich's Jewish community had a rich variety of clubs and associations. According to contemporary statistics that were reassessed and reprinted in Hans Lamm's *Von Juden in München* (1959), the following associations existed between 1915 and 1932:[7]

TABLE 7.1

	1915	1932
Religious and charitable associations	20	38
Student associations	6	3
Scientific associations	3	3
Youth and sports clubs	4	9
Social clubs	1	4
Lodges	1	2
Local chapters of national Jewish organizations	9	9
	44	68

This table requires some comment. Above I already called attention to the Munich Lodge and the Jesaia Lodge of the independent order of B'nai B'rith. The names of three student associations were Licaria, Thuringia, and Jordania. Ideologically, the first was German-Jewish, the third Zionist. Thuringia, on the other hand, did not call itself Jewish because it had some non-Jewish members. There was also an Association of Democratic Students which had mainly Jewish members. Among the academic associations, the most noteworthy was the Association for the Statistics of Jews. The conspicuous increase in the number of youth and sports clubs—from four to nine in seventeen years—marks a phenomenon of great significance, namely, the inroad of the youth organizations into Jewish communal life. Originally, many young Jews were enthusiastic participants in the general German youth movement in the aftermath of World War I, from which they were gradually excluded and finally formally expelled. As a result, they joined in ever increasing numbers the existing Jewish youth associations and alliances, such as the Zionist

Blau-Weiss and Bar Kochba, as well as the Orthodox Esra. Members of the first two alliances were mainly from among the children of east European families; now the children of more prominent families joined them. The Jewish Youth Association, not a Bund really, was officially neutral, but it became more and more sympathetic toward Zionist ideology in the course of the 1920s. Martin Buber's address, "How Does Community Become Real?" at the Congress of the Jewish Youth Associations of Germany held in Munich in 1930, is a good example for the absorption into Jewish consciousness of German sociological theories in the garb of Hassidic-socialist formulations. Buber himself married a Christian woman of Munich, Paula Winkler, a convert to Judaism and Zionism; through her, Buber felt a personal attachment to Munich. He loved, he stated, the "crafty air of Munich," and the youth of Munich loved him in return.[8]

The actual Buber circle grew out of the Bund Kameraden, ideologically German-Jewish and oriented to the general German youth movement. Its members came from neither the east European nor the elite old families milieu but from the solid middle class. Under the threat of approaching Nazism, the circle split into three distinct groups: 1) the Schwarze Fähnlein (Black Banner) was scout-like and German-nationalistic; 2) the Rote Haufen (Red Crowd) was socialist and communist; 3) the Werkleute (Working People) was Jewish-oriented and later became part of the Haluz-Zionist movement. The Kameraden of Munich eventually joined this third group. Having said all this, it must be stated that these clubs and associations attracted not all—or even the majority—of Jewish youth in Munich. The majority was and remained individualistic to the bitter end. It was the members of the Bünde and associations— along with some adults—who filled the seminars and lectures of the newly established Lehrhaus (House of Jewish Learning) under the leadership of Dr. Ludwig Feuchtwanger; the Lehrhaus was modeled after the Frankfurt Lehrhaus established by Franz Rosenzweig in the 1920s.

Significant among the branches of larger Jewish organizations were, for example, the Self-Help Association of German Jews, (Hilfsverein der deutschen Juden), the Council of Jewish Women, (Jüdische Frauenbund), the Zionist Organization, the Zionist Revisionists, the Organization of Jewish Veterans, and the Centralverein. There existed during the 1920s a small but significant group of nationalist German Jews, consisting mainly of wholly assimilated academics who did not partake in any kind of Jewish community life. Sociopolitically speaking, the most important organizations were the Centralverein and the Frauenbund. (I am going to discuss the Centralverein and the Organization of Jewish Veterans in more detail at a later point.) The Zionist Revisionists were a small but very active and aggressively polemic group whose members came almost entirely from the east European portion of the community. The local branch of the Zionists was led by the brilliant lawyer Eli Straus, who had moved from Karlsruhe to Munich. Before World War I, the few Munich Zionists displayed an aggressively secular-nationalist orientation; an outstanding representative of this group was Dr. Felix Theilhaber, a physician, who achieved fame through his demographic monograph, *Der Untergang der deutschen Juden* (The Decline of German Jewry), published in 1921. On account of their orientation, the Zionists were not only shunned by the liberals but also by the orthodox in Munich. The liberals' appeal was to patriotism, the appeal of the orthodox to the *Yichus* of Jewish tradition. Eli Straus, himself a member of the Orthodox community, led the Zionists into a coalition with the Orthodox and the *Ostjuden* and named it the Jewish People's Party (Jüdische Volkspartei). Placing their emphasis on social and charitable activities (as against limiting their activities to ritual matters), the Jewish People's Party and the B'nai B'rith joined hands, even though the members of the lodge voted the Liberal ticket in the community elections. In the elections of 1920, the Liberals elected 68, the People's Party, 32 representatives. After their agreement of 1925, the picture remained basically the same: 67 and 32, respectively. The administration of the community lay in the hands of Oberlandesgerichtsrat Dr. Alfred Neumeyer from 1920 on, but Eli Straus became its vice chairman and head of the newly founded Welfare Office. In this way, former conflicts between Liberals, Zionists and the Orthodox, as well as those between eastern and western Jews were largely eliminated, giving way to a rarely disturbed cooperation in the face of the approaching danger of radical-nationalist and antisemitic movements. Dr. Neumeyer's conscientious legal and political work served the same consolidating purposes that led to the establishment of the Union of Bavarian Jewish Communities in 1920.

Concerning their political orientation, the Jews of Munich were liberal in the spirit of Bavarian liberalism which, regardless of its loyalty to the monarchy, favored German unity and anticlericalism. This was, to be sure, a general attitude and not to be confused with political activism. The Jews of Munich participated in the genius loci of the city, which is of a private nature and prefers artistic preoccupations to civic activities. But there existed a minority with more active concerns. Shortly before the outbreak of World War I, a more left-liberal trend asserted itself among a sizeable group of people, my father among them. He and his friends gathered around Professor Ludwig Quidde, the Nobel Peace Prize winner. They were closely associated with the Swabian People's Party and the famous daily, *Frankfurter Zeitung*, and rejected the old-fashioned nationalist liberalism. Actively involved were a number of Jews, among them the long-time legal advisor to the Centralverein, Wilhelm Levinger. Following World War I, these liberals became part of the German Democratic party, which shortly after its rapid rise declined no less rapidly. In the person of Adolf Strauss, the Democratic Party had a

Jewish representation on the City Council. In the 1920s many Jewish academics and also some businessmen turned to the Social Democratic Party. Some of them became very active members, such as the economist Carl Landauer, the lawyers Philipp Löwenfeld and Max Hirschberg, the director of the local brewery, Joseph Schülein, as well as City Councillors Nussbaum and Epstein—the latter a well-known physician of Russian origin. Members of the Orthodox community started to move toward the Bavarian People's Party, especially so after the debates on the ritual slaughtering of animals in the Bavarian Diet in 1930, where the Social Democrats in large numbers supported legislation prohibiting such ritual slaughter commanded to observant Jews. It should be noted that Jews were playing important roles in several progressive organizations, such as the German Peace Society, the Society of Women Voters, the Society of Ethical Culture, and others.

Among the forty-five members of the Munich Chamber of Industry and Commerce were seven Jews, five representing wholesale trade, one retail trade, and one industry. Naturally Jews participated in many professional organizations. Graduates of the Munich schools, and then members of the academic professions joined their former classmates in class reunions and regular professional meetings. They were members of bowling clubs as well as sports clubs and *Wanderbünde* (hiking clubs). Assimilated Jews went hunting with their Christian friends and colleagues. At the purely social level and in domestic entertaining, however, things were markedly different. Jews could become members of Odd Fellows' Lodges but more often than not these lodges were heavily Jewish; other societies of this kind often remained decidedly *judenrein* (free of Jews). One of the more striking examples in sociological terms is the Insel Klub (Island Club) that was established in 1909.[9] This club was strictly a social club with an almost exclusively Jewish membership that nevertheless eschewed all Jewish–oriented social or cultural activities. About twenty to thirty prominent Jewish businessmen and professionals met weekly at the fashionable Regina-Palast-Hotel or later at the Restaurant Schleich in Brienner Street; there, they indulged in high-stake gambling and eating and drinking bouts. On occasion they invited highly paid artists or scholars for lectures. Thomas Mann and Professor Moritz Bonn were among the speakers. Members were selected on the basis of wealth and status; consequently, merchants who served their customers in their stores were not considered respectable enough to join.

At social gatherings in their homes, Jews entertained mostly Jews. Mixed couples, in most cases Jewish husbands with Christian wives, or artists and writers who in many cases were married to Jewish women were welcome at these Jewish gatherings. In the homes of upper-class Christians one would not expect to meet any observant Jews, and only occasionally any converted Jews. In short, one might say that personal contacts between Jews and Christians diminished in the degree that the intimacy of the encounter increased. They would meet at their clubs, not in their home.

Antisemitism and Jewish Reaction

Having sketched the structure and stratification of the Jewish community, as well as the nature of the half-Jewish and quasi-Jewish groups, in Munich, we must now turn attention to the rising wave of hostility that threatened this community. Since the enmity assumed different and ever-changing forms, and because different people experienced this enmity differently, my report henceforth will be largely autobiographical in character.[10]

When in the morning of 8 November 1918 it became known that Kurt Eisner had proclaimed the (Bavarian) Republic the night before, my father said he was going out to see what was happening in the city and asked me whether I wanted to join him. I was a 16-year-old Gymnasium student and had mixed feelings about the whole thing. I painfully realized that the war was lost. The kaiser was not beloved in my family, but as far as Bavaria was concerned, I was a monarchist. When we returned from downtown and alighted from the tram at the Rondell Neuwittelsbach, my father asked a man who was also getting out, "What do you think about the situation?" He answered, "The Jew is sitting on top!" Suddenly, it became clear to me where I stood. I realized that the fate of the Jews was linked to the fate of the republic. This connection could be recognized earlier and more clearly in Munich than anywhere else in Germany. The theme of antisemitism that existed traditionally grew into a political device of explosive force.

Eisner's extremely short-lived regime was followed by the Communist Republic of Councils (Räterepublik). From its inception it was branded a "Jewish republic" because one of its two leaders, Eugen Levine, was a Russian Jew (Max Levin was of Baltic-German extraction), and several Jewish literati, among them Ernst Toller and Erich Mühsam, were among its vocal advocates. Gustav Landauer's participation was owed to his utopian socialism. The far more significant participation of Jews on the other side was never even mentioned: Carl Landauer, Dr. Fritz Stern, Franz Gutmann, and Walter and Philip Löwenfeld, who were Social Democrats; Sigmund Fränkel, a spokesman for the Orthodox and the Jewish citizenry in general; many Jewish members of the Freikorps, among them Leopold Ballin, the much-decorated fighter pilot of World War I, and member of the Richthofen Squadron. And I was one of those who distributed propaganda leaflets against the Räterepublik in the streets. After the collapse of the Räterepublik we were deeply shocked by both the brutal murder of Gustav Landauer and the previous shooting of the members of the so-called Thule Society. At that time, all I knew about the Thule Society was what was published in the papers, but one could hardly miss that their members were consumed by racism. And I was so upset by all this that I was unable to do justice to my school work and was held back one year; my parents then transferred me to the Römer-Institute on Kaulbachstrasse, which was known for its strictness. But what my parents did not know about the institute was the fact that it was the citadel of racial nationalism. Graduates of the institute were among the leaders of the Freikorps. Although the school atmosphere was one of brutal arrogance, I was not physically harmed. I was a quiet boy, went about my business in an inconspicuous way, and showed myself unafraid. Likewise, when I returned to the Max-Gymnasium, for the following years, I remained a friend among friends; indeed, I am grateful to the Absolvia Maximiliana for all those friendships that have endured to this day through very difficult times. But it became obvious to any observer of the scene that Jewish students at the lower forms of secondary schools (*Mittelschulen*) did have a very hard time. Once I even had to rescue a young boy who was the only Jewish pupil in his class from one of his attackers and had to escort him home amid screams and shouts. This incident left a deep and lasting impression on me. Way back when I was a 12-year-old, I was so influenced by certain persons and books that I became a Zionist. During the years of war and revolution, new impressions overshadowed those influences. Now I felt I had to teach my young charge that a young Jew must be a Maccabee, and that he would never again feel alone and defenseless if he knew that he belonged to the eternal Jewish people.

It should not come as a surprise that young people were extremely agitated at that time.[11] There was an open call for the murder of Jews; one only needs to recall the song "When Jewish Blood Drips from the Knife." Pasted on the advertisement pillars one could see the huge red posters of the Nazi Party with the added slogan: "Admission of Jews is forbidden!" The police authorities, whose highest posts already were occupied by Nazi sympathizers like Pohner and Frick, did not interfere. Dr. Neumeyer reports in his "Memoirs" that when he confronted Frick—whom he characterized as an "elusive guy" (*Aalglatt*)—he was told that admission or exclusion was a matter of rightful judgment (*Hausrecht*) of any party. In fact, the right of free expression was forcibly eliminated. Meetings of other parties or displeasing associations were disrupted. When Rabbi Dr. Bärwald tried to speak up at a meeting of the Nazi Party in October of 1920, he was shouted down. His companions from the Reichsbund Jüdischer Frontsoldaten (National Association of Jewish Veterans), among them Karl Stahl, a captain of the reserve and recipient of the Iron Cross Class I, were beaten up and thrown down the stairs. It became apparent that any such kind of open "resistance" was hopeless. In the meantime, the other side abused the right of free speech in its special way. I once witnessed the practice at a meeting of the Democratic party which I attended with my father in order to hear Senator Carl Peterson of Hamburg, the main speaker of the meeting. Adolf Hitler also attended the meeting and took part in the discussion; he attacked the speaker in the most vulgar manner, and when a member of the audience called out to him, "Take your hands out of your pockets when you address another person!" Hitler started to wave his arms about and shouted back in his kind of German: "I can talk with my hands too, just like the Jew Senator" (*I kann aa mit dö Händ reden, wia der Jud, der Senator*), and with that he quit. I asked my father afterwards: "How does he get to call the Senator a Jew?" to which I received the answer that Senator Peterson was, indeed, half-Jewish. That gave me something to think about; I realized that there was no escape from the Nazis.

At the time, there lived in Munich a man of Jewish origin, although baptized into the Catholic faith, who just did not wish to see the writing on the wall: Professor Paul Nikolaus Cossmann. He was cofounder in 1903 of the famous journal *Süddeutsche Monatshefte*, and became its editor from 1904 to 1933. In this capacity, Cossman propagated an extremely nationalistic view during World War I, advocating a so-called *Siegfrieden* (victory peace). In 1920, Cossmann's backers bought up the respectable newspaper, *Münchner Neuesten Nachrichten,* and he became head publisher as well as political advisor of the daily. Adopting a lofty standpoint toward everything, Cossmann opposed Hitler and his race theories. But that did not prevent him from providing the Nazi movement with a rousing slogan and a terrific impetus through his passionate and very personal fight in the question of war-guilt (and reparation). Cossmann's infamous roles in the "war-guilt-trials" of 1922 and in the lawsuit (1925) against the newspaper *Münchner Post*, which was accused of fifth-column activities during the war, are well-documented in Philipp Löwenfeld's "Memoirs," (at the Leo Baeck Institute in New York City). Although Cossmann's lawyers failed to prove that either Kurt Eisner, or his secretary, Fechenbach, committed "fraud" or "treason," Cossmann was acquitted because it was considered that he acted in the public interest and also because public opinion was solidly behind him. Fechenbach, on the other hand, unjustly accused of falsifying documents, became the victim of a blatant miscarriage of justice. He was sentenced to eleven years in prison and civic degradation; he was released much later, only thanks to the intervention of the Supreme Court. In 1933 Fechenbach was shot dead by the Gestapo "while trying to escape."

Cossmann's article about the Fechenbach trial in the *Süddeutsche Monatshefte* was characterized by the court-appointed scholarly experts as a "falsification of history," but the presiding judge Frank—later a Nazi judge— declared that Cossmann was "acting in the public interest," thus insuring that Cossmann's fanciful *Dolchstosslegende* ("stab-in-the-back" scenario) became an effective weapon of Nazi propaganda. It is true Cossmann rejected the hysterical antisemitic scenario, according to which the Jews aspired to world domination via "Jewish war" and "Jewish revolution." Cossmann's special kind of antisemitism operated on a "higher" level, as he was fighting against the so-called "antinational" ideas of his opponents not because they were Jews but because he deemed them "traitors." In the eyes of the Nazis it was one and the same thing, and they naturally rejected any cooperation with Cossmann. He was placed under arrest for over a year after the Nazi takeover in 1933; from 1935 to 1941 he lived in retirement in Ebenhausen/ Isartal. He was rounded up in 1941 and sent to the Munich ghetto located in Berg am Laim. In her memoirs, Else Behrend-Rosenfeld, a fellow inmate, speaks of him as a "saint," who bore his fate without complaint of displeasure, deeply pious, and generally revered. He died in Theresienstadt.

More important even than Cossmann himself was the so-called Cossmann circle. What I knew of this circle was what my father's political friends used to report about it. I referred above to the threatened takeover of the Munich newspaper (*Münchner Neueste Nachrichten*) by a reactionary group. A few wealthy Jews, among them our relative, Kommerzienrat Heinrich Marx of the banking firm Heinrich and Hugo Marx, tried to come up with an offer to prevent this but had to yield to the financial superiority of the nationalists. The new powerful backers were the Gute Hoffnungshütte concern along with Kommerzienrat Seitz and Consul Scharrer, a big landowner. These names may mean nothing today, but at the time they had a powerful following among an elite group of men who worked together in an exclusive and extremely private club called Gaea. Franz von Gebsattel, personal secretary to Cossmann, was the general manager of this secret society, and its president was the Duke Eugen zu Oettingen-Wallerstein. Among its members could be found well-known industrialists, such as Dr. Karl Haniel, Dr. Alfred Hugenberg, Dr. Paul Reusch, Dr. Albert Vogler, Dr. Sorge, and Dr. Clairmont; members of the aristocracy, such as Prince Ysenburg-Birstein, Baron von Frankenstein-Wangenheim, Baron von Kenkerink zu Borg (chief of staff of Crown Prince Rupprecht of Bavaria), Josef Maria von Soden-Fraunhofen, and the like. From the military, there was Admiral (retired) von Tirpitz and General (retired) von Lettow-Vorbeck; from the political arena, there were mostly members of the Bavarian People's party, such as Dr. Georg Heim, Sebastian Schlittenbauer, Gustav von Kahr, and Fritz Schäffer; the Church was represented by the future Cardinal of Berlin, Konrad Count von Preysing, and Abbot Alban Schachleiter. Among sympathizing scholars were men like Oswald Spengler, Karl Alexander von Müller, and the astronomer Hugo von Seliger. Cossmann thus summoned the spirits that he could not control. These gentlemen of the Gaea-Club made good use of Cossmann's pretentious ideas and lofty idealism, but their objectives were different. They wanted to reinstitute the leading role of the military in German society, keep down the trade unions and—as far as the Bavarian state government, including Minister-

President von Knilling, was concerned—they wanted to preserve the Bavarian state's rights vis-à-vis Berlin. In order to reach these goals, Hitler came in handy as the "drummer," and the Jews as the sacrificial animals to be surrendered to popular passion on the altar of public interest. In the end, the drummer outwitted all these generals, politicians, aristocrats, and industrialists, as the history of the Third Reich has shown.

Hitler certainly was shrewder than Gaea representative Gustav von Kahr, who was appointed Generalstaatskommissar of Bavaria on 26 September 1923. Kahr rescinded the law for the protection of the republic, refused to enforce warrants against perpetrators of high treason, and dissolved Social Democratic self-protection associations. And he worked hand in hand with Nazi groups. In competition with Hitler, and to go one better in currying favor with antisemite elements, Kahr proceeded against the Jews of foreign nationality. Aliens had no legal claims to residence or permanent stay and could, therefore, do little against his arbitrary and capricious expulsion orders other than appeal to the human understanding and good-will of Kahr's office or police headquarters. Kahr assured Rabbi Ehrentreu that he was no antisemite; he only wanted to get rid of "parasites." What kind of parasites Kahr had in mind may be seen from the expulsion order against a 60-year-old tobacco manufacturer cited by Löwenfeld:

> You came to Munich in 1887 as an impoverished tobacco worker. It has now been established and documented that you are the owner of a flourishing factory and three apartment houses. During a police search of your premises we found two gold watches. Therefore, you are a parasite of the Bavarian people and will be expelled. . . . Within a week, you must wind up your business and turn over your factory to a sequestrator to be appointed by the Generalstaatskommissar. Otherwise, it will be seized without compensation for the benefit of the people of Bavaria.[12]

Orders of this kind did not prevent Hitler from holding a gun against Kahr's head at the infamous rally in the Bürgerbräukeller; at his orders, Kahr was beaten to death on 30 June 1934.

In the fall of 1922 I entered the University of Munich, first as a student of law but soon changing over to political science. The first lecture I attended was given by a visiting professor, Zittelmann of Bonn University, who spoke on "The Philosophy of Law." Zittelmann developed the following ideas: If you want to study and practice law, you must first acquire a clear notion of the nature of man. Should one subscribe to the notion of any of the trendy philosophies of the time that man is by nature good, things like law and justice would be superfluous. If, on the other hand, as good Christians, you hold that man is sinful, then you know at least why laws and justice are necessary. In that case, it made sense to study law. Although not a Christian, I was impressed by such a conservative strain of thought, especially after the experiences I had had so far. Other lectures I attended did nothing to contradict Zittelmann's argumentation, albeit one might supplement it with Nawiasky's maxim: "Law is what the judge says it is." The most thrilling expansion of this idea was contained in Hugo von Hoffmansthal's guest lecture, "Literature as Spiritual Space of the Nation." He spoke at the Auditorium Maximum of the university on 10 January 1927. After a highly ceremonious introduction, the speaker talked of a process "in which we find ourselves confronted with a synthesis that evolves slowly and magnificently if one viewed it from the outside—but more sinister and probing if one sees it from within . . ." He called it a "conservative revolution whose goal is not chaos but form . . ."[13] This kind of thinking was quite familiar to me from my days at the Max Gynmasium.

At the university, I took part in the seminars of Jakob Striedter and Otto von Zwiedineck-Südenhorst. The former was a conscientious researcher whose Christian piety was not shaken by his immersion in the history of early capitalism. Zwiedineck was of a more complex nature. His seminar treated the themes and history of economic theory, including the history of socialism and social legislation with special emphasis on wage policies. Zwiedineck did not demand from his students that they tow the line. One could come up with sense or nonsense and have good discussions. His seminar was attended by northern and southern Germans, Christians, Jews (in fact, there were four Jewish female students among the participants), and even two Nazis, First Lieutenant Bruckner and Rudolf Hess. Bruckner was a broad-shouldered gorilla—it was best to avoid him. In contrast, Hess with his bushy eyebrows and his sometimes penetrating, sometimes dreamy eyes took part in the discussions from time to time—in an always abrupt and explosive manner and always coming back to his central theme: "What is Othmar Spann's opinion on this?" and "What is the universalist point of view?" Slowly I gained the impression that has since grown stronger that Hess was not so much a Nazi as a Spannian.[14] His attachment to the Führer, whom he possibly wanted to convert to universalism, was purely personal, like the attachment of a faithful house dog. Unquestionably, Hess was also devoted to Zwiedineck, whose tolerant scepticism and readiness to always listen carefully to what his students had to say assured him a loyal following. As we later learned from Zwiedineck's essay, "Feeling, Willing, Knowing" (*Erfülltes, Erstrebtes, Erkanntes*), Zwiedineck had been helped by Hess out of a very dangerous situation during the Nazi period.[15] As for myself, I am convinced that my release from police custody in January 1934 was the direct result of Zwiedineck's intervention with Hess and subsequently of Hess's intervention at police headquarters in Munich.

My own viewpoint developed to a large extent under the influence of two ennobled Austrians, Zwiedineck and Hoffmannsthal. As far as Zwiedineck was concerned, there were only two kinds of Jews: self-assured and proud Jews, like the obstinate *mitnagdic* rabbis of the East or Zionists like Theodor Herzl; and Jews deserving only contempt, because they failed to own up to their Jewishness. I more or less accepted Zwiedineck's position, but in a conversation with him made the additional point that a German Jew was not really an "assimilationist"; rather, he was German born and educated and consequently felt that way. Zwiedineck accepted this modification but otherwise stuck to his entrenched Austrian view. A likely additional influence on my views derived from the fact that I was an enthusiastic member of the Political-Academic Club (*Politisch-Akademischer Klub*). It was the purpose of the club to invite politically interested students and adults to hear and discuss the views of politicans of diverse orientations, from Papen to Severing. The leader of the club was a good friend of mine from the Zwiedineck seminar, Albert von Borsig, scion of the Berlin industrialist family. Of the members I remember Albrecht Haushofer who, like Borsig, became a victim of the Nazis, further, R. A. Seuffert and Wolfgang Hallgarten, the latter a son of a prominent, highly cultured Munich Jewish family that had no contact whatsoever with Jewish circles; and Johannes von Elmenau, who was of "mixed race," something that was of no significance to us at the time. Neither communists nor Nazis participated. Privately, I once talked to one of the more accessible Nazi students to induce him to bring a couple of his friends to our club meeting to discuss the "Jewish Question." He confessed that he personally liked my attitude but that he would not even dare to mention a conversation with me to his friends; the party had given strict orders not to engage in talks with Jews. That made it absolutely clear to me that the enmity between us was inexorable. It was a confirmation of this conviction when I read in a special issue of the *Süddeutsche Monatshefte* (September 1930) the article penned by Count Ernst Reventlow that contained the programmatic statement that the solution of the Jewish Question was a matter of "complete separation and annihilation."

My own position during these years, that is, the pre-Nazi and early years of the Nazi period, is well documented.[16] Between 1926 and 1938 I published seventy-eight papers, essays, and memorandums, as well as many book reviews, short essays and belles lettres. Of the seventy-eight articles only ten were on economic and demographic topics; the others dealt with Jewish themes: the sociology of Jews in Germany and the Danube basin, problems relating to Palestine, and politics in the Orient. Among the pieces on the situation in Germany and/or Austria are my essays of the 1930s, such as "Jews in the German Regions" in *Der Morgen* (1934) or "East and West" in the same journal (1937); and my articles on Herzl, Rosenzweig, Heine, Wassermann, and Hoffmansthal, all aiming to serve Jewish self-awareness, as were my essays on Palestine. My pamphlet, *Völkische Rassenlehre—*

Darstellung, Kritik, Folgerungen (Nationalist Racial Doctrine—Description, Critique, Consequences) was published by the Philo Verlag in 1932. Commissioned by the Centralverein it deals with the pseudo-scientific book by Hans Günther and with partisan polemics. I should note in this connection that I had attended the lecture on "Racialism" by Professor Friedrich Lenz of the University of Munich, and it was there that I gained a devastating impression of the intellectual poverty and obstinacy of this racial theory which was spreading like a cancer at that time. With beastly earnestness Lenz argued that it was possible to draw hard and fast conclusions about the spirit of a people from items of physical appearance and to formulate national policy (*Volkspolitik*) accordingly. My article "Judentum und Volksgemeinschaft" (*Der Morgen*, 1926) was written under the impact of this situation and had a personal-programmatic and youthful-confessional tone. I argued against the liberal notion that it was sufficient to treat the eligibility of the Jews in terms of their equality as human beings and citizens. The idea of peoplehood must not be ignored. The Jews should be accepted as Jews—as a people with their own tradition and *as such* integrated into the German nation, with the same inalienable rights to home and country. Beyond that, there was such a thing as the fellowship of nations and human groups. This line of thought, I noted, represented one possibility, and I added: "Whether that possibility could become a reality, is, as all future, still veiled in darkness; its realization depends on the will of men."

But just how *did* men feel about it? In retrospect, I think it is safe to say that the Jewish community council had tried to do justice to the situation. The Bavarian Association of Jewish Communities had been established, the social welfare system reorganized, and the lectures at the Lehrhaus were a permanent fixture by 1926. But the number of participants, whether adult or young, remained relatively small. Most of the young Jews I knew were preoccupied with personal and professional problems. Moreover, in good Munich tradition, they were rather absorbed in music, literature, and the arts. In Munich, *Kultur* was the religion. Interest in, and understanding of, politics was not widespread. Within the general student body, however, a growing minority with an aggressively political bent began to confront the politically indifferent majority. In the centenary year of the university (1926), the rector, Professor Karl Vossler, saw himself compelled to appeal to the Board of the United Student Fraternities to rescind the exclusion of Jewish and non-sectarian fraternities from the general meetings of the incorporated student body, or, if this proved unacceptable, to abstain from representation at future festivities. The first alternative was not supported by enough votes, so that the second remained the only viable one.[17] As a result, Jewish firms withheld their advertisements from university-related publications, and the mutual estrangement became palpable.

Contributing to the estrangement was the fact that there were only very few men like Vossler around the university. There were, to be sure, the eager beavers of the NSDP (the Nazi party), some well-meaning men who tried not to become too conspicuous, and a few who were outwardly sociable, but inwardly seething with hostility. The most striking incident was connected with the resignation of the Nobel Prize–winning chemistry professor, Richard Willstätter. In the spring of 1924, the retiring zoologist, Professor Richard von Hertwig, felt constrained not to appoint a Jewish (or "non-Aryan") as his successor, remarking to Willstätter in a resigned tone: "We must take into consideration the mood of the time and the mob in the street." In the fall, when the question of his own successor came up, Willstätter recommended another Jewish professor, Viktor M. Goldschmidt of Oslo, who was not even included on the list of possible candidates to be considered by the faculty. Those who objected never even mentioned the words "Jew" or "non-Aryan," but referred only to "foreigners," Willstätter reported disgustedly. On the very evening of the voting, he resigned from the faculty. The story of his resignation was only a prelude. Willstätter was correct in stating in his memoirs that the universitites and learned societies were the most fainthearted in their stand against the "cruelest, most vicious, and rapacious anti-semitism."[18]

Nevertheless, the Jewish fate remained in the balance for another decade. Howard John Fields (formerly Hans A. Feibelmann), law student at Munich University (1930-33) and representative of the Jewish and non-sectarian fraternities as well as of the Club of Democratic Students in the ASTA, the official organization of the student body, during the academic years 1931–32 and 1932–33, reported in an (unpublished) interview that the mind and heart of the students had been thoroughly poisoned by the Nazis well before the *Machtergreifung* (seizure of power).[19] The following right-wing organizations were active within the ASTA: the National Socialist German Student Association, the German Armor Bearers (der Waffenring Deutscher Art), the Association of Catholic Fraternities, both wearing colours (CV) and without (KV). Fields was the only Jewish member of the ASTA out of a total of forty student representatives. At the time of election campaigns for ASTA, there were so many bloody uproars at the meetings that the police had to disperse the unruly crowds. Fields thought it advisable to show up at the meetings in the company of fraternity brothers (Likaren), as he was often subjected to abuse and jostling. On one occasion, when wreaths and ribbons had been removed from a memorial tablet for the fallen, the Nazis moved that condemnation of this "cowardly act" be officially adopted by ASTA. Fields, expressing his support of this condemnation, declared that he would have welcomed a like demonstration of indignation when the graves of Jewish soldiers killed in World War I were desecrated in the Jewish cemeteries. The response was a stormy tumult. Fields was accused of defaming the memory of the fallen by comparison and was treated to shouts like: "You will be strung up soon!" When the members of *Licaria* came into restaurants or beer halls, they frequently had to endure molestation by "couleur" students. They were welcome only in the Jewish restaurants Hungaria and Schwarz. At processions, when students marched as representatives of their fraternities, the Jewish fraternities had to march at the tail end, or at a distance from other fraternities. At the university, the defamation and isolation of the Jewish students was in full swing by 1930. The house of learning stood way out in front: society was to catch up.

The Centralverein of Munich

Dr. Ludwig Holländer, secretary general of Centralverein, approached me in 1930 with an offer to work for the Centralverein. He then recommended me to the Board of the Bavarian branch for the position of *Syndikus* (legal representative) and told me on this occasion: "Look, I am well aware of your Zionistic leanings. That doesn't disturb me a bit. I'll tell my friends in Munich that they will have to get used to it. It think it altogether a good thing to proceed this way."[20] Most of the Licaria members at that time were from northern Germany, and Dr. Holländer thought my Bavarian-Swabian accent would be a great asset in dealings with ministry officials. My appointment went all the more smoothly because the president and vice president of the Munich branch, Dr. Fritz Baron and Eugen Neustädter, both German nationalists and assimilationists, had just resigned. The new president, Dr. Alfred Werner, was a Social Democrat and close to the pro-Zionist Jewish Agency wing of the Centralverein. Dr. Werner was a man of clear vision, straight talk, and quick decision, and we always worked together without any problems and double-talk. My duties consisted of dealing with government authorities, institutions, and persons in public life, with matters concerning speaking engagements, organizational developments, and youth welfare; I also acted as counsellor to Centralverein members in personal and financial problems. Our legal affairs were handled by Dr. Wilhelm Levinger, lawyer, well-versed in dealing with boycotts and such. Other prominent members of the Munich branch were the pediatrist Dr. Ludwig Kaumheimer and Justizrat Julius Heilbronner. It was clear to me that as Jews we were confronted with roaring waves of hatred. In my inaugural address at the meeting of the Munich branch, I stressed the need to band together in the "defense of our homes." My duties were first and foremost those of a social worker, especially in the small towns of Franconia, Swabia, and the Upper Palatine, which I visited frequently. I was treated everywhere with the warm hospitality characteristic of the countryside. In return I tried to uphold their morale by assuring them that our people in Berlin and Munich were well informed of their predicament; that they were aware of the danger to the Jews in the villages and small towns, the threat to their businesses, their children's future, their very existence; and that they were doing everything possible to ease their burden. I counselled the local leadership—in most cases, teachers whose devotion cannot be praised enough—about possible local avenues to provide relief, but I must admit in all honesty that I learned more from them than they could from me.[21]

One of the main tasks of the Centralverein was to encourage its members actively to participate in social and professional associations even under the most difficult of circumstances. It was too late for that in the countryside, especially of central Franconia, which had been set aflame by Streicher's propaganda campaigns. Isolation of the Jews had increased to the point of no return. The same was true of the youth movement. Before 1918 I myself was a member of Squad 11 of the Wehrkraftverein in which about 10 percent of the members were Jews. Among the members were, however, many who later became Nazis, such as Edmund Heines, future police chief of Breslau and a close friend of Röhm, and the future SS general, Demlhuber. Walter Koch, a good friend of mine, gave an account in his memoirs of a meeting of the South German Youth Bünde at the Hals ruins at Passau, where representatives of the Austrian Boy Scouts raised the *Judenfrage*. Almost half of the Viennese Boy Scouts were Jews, as were most of those from Prague. Martin Völkel, leader of the Youth Movement, stated that he was no antisemite; however, Jews were not Germans, and could not be accepted as members of a German *Jugendbund*. There still should have been ways to cooperate with the Jewish Bünde so identified, but in reality the statement signified a final break.

With the exception of student organizations, participation of Jews in clubs and charitable organizations was possible in Munich until 1933. The 1926 Annual Meeting of the Munich Section of the Alpinists, however, was symptomatic of the situation. The minutes of the plenary session are extant. They were corroborated by my father, who gave a similar account—albeit from a somewhat different angle—of the event, as well as by other reports, such as the article on "Munich's Jewish Mountaineers" by George E. F. Bergmann and the description by R. A. Michael Siegel.[22] The board had to vote on a motion to introduce a *numerus clausus* by effectively limiting the acceptance of new Jewish members. The percentage of Jewish members of the Munich Section was not to exceed the percentage of Jews in the general population of Munich. Those arguing against the motion were Justizrat Julius Heilbronner and Dr. Wilhelm Levinger, both representing the Centralverein. R. A. Michael Siegel protested as a private member. Heilbronner was not only a highly regarded professional and modest man, he was also one of the best Alpinists of Munich, with record-setting achievements. According to the minutes, Heilbronner spoke quietly and showed his love of the Alpinists and the mountains;

however, he was able to demonstrate the real reasons for the motion. Dr. Levinger further tried to show how the exclusion of such prominent Alpinists as Heilbronner, Cohen, Merzbacher, et al., would hurt the club itself. Siegel, on the other hand, expressed his annoyance that such a motion could seriously be considered. He stood up and stated that he would not stand for such discrimination and exclaimed: ''I won't let you shit on my head!'' With that he left the meeting and the motion was passed handily. All the other Jewish members resigned and Siegel was reprimanded by the lawyers' association for his unseemly expression, as there were ladies present. Although my father thought otherwise, Siegel was convinced that the voting would have gone the same way without his outburst. A similar case happened shortly before the curtain went down: The Turnverein for men had instituted the practice— without any formal vote-taking—in 1932 not to disturb old members, but to bar the acceptance of any new Jewish members. When the local Zionist organization demanded a clear policy statement, the next meeting of the board adopted the formal decision of barring Jews; moreover, it now asked the old members to resign from the Turnverein. These and similar incidents proved beyond any doubt that neither the conciliatory nor the more demanding defensive tactics of the Jewish community were any match against the growing Nazi steamroller.

To round out the picture, a later incident involving Dr. Siegel deserves mention: On 11 March 1933 he went to police headquarters as legal representative of the Association of Retailers in Bavaria in order to deliver an appeal. He was dragged down into the cellar, beaten, and forced to march barefoot through the streets of Munich to the central railroad station, with his pants cut and holding a placard with the text: ''I will never again complain to the police!'' At this time, it was surely too late for confrontational tactics.

The time to fight and exert influence on people was in the 1920s; the question was, of course, whether one could find nationwide allies. The National Association of Jewish Veterans was willing to participate in parades and demonstrations. As to the Centralverein, the need for political action had since been clearly recognized, but the situation in Bavaria was different from the rest of the nation. In the country as a whole the Democratic party had lost its influence; the only allies the Jews could count on were the Social Democrats and the Reichsbanner. In Bavaria, however, the Social Democrats were in hopeless opposition. For almost a decade, the Bavarian Volkspartei under the leadership of Kahr and Knilling—and somewhat less even under Lerchenfeld—had labored under fatefully false conceptions that in fact paved the way for extreme nationalism. Toward the end of the 1920s it became clear to the cardinal of Munich and to other princes of the Church that the race doctrine was pagan, the Nazi party anti-Church, and the constitution but a heap of junk for Hitler and his sort. Now was the chance to approach and try to make common cause with the Volkspartei. Alfred Werner, himself a Social Democrat, agreed with me that there was no other alternative but to cooperate with the Bavarian Volkspartei. Our Nuremberg office, led by Dr. Julie Meyer and Dr. Walter Berlin, already had good contacts with the Social Democratic party. The leader of the office in Munich, Dr. Ludwig Wasserman, was already close to the Bavarian Volkspartei. Our liaison to Diet and BVP was Dr. Franz Schlittenbauer, who had since recovered from his Gaea infatuation. The same could not be said of Dr. Fritz Schäffer who was usually friendly and cautious when I dealt with him in the ministry, but whose hidden antisemitic feelings surfaced now and then. The head of the city library, Hans Ludwig Held, and the city pastor Muhler proved very valuable allies in the good cause. The latter helped me to organize a circle of Jewish and Catholic students willing to address the burning issues of the day. Among the Jewish participants were the aforementioned Hans A. Feibelmann (AKA Howard John Fields), Otto Walter, Franz Winkler, and Max Schwarz; prominent among the Catholics were Stalf, son of the director of the Loden-Frey factory, and the Jesuit Dr. Stürmann. I recall two of the discussion meetings that focused on the 1) rejection of the race doctrine by all the participants; and 2) the abuses of capitalism and the role of the Jews: Was Jewry necessarily involved—or only individual Jewish capitalists? Those were the questions debated. Not capitalism as such was in the center of interest, but rather materialist thought and attitude.[23]

Dr. Schlittenbauer was instrumental in bringing us together with Dr. Alois Hundhammer, then general secretary of the Bavarian Union of Christian Peasants and delegate of the Bavarian Volkspartei, and also with Dr. Josef Baumgartner, who was likewise an official of the Bavarian Union of Christian Peasants. Thus began a long-time political alliance that lasted way beyond the Nazi period. Alois Hundhammer, himself of peasant stock, was a highly educated jurist, economist, and philosopher, with a pleasant personality. He was, moreover, very articulate, decisive in action, and a good Christian, free of antisemitic feelings as far as I could judge. Naturally we did not always see eye-to-eye in political matters, but we were united in our fight against the Nazis. Alois Hundhammer was a friend.

The test came in 1932, when two election campaigns for the presidency and two for the Reichstag had to be fought. None of the political parties was unprepared for the test.[24] Especially in the case of the second election for the Reichstag, the crucial issue was to block the seemingly irresistible advance of the Nazi Party. In this test, the Social Democrats appeared simply helpless; the organizational set-up of the Bavarian Volkspartei and that of the Bavarian Bauernbund proved inefficient. The Social Democrats were still more skillful and better informed; in the other two parties, they hardly knew what hit them. Since the party organizations seemed unprepared, it was the locals of the unions and agricultural associations who had to shoulder the campaign work. The Centralverein took on some tasks because it had amassed a wealth of data about the Nazis in a special archive in Berlin; its archive was the sole repository of comprehensive and dependable data on the Nazi movement. Based on the materials so collected, speakers of the anti-Nazi parties and newspaper editors could be informed; articles and political pamphlets could be written, such as the "anti-Nazi" handbook, which would fit into the pocket of every speaker. I was the co-author, with Dr. Baumgartner and the assistance of Dr. Hundhammer, of a brochure, entitled *National Socialism and Agriculture,* of which two hundred thousand copies were distributed in all of southern Bavaria. (Unfortunately, thus far not a single copy of this brochure has been found, in spite of an intensive search.) The following persons participated actively in the campaign and formed a kind of informal campaign committee: Dr. Werner Cahnman (Centralverein), Dr. Alois Hundhammer, Dr. Josef Baumgartner (Christian Union of Farmers), Professor Karl Simbeck (Bavarian Bauernbund), and Adolf Dichtl (Free Trade Unions and Reichsbanner). These five maintained steady contact in the summer and fall of 1932. Professor Simbeck and Dichtl showed up individually at my office almost every day; Dichtl was secretary of the Munich Social Democrats and had to fight a two-front war, against the Nazis and the Communists. Karl Simbeck, a Gymnasium professor and one of the few intellectuals in the Bauernbund, was very sensitive to popular feelings in all regards. He taught me a lot and in turn sought my advice in political party matters. He disappeared without a trace during the Nazi era. Dr. Werner was also very active during that time. I know that at a meeting of Jewish lawyers he warned everybody that it was a matter of life and death now, and such a situation demanded that they were generous with their pocketbooks, backing the proper political parties, especially the Social Democrats. It is a matter of record that in the 1932 elections for the Reichstag the number of votes for the Nazi party declined notably in southern Bavaria.

It was about that time that Dr. Hundhammer brought me an invitation from Geheimrat Dr. Heim for a personal talk in his home in Söchtenau at the Chiemsee. Dr. Heim told me that in the light of the political developments in Berlin, he was working on a plan to "encapsulate" Bavaria with the help of a paramilitary Bavarian Guard (*Bayernwacht*). He expected, he said, to raise 100,000 RM (*Reichsmark*) from among the Bavarian clergy and would appreciate the help of the Centralverein to the tune of 50,000 RM. When I voiced my doubts that such a large amount could be raised fast in Bavaria, he replied that surely some heavy backing would be forthcoming from Jewish sources without. I told him straight that we could not expect any money from American Jews. He thought that was incredible. So I said: "Charitable contributions after the catastrophe: Yes!—Political assistance before the catastrophe: No!'' Dr. Heim retorted that he would have never thought Jews were so shortsighted. I also suggested that his plan might be construed as high treason. He replied that he was basically no separatist; what he had in mind was a "temporary encapsulation" only until the intervention by the Western powers put an end to the spook. I promised to inform Dr. Alfred Werner of this plan without delay.

Dr. Werner recognized the tremendous importance of Dr. Heim's conversion from Nazism to anti-Nazism. He went to Berlin the very next day in order to carry the message to Centralverein headquarters. Dr. Hermann Schülein, director of the Löwenbrau Brewery and a cousin of my mother, happened to be on the same train. He promised to back us up at headquarters. In addition to Secretary General Dr. Ludwig Holländer, two prominent public figures, friends of the Centralverein, listened to our report: both Dr. Bruno Weil, a lawyer, and Georg Bernhard, editor in chief of the influential paper *Vossische Zeitung,* were highly sceptical. As you would expect, Dr. Weil objected because of the high treason aspects of the plan; and Bernhard rejected every kind of "local patriotism.'' Dr. Holländer, however, who had an intimate knowledge of the Bavarian situation and was persuaded by our argumentation, gave us 20,000 RM, which through Dr. Hundhammer, was handed over to Dr. Heim. In the meantime, Dr. Heim, who had been refused any help by the Stuttgart industrialist Bosch, was highly pleased with our contribution. This shows that the Centralverein did not fail in its duties, which, alas, cannot be said of the Bavarian Guard; without resistance the arsenal of the Bayernwacht was confiscated by the Nazis in March 1933.

The turning point came in January-February of 1933. The dice were cast in Berlin. But now, when the rest of the nation became Nazi, Bavaria wanted to be anti-Nazi. Paul Nikolaus Cossmann and his co-editor, Baron Erwin von Aretin, published a special issue of their journal, *Süddeutsche Monatshefte,* entitled "King Rupprecht.'' The behind-the-scene negotiations were drawn out mainly because of the financial demands of the Prince, so that nothing came of the efforts to re-establish the monarchy in Bavaria. The Bavarian minister of the interior, Dr. Schäffer, warned the Reichskommissar that he would be arrested as soon as he crossed the Bavarian "border.'' Apparently he did not know that the future Reichskommissar in the person of General von Epp was already in place. In these twilight weeks a wave of refugees came from Berlin to Munich. Among them were Georg Bernhard, the deposed editor, who no longer objected to "local patriotism,'' Fritz Borchardt and Hans Reichmann from Centralverein headquarters, and also Walter Gyssling of the Centralverein's Wilhelmstrasse office.[25] With the help of my secretary, Cilly Goldschmidt, I began to destroy politically explosive files, especially those relating to election campaigns and political negotiations, which could possibly incriminate friends like Schlittenbauer, Hundhammer, Baumgartner,

Muhler, Simbeck, Dichtl, and others. Our Berlin officials requested that I take possession of the B.W. (anti-Nazi) archive and either hide it in a safe place or try to smuggle it abroad. How it was to be done was my problem. I asked Dr. Hundhammer's advice, who referred me to Dr. Georg Heim Jr., then a lawyer in Munich. Dr. Heim agreed to take the archive to a warehouse of the Bavarian Christian Bauernverein in the country; he then had second thoughts about some of the people working there, that is Nazi infiltration, and did nothing. I learned about the matter too late, when there was no time left to save the archive. With the help of a Centralverein member, owner of Wolf's Used Paper and Recycling, the archive was taken to Puchheim and burned. This happened on 8 March 1933, two days before the Nazis seized power in Bavaria.[26]

I was in the city and in my office in the evening of 9 March and could see the SA marching up and down without any hindrance. I left the premises shortly after midnight. When I entered the office the next morning, 10 March, I found the place in disarray, partly demolished, and the files scattered about. According to the superintendent, the "burglars" came at 12:30 A.M. Luckily I missed them. I asked the photographer Biberkraut to come to the office. He had hardly finished taking the pictures when the police arrived, confiscated his negatives and made out a report, completely disregarding my protestations. Dr. Werner was asked the same morning by a passer-by where his office was located. He gave the address, went home, and within hours crossed the border into Switzerland. I was left completely on my own; I had my hands full with calls coming in all day from the countryside, with visitors, especially businessmen, asking for advice and/or help. I still remember the many sessions with, for example, the owners of the Haimann Silk Factory, with the head of the Pauson store (kitchen tools), and with Carl Bach (men's wear, on Sendlinger Street). To escape arrest, I spent the nights in the apartment of the superintendent of the Bärlocher Chemical Works in Moosach. I transferred my checking account to a Catholic priest recommended to me by Dr. Hundhammer. I was assisted in my work not by any member of the Centralverein Board but by outsiders willing to help, such as Julius Hechinger, a banking clerk, who later played a role in the Jewish community council, Max Adler, a teacher, and R.A. Leo Lemle. Max Adler was a member of the Orthodox congregation and in time became its president; he saw things clearly, was always ready to help, and was a man of great courage. Lemle was married to a Christian and had since kept distance from the Jewish community. Like Adler, Lemle was born in a neighboring village, had the temperament and inclinations of a peasant and was unwilling to put up with lawlessness. All three sacrificed themselves on their posts. As for myself, I often had to report to police headquarters and officials of the ministries. On 12 May I was called back to my office from a visit to the ministries. Two Gestapo officers were waiting for me with an order to close down the office. When they asked me to put my signature on their document, I stated that orders could be issued and enforced, but no consent thereto expected; in any case, only an official of the regional Centralverein had the authority to sign a consent. The following day, *Justizrat* Eugen Strauss of Augsburg and I went to police headquarters but failed to achieve anything. Strauss, as third director of our regional executive committee, also refused to give his signature. I told him that I would continue my work in private. He gave his consent with the admonition not to use the stationary and address of the Centralverein. I performed my duties from May to December 1933 in the office of Dr. Levinger, which was across the street from police headquarters, and also in the house of my parents, at 12 Sophie Stehle Street; all of my correspondence was done from this address. Dr. Levinger's collaboration remained hidden from the police.

I still have the copies of my correspondence of these seven fateful months.[27] There is not much in it concerning Munich; most of my discussions and counselling (relating mainly to vocational problems and emigration) were conducted orally. Apart from few exceptions, such as cases in Starnberg and Wolfratshausen, most correspondence dealt with local affairs of the region north to the Danube: Ansbach, Altheim, Burgbernheim, Ellingen, Ermetzhofen, Hersbruck, Hilpolstein, Ickelheim, Neustadt/Aisch, Oberndorf, Ostheim, Roth, Scheinfeld, Spalt, Weissenburg and Windsheim in central Franconia; Brückenau and Würzburg in Lower Franconia; Zwiesel and Weiden in Lower Bavaria, and in the Upper Palatine.[28] A heavy concentration of problem localities in Central Franconia strikes the eye. No wonder: it was the fiefdom of Julius Streicher. Streicher's Nuremberg was the center of the most primitive and virulent antisemitism, from the 1920s to the "Final Solution." There were hardly any antisemitic measures which were not tried first in Franconia under the slogan: "Franconia first!"[29] If Munich was the place that promoted Hitler, Franconia was the field of action for dubious characters, the dissastisfied lower-middle classes, and a frightfully large number of greedy, power-hungry, and brutal upstarts.[30] There one could find many small-town public school teachers among the Nazi spokesmen.

Our friends in the countryside informed me (and in even more detail reported to Dr. Berlin, the Centralverein official in Nuremberg), of numerous official and unofficial measures designed to destroy completely the Jewish retailers and cattle dealers. The measures ranged from a ban on advertisement, exclusion from the Christmas business, and appeals to boycott Jewish stores to verbal intimidation and abuse of shoppers, which included taking their photos as they entered or left the stores. Those seen entering a Jewish home or greeting Jews on the street were proscribed and/or denounced in the newspapers; the names of shoppers and suppliers of Jewish businesses were frequently posted in public places; repair work in Jewish homes and the delivery of food to Jewish homes were inhibited by public and covert threats. Jews were denied service in restaurants and their children accosted on the streets. No one was held accountable for mischievously damaging or destroying Jewish property. In short, open season was declared on the Jews. Most markets and whole localities were closed to Jewish traders and peddlers. There was little that could be done for the victims against such massive terror, other than through delaying tactics and some moral support by letting them know that someone will at least protect their retreat. In most cases I sought such protection at the State Ministry for Commerce, or the State Chancellery of the Free State of Bavaria, the Trustee for Work of the Economic Region of Bavaria and, at least in one case, assisted by Dr. Lemle, the governor of Upper Bavaria; once in a while, I even approached the political police.

All of us laboring in the cause preferred to work through government agencies—never through party channels, in the vain expectation of using the former against the latter. In Nazi Germany there were two governing bodies, the government bureaucracy and the party, the latter being the more aggressive and the mostly victorious partner. In the case of Neustadt an der Aisch, for example, I sent my appeals to the State Ministry of Commerce (dated: 6, 8, 11 and 15 May 1933) and on 26 May I was informed by our Nuremberg office (Dr. Julie Meyer) that the posting of names and the surveillance of Jewish stores had ceased; on the other hand, the boycott of deliveries continued. A partial success! A few days later, however, I had to report that the county propaganda chief, Gessner, openly declared to a meeting of the Peasant Union that only a total boycott of the Jews would do, adding that should there be any interference by foreign governments, the Nazis will see to it that "no Jew will survive!" Addressing both domestic and foreign "enemies," he assured them that the Nazis would not let themselves be deterred from the final goal: complete victory. My frequent appeals resulted in a subpoena: I was ordered to appear at the Political Police on 7 June 1933 and assure them that my only aim was "to insure the smooth cooperation between the Christian and Jewish populace in Neustadt an der Aisch."

Realizing that party officials alone had the last word in all matters, I decided to approach Herr von Conta, chief of the commerce section in the offices of the deputy of the *Führer*. As usual, I submitted that it was against the national interest to disturb the economic life of the country, to destroy the existential basis of the middle class, and to increase the number of unemployed by permitting the destabilization of "Einzelhandlungen," as they were called. Herr von Conta referred my brief to both a government and a party office. The Berlin office of the party sent the brief back to Munich and that was that. The government official, an engineer named A. Pietzsch, was well-meaning but powerless. Herr von Conta was no longer accessible. On 22 December 1933 I was arrested and taken for interrogation to the Bavarian

Political Police in the Wittelsbacher Palais. In my defense I declared that the closing down of the Centralverein office did not, as far as I could see, declare my activities to be illegal. After my interrogation, about which I later wrote a detailed account, I was taken to the police jail on Ett Street. About the role of Rudolf Hess in this connection I have reported above. I was released on 4 January 1934.[31]

What transpired in the channels of the bureaucracy and what kinds of material about the activities of the Centralverein fell into the hands of the police, I often wondered. Some of the materials have been preserved in the official archives and are still available for research.

According to the documents, the course of events was as follows: Immediately after the police raid on our offices during the night of 10 March, 1933, the vice president of the Munich branch of the Centralverein, Dr. Ludwig Kaumheimer, and myself went to the Political Police for an interview with Ministerialrat Dr. Sprick; stressing the patriotic orientation of the Centralverein we requested the return of the confiscated material.[32] Even after the closing of our offices on 12 May, we called on the Political Police again. At the same time, Dr. Neumeyer cabled to the Reich Commissar (Reichsstatthalter) the protest of the Munich Jewish community against the confiscation of its files, correspondence, minutes, monies, saving accounts, as well as against the dissolution of fifty-four associations, among them six synagogue and prayer hall associations, the Orthodox congregation Ohel Jakob, several social welfare organizations, youth clubs and other organizations, such as the Association of Jewish Museums and the National Association of Jewish War Veterans. He called particular attention to the desperate situation of the Aid to Youth Association and the Apprentices' Union.[33] The Centralverein was not even mentioned. Nevertheless, a letter to the State Chancellery from the Headquarters of the Political Police of Bavaria of 30 May 1933 stated, with special reference to the activities of the Centralverein, that Dr. Neumeyer's protest message about the charitable and religious activities of his organizations was a "blatant untruth." With some vague reference to "confiscated files" it characterized the Centralverein as the decision-making organization of all Jewish associations, including the charitable ones. On 21 August 1933, a petition was forwarded to Gauleiter and Minister of the Interior Wagner, who had jurisdiction over the Political Police (and Heydrich), for the release of all confiscated material including the bank accounts, of the Centralverein. A copy of this petition was sent to the office of the Reichsstatthalter on 22 August 1933. In order to prove the patriotic stand of the Centralverein, excerpts from the charter of the association were included as well as citations from documents relating to our protests against the so-called "atrocity propaganda." I was against this kind of servile argumentation and expected the rejection that was promptly forthcoming. On 31 August 1933, the Reichsstatthalter asked the offices of the Gauleiter for a report on the matter; in fact he repeated his request to write four more times: 4 October, 9 November, and 7 December, 1933, and finally on 7 February 1934. The process clearly demonstrated the antagonism between him and the Gauleiter. In the end, the minister-president himself had to ask for the report. What alone remained from the stage of the procedure was the report from the headquarters of the Bavarian Political Police under the office of the Gauleiter dated 15 February 1934 to the Reichsstatthalter. Attached to this report were seven documents, clearly part of the confiscated material, selected to demonstrate the subversive tactics of the Centralverein. The rest of the exchange, as well as the confiscated files of the Bavarian branch of the Centralverein transmitted to the Gestapo in 1936, must be declared lost.

The above-mentioned documents related to the following activities and procedures of the Centralverein: assistance to several Social Democratic women and union organizations in the early 1920s and assistance to the German Republican Student Bund in 1930 (nos. 1–3); documents 4–7 related to my own activities as an official of the Centralverein. Among the documents was a request dated 1 June 1931 by R.A. Max Hirschberg of the firm Hirschberg, Löwenfeld, and Regensteiner to my office that we forward to Berlin, and eventually America, an article for publication. That article, entitled "The Hitler Movement in Germany," critically analyzed the Nazi movement and declared both right and left extremism to be an international problem. It also forewarned that, without international cooperation in the struggle against fascism in Germany, political and economic chaos would ensue. The article was sent to the American Jewish Committee in New York but, as I said in my letter of 9 November 1931 to Dr. Hirscherg, it was "inexplicably ignored." I should have destroyed this correspondence, but since Dr. Hirschberg escaped Germany in March 1933, I did not feel so bad about it. Documents nos. 6 and 7 relate to the discussion in January and December of 1932 with Rabbi Dr. Wiesner and five young eastern Jews of Munich about mobilizing their generation to take an interest in German political problems. Since only "German citizens" could become members of the Centralverein according to its charter, I sought to enlist the cooperation of our eastern brethren through informal channels—with the full consent of Alfred Werner. The police commissioner interpreted my attempts to facilitate the integration and naturalization of eastern Jews as an attempt to "inflict the greatest damage on the German national body." It was thus the logical conclusion that the Bavarian Political Police proposed the disbanding of the Centralverein and the confiscation of its assets according to the decrees of 26 May and 14 July 1933 and the proclamations of 19 September 1933 by the state ministries of Interior, Justice, and Finance. I received the orders orally at a meeting with Inspector Schall of the Bavarian Political Police to cease all and any activities on behalf of the Centralverein in Bavaria. The Centralverein in Berlin made no attempt to have the order rescinded.

I remained in contact with the Catholic underground, partly through Dr. Alois Hundhammer, who had since been released from Dachau and maintained a small shoe-repair shop on Schwanthalerstrasse, partly through Franz Elsen, later a Director of the Bavarian State Bank, and partly, through Maximilian Fuchs, the owner of the French Travel Bureau at Maximiliansplatz. In the spring of 1937 I decided to go to Vienna, partly for personal reasons, partly in order to gather information about the situation of the Jews in Vienna for the *CV News*. Maximilian Fuchs put me in touch with a Munich writer, Eugen Gürster, who had emigrated and lived in Basel. Gürster, in turn, made arrangements with Austrian and Swiss railway personnel so that I could cross the border without valid passport. Baron Nostiz in the Ministry of Interior in Vienna saw to it that no entry was made in my passport. Subsequently, I could visit Basel and also went to Paris, had many discussions with Jewish personalities and also with Heinrich Funder, editor of the *Reichspost*. Nothing of this ever became known to the Gestapo.[34]

Isolation, Atomization and Extermination

If one wished to characterize the fate of Jews in Germany, and in Munich, during the period from the end of World War I until the "Final Solution," three stages may be distinguished. First, Nazi propaganda and party activities aimed at the separation of Jews from the rest of the populace through defamation; second, they furthered the isolation process up to atomization by means of legislation; and, finally, after the collapse of moral resistance, they completed the job by physical annihilation. In the preceding chapters, I tried to describe the process of separation and the attempts of the Jews to stem that process. I now turn to the second stage, the isolation and atomization process.[36]

To be sure, isolation of the Jews has had a long history. The German Student Fraternities in Vienna issued "Aryans only" by-laws way back in 1878-83.[36] At the time I started out as *Syndikus* of the Centralverein, the exclusion of Jews from organizations in central Franconia was well on route. We advised our members to remain in their respective organizations as long as possible but their participation often degraded to but a "silent" partnership. Similar trends cropped up in Munich, but so far remained isolated incidents. In the spring of 1933, however, what was simmering under the surface burst forth with the force of an explosion. Expulsions from organizations—even from professional associations—became the norm.

For the masses, the boycott of Jewish stores on the 1st of April 1933 became the symbol of ostracism and prescription.[37] Yet, the boycott did not quite achieve its intended objectives. To be sure, hundreds of Jewish stores as well as offices of lawyers and doctors were closed down in a nationwide action led by the party under the direction of Gauleiter Julius Streicher from Franconia, whose headquarters were in Munich. But the attitude of the populace fell short of the expected national "awakening." Preceding the day of the boycott, shoppers made such a run on Jewish stores, especially in the inner city, that the organizers of the boycott in some cases had to withdraw their guards from the doors of the Jewish stores. On the day of the boycott, the pogrom and looting so feared by the Jews did not take place. The business district was full of rather passive and curious folk; in some cases the throng even demanded the opening of certain stores. Nazi propaganda was discredited for the time being. The naive belief of many Jews—and Christians—that the worst was over turned out to be cruel self-deception. Just the opposite: I happen to believe that the passivity of the populace helped to convince the top leadership of the Nazi party that only the most radical legislative and administrative measures could guarantee their real goal: the elimination of Jewish influence and then the annihilation of Jewry.

Indeed, as early as the end of March, the executive power was transferred from the office of the Reichstatthalter to the head of the Political Police in Bavaria in his capacity as the political section chief in the office of the Gauleiter. This appointment of Himmler as head of the Political Police meant that with one single move, that was to affect the whole Reich, the state fell into the hands of the party.[38] This shift in the power structure was mirrored in my own experiences in the last phase of my activities as a Centralverein official. This single move robbed the Jews of their noblest instrument of defense which all the Jewish organizations had successfully relied on since the days of the Austrian Edict of Tolerance, the Prussian Legislation of 1812, and especially the French Revolution and Napoleon's calling up of the Sanhedrin. When faced with feudal, clerical or estate resistance, or coming up against popular prejudice, Jews could fall back on the growing power of the state and state interests. But now the state was reduced to a nominal power in the form of the continuance of a state bureaucracy. In reality, the state was taken over by the party and political decision making was transferred from the state to the party. All that followed was a matter of execution.

The Church was on the side of the Jews, but only in a half-hearted way. However, the Lutheran clergy, particularly in Franconia, was wholeheartedly nationalistic, and almost completely Nazi. I know of no exception. Things were different with the Catholic Church, for the simple reason that it never embraced nationalism. (The Church always came first.) This does not mean, however, that leading members of the Church were not antisemitic, or that they rose as one man in defense of the Jews. It was therefore all the more surprising—and amounted to a sensation—when Cardinal Faulhaber gave his four Advent sermons and the New Years's sermon in the St. Michael's Church of Munich.[39] The Cardinal called for the upholding of Christian values against modern-day paganism; he addressed Christian believers, but possibly his sermons found an even greater echo in the Jewish community. In magnificent wording, the Cardinal reminded the Christians of Christianity's indebtedness to the Old Testament, that is, its ethical and social values. He thus gave a spiritual weapon to the Christians; at the same time, he provided a source of satisfaction to the Jews. And yet, the Cardinal avoided any direct reference to the Nazis' hatred for, and persecution of, the Jews. He even stated that the "dislike of the Jews of today" should not be extended to the Holy Writ of the Old Testament. The Volk Israel was a bearer of divine grace and Jesus was a Jew; but the Jews after Christ could no longer be regarded as chosen. Although the Cardinal failed to mitigate the isolation of the Jews, he must be credited for mobilizing Christian resistance. That this was the case is documented and remarked upon in reports by the police as well as by the office of the minister-president. How far this resistance extended to the defense of all who professed the Jewish faith remains unclear. With the most liberal interpretation, one can only speak of a few individual cases. A Gestapo report of 14 July 1937 complains about the fact that there were still fellow Germans who feel they have "to break a lance for Jewry."[40] Especially in the countryside, so says the report, priests still speak of the Jews as the chosen people and in some cases even recommend that people should buy at Jewish stores. It should go on record that Father Hermann Muckermann, in his Advent sermon of December 1934 at Munich Cathedral, categorically denied the right of the state to kill. By contrast, the same Father Muckermann in a sermon of December 1936 entitled "The Church and the Present," rejected the idea of abolishing the Old Testament, but added the warning that the teachings of Christ were in opposition to Judaism. These and similar statements support our contention that the position of the Church was and remained ambivalent.

And what about the populace? Did it hate the Jews? Is this the right question to ask? Shouldn't we put it this way: Who hated the Jews? Here we touch upon an important problem, namely, whether our behavior is determined by our environment—in this case, the Nazi environment—or we act according to our free will. From time to time there arise mass psychoses and fashionable trends, and there are always a multitude of people who let themselves be carried away by the current and counter-current of public opinion. And in each instance, the tendency toward the development of a dominant streak is unmistakably there. As early as the 1920s, the tendency toward proscription of the Jews was clearly recognizable, but it ran parallel with the counter-currents. In the face of actual or presumed terror, as during the Hitler era, the trend toward proscription became well-nigh irresistible. Still, as the following examples demonstrate, both the conditions set by the (social) environment and situational differences based on interest create varying possibilities and room for personal choice and decision.[41]

There are numerous references in the reports by the government, police headquarters, and the Political Police about their success in first obstructing, and then completely paralyzing Jewish business activities, especially of cattle-dealers but also of doctors in resort hotels and spas all over Upper Bavaria. The case of Dr. Rosenmeyer, a physician who was a volunteer in World War I and practiced in Grünwald, is mentioned: First, he was brutally beaten by roaming SA men, then his safety and his practice was vouched for by the NSDAB (Association of Nazi Physicians), and six months later, his license was revoked by the local community.[42] On the other hand, the residents of the communities Peiss and Dürnhaar defaced the Party billboards the following way: in the sentence *"Juden sind hier unerwünscht,"* the *un* was deleted to make the text read: *"Juden sind hier erwünscht!"* —altering "Jews are not wanted here" to "Jews are wanted here." In its monthly report of 1 August 1937, the Gestapo complained that in some localities Jews were still doing business as cattle-dealers because the peasants were "infected" by the teachings of politicized Catholicism and were sadly lacking in "racial consciousness." It noted that only financial disadvantages would persuade the peasants to do their business with "Aryan" cattle-dealers. The final removal of the Jews did the rest.

Concerning the city itself, I have in my possession reports of firms and schools, supplemented by my own experiences and official reports.[43] A few cases will illustrate the situation. In the Isaria Chemical Laboratories where my father worked, a grotesque situation developed. Nobody there knew that the manager was a Viennese Jew who had converted to Catholicism—except the Political Police. One day a squad of SA men stormed the premises and demanded that the manager as well as my father be fired immediately. What made it a theater of the absurd was the fact that the leader of the squad was the son of the senior owner of the laboratories who was a Christian himself but whose wife was Jewish. The SA knew nothing of *this* fact. The young man became the new manager of the firm, but lacking in money, business know-how, and intelligence, he succeeded in ruining the firm in no time. Then there was the case of the Ballin Furniture House, with its large sales and showrooms on the Promenadenplatz and a factory on Deisenhofer Street. It was one of the leaders of Munich's skilled crafts. In addition to furnishing apartments and houses all over Munich, it outfitted business establishments, hotels, villas and castles, yachts and oceanliners. Like the firm Isaria that supplied retailers on the countryside, the Ballin Furniture House had already felt the adverse effects of antisemitic propaganda well before 1933. After 1933, the systematic boycott made it impossible for a large segment of the firm's customers— especially officials and civil servants—to even enter its premises. The manufacturing part had to be closed down soon because of declining sales. Finally, the Bayerische Vereinsbank foreclosed the firm's longstanding credit in order to get hold of the business, and in 1936 the firm was "Aryanized."

We can find similar examples in the correspondence of Carl Bach, of the firm Isidor Bach, with the Bavarian Ministry of Economics, the president of the Chamber of Industry and Commerce, and the Centralverein. The firm I. Bach not only had a retail store on Sendinger Street but also had a manufacturing plant and a wholesale division in men's clothing. In his letters, Bach calls attention to the following conditions: the sales of his firm declined by more than a third between April and July of 1933—while the sales volume of "Aryan" firms rose by 6 to 21 percent (or in some cases, declined by approximately 10 percent only). Customers of the firm were scared away by propaganda and threats at buying at a "Jewish firm," on the one hand, and through verbal confrontation in the street or even in the store itself, on the other. Bach reports how faithful customers felt compelled to remove the firm's label from their packages in order to avoid possible harrassment: he describes the virulent antisemitic propaganda in the pages of the official journal of the Association of German Textile Workers distributed gratis among the firm's workers, and how the Association of Aryan Manufacturers advises both in print and on the radio all the firms to patronize only Aryan suppliers in the clothing industry. He mentions the stipulation (*Arierparagraph*) that uniforms for the *Arbeitsfront* (Labor Front) may be purchased from Aryan firms only. Like other complainants of those times, Carl Bach calls attention to the disturbance of the economy and likely repercussions on the labor market because of such propaganda measures. He thinks that the existence of the firm is at stake.

Among the most popular stores were the firms of Karl Uhlfelder in the Rosenthal and Sally Eichengruen on the Karmelitengasse, the former a large department store and the latter a fabrics shop, both enjoying large sales volumes. In March 1933, throngs of prospective customers lined up in front of both stores. To shop at these stores was a symbol of opposition against Nazi propaganda. According to police reports and Gestapo records, as late as February and July of 1936 a horde of women descended on these stores, bent on taking advantage of the inventory sales. The police report noted that all those women obviously failed to grasp—or did not want to—the Führer's guidelines regarding the "Jewish Question." Moreover, the 250 employees of the firms for a long time rejected the organizing efforts of the Nazi party; only around 1935 did the Party succeed in finding one (!) employee who was willing to undertake an organizing drive. Finally, one day, five or six party functionaries in civilian clothing stormed into the store and accused Sally Eichengruen of violating one or other regulation; when the old man denied the charge, he was hit in the face and would have fallen had not one of his employees supported him. Eichengruen lived for his business only, to the extent that he could not even imagine of voluntarily giving up his store; he was finally forced to hand it over for a pittance to Loden-Frey, an "Aryan" firm. He escaped and arrived at the Swiss border with 10 RM in his pocket—thanks to his children's having bribed a Nazi bureaucrat to the tune of 2,000 RM. Interestingly, earlier in 1936, he was able to visit his dying wife in Zurich because a friendly and well-meaning police inspector advised him to follow a certain route and so escape detection. The Eichengruen story demonstrates that even under conditions of terror, human beings can and will make free decisions; it is also true that only a handful did so.

The question whether and to what extent terror can account for people's behavior demands a more incisive analysis than can be undertaken here. We must restrict ourselves to contributing a few basic observations. There is the phenomenon of the "captive mind" that seriously believes that the prison guard is a genius. I know of cases of officers assigned to the *Führer* who were convinced of the absolute superiority of the man, asserting at the same time not to be close to the Nazi movement as such. There also are people who in all times and places have taken pleasure in plundering a man bound hand and foot. And there is a multitude of people who worry about their livelihood. Furthermore, the threat of arrest and Dachau was in fact hanging over the heads of those perceived to be of oppositional spirit—and this was a well-known fact in the Hitler era. In Neustadt an der Aisch, for example, people who hesitated to partake in the boycott against the Jews were threatened with being sent to Dachau. In fact, not only the city but the whole country was in the hands of terrorists, of people whose arrested aggressiveness is released when the system of government encourages aggression instead of curbing it. This does not mean, however, that the good in man cannot find expression, even if it may lack the power to achieve results. In the following I will try to identify such alternative modes of behavior.

SA Obersturmbannführer Kurt Bär of Gunzenhausen in central Franconia was the very embodiment of aggressivity in Bavaria and at the same time an example of how the Party superseded the state government.[44] In Gunzenhausen, an innkeeper couple by the name of Strauss and their son were taken into protective custody by Bär and his men, accompanied by a mass of people gone wild; the couple was mishandled, their son beaten into unconsciousness. The aroused and hooting mob arrested 30 more Jews, dragged them around, and beat them severely. Two bloodied men were released, then threatened again with arrest, were driven to commit suicide. Kurt Bär was sentenced to serve for disturbing the peace by the District Court in Ansbach, but even that mild sentence could not be enforced by Regierungspresident Hofman against the objections of Gauleiter Wagner. Kurt Bär then took revenge by shooting to death both Strauss and his son. In the following trial, the attorney for the defense reminded the court of Bär's "youth" (he was twenty-two years old) and pointed to his "unusually activist bent" as a mitigating circumstance.

Similarly, the actions of the local schoolteacher in neighboring Bechhofen, in setting fire to the famous wooden synagogue of Eliezer Sussmann during the Kristallnacht (1938), is a striking example of dormant aggressivity released. Numerous reports by both the police and government agencies provide summaries of brutal impediments to Jewish business activities in Munich. Potential customers were accosted and jostled, windows broken, and offensive slogans, such as *Saujude* or *Juda verrecke!* were smeared with red paint or silicic acid on shop windows and doors. Large open boxes with heaps of Streicher's particularly offensive paper *Der Stürmer* were displayed all over the city. In May 1935 there were visibly more "individual, spontaneous" actions against Jewish retail stores by offenders "unknown." When on 18 May and 28 May they evolved into a systematic boycott, both the police and the government remained passive onlookers. Nobody was arrested or even warned; it became obvious to all that Gauleiter Wagner had given his unconditional approval.[45] The populace was convinced that the "individual, spontaneous" incidents, the preceding brutal demonstrations, and the "spontaneous" action during the Kristallnacht, had been organized by the Nazi party.

Cultural institutions were not spared either. On 24 November 1934 students and young thugs who claimed to be students disrupted the performances of the famous cabaret Simplicissimus on Türkenstrasse. This happened in spite of a completely "Aryan" ensemble, since the Jewish artists had been fired well before that. The student mob insisted that the program still clearly showed "Jewish influence." Criminal inclinations had received the green light and more than once the audience was forced to run the gauntlet as it tried to escape the marauding mob. The fear of physical brutality enveloped the city in a heavy dark cloud. Still, the city of Munich and most southern Bavarian localities were spared the kind of excesses that took place in Gunzenhausen.

But then there was the other side of the coin; a good illustration is the case of the horticulturist Frank Kreitmayr, who was denounced by fellow citizens for having remarked that Germany would be a better place, a more honest country, if it had more Jewish citizens. His license for teaching young Jews gardening skills was revoked—a measure in the drive to isolate the Jews. All the denunciations and convictions for committing *Rassenschande* belong under the same heading of "isolation." Numerous police reports were filled with such cases.[46] It was morally reprehensible for a Jewish male to befriend a Christian female. Not so clear was the issue the other way around. One of the police reports made note of the case of a Sybille Schlesinger (a Jewish girl) and Konrad Mann (an "Aryan") of Starnberg, with the added remark: "Unfortunately, the Jewess cannot be apprehended." I personally know of a case when a young Jewish woman saved her life by committing *Rassenschande* with an Obersturmbannführer. After the legislation of 15 August 1935 banning intermarriage and extramarital traffic between Jews and Aryans, in order to "protect the purity of German blood and family," there came other regulations forbidding even the employment of "females of German or related origins under the age of 45" in Jewish businesses and households. As a consequence, the police received numerous appeals by household employees who yet wished to stay in Jewish employ. Of course, all of these appeals were rejected. Those employed by Jewish families knew that they were well off, but that was exactly one more reason to undercut the continuance of friendly relations.

Considering the rigorously enforced policy of isolation, it is the more astonishing that people of most modest circumstances found ways and means to lend a helping hand. Thanks to them, it was possible for my youngest sister to start her apprenticeship in the ceramics craft at the factory of A. & E. Königbauer as late as 1937 (!) and stay on until the Kristallnacht, although among the workers were an SA and an SS man. It was possible because the master as well as most of the workers were anti-Nazi and, in good Bavarian tradition, anti-ideological. All of them tried to make it as pleasant as possible for this young Jewish girl to work at the plant until the fateful day in November 1938 when the SA arrived and posted bills with the words: "*Juden ist der Zutritt verboten!*" (Jews are forbidden to enter here all over the premises).[47]

Even after 1939, when Jews were proscribed from entering foodstores, there were many Christian storekeepers and neighbors who brought food to Jewish families—in some cases without reimbursement. I know of the case of the courageous administrator of the Jewish cemetery, Lina Angermeier, who daily visited Jewish families with her rucksack full of provisions; there were maids in Jewish households who gave up their ration cards to help.[48] Needless to say that such cases of individual solidarity did not suffice to avert the ultimate fate. Even this last flare up of humanness was extinguished when the isolation of the remaining Jews of Munich commenced, first by transporting them to the ghettos of Milbertshofen and Berg am Laim, and then by deporting them to the death camps.

In the schools, too, the isolation process was at work. Describing her own and others' experiences in the 1930s, my friend, Ruth G., recalled how, between classes, she had to stand alone in one corner of the schoolyard and not mingle with her peers, because they were forbidden to talk to her. One day a schoolmate of hers came up to say: "You know, Ruth, I really would like to be your friend, but my father is a high government official and should somebody report that I am fraternizing with a Jewess, he would have serious difficulties." The psychological pressure of the school was reinforced by the additional pressure from the family. Ruth was not allowed to partake in the chess lessons or school excursions, or to dance with a teacher at the graduating prom, because of possible *Rassenschande*; she herself had to petition for exclusion from physical education classes where the students were harangued with antisemitic hate propaganda. Frequently she received failing grades on her German essays with the remark that a Jewish girl just would never be able to write a good German composition. Some of her classmates belonged to the Bund deutscher Mädels and came to school in brown uniforms; the others tried to conform. It came to pass that members of the Bund disturbed the Catholic mass one day with noisy demonstrations because the ministering priest, who was also a teacher at the school, rejected Nazi ideology in his religion classes. On one occasion, that teacher came up to Ruth saying that he was well aware of her predicament and that he, too, was having a bad time; but, she should keep the faith that one day this nightmare would pass. On another occasion, the French and English teacher approached her on a lonely street and invited her to come to her house on Sunday for coffee and cake. The invitation was repeated time and again and Ruth's faith in humanity sustained.[49] It becomes clear from such cases that generalizing judgments are wrong and that individuals must be judged on a case-by-case basis.

The above descriptions, but a small selection from a huge mass of situation reports, do permit, I believe, an appreciation of the isolation process as an overture leading to the "Final Solution." They have to be comprehended against a specific background: against a system of legislation of the most brutal, most abject and rigorous kind—with the word "legislation" a cruel misnomer that had no relation to anything just or lawful, a facade for the rule of the vilest terror. The maze of this legislative and administrative machinery was too complex and many-faceted to be fully dealt with here. It meant the exclusion of Jews from the civil service and economic life; it meant banning them from restaurants and hotels and driving them from their homes; and it meant preventing them from sitting on park benches and even using the tram. From the humiliating Nuremberg Laws the path led directly to the confiscation of Jewish property and the Kristallnacht. And at the final stage, the machinery collected the Jews and took them into "protective custody" (*Schutzhaft*), until the days of German Jewry were over and they were deported and gassed. The history of the Jews in Munich during the Third Reich, said Peter Hanke, is the story of legalized terror. And he adds that the laws and regulations were defined and enforced in the harshest and most brutal manner both by the Nazi city government of Munich under Fiehler, and by the Munich-Upper Bavaria Gauleitung under Gauleiter Wagner. In fact, both governing bodies instituted such measures at their own discretion long before legislative enactment.[50] Humanness and individual good will proved powerless against the capricious despotism of the Nazi party and state.

Escape and Death

To the question of the Jewish response to the Nazi terror regime there is no unambiguous answer. Indeed, it begs another question: Do we mean the *Israelitische Kultusgemeinde,* the organized Jewish community, or individual Jews—or distinct groups of Jews?

As for the members of the Jewish community of Munich, at least an answer may be given in statistical terms.[51] Sometime during the year 1937, I suggested to the Gemeindeverwaltung (administration of the community) that an evaluation of community strength be made on the basis of the existing file of membership cards, and that a new card file system of those who had in the meantime left the city be introduced. I argued that on the basis of data gained from comparative statistics, the Gemeinde would be able more efficiently to counsel those who planned to emigrate. My unstated motivation was, moreover, to obtain an historical document and not let the Gemeinde disappear without a trace. The proposed stock-taking of the archives served the same objective. The Kultusgemeinde entrusted the stock-taking of the archives to Dr. Bruno Finkelscherer and myself.[52] We assembled some 806 community files, 199 files relating to Bavarian communities outside of Munich, as well as 250 pennons, wrapped them and readied the material for mailing. Our work was finished on 9 September 1938. Had the boxes immediately been sent to Berlin, that is, in October, the material might have been saved. I succeeded in saving five files of which two have since been published.[53] There was no time left for the compilation of statistics as proposed. My report on "The Jewish Population of Munich on 16 May 1938" (in this volume) was transmitted to the Gemeindeverwaltung at the end of August and published in the 1 October 1938 issue of the official journal of the Bavarian Jewish Community. Subsequently, I prepared a report on the "Emigration of Jews from Munich, 1933–38" and gave it to the *Gemeindeverwaltung* on 4 November 1938, just a few days before the Kristallnacht. I retained a copy "in order to hand it over to the Kultusgemeinde at some better future time." Thus, the reports were saved. My work on the "Emigration" paper had to be done under the most difficult conditions, when the main synagogue was being demolished and the administration of the Jewish community forced to vacate its premises and move to Lindwurmstrasse.

What do the statistical data amount to? During the period dealt with in my report, the number of emigrants totalled 3,574, that is, in the course of five years the city lost about one-third of its Jewish population. A substantial number, especially persons in their thirties and forties, reacted in the most direct way to the Nazi seizure of power by emigrating on the spot, neither seeking counsel nor waiting for directives from the Gemeindeverwaltung or from the national Jewish community representatives in Berlin.

While the younger generation saw emigration as the most viable response, many heads of households of the over forty segment of the community pleaded for *Aushalten* (hold out)—at least until the catastrophic year 1938. They reaffirmed their historical ties to Germany, the land, the language and the place where they earned their livelihood; they feared to surrender their economic independence. They realized only too late the deadly threats awaiting them. I find it difficult to describe my own attitude during those years. Whenever someone turned to me for advice, I urged him to emigrate, but I felt it my duty to remain at my post. My family history, my childhood experiences, and my relation to the city of my birth proved such a strong bond that I made every attempt to make the inevitable separation process as slow and painless as possible. Friends have told me that I used to remark at the time: "Emigration is easy, but to leave Munich is difficult." After the *Anschluss*, I saw that was inevitable, but then I discovererd that I was way down on the waiting list for an American visa. Not before June 1939, on the eve of World War II did I succeed in leaving for England, thanks to the generosity of an English cousin of my father's.

We must not forget that by that time many of the remaining Jews of Munich desperately wanted to emigrate but could find no country that would accept them. Rich Jews or famous scholars and scientists were generally welcome, but for the poor and those who had been robbed of their wealth, the welcome mat was not out. On the other hand I would be the last to cast a stone on those who could not bear the thought of separation. I remember meeting Professor Karl Neumeyer on the street one day; this well-known scholar, a codifier of international administrative law, told me how happy he was to know both his sons abroad. When I asked him about what *he* was going to do, his answer was: "My friend, I was born here and grew up in this city; I did all of my work here and I'll die here!" The day they were ordered to leave their home in Königinstrasse, Karl and Anna Neumeyer committed suicide.

There was no more opportunity for Jews to publicly demonstrate their sense of German identity, first, because the situation itself demanded self restraint and, second, because the Nazi authorities thwarted any organizational display of such sentiments, as expressed by the Association of Jewish War Veterans. By contrast, Zionist sport organizations were allowed, and state-Zionist (revisionist) functions even encouraged. To be sure, Zionist political activities were both denounced because they aimed at "Jewish world dominance" and ridiculed because of the inability of Jews to function positively and constructively.[54] Such contradictions were part of the nihilistic world view of National Socialism. Although there were more than a few agitators, State Zionism did not find many converts among the Jews of Munich. There were fanatical as well as romantic and practical Zionists—the latter group abandoning the idea of going to Palestine when the chance to emigrate vanished.

But the majority of the young generation were individualists plain and simple—including most of my friends. After 1934, I was attracted to the *bündisch* and *chaluz* kind of Zionism and cultural nationalism, especially the anchoring of Jewish personality in the Hebrew language. My publications of the time, such as "Warum Hebräisch lernen?" (Why learn Hebrew?) may serve to document this.[55]

Only a small segment of Jewish youth was organized in the *bündisch-chaluzic* youth movement, but, in my opinion, it was the cream of the crop. The most interesting group was the Kameraden (Comrades), because they most clearly reflected the shift in mood and perception of the period.[56] At the time my youngest sister joined the group (1931), it was Jewish in the sense only that its members were excluded from all other groups and thus thrown together. The group had limited aims: to go on hikes, play games, sing songs, and in the evening discuss personal and social problems. The fermentation process began in earnest in 1932, amidst an atmosphere turned hostile, and when Jewish children were accosted in the streets. Now the Munich Kameraden joined up with the Zionist Werkleute. Now these young people of good and assimilated middle class background embraced Jewish custom and thought. The tribulations of everyday life were easier to bear because of those intoxicating things done together: the lighting of the Sabbath candles, the singing of Sabbath songs, attending Bible courses, discussing problems of reconstruction in Palestine, and, lastly and most importantly, the combining of Hassidism and socialism as exemplified in the person of Martin Buber. Needless to say, all the Jewish groups were under police surveillance; their joint activities, such as excursions and camps, were curtailed from time to time—but the Bünd existed. Their small-scale activities were recreated on a much wider scale at the community Lehrhaus and the young people of the Bünde contributed to it. I was active at the Munich Lehrhaus either as lecturer, discussion leader, or simply one of the audience. I also attended Hebrew classes taught by Dr. Mordecai Ehrenkranz. The Munich Lehrhaus became an integral part of the Mittelstelle for Jewish Education, and Martin Buber returned from Jerusalem to Germany in order to enhance its work through his leadership. I still remember vividly the evening when he went through the Book of Jonah with us; he discussed the Hebrew text word-by-word and also etymologically. He then proceeded to provide the historical background, and analyzed the role of the prophets and the power constellations of the ancient Middle East. Finally, Buber presented the whole book in the manner of a great orator; when he came to mention "Niniveh, the great city" and God's concern for its inhabitants as soon as they turned away from evil, we felt the prophet had spoken about us and our city.

Such were the moments when we became a true Gemeinschaft (community). The Sabbath services received new meaning. For a larger circle, the same objectives were achieved by the lectures and musical performances offered by the Kulturbund. These cultural offerings had to be limited to members of the Kulturbund only at the order of the Nazi authorities, who wanted to prevent attendance by our Christian friends and the maintenance of contacts.

On the occasion of these concerts and lectures one could meet people who never before—or only rarely—had attended the synagogue. Since we were forbidden to play "German" music, we saw ourselves compelled to turn to the classical composers designated as Jewish, such as Felix Mendelssohn, or modern composers like of Darius Milhaud, as well as to synagogue music. Conductor Erich Erck did his best to maintain the high standard of the performances. We even had a Jewish puppet theater under the competent direction of Maria Luiko and Alfons Rosenberg. The executive committee of the Kulturbund, of which I was a member, was chaired by Dr. Alfred Perlmutter, one of the noblest and best-educated members of the Munich community; after Eli Straus's emigration, he was one of the leaders of the Zionist organization in Munich. I should mention that among the cultural organizations seeking to meet the educational and cultural needs of Munich's Jewish community was the Jewish elementary school, founded in 1925 by the Orthodox congregation Ohel Jakob. In 1934 it was transformed into an eight-grade community school. It may be looked upon as a symbol of isolation, and it would have been so regarded by the liberals of our community. By this time, however, the school had become a haven for Jewish children and a place of refuge for cultivating things Jewish. I admit to serious disagreement with those who saw in the creation of the Bünde-Lehrhaus-Volksschule-Kulturbund an attempt at euphoric self-deception, providing a false feeling of security and normalness, that was wholly at variance with the perceived need for emigration. In reality, the newly gained moral resistance of the Jews in the face of insult, threat, and fear of death manifested itself in each and every case as self-knowledge and self-consciousness. When after 1938 all these organs of self-knowledge and self-consciousness were dissolved, the process of isolation had turned into the process of atomization. The soul had gone out of the body and now the body could be destroyed.

As a result of Nazis' pattern of trying out their anti-Jewish measures in the city of Munich before employing them in the Reich, the destruction of the synagogues during the Kristallnacht had already taken place in Munich in June 1938. The beautiful main synagogue, once an ornament to the city's skyline, was torn down within a few hours. This happened for the "compelling" reason that Hitler sighted the synagogue when looking out of the window of the Kunsthaus and found the sight repulsive.[57] The president of the community, Dr. Alfred Neumeyer, was notified only at the last minute; he had to call upon the young men of the Home of the Jewish Apprentices hastily to rescue some of the sacred objects. Fortunately, the Torah scrolls had been removed the preceding evening (8 June) in a solemn procession. I was at the time working at the *Karteistelle* of the community administration. On 9 June we were ordered to guard all doors leading to the synagogue during the demolition; I posted myself at the side entrance on the south side of the building. A number of hefty German youths were loitering about the place and heckled. Soon they asked me why they could not enter. I told them that the Gestapo forbade it and they should ask them for permission. As the situation grew more tense, I said I would allow them to enter the synagogue one by one for half a minute only. One after another they came out of the building visibly shaken and wondering why a "building so solid and nice" had to be torn down. They left quietly—and in some bafflement. It so happened that a meeting of the Association of German Rabbis was held in the conference room. The rabbis broke up their meeting and filed out in silence to witness the demolition. I can still see them: Rabbi Bärwald of Munich, urbane and composed; Rabbi Grünewald of Mannheim, erect and determined; Rabbi Eschelbacher of Düsseldorf, with the face of an avenging angel; and Rabbi Baeck of Berlin, with the martyred look of a saint undaunted by fate. I have never in my life seen such a drama played out before me.

Compared to the immediacy of this experience, Dachau was like the echo of the thunder. My Dachau experiences and the events leading to it have been described in some detail in my essay, "In the Dachau Concentration Camp" (in this volume).[58] To be sure, the Dachau concentration camp of 1938 must not be compared with what happened in the extermination camps. But it was inhuman enough. I wish to go on record—as stated in my Dachau paper—that we in Dachau held on to the illusion that Britain, France, and the United States would not long tolerate the National Socialist regime of terror. In this we were bitterly disappointed. The democratic powers were not interested in the fate of the Jews, although Hitler delivered warnings which were unambiguous enough. While many a friend still languished in Dachau, I heard Hitler state loud and clear on the radio: "Should international-finance Jewry in Europe and abroad succeed in plunging the nations into another world war, the outcome would not be the victory of bolshevism—and thereby the victory of international Jewry—but the annihilation of the Jewish race in Europe."[59] The death threats against the Jews were ignored by all concerned. No one was willing to recognize the threat against world peace that started with the attack on the Jews as the point of least resistance. It should come as no surprise that post-Dachau and post-Auschwitz Jewry has since lost faith in declarations of good will—or even in guarantees and formal declarations of intent.

Finally, I should say a word about the character and fate of the Kultusgemeinde, its organizational make-up, and its courageous leaders, the men and women who guided it in the last phase and whose sad duty it became to serve to the end.[60] I can only partly accept the evaluation of Peter Hanke about the gulf between the members of the community and the administrative leadership. To emigrate or not: this difficult choice had to be left to the individual. The administration of the community adhered to the guidelines of the Reichsvertretung regarding the vocational and professional retraining of the younger generation and assistance of their emigration, especially to Palestine; as to the older generation, they were to be cared for in their home country. That total annihilation would be the fate of all who stayed behind was a thought too difficult for most to grasp. The few who did, knew not what they could do about it. This situation was compounded by the fact that in Palestine as well as in other countries the would-be immigrants encountered increasingly stiff bureaucratic measures and obstacles. The Gemeindeverwaltung was able to perform a sound job in counselling people, but it was unable to provide a country of refuge for them!

The top leaders of the Kultusgemeinde were two prominent jurists, Oberlandesgerichtsrat Dr. Alfred Neumeyer and Justizrat Carl Oestreich. Both were liberals but highly respected by the Zionists, the Orthodox, and the eastern Jews alike. Dr. Neumeyer was well-known in government circles and among many high-ranking Bavarian bureaucrats—a fact that served him well, at least until 1935. It enabled him to escape with his wife as late as 1941. Fundamentally, however, the situation was such that, to the extent to which the *Rechtstaat* was supplanted by the *Unrechtstaat* of the NSDAP and the rule of lawless terror, mere legal approaches to political events became increasingly futile and worthless, which in turn produced the impression of utter helplessness among the members of the Gemeinde, an impression probably justified in form, though not in substance. Soon two oppositional forces emerged from within the community, the first led by Georg Josephtal, the other by Julius Hechinger. The former, scion of a prominent Nuremberg family of jurists, was the charismatic leader of the *chaluzic* youth groups. He demanded with forceful eloquence that all energies be deployed for retraining and then emigration to Palestine, without any ifs and buts. Hechinger, a former bank official and restive man whose views echoed those of the lower middle class, eschewed the subtleties of lawyers. He held that you could not impress the Nazis with legal arguments, but with folksy talk and emotional appeals, if at all. Josephtal emigrated, and Hechinger remained, persisting under severe humiliations until he was deported to the east in 1942 and disappeared. After the emigration of Dr. Neumeyer in 1941, Karl Stahl, an engineer, stood at the helm. He was a member of the Munich branch of B'nai B'rith before 1933 and also of the Jewish War Veterans Association. Moreover, he was a close friend of my father's. He was a resolute, fearless man, and quite used to the discipline of military organizations.[61] Alas, there remained nothing else for him to do but to carry out orders, including the order to prepare lists of those to be deported. The only compromise he was able to achieve was that he delayed once in a while the deportation of one or another person whose work was absolutely essential for the community. The day came when Stahl himself was deported to Theresienstadt and from there to Auschwitz.

Jewish community activity before 1920 was almost exclusively oriented toward Kultus, religious instruction, and cemetery care. In the era of Eli Straus, welfare and relief concerns assumed a center place in the activities. After 1933, the shift was toward the tax office, next to the welfare office.[62] Dr. Otto Weiler was the person responsible for the welfare and relief office, the old age homes, the soup kitchen, the YM and YWHAs, the hostel, and the home economics school at Wolfratshausen. Soon, the professional and vocational counselling services occupied the most prominent place among the services including *haksharah* for Palestine. After 1938, the same office attended to the distribution of ration cards. The devotion of the female social workers was legendary. In my capacity as member of the executive committee for the Horticultural Training Center at Feldmoching, I was also attached to the Welfare and Relief Office. To appreciate the whole range of problems facing Jewish social work in Munich, one need but scan the extant correspondence of the few young social workers.[63] In the center of their labors was the care of the aged and the children. As they could not bear letting those children go alone, two of them, Hedwig Jacobi and Alice Bendix, accompanied the last twelve boys and girls to the death factories of Auschwitz in 1943. The Revenue Office was the responsibility of Hechinger, and his assistant was R. A. Fritz Silber (Fred Silber), who managed to escape to the United States in the fall of 1941. Before 1933, the church tax was payable together with the income tax and was set at 10 percent of the latter; the same regulation applied to the Jewish community. After 1933, each church had to take care of its own revenues. Things changed again after 1938 when the state's revenue system sent out the lists, but the local Revenue Office had the responsibility of collection. This way, even the Gemeinde affairs became part and parcel of the Nazi party's apparatus. As a consequence, the sense of community was dissipated; especially after the enactment of the Nuremberg Laws (1935), there arose disagreements and conflicts because everyone declared *Volljude* had to pay the "church" tax whether or not he was a *Glaubensjude* or member of the community. The establishment of a litigation court, which was called Rechtsreferat after 1938, was supposed to ease the situation. All of these considerations became irrelevant after 1939. In spring 1939, Gauleiter Wagner established a so-called "Office of Aryanization" (Arisierungstelle) in Widenmayerstrasse (chief: Wegner; assistant: Kugler), which in due course turned into an overseer that had to account to no one. Wegner or his henchmen often raided houses to see whether everyone in the household was at home after the eight-o'clock curfew, for example. Even the Gestapo—not to speak of the

City Council—was powerless against Wegner's office. Hechinger was the middleman between the Gemeinde and the Arisierungsstelle; he soon could not bear the burden of his office. His successor, a man named Koronczyk, was an agent of Wegner; he managed to survive. The Arisierungsstelle symbolized the transitional stage from the party-dominated state to the reign of terror.[64]

Mention should be made of two important committees within the community administration: the Rabbinical Council and the School Council. Other councils, such as the one in charge of private endowments, libraries, Lehrhaus, community newspaper, and cultural activities ceased functioning by 1938, or 1939 the latest. They would have impeded the atomization process and were therefore eliminated. Things were different with the Auswandererhilfe, the Advisory Office for Emigration under the leadership of Judge Schaeler. That office, however, was removed from the jurisdiction of the Gemeinde and maintained by the Central Office for Emigration under the Reichsvertretung der deutschen Juden in Berlin. The Auswandererhilfe kept the waiting lists for American visas issued by the American consulate at Stuttgart and facilitated the issuance of transit visas for Spain and Portugal. It also administered the transients on their way to other countries, especially with its travelers' aid committee at Munich's main railway station. Most of the travelers were put on trains to Vienna, where the Gestapo demanded extremely high payments for loading them on rickety Danube boats. My youngest sister was on the last transport to Palestine in August 1940. The British regarded such transports as illegal and, after long delays in Haifa, sought to force the passengers onto another ship, the *Patria*, that was to take them to Mauritania. As is well known, the *Patria* was blown up, and those able to jump ship did finally reach their new homeland.[65]

I left Germany a few days before World War II broke out. Thus I was spared the experience of the very last phase, total atomization and physical annihilation. I should like, however, to say a word about the symptomatic process of relocations—from roomy comfort to increasingly cramped quarters—based on my own family's experience. Before the Nazi takeover, we were a happy family living in a beautiful house of fourteen rooms on the Sophie-Stehle-Strasse in Neuwittelsbach, the outskirts of Munich. In 1938 we had to move to a three-room apartment on Teng Street. Bent on the separation of German and Jewish populace, the Arisierungsstelle issued a decree in April 1939, entitled "The Housing of Jews and Non-Jews," which gave them a free hand in ordering the immediate eviction of the Jews from their dwellings. In the winter of 1939 my parents and my youngest sister lived in the Teng Street apartment without heat and electricity. Now they were "voluntarily" vacating these premises. A friend of my father's offered them a room with a kitchenette (but no bathroom) in the attic of his house on Paul-Heyse-Street. My sister

later told us about the intimate togetherness of those days, filled with alter-
nating moments of happiness, worry, fear, and love, all experienced in concentrated form. She recalled her departure in these words:

> It was at the door of our tiny place that I saw my mother the last time. I said
> good bye to her forever! The separation from this graying, unselfish, and kind
> woman who stood there without tears and lamentations left a never-healing
> wound in my heart. She could not get herself to come to the station to see me
> off. Thus the farewell scene was the last unforgettable picture I have of her![66]

Even this last refuge of my parents had to be surrendered in March 1941.
Seven kilometers from the center of the city, on a large plot on the Knorr
Street, a camp of wretched hovels had been hastily erected. Another soon
followed in Berg am Laim, on the premises of a convent. The Nazis called it
Heimanlage.[67] In the recollection of a survivor, the nuns were "generous,
helpful, even friendly" in spite of Nazi warnings against any contact with the
camp inmates. The camp held all kinds of Jews, rich and poor, orthodox and
liberal, converts to Catholicism and Protestantism, all closely penned together
in mortal fear. I do not think that my father was in that camp. He died in
January 1942 after all attempts at emigration had failed. He left behind an
immensely touching farewell, an "ethical testament," as such documents are
called in Hebrew literature.[68] My mother was in the camp at Berg am Laim,
and my aunt in that of Milbertshofen. My mother was deported in the spring
of 1942 and perished in Piaski, Poland; the day of her death is not known. But
we know of the unimaginably horrifying conditions of life and death in Piaski
through the publication of salvaged letters and reports.[69] Nobody returned
from Piaski. The case of my mother was only one of many.

There is a courageous and moving letter of a young rabbi, Bruno Finkelscherer, to Alfred Neumeyer in Argentina. Dated 30 November 1942, the
letter contains the names and fate of several people close to me, among them
my father and my secretary, Cilly Goldschmidt.[70] They were listed among the
deceased. You may also look upon the letter as providing a "List of the
Happy Ones." Of the 630 Jews left in Munich in 1942, very few returned
after the war. The deportations that destroyed a flourishing community in
Munich were only one form of physical annihilation. I think we should not
forget another form of death which at the same time symbolized resistance:
suicide. There are no definitive statistics about the suicides committed during
the period, 1933–43, more especially 1938–43. Contemporary police reports
mention many cases of suicide. For the months of June and July 1942, for
example, the reports list 17 suicides of 30 and 25 deaths respectively.[71] The
year of 1942 was an especially cruel year. Fred Herbert (AKA Fritz Hirschberg) notes in his memoirs that among his circle of friends there, 53 persons
were lost; of these, 3 died in Dachau, 35 in other death camps, and 17

committed suicide.[72] That would suggest, I submit, that the list of martyrs is much longer than previously believed. The total number of victims of the "Final Solution" is underestimated if we omit the many who died by their own hand. The high number of suicides is proof positive that as the last resort, the choice between life and death cannot be denied as a valid manifestation of free will.

1979

Notes

1. To the best of my knowledge there exists no qualitative structural analysis of the Jewish population of any of the great cities before 1933. The following account is based on many diverse sources; first and foremost, it is based on my personal experience. I was born and educated in Munich. From my great-great-grandfather on, I am the descendant of an old Munich Jewish family — at least on my mother's side. I started my professional career in the same city as the *Syndikus* of the local branch of the Centralverein. I was privy to the personalities and ways of the intellectual and artistic circles of Munich, as my uncle was one of the cofounders of the New Secessionist movement in Munich, while my father's sister was a known writer. During my Centralverein tenure I came into contact with many political personalities of the time and place. My younger brother and sister were active members of diverse Jewish *Bünde*, and I came to know many of their peers and their families. Both at the Gymnasium and the university I have had many Christian friends and also some of "marginally Jewish" families. After the early 1930s, I was seeking out and subsequently established close contacts with many Zionists and *Ostjuden*. All in all, I can state without exaggeration that I came to know intimately the widest possible segments of the Jewish community of Munich.

2. I have made good use of the following additional sources: the memoirs of Philipp Löwenfeld, Alfred Neumeyer and Fred Herbert (formerly: Fritz Hirschberg); the published autobiography of Rahel Straus, entitled *Wir lebten in Deutschland* (1962). I found my talks with Paul Weinberger and Karl Rosenthal enlightening with regard to their early years in Munich. Concerning the *Ostjuden*, the following publications were consulted: Jakob Reich, "Eine Episode aus der Geschichte der Ostjuden Münchens," *Von Juden in München—Ein Gedenkbuch*, ed. Hans Lamm (1959), pp. 318–22; Martin Buber, "Wie kann Gemeinschaft werden?" in *München ehrt Martin Buber*; ed. Hans Lamm (1961). Finally, there is an interesting *Festschrift*, entitled *50 Jahre Hauptsynagoge München 1897-1937* (München,1937); especially chapters 3 and 4 contain useful data.

3. Reference is to Ritter Gustav von Kahr, Bavarian Prime Minister after World War I. See relevant treatment of the *völkisch* sentiments and calls for the expulsion of the Jews in Herbert A. Strauss, ed., *Jewish Immigrants of the Nazi Period in the U.S.A.*, vol. 6, *Essays on the History, Persecution and Emigration of German Jews* (New York München London Paris: 1987), pp. 142–76.

4. The synagogue music of Emanuel Kirschner has been published under the title *Tehilloth-le-El-Elyon, 1897-1926.*

5. I have consulted the following sources: *Statistik des Deutschen Reiches* 1925, vol. 150, no. 2: *Die Glaubensjuden im Deutschen Reich* (Berlin, 1928); *Statistik des*

Deutschen Reiches 1933, vol. 150, no. 5: *Die Glaubensjuden im Deutschen Reich* (Berlin, 1935); *Zeitschrift des Bayerischen Statistischen Landesamts,* vol. 66, nos. 3-4 (1934); Hans Wipplinger, "Die Glaubensjuden in Bayern auf Grund des Volksund Berufszählung, vol. 16, June 1933, in *Ibid.*, vol. 70, nos. 3-4; further, Erich Rosenthal, "Jewish Population in Germany, 1910-1939," in *Jewish Social Studies,* 3 no. 3 (1941): pp. 285-300; Felix A. Teilhaber, *Der Untergang der deutschen Juden—Eine volkswirtschaftliche Studie* (Berlin, 1921); and Helmut Genschel, *Die Verdrängung der Juden aus der Wirtschaft im Dritten Reich* (Göttingen, 1968), pp. 20, 210, 274.

6. Some of the prominent baptized Jews were either professionals, such as the lawyer Nawiasky, or members of academia, such as the physics professor Fajan. The brothers Thomas and Heinrich Mann had Jewish wives. The well-known painter Hans von Marées and the sculptor Hildebrandt were *Rassenjuden.*

7. See especially the contributions, "Das jüdische Vereinsleben in München 1915 und 1932," and "Industrie-und Handelskammer München: Verzeichnis jüdischer Kammermitglieder und Handelsrichter 1932-33," in H. Lamm, *Von Juden in München* (München, 1959); also pp. 69-90 et passim. For a historical overview see W.C. Cahnman, "Die soziale Gliederung der Münchener jüdischen Gemeinde und ihre Wandlungen," in the same volume, pp. 31–42.

8. According to Martin Buber's statement to me, Paula Buber's conversion to Judaism took place under the guidance of Rabbi Warschauer of Berlin. She is buried at the Jewish cemetery of Venice.

9. See Fred Herbert, *Mein Leben.* Deposited at the Leo Baeck Institute Archives, New York City.

10. This chapter is a strongly autobiographical one. I have also drawn on a wide assortment of literature of that period such as books and newspaper and magazine articles. For reflections on the *Räterepublik,* see Lamm, *Juden in München,* especially the contributions of Buber, Carl Landauer, Sigmund Fränkel, and Immanuel Birnbaum. See also Erich Mühsam, *Von Eisner bis Leviné—die Entstehung der bayerischen Räterepublik,* (Berlin, 1928); further, Josef Hofmiller, *Revolutionstagebuch, 1918–19* (Leipzig, 1938). The last two accounts represent two oppositional viewpoints. As for Gustav Landauer, it should be noted that he was a thoroughly ascetic socialist who let himself be drawn into politics by his impatience to see his visionary utopia realized. He then did a lot of damage and was, in turn, destroyed by the events. Landauer wanted to have the messianic future here and now, a position hardly compatible with political realities. In addition, he had forsaken the basis of his messianic faith, the Jewish communal life. In that, he chose a different road from that of his friend, Martin Buber. His grave was desecrated in 1933, after which his daughters appealed to me to intervene with Rabbi Bärwald in order to find a new place for him in the Jewish cemetery at Garchinger Street, which was done.

11. The seed of what was to come to fruition in 1933 was already in place between 1919 and 1924. One of the earliest and keenest observers of the approaching Nazi tide was the journalist Konrad Heiden. His *Geschichte des Nationalsozialismus* was published in 1932. Refer to the memoirs of Alfred Neumeyer at the Leo Baeck Institute Archives, New York City. Concerning the fateful role that Paul Nikolaus Cossmann played, consult the memoirs of Philipp Löwenfeld, also at the Leo Baeck Institute. See Wolfram Selig, "Paul Nikolaus Cossmann und die *Süddeutschen Monatshefte* von 1914–1918," *Dialogos,* 3 (1967).

12. See the memoirs of Philipp Löwenfeld.
13. Hugo von Hofmannsthal, *Das Schrifttum als geistiger Raum der Nation* (München,1927).
14. My own impressions of Rudolf Hess are confirmed by the article of John Haag, "The Spann Circle and the Jewish Question," in *Leo Baeck Year Book,* 18 (1973): 93–128.
15. Otto von Zwiedineck-Südenhorst, "Erfülltes—Erstrebtes—Erkanntes," in *Mensch und Wirtschaft* (Berlin, 1955), pp. 1-37. Also Otto Neuloh's article, Ibid., pp. 23-87.
16. Reference is made to diverse unpublished essays in my possession, such as a four-page "Lebenslauf" (Record of a Life) and a twelve-page "Bibliographie"; these two writings were put together in the course of my preparation for emigration.
17. See Karl Vossler, "Ansprache an die im Korporationsaussschuss vereinigten Studentischen Verbindungen," in Lamm, *Von Juden in München* Munich, pp. 331-33.
18. Richard Willstätter, *Aus meinem Leben* (Weinheim, 1949), pp. 338–46. For a statement on the universities, see p. 397. For an extremely informative and insightful description of the harrassments and pains inflicted upon a Jew about to emigrate, see pp. 401-7.
19. The unpublished statement by Howard John Fields, Esq. (formerly: Hans A. Feibelmann) is in my possession.
20. There exists no monograph on the history of the Centralverein as of the date of this essay. Concerning the political activities of the Centralverein, see Arnold Paucker's account, *Der jüdische Abwehrkampf in den letzten Jahren der Weimarer Republik* (Hamburg, 1969). The pamphlet of the assimilationist Raphael Löwenfeld, entitled *Schutzjuden oder Staatsbürger?* (Berlin, 1893), tells about the founding and early development of the organization. Even Paucker's story is largely limited to the political activities of the Berlin office. The other district and local centers are hardly even mentioned. The person most interested in and acquainted with the work of these latter group was Dr. Ludwig Holländer; unfortunately, he ceased all activities around 1932 because of illness. Chief Counsel Julius Brodnitz, whom I had known as well as Alfred Neumeyer, was preoccupied with the Berlin group. All the younger *Syndiken* were activists and eager to "mobilize the masses" against the Nazis, obviously a utopian endeavor. They regarded Bavaria—and Munich—as a case of *quantité négligeable*. This essay thus serves as a contribution to the still-outstanding story of the Centralverein, albeit from the viewpoint of a man trapped in the trenches.

At the very beginning, under the leadership of Raphael Löwenfeld, Centralverein displayed an enlightened-patriotic spirit, but by the 1930s there was an ongoing debate as to the ideological direction it should take. Professor Chaim Weizmann succeeded in establishing a Committee of Non-Zionists within the Jewish Agency and in securing the cooperation of leading members of the Centralverein, among them Dr. Leo Baeck, Ludwig Tietz, and the banker, Oskar Wasserman. It thus became possible to be a Zionist in a non-Zionist framework, that is, without belonging to a Zionist party. The same constellation was realized in Munich with the participation of Levinger, Werner, and myself. As a consequence, we were spared the infighting that characterized the northern-German branch. My own critical stance toward the dominant ideology of the Centralverein is documented in my correspondence to Dr. Ludwig Feuchtwanger (see my letter of 31 August 1932, especially) who was even more sharply critical of the Centralverein.

21. See my essay, "The Nazi Threat and the Centralverein—A Recollection," in *Conference on Anti-Semitism,* ed. Herbert A. Strauss (New York: American Federation of Jews from Central Europe Publ., 1969), pp. 27-36. See also Herbert A. Strauss, "Jewish Reactions to the Rise of Anti-Semitism in Germany," ibid., pp. 7-26. Strauss stated that the Centralverein treated the symptoms instead of taking a look at the illness itself. In my opinion, that was due to organizational politics.

22. Characteristic of the situation was the Council Meeting of the Centralverein held on 17 December 1924 (*Jahresbericht 1924,* 22: 10–13) at which a heated discussion took place about the renewed acceptance of Jews in the Association of Alpinists. The Centralverein speakers argued in either an emotional-rational tone while Dr. Siegel attacked the principle of discrimination. Both sides had their positive impact but were equally unproductive. In 1924 it seemed to be a matter of dispute, but in 1932 it became tragically clear that neither the contributions of the Jews to German national life and culture nor the principle of equality counted much in the eyes of the Nazis. With regard to the Alpinist affair, see the documentation in Lamm pp. 220–23.

23. It is assumed that the files of the Munich branch of the Centralverein are lost, with some exceptions to be discussed at a later point. I have reconstructed the discussion between Catholic and Jewish students with the help of Hans A. Feibelmann (aka Howard John Fields).

24. For an account see "Niederschrift über ein Gespräch mit Herrn Professor Werner J. Cahnman am 1. April 1973 in New York," in my possession (and in that of Ms. Elisabeth Zauner, who was working on her dissertation on Dr. Alois Hundhammer). A copy is deposited at the library of the Institut für Zeitgeschichte.

25. Walter Gyssling, a journalist, was not Jewish; he worked as an archivist at the Büro Wilhelmstrasse. Gyssling and Konrad Heiden were the most knowledgeable experts on National Socialism.

26. It is to be noted that the report on the fate of the Berlin Archives in Arnold Paucker's book, *Der jüdische Abwehrkampf,* pp. 126 and 281, is absolutely incorrect. The Archive was never hidden in a farm, nor was it ever left in the yard of a factory. And it was definitely not recycled in a paper factory.

27. The correspondence of the *Centralverein* consisted of eight headings: 1) Zwiesel/ Lower Bavaria; 2) Office of the Deputy of the Führer (von Conta), including a copy of the report of Carl Bach to the state secretary in the Ministry of Economy, dated 3 October 1933; 3) Christmas Business; 4) Embargo on Advertising I; 5) Embargo on Advertising II; 6) Neustadt ander Aisch; 7) Würzburg; 8) Collection of Newspaper Clippings.

28. The following report should be consulted in case of follow-up: *Geheimes Staatsarchiv* MA 106410 (Munich). It contains the remarks of the president of the Chamber of Commerce in Munich addressed to the Regent, dated 14 March 1933, in which he asked for an assurance toward Jewish businessmen. The appeal went unheeded.

29. Helmut Genschel reports on the exploitation, corruption, and greed of Frankonians in *Verdrängung der Juden aus der Wirtschaft im Dritten Reich* (Göttingen: Göttinger Bausteine zur Geschichtswissenschaft, Bd. 38), pp. 240–48.

30. For an account of the "society" patrons of Hitler, see Hellmuth Auerbach, "Hitler's politische Laufbahn und die Münchener Gesellschaft 1919-1925," in *Vierteljahreshefte für Zeitgeschichte,* 1 (1977): 1-45. I would turn around Auerbach's argumentation and say that Hitler was no "operational accident" in German history, but that the "radical charisma" of his personality had put its stamp on National Socialism in a very special way.

31. I have an unpublished account of my incarceration (from 22 December 1933). In addition to these thirteen pages, I also have copies of my agreements and discussions with Inspector Schall of 9 January 1934 and 9 February 1934, as well as a report to Alfred Hirschberg of the Berlin branch of the Centralverein dated 27 March 1934.

32. For the Centralverein appeal see "Archivinventar," vol. 5, *Geheimes Staatsarchiv München* (Reichsstatthalter 432/1-4); the correspondence and appeal contained in this State File are the only Centralverein documents existent after the confiscation of Centralverein files.

33. Refer to the letter of protest written by Dr. Neumeyer on 31 March 1933 to the office of the Reichsstatthalter. In addition, an appeal was sent, signed by Dr. Neumeyer and Rabbi Dr. Freudenthal, asking for the cessation of harassment against Jewish citizens; it also expressed the hope that the "renewal of German national life would not be accomplished by the repression of Jews."

34. See Peter Hanke, *Zur Geschichte der Juden in München zwischen 1933 und 1945* (München: Miscellanea Bavarica Monacensia, Heft 3, Stadtarchiv Series, 1967). It is a very good reference source also with regard to the period between 1930 and 1934. Mention of my name and work is made on pp. 41–44, 53, 56, 65, 71, 75, 81, 105, 115, 166, 171–73, 177–78, 180 and 205.

35. For my three-stages theory of the destruction of German Jewry see "Jewish Morale in Our Time" in *Social Forces,* 20, no. 4 (May 1942): 491–96.

36. For anti-Semitism in Austria and its political significance see Paul Molisch, *Politische Geschichte der deutschen Hochschulen in Österreich von 1848 bis 1918* (Wein-Leipzig, 1939); further, Oskar Karbach, "Die politischen Grundlagen des deutsch-österreichischen Antisemitismus," in *Zeitschrift für die Geschichte der Juden,* nos. 1–4. (Tel-Aviv, 1964).

37. For a detailed discussion see Peter Hanke, *Zur Geschichte,* pp. 83–87. Refer also to Baruch Ophir's account of the traumatic experience of 1 April 1933, deposited at the Institut für Zeitgeschichte.

38. Hanke, *Zur Geschichte,* pp. 87–89. Himmler developed the operation of the Dachau concentration camp and with that all of the other camps. The suppression of the Centralverein was Himmler's doing.

39. Cardinal Faulhaber's advent sermons were devoted to the following themes: 1) The Old Testament and Its Fulfillment in Christianity; 2) The Ethical Themes of the Old Testament and Their Elevation in the Evangelium; 3) Social Ideas in the Old Testament; 4) The Cornerstone between Judaism and Christianity; 5) Christianity and Germanic Nationhood.

40. Reports on Muckermann and other priests are to be found in the monthly reports of the police headquarters in Munich (December 1934, December 1936) and also in the monthly report of the State's Secret Police, dated 14 July 1937.

41. Much of the information was gained from the States Archives, Closed Material Section, for which permission was kindly granted to the author.

42. Ibid., MA 106689, MA 106690, MA 106697, *Archivinventar* vols. 1, 2.

43. My account is based on the written report of Max Ballin and Hedwig Eichengrung Stern and used with their kind permission. Copies of Carl Bach's appeals of 3 October and 7 December 1933 are in my possession. For information on Eichengrün and Uhlfelder see MA 106685, MA 106688 and MA 106697.

44. For Gunzenhausen, see Jochen Klenner, "Verhältnis von Partei und Staat 1933-1945, dargestellt am Beispiel Bayerns," (München: Miscellanea Bavarica Monacensia, Vol. 54 of the series, 1974), pp. 235-42. See also MA 106694.

45. Concerning boycotts and demonstrations, see the following files: MA 106411, MA 106671, and MA 106685; as for *Simplicissimus,* see MA 106685. On Franz Kreitmayr, consult MA 106690.

46. Concerning cases of *Rassenschande,* see MA 106677, MA 106685, MA 106687, MA 106688, and MA 106690; also monthly reports of the BPP.

47. For the case of A. & E. Königbauer, I am indebted to Lilo Cahnmann Dotan. I have also used the reports of Ruth Goldschmidt Meros, Hugo Marx, and Fred Silver on the distribution of food by Christian neighbors and businessmen. See Else Behrend-Rosenfeld, p. 114.

48. On Lina Angermeier see "Man nennt sie die Mutter der Toten," in *Süddeutsche Zeitung* (23 June 1964).

49. Report on the school was written up by Ruth Goldschmidt Meros; similar reports by Lilo Cahnmann Dotan and several letters of Franconians are in my files.

50. Peter Hanke, pp. 299–300.

51. The files entitled "Israelitische Kultusgemeinde München—Kartei der Ausgewanderten" contain my report to Dr. Weiler (23 August 1938) and my "Report on the Emigration of Jews from Munich 1933–1938" with an accompanying letter (4 November 1938); further, the 1 October 1938 issue of the *Jüdisches Gemeindeblatt* with my article, "Die jüdische Bevölkerung in München am 16. Mai 1938"; and many other items regarding communal affairs.

52. See "Archiv der Israelitischen Kultusgemeinde München; Aufstellung betr. Nachtragsverzeichnis von Akten bayerischer Verbandsgemeinden," signed by Dr. Werner Cahnmann and Dr. Bruno Finkelscherer; further, a letter to Dr. Ostreich, dated 28 September 1938. Also, Werner J. Cahnman, "Munich and the First Zionist Congress," in *Historica Judaica,* 3, no. 1 (April 1941): 7-23.

53. Ibid.

54. For Zionism and other organizations, see *Geheimes Staatsarchiv,* MA 106687, MA 106688, MA 106689, and MA 106690.

55. Werner Cahnmann, "Warum Hebräisch lernen?" in *Frankfurter Israelitischer Gemeindeblatt,* no. 6 (1937); further, in *Monatsblätter des Jüdischen Kulturbunds,* no. 6 (1938).

56. Concerning "Werkleute," I am indebted to Lilo Cahnmann Dotan. My oldest sister, Eva Cahnmann Mansbach, was member of the Jüdischen Jugendvereins, and somewhat later on, of Hechaluz. My brothers were members of the general Jugendbewegung. Archival references, MA 106670, MA 106682, MA 106691, and MA 106697.

57. Description of the destruction of Munich's central synagogue in Hanke, pp. 204ff.; Lamm, *Von Juden in München*; Carl Ostreich, "Die letzten Stunden eines Gotteshauses," ibid., pp. 349-50; Emanuel Kirschner, "Abschied von der Münchner Hauptsynagoge," ibid., 348; and Alfred Neumeyer, "Erinnerungen,"

58. For "In the Dachau Concentration Camp," see present volume.

59. Max Domarus, *Reden und Proklamation 1932–1945.* Kommentiert von einem deutschen Zeitgenossen, vol. 1 (Neustadt ander Aisch, 1963), p. 1058.

60. For the story of the Israelitische Kultusgemeinde in Munich, see Peter Hanke, p. 263 et passim; further, my interview with Fritz Silber (Fred Silver) and several essays in Lamm, esp. those by Julius Spanier, Elisabeth Kitzinger, Julius and Helene Weil, and Lotte Stein Pick. See also A. Neumeyer, "Erinnerungen."

61. Concerning Karl Stahl, see Else R. Behrend-Rosenfeld, *Ich stand nicht allein* (Franfurt am Main, 1963), pp. 93, 105, 132, 153 et passim. The last report of Karl Stahl to Alfred Neumeyer is reprinted in Lamm, p. 360ff.

62. For information on communal organization and activities, see Peter Hanke, p. 263ff., interview is by Fred Silver.

63. See the Ernst Kitzinger Collection, deposited at the Leo Baeck Institute, New York City. There are letters by social workers, among them Alice Bendix, Hedwig Jacobi, Clara Mayer, and Anna Renner, from the years 1939–41 addressed to E. Kitziner. From 1933 to the time of her emigration to Palestine, E. Kitziner was the social worker responsible for Jewish youth. A letter by Carola Castau of 15 August 1947 describes the last transports leaving Berg am Laim in 1943. Castau was a Christian Red Cross worker.

64. On the offices of "Aryanization," see Hanke, p. 275ff.; Else Behrend-Rosenfeld, et passim; the interview with Fred Silver. Concerning Hechinger and Koronczyk, see Hanke, p. 278.

65. Based on conversations with Fred Silver and Lilo Cahnmann Dotan.

66. Ibid.

67. See Hanke, p. 279ff.; Else Behrend-Rosenfeld, p. 104ff.

68. The ethical testament of my father has finally reached us, that is, a copy of it. It was brought out via Stuttgart, Zürich, and London. The English translation was published under the title, "An Ethical Will and a Memorial Tribute," in *The Reconstructionist*, 9, no. 10 (25 June 1943): 29–32. Both an English and German version are deposited at the Leo Baeck Institute in New York City and in the Museum of the Dachau Concentration Camp.

69. Else Rosenfeld and Gertrud Luckner, eds., *Lebenszeichen aus Piaski—Briefe Deportierter aus dem Distrikt Lublin, 1940-1943* (Munich, 1968). See also Adalbert Rückerl, *NS Vernichtungslager im Spiegel deutscher Strafprozesse* (Munich, 1977).

70. Letter of Bruno Finkelscherer, dated 30 November 1942, is reprinted in Lamm, pp. 361–63.

71. See *Archivinventare* (Munich), vol. 2: *Repertorien und Spezialinventare zu den Beständen NSDAP und Gestapo Leitstelle München* (Munich, 1975). The volume deals with the period from 20 July to 13 August 1942.

72. Fred Herbert, "Mein Leben." Manuscript is deposited in the library of the Leo Baeck Institute, New York City. Photocopies of the memoirs of Löwenfeld, Neumeyer, and Herbert are deposited at the Bavarian State Library (Bayerische Staatsbibliothek), Munich.

8

In the Dachau Concentration Camp:
An Autobiographical Essay

Arrest and First Day

About 7 A.M. on 9 November 1938 my mother received a phone call from
a friend of our family, a retired doctor, who said he had just been warned by
a former patient, then an official in the Gestapo(!), that mass arrests of Jews
were imminent. We urged father to leave for his sales route as soon as
possible. I spent the day downtown but returned in the late afternoon, when
I assumed that the storm had blown over. I found a limousine in front of the
house and the door open. Upon entering, I heard my mother talking agitatedly
to two men. She said that her husband was not at home and that she did not
know when he was going to return. She also said that she did not know where
I had gone. I considered the situation for a moment. Nobody had seen or heard
me. It would have been easy to leave the house once again and be gone for
the night. In that case, I reckoned, my father would certainly be arrested. I
thought I could avert this if I were to offer myself instead. Consequently, I
stepped forward and said: *"Meine Herren, wollen Sie etwas von mir?"* Yes,
they replied, they wanted me for a brief interrogation, possibly lasting through
the night. I should take a toothbrush along. My mother looked aghast. As we
raced toward the city, I saw my father pedaling slowly homeward on his
bicycle, looking pensive and downcast. Nobody ever came to ask for him
again.

I was brought to the Wittelsbacher Palais which then served as Gestapo
headquarters. There were hundreds of people standing in line and being
shoved from one formality to another. In the intervals, there was waiting,
waiting, waiting, shouted commands, and hushed talk. In the early morning
hours of 10 November we were loaded into buses and trucks. It was a grey,
foggy day. After about one hour's drive we were ordered out. As I had a
notion as to what was awaiting us, I jumped to the ground very quickly and

thus escaped the kicks of an SS man who was standing beside the door. But older and heavier men were knocked down and kicked repeatedly before they could move on.

We knew that we were in Dachau. We were marched around, kept waiting, interrogated, abused, marched around again, kept waiting again, and so forth, ad infinitum. We were deprived of all our belongings, which were, however, painstakingly registered. Then our heads were shaved. Finally, stark naked, we were herded into shower rooms. After that, we were ordered to run through a long corridor, around various corners, to another room, for a "medical examination." On every corner stood an SS man who kicked each prisoner, as he passed by, with his boot or with a stick; if a prisoner was slow, he was kicked repeatedly. Again I succeeded in squeezing by so quickly that I escaped injury. The examination, of course, was a farce. One had to turn on one's heels several times (for inspection), and that offered another opportunity for kicking and whipping. I received a good kick on that occasion, but pretended indifference. However, several elderly men stumbled and fell to the ground and were mercilessly trampled upon. We were then ordered into a room where we received prisoner's clothing. We waited again in line, once more enduring a great deal of verbal abuse. In the meantime, several SS men amused themselves by asking one or the other of us whether he knew why he was in Dachau. The reply—"I do not know"—was another occasion for slaps and kicks. People were made to say: "Because I am a traitor"; "because I am a war-monger"; "because I am a criminal"; and similar remarks. One fellow, however, got away with only a token kick because he replied, standing stiffly to attention: "I beg for information, sir."

It was toward evening when we were led to the barracks. Most of us had not eaten anything for a period of about forty-eight hours. Hardly had we gotten into the barracks, before we were ordered harshly out again to line up for the evening meal. It consisted of two potatoes and a herring. Although exceedingly hungry, I could not eat the herring. Noting that my brother-in-law, Leo M., was in the adjoining barracks and that he was receiving his portion at the same place, I gave him the herring and received from him another potato. I swallowed my three potatoes, to the accompaniment of a brown something called "coffee," within not more than three minutes. This was a good thing because we were instantly ordered into the barracks again to get ready for the night.

Life in the Camp

During the night we were packed tightly like sardines on thin straw mattresses, spread over a cement floor. Space was at a premium, so much so that one was unable to lie on his back—he had to rest sideways. Whoever had to go to the toilet inevitably had to step across rows of sleepers. Quite a few people breathed and snored heavily, and the noise never abated. The air was exceedingly sticky.

We were awakened before daybreak. We had to fold the mattresses, store them in certain places in orderly heaps, take towel, soap, and toothbrush from drawers alloted to each of us, wash ourselves, go to the toilet, and be ready for breakfast within, I believe, fifteen minutes. Since there must have been several hundred persons in each barrack one can imagine the demeaning bedlam that was occasioned by all of this. There was shoving, pushing, yelling, and cursing among the prisoners. Especially besieged by the impatient crowds were the toilet seats, which were arranged in an open row along the walls. If I remember correctly, no one was allowed to use the toilet except in the morning and during the night. In short, we had to organize every step very accurately if we wanted to go through all the motions in time. Failure to do this drew verbal abuse and, if the whim of the supervisor was inclined toward it, corporal punishment.

However, once lined up outside the barracks for breakfast, one had to wait. This enervating shift from rush to wait and back to rush again was part of the system. Likewise was the insistence on minutiae. Anyone observed having omitted brushing his teeth or washing his hands or not folding his mattress in the prescribed way or not organizing his drawer properly was severly reprimanded by the SS man in charge, ordered to start all over again, called a "swine," "trickster," "Jewish sow," and so on, and occasionally slapped, kicked, beaten, or otherwise punished.

We were not detailed to any work group. Instead, our days were passed with standing at attention either in front of the barracks or, once a day, on the parade grounds (*Appelplatz*), where we were counted, and with marching, running, exercising, and singing. We marched dozens of times in the mornings and then again in the afternoons up and down the main road of the camp, along the side lanes, across the parade grounds, with hardly a break. And we had to sing! Not "the songs of Zion" though, but various German folk songs that seemed appropriate to the occasion. I remember that we sang *"Das Wandern ist des Mueller's Lust"* hundreds of times. This song was considered especially appropriate because it was designed to turn our thoughts toward emigration. At various times, SS officers yelled at us: "Why are you still here?"; "Why don't you get out of the country?"; "You can't exploit innocent *goyim* any more!"; "No more profiteering permitted!"; "The time for gypping has run out!"; and so forth in the same vein.

Of course, every sign of weakness was fatal. Many elderly or infirm men stumbled and broke down. In slight cases, they were kicked and pushed up again; in more severe cases, they were carried away and seen no more. Manifestations of compassion, such as supporting a man who was on the verge of collapse, were punished. On the parade grounds, the slightest move from a rigid position was an excuse for slapping and beating, if not worse. Once, on a cold, windy evening, we had to stand motionless for several hours. On that day, dozens who fainted or fell or otherwise aroused the displeasure of the SS were dragged out of sight, never to be seen again.

Gas chambers were not yet in evidence, but the death toll was nevertheless appalling. We saw crude coffins and corpses on stretchers carried across the camp at all times. Some people were beaten to death; some contracted fatal illnesses; some were tortured.

My friend Hans S., who suffered from diabetes, died within one day for lack of insulin. A Munich lawyer (a member of the Orthodox congregation Ohel Jacob), a frail and nervous little man, began to wail hysterically during one night. He was dragged out into the open, and, in order to exorcise his fear complex, he was doused with buckets of ice cold water; the more he shrieked, the more he was doused. He was left lying on the ground during the rest of the night. He contracted pneumonia and died within hours.

The story of Felix F., a leading personality in Ohel Jacob and in the München Loge of B'nai B'rith, I know only from hearsay. Wearing a long, black beard, he was conspicious and hence manhandled and mistreated. His beard was first pulled, then shaved, and he was beaten in a most barbarous manner. Finally, a human wreck, he was released. When he arrived at his home, in pain, his wife failed to recognize him and closed the door on him. Upon his whimpered pleas she recognized him, however, and put him to bed. He died a few days later. I find it painful to relate more incidents of this kind.

But I must relate the story of my cousin, Jacob M., of Rheinbischofsheim in Baden, my father's birthplace. One day, during the brief noontime intermission, he turned up at our barracks. The grapevine had told him I was there, and he wanted to see me. He had a large blue spot near one eye and smaller spots elsewhere. He said that the Jewish men had been lined up in the village and interrogated. As each man stepped forward, the "interrogation" began. It consisted of shouted abuse, followed by slaps across the face, kicks over the head, and so forth. When the victim fell to the ground, he was rudely helped to his feet again and the procedure repeated. Similar scenes occurred on the long train and bus ride from Kehl to Dachau. Fatalities were thrown out of the train windows. He reported these things quietly, in a matter-of-fact way, and asked me to greet his family in case he should not be able to leave the camp. He was later released but could not secure a visa to any place where he could have emigrated. As a result of the treatment which he had received, he lost his eyesight. In this condition he was brought to camp Gurs in France, and from there transported to a death camp in Poland, together with his wife and daughter. One must multiply such stories a millionfold in order to comprehend what happened in those dark years.

The morale of the Jewish prisoners, which has been subjected to severe doubts by authors like Raoul Hilberg and others,[1] seemed to me high at the time. I would say the same thing in retrospect. Of course, there were shades and grades. There were petty jealousies, egotistic attitudes, despondency, lack of comprehension. On the whole, intellectuals and persons from the upper class, as well as persons from the laboring classes, stood the test better than persons from the middle classes, that is, owners of medium-sized businesses, and so forth. The petit bourgeois simply did not understand what was happening to him. Upon being kicked or abused verbally, he would turn around, staring uncomprehendingly—and that was his undoing. These people were more often than not physically awkward and became the butt of practical jokes—Nazi style.

People from the laboring classes, on the other hand, were helped by their sturdy physique and by a culture pattern which was less individualistic and more inclined toward mutual help. There were, of course, only a few of them. One of this group, a blond Galizianer boy, who used to work in the stockroom of a Munich textile house, was physically indistinguishable from the guard. He was never touched.

Intellectuals and persons from the business elite were more numerous. They were helped by their inner resources and their keen grasp of the situation. Dr. Bruno Finkelscherer, a few years younger than myself and destined to become the last rabbi of the old Munich Jewish community (he died later at Auschwitz), was a marvel of quiet dignity and resigned cheerfulness. With great affection I remember the philosopher Professor Hoenigswald, the art historian Professor Franz Rapp, and an electrical engineer, Dr. Galitzenstein, all three, by the way, baptized and intermarried Jews.[2] While waiting for a meal or during the precious intervals between one activity or another, we sustained ourselves by means of philosophical and political discussions conducted at half-voice. I thought that Zionism seemed justified by the events we witnessed, while Hoenigswald maintained that the unity of mankind would emerge victorious in the end. As I see it now, we were both right and I believe we admitted it to each other right then and there.

The most remarkable thing happened with Carl B., owner of a large Munich clothing enterprise, who was of my size and height and was marching by my side all of the time. One day while we were marching, he whispered into my ear: "As an educated man, doctor, can you answer a question? Do you believe in God?" I replied: "That is hard to say. I believe in a force, whatever its name, that shapes our lives." He said: "Alright, but what I mean is, do you believe in a God of Justice?" I replied: "I do not know—but, eventually, yes." Such shy exchanges contain the stuff of which morale is made.

Speaking of morale reminds me of another incident. During a noontime intermission (*Essenspause*), I encountered a friend and lodge brother of my father, an elderly Munich manufacturer. He looked drawn and haggard and had a whipped-dog visage. He said: "My dear doctor, it's terrible, it's hopeless. We won't get out of here." I flew into a rage. I said: "If you want to go to the dogs, go ahead and do it. But as far as I am concerned, I'll get out of here, I assure you." He stared at me in bewilderment, apparently taken aback by the rudeness of my outburst, but he collected himself and replied: "Perhaps you are right." Of course, if the gas ovens had been in operation at that time, neither resignation nor defiance would have helped us.

At that time, prior to the outbreak of the war, the Nazis tried to profit from us by permitting our families to send us money which we could spend at the "canteen." As I remember it, this was a place resembling a large army store. The trouble was that there was hardly time to get there during the brief noontime intermission. But the very expectation did serve to keep a man's spirit alive. Another difficulty was that a great many items on display at the store were of no use to us. If one succeeded in getting them to the barracks before the afternoon drill started, they might be stolen by a greedy fellow inmate. If one was late, the things bulged in one's pockets and aroused the ire of the SS. I never purchased anything which I could not consume on the premises. One day I observed that a large jar of honey was on sale on one of the counters. I bought it, asked for a spoon, and emptied the jar in no time. No bear in the forest could have done better. The thin soups, hard bread, stale potatoes, and nondescript coffee that used to be the mainstay of our daily diet had reduced us to hungry beasts. People had hunger reveries, daydreaming about roast beef, veal, and goose. I was a lanky, skinny, rather underweight fellow when I entered the camp. Still, I lost about twenty pounds during the five weeks of my imprisonment.

Naturally, the place was rife with rumors. Why we had been brought to the camp was clear to us. But whether and under what conditions we would be released was a matter of wild conjecture. Those who had visas for foreign countries, those who had families, those who were over sixty years of age, those who were ill, those who were healthy, those who were veterans of the army — all such possibilities of being released, and innumerable combinations of these, were mentioned. Everybody favored the category that put him ahead of the queue. One day, towards the end of my stay in the camp, I heard a man in his sixties complain bitterly about the fact that a man in his twenties, who had been in his group all the time, had been released before him. I reminded him that it was perhaps more important that young people be saved than old ones, if there was to be a choice. Hardly anybody understood that there was no rhyme nor reason in the whole thing. Our families worked for our release, but success or failure was like a game of dice.

While only a few of us were wise on that score, we were all foolish when it came to a consideration of foreign intervention. We were quite sure that the "civilized world"—Britain, France, the United States—would not stand for the mockery of justice and the contempt for human rights to which we were exposed. We were even more certain that the statesmen of the world would realize that the Nazi regime was inexorably drifting towards war. It seemed to us that it was a matter of self-preservation for the democratic powers to slay the ugly dragon before he could rise and devour them. Little did we imagine that many influential people in the West lived with the illusion that they could accommodate themselves to Hitler, and that our fate was a matter of extreme unconcern to practically everybody.

Bruno Bettelheim and others have theorized about the tendency of those in "extreme situations" to adopt the values of their tormentors as their own.[3] Undoubtedly, that phenomenon could be observed. But to do in Rome as Romans do is not unusual in the world-at-large. In the distorted world of the camp, it was a matter of sheer self-preservation. To march in step, to observe the pedantic etiquette of cleanliness, to assume an erect posture when talked to, to stand motionless during the roll call in the evening—these were things that, if disregarded by one of us, might spell disaster for the rest. Consequently, we urged deviants to comply. But I don't think that many of us confused those means to an end with ultimate values. And we admired those in the camp who were Jehova's Witnesses (*Ernste Bibelforscher*) for their uncompromising stand. We did not share their credo, but we were sure that it was superior to the monstrous excrescences of the Nazi mind.

It may be retorted that we were not "old prisoners" and that time would have told on us if we had stayed in the camp for a prolonged period. But some of our supervisors were precisely such old prisoners, and their behavior was recognizably different from the behavior of the SS. They were outwardly harsh, but not brutal. With gratefulness I remember one of them, a young Sudeten-German, who told us under his breath that he used to be a trade union man. When he commanded our unit, he skillfully directed us away from the main road in the camp and into deserted lanes between the barracks, where he felt that he could safely permit us to rest our aching limbs and sore feet for a few precious minutes. Whether he was able to retain his integrity in the long run, I do not know. He had arrived in the camp only a few weeks before us. I am inclined to agree with Primo Levi[4] that the concentration camp was not so much a place where values were reversed as a place where they were totally corroded. Normlessness ruled supreme.

It must be added that the young Sudeten-German was an exception at any rate. But even among the SS, there was a whole range of types, from the all-out bloodhound to the contemptuous sadist, and from the moral monster to the man who appeared to merely do his duty. It is easy to generalize, either from limited observation or because one wants to prove a pet theory to be right, always and everywhere. I believe that the exception is as important as the rule. Ultimately, perhaps, it may count for more.

Release and Rescue

I was released on 16 December 1938. I was called to the central office and told that I had a visa for Paraguay. (My mother had secured such a document which, however, had no value other than to effect my release.) I was sternly advised that I would be arrested again if I failed to leave the country in due time. I was handed back my civilian suit, shirt, shoes, and other belongings. I arrived at home on a Friday evening, shortly before dinner time. After dinner, I was shown letters from abroad pertaining to emigration, but I felt that I was unable to concentrate on reading them, and I said so. When my father admonished me to try to read the letters nonetheless, I rose from the table, red with anger, and slammed the door. For weeks afterwards I could not even bring myself to read a novel or a detective story. The letters would dance before my eyes, and I would break into a sweat. I was certain that I was hovering on the verge of a serious mental disorder. But I finally climbed out of the hole, mentally as well as physically. I left Germany on 20 June 1939. On that day I was born into a new life.

1964

Notes

1. Raoul Hilberg, *The Destruction of European Jews* (Chicago: 1961).
2. Hannah Arendt asserts in her *Eichmann in Jerusalem* (New York: 1963) that many Jews could have escaped arrest, deportation, and death if Jewish community leaders had not diligently preserved the lists of their members. The fact that baptized and intermarried Jews were arrested with bona fide members of Jewish communities (congregations and related organizations) goes a long way to prove the conjectural character of that assertion.
3. Bruno Bettelheim, "Individual and Mass Behavior in Extreme Situations," *Journal of Abnormal and Social Psychology*, 38, (1948): 417–52.
4. Primo Levi, *If This Is a Man*, Stuart Woolf, trans. (New York: 1959).

Part III

Profiles in Jewish Courage and Vision

9

Scholar and Visionary:
The Correspondence between
Theodor Herzl and Ludwig Gumplowicz

I

As is well known, Theodor Herzl, in the eight years between the conception of his rousing paper "The Jewish State" and his death, was indefatigably trying to interest the high and the mighty of this earth for the Zionist cause. But as an intellectual of far-flung pretensions, he was equally eager to attract the attention of leaders in the field of thought. Deeply convinced as he was of the ultimate validity of the idea of the Jewish state, nevertheless, as the true child of a science-pious generation, he craved the approval of men of academic and literary distinction. But the scholar and visionary are not likely to speak the same language. It is in the light of this thought that the brief encounter by correspondence between Herzl and Professor Ludwig Gumplowicz ought to be evaluated.

An analysis of the life and thought of Ludwig Gumplowicz is very much worthwhile. One of the most notable of the Jewish contemporaries of Herzl, he takes his place in the galaxy of unforgettable characters that added to the fascination of the last decades of the Habsburg monarchy. He was an author of world-wide fame in the fields of political science and sociological theory; his influence on American and European sociology is increasingly recognized. Born in Crakow on 3 March 1938 as the son of Abraham Gumplowicz, a prominent businessman and president of the Jewish community, and Henryka Inlender of Brody, he came from the background of the higher Jewish bourgeoisie in Galicia, and as such was placed in the midst of the bitter nationality struggle of his time.[1] While the poverty-striken Jewish masses remained true to the Yiddish language and the internal rule by Hassidic Rebbes, a thin but influential upper crust, especially in Brody and Lemberg (Lvov), adhered to the idea of German enlightenment. Moreover, Krakow,

which was annexed to Austria only in 1846, was a seedbed of Polish nationalism, and young Gumplowicz, who had studied law and economics there and
in Vienna (1858–61), belonged among those Jewish intellectuals who ardently
advocated the fusion of the historically antagonistic social groups of gentry,
peasantry, and Jews into a new Polish nationality. He was drawn into the
excitement around the Polish rebellion against Russia in the early 1860s. In
his "Eight Letters from Vienna," written about that time, he condemned
"artificial, multilingual, dynastic states," such as the Habsburg and Ro-
manoff empires, and advocated unified national states and their voluntary
association in larger entities instead.[2] The sociological theories which Gumplowicz developed more fully later are already indicated here, and their basis in
actual life experiences stands revealed.

From this period, when the hopes for Polish-Jewish fraternization were
raised high, we have a letter written by Gumplowicz which illuminates the
state of his Jewish consciousness like a flash of lightning in a dark night. It
is addressed to Philipp Mansch of Lemberg, a fellow law student and one of
the earliest proponents of Jewish nationalism in Galicia.[3] In Lemberg, where
the large Jewish population lived dangerously on the borderline between Poles
and Ruthenians (Ukrainians), the idea caught on first among Jewish youth that
the most natural, as well as the most dignified, response to the challenge of
the situation would be to identify themselves neither with German centralists
nor with Polish nationalists (and certainly not with Ruthenian peasants), but
to declare themselves of Jewish nationality and to defend their rights under
their own flag. Philipp Mansch, who later became a president of the Lemberg
kehillah, a founder of the society Shomer Israel and an editor of the weekly
Der Israelit, was one of the leaders of this group. His own letter to Gumplowicz has not been preserved, but Gumplowicz's reply makes the nature of the
controversy explicit.[4]

Krakow, 12 November 1861

Dear Friend:

Your letter of Sept. 1 of this year is still before me, unanswered. Reason: much
work—I had to undergo the *examen rigorosum*. A propos! Recently I learned—
you didn't write about it!—that you are already Doctor Juris—belated but
heartfelt congratulations!

To come to the point—rather, to return to the cause: perhaps a sense of defeat—
because, to put it bluntly—your last letter ["Jews are a nationality"] has given
me a bit of a jolt. You are right—we are, sorry to say, still a nationality! But,
in admitting this, shall I take back what I have said about Jews in Poland—no!
Because, where is the cause of my mistakes—and your victory? In that you,
speaking about Jews, look backwards—into the past—while I look into the
future. And regrettably we are still stuck in the past and the future rides slowly
and tarries a damned long time. Yes! You have hit the nail on the head. *Civil
marriage*! My reply: that is supposed to be part of our striving—that has to

come. You have read the motion of the Commission for Religion—decided by Smolka. You are finding that "religion is no obstacle to matrimony!" Dear Friend! *That* future which knocks already at the doors of the Austrian Parliament cannot be far off—and, I hope, you are not less of a freethinker than Smolka?

Give me your word that we shall marry the most beautiful Christian girls—alias *shikses*—in case that motion becomes law! I am joking and yet the matter is no joke. The day is not far where even this last wall of separation is *bound* to fall—and we are compelled to take leave from this shadow of our nationality which is long decayed but which for centuries keeps creeping after us like a vampire, sucks our blood and destroys our vitality. It's from this vampire that we have to take leave and then we shall say: "Sehe jeder wie er's treibe, sehe jeder wo er bleibe—und wer steht, dass er nicht falle!"

Then the parole will be—*Anschluss* [merger] with those nationalities among whom *one lives*—that this be made possible, I demand—and here is my program:

1. *Acceptance* of the language of the *people* among whom *one* lives and (this you have already conceded in one of your letters)

2. A political behavior which doesn't push us into stark opposition and enmity to the people among whom we have to live—to the contrary—a behavior which brings us sympathy.

Maybe I have used the word "political" in a bad sense here—I would like to have it understood in the sense of *wise* behavior: with "Emigration and Paris," as you say, I am far from sympathizing—and I don't ask that any Polish Jew—generally, I don't ask for political machinations—I have no idea of political independence and I am convinced that we are safer under Austria— perhaps. But I demand that one doesn't oppose oneself to the Poles as a German element, that is, as a clearly hostile faction, because it isn't clever—and because it destroys the hope for unity *in the future*. Rather, we ought to attempt to make good what a sad past has frustrated—by *bringing together what has been separated* in the past! If we accept the Polish language, then the lifting up of a generation of Poles must be near to our heart as *our own* cause, and justice for the Polish people must be near to our heart as the people with whom our descendants shall dwell together peaceably, and the moral uplift and civilization of the Polish *people* must interest us as much as those of our own coreligionists.

This is my program—the two most important points—and I believe we will in the end agree on it—and if that should be the case, I have already a plan for the future, e.g. an association, etc. But about this some other time—I am sure I shall make a trip to Galicia shortly—then we shall see each other and talk about all sorts of things.

Now, one more thing: In D. I read today: the Jewish students in Lemberg bring in a motion to the effect that the principle should be accepted that there should always be a Jew coopted to the Committee of the Ministry of Education—what nonsense! A *Jew* shall be elected? Shall the damned religious discrimination be introduced into the University? May Jewish students gain the respect of their colleagues—in that case they will be elected. How is it with us? Yesterday was a plenary meeting of the University, for the purpose of electing the chairman of the Welfare Association, and nobody even dreamt of accepting the principle that a Jew shall be elected—that would sound ridiculous here—and yet, without all this, a medical man, Blumenstock, Jew, got 250 votes and became with the majority the vice-president of the association! Last year, when I was in Vienna, the Polish students (60 of them) elected a deputation to go the Smolka—nobody dreamt of principles—and my Christian colleagues liked me in the deputation—but in Lemberg terrible things are happening at the University—and the Jews are to be blamed!

Did you make propaganda for Jutrzenka? What are you doing? What are you working on? And how are you—don't let me wait for a letter long. You don't need to enter *rigorosa*! You are lucky!

A propos! Eichbonack's writings were of no use to me—I did my *rigorosa* with Demelius. However, since to-date I still belong by descent and birth to the Jewish nationality—and the national speculative spirit has not left me in spite of the fact that I am polonizing myself—I have sent Zietonack's writings to Lemberg, in order to sell them there. I gave them to my friend Dr. Wagner, medical practitioner at the railroads in Lemberg. They are now with them. Perhaps you know buyers—I sell a *tout prix*—to be had at Dr. Wagner's.

Having finished my letter in a truly national way, I am merely adding my heartfelt greetings to you and remain your friend

L.G.

In this letter we have the liberal position of the mid-nineteenth century before us, classically expressed. Moreover, the workings of the Jewish mind are revealed not only, as the writer thought, in its "speculative" bent but in its eternal optimism, its ever-readiness to accept the hand-clasp of brotherliness. But the hopes that had been raised so high when the Polish people rose against their oppressors were soon to be shattered. In the wake of the revolutionary excitement, Ludwig Gumplowicz had attached himself to the circle around the "red" Prince Adam Sapieha and a group of the young literati who stood for a radically democratic nationalism, cultural progress, and free thought (The Young Poles). In 1869, the periodical *Kraj* (Land) was founded, with Ludwig Gumplowicz as a fiery editor; in 1870, the *Political Circle* (*Kolo Polityczne*) was created, to carry the fight against servility and apathy to the masses. But by 1874 the whole enterprise collapsed, as Prince Spaieha realized that the alliance of gentry, church, and monarchy was unbreakable. Our dreamer from the ghetto was left high and dry, cursing the "frankness that didn't care how strong the opponent was," and the indifference of the majority. "The manliest, the most pulsating years of life, the years of the freshest, the most vital thoughts and impulses, of the most powerful pathos and the most conquering eloquence—they were past and gone and nothing remained but a boat that had foundered a pen that was broken and an inkpot full of bitterness."[5] These were the young man's own words, as he left his native town, to which he never returned. On suggestion of his former teacher. Professor Ernst Demelius in Vienna, he applied for habilitation at the University of Graz, presenting a scholarly paper on "Race and State." He was accepted as Privatdozent in 1876 and appointed ordinarius for constitutional law in 1893.[6] He remained in Graz until his death in 1909.

In these decades, Ludwig Gumplowicz became a European celebrity, even without his ever leaving the provincial capital of Styria. The first edition of his *Rassenkampf* (Race Struggle) appeared in 1883, his *Grundriss der Soziologie* (Outline of Sociology) in 1885, his *Soziologische Staatsidee* (The Sociological Conception of the State) in 1892, and his *Allgemeines Staatsrecht* (General Constitutional Law) in 1897. Apart from these and lesser known works, he published numerous papers in scholarly and general periodicals. One of his articles, bearing the biting title "Der Rechtsstaat—Ein Nekrolog," which appeared in the same year as Herzl's *Judenstaat*, was widely commented upon and bitterly opposed by historians of law and constitutional lawyers in Germany and Austria, because it attacked the most cherished notions of the day, the rule of law as an independent entity and the paramount importance of the heroic individual in the historical process. Briefly put, in the frustrating Austrian environment and the turmoil of the nationality struggle, the former liberal idealist, the fighter for the resurrection of Poland and the fraternization of peoples, had been transformed into a sceptical observer of the social scene. It is not that he betrayed the dream of his youth and the love of liberty, but as one of his pupils, the Italian Franco Savorgnan, keenly observes, his attitude became ambivalent: as a scholar, he recognized that the iron laws of societal development overruled his wishes and the desires of individuals, but as a human being he hoped that the knowledge of these laws would enable the individual to regain once more the mastery of his fate.[7]

In Gumplowicz's opinion, all social and cultural evolution is the product of group conflict. He offered a polygenic hypothesis about the origins of mankind: In the dawn of human organization, he thought, numerous kinship groups existed in comparative independence, held together by blood ties and common interests. The progress of civilization meant that contacts between groups, and hence actual and potential situations of conflict, became more frequent. In the course of the struggles that followed, the powerful subdued the weak. At first, the defeated groups were exterminated, but later it was found more advantageous to enslave the conquered and to exploit them economically. Gumplowicz saw in this superimposition of one ethnic group upon another the cause of social stratification and the origin of the state.

At this point, the conflict situation takes on a twofold aspect. On the one hand, as states compete with other states for expansion, intergroup conflicts are widened into a clash of rival imperialisms; on the other hand, intragroup conflict, that is, the struggle of social classes, arises within national states. As a result, the class in power realizes that, to maintain its dominance, it must establish legal and political institutions. However, Gumplowicz concludes, a feeling of synergism, or consciousness of kind, exists only *within* groups, not *between* groups. It should be added that, in calling these groups "races," Gumplowicz refers to historical, not biological, entities.

Without attempting a thorough analysis of Gumplowicz's theoretical position, it can be seen that it entails a transposition of the Darwinian idea of the "struggle for existence" from the individual to the group, and that, in its emphasis on ever widening economic conflict situations, it has stong affinity to Marxist thought.[8] But a third element, namely the influence of the immediate environment, must not be overlooked.[9] The Habsburg monarchy was a multi-national state where the interests of those who supported the central government and of those who adhered to ethnic loyalties frequently pointed in opposite directions. Moreover, the nationality problem in Austria was a problem of social and political democracy inasmuch as the rise of the middle and laboring classes was identical with the rise of the submerged or, as they were often called, the "ahistorical" nationalities, meaning those which had no political history or whose political history had faded into the remote past. Thus, Germans and Magyars were considered paramount; Italians, Czechs, and Poles were judged to be capable of regaining their historical consciousness, with the Poles, however, confronted with the additional problem of overcoming their own internal cleavage first. But Ruthenians, Rumanians, Slovaks, Slovenes, Croats, and Serbs had to create their middle classes and their intellectual leadership entirely from scratch; among them, the emergence of the class struggle coincided with the rise of an ethnonational ideology.

With this interlockiing pattern of inter-cultural relations in mind, Gumplowicz demanded a federated Austria. He declared that political liberty and a policy of denationalization were mutually exclusive because the strength of a nationality rested with the masses of a people.[10] At this point, however, the objective scholar in Gumplowicz departs, and the Jew who feels ill-at-ease being a Jew comes to the fore. Logically, those Jews who considered themselves a nationality should have been permitted to do so and denationalization against their will should have been decried in their case as well as in other cases. Instead, Gumplowicz inserted the observation that the masses of a people that lays claim to national status must be rooted in their native soil and occupy a clearly defined territory. Under the circumstances, this was a *lex contra Judaeos*. The Jews, a historical people, found themselves deprived of any claim to historicity; their political independence, so they were told, was lost, and they had retained neither a common language nor a circumscribed area of settlement. Their stubbornly continued existence as a nationality was considered irritating, an anachronistic fossil, as Gumplowicz had already maintained in his letter to Philipp Mansch; in his *Rassenkampf*, he regretted expressly that they had not disappeared long ago.[11] It is worthy of note that on this point he agreed entirely with Otto Bauer, the eminent Marxist theoretician of the Austrian Social Democracy and likewise a Jew.[12]

II

In the issue of 9 December 1899 of Maximilian Harden's influential German weekly *Die Zukunft* appeared an article entitled "Soziologische Geschichtsauffassung" (The Sociological Interpretation of History) by Ludwig Gumplowicz. In this article, the famous author opposed both the "idolatry" of a heroic interpretation of history and the concept of historical materialism. He pointed out that states, or governments, arose out of the struggle of heterogeneous ethnic elements and that the unfolding of this struggle was the content of all history. He went on to say that the origin of political power and nationality, but also of the class struggle, from war and conquest rather than from peaceful contract, was now acknowledged by leading scholars, such as the psychologist Wilhelm Wundt, the sociologist Gustav Ratzenhofer, and the geographer Friedrich Ratzel. He quoted Ratzel for confirmation that even where the origin of a nation was coincidental with colonization and settlement rather than with the forcible occupation of a territory, the element of coercion and conflict was nevertheless present. He concluded:

> From the nowadays rarely contested fact of original polygenism, that is, the cohabitation of heterogeneous groups that are differently endowed by dint of differing environmental conditions, and from the further fact that each of these groups is imbued with a drive for self-preservation, we arrive at the inescapable conclusion that the clashes of stronger with weaker groups constitute the force which carries forward the evolutionary processes of mankind. From this fact of a universal polygenism and the variations among particular human groups . . . derives with necessity the stream of history, or rather, the great variety of streams of history in all habitable places about the globe: everywhere, human groups are drawn into this whirlpool, in accordance with one and the same social law. The name of the law: the strong are the masters.

In a second article under the same heading which appeared in the 16 December 1899 issue of *Die Zukunft*, the idea was further elaborated that at the core of a sociological interpretation of history lay the drive for self-preservation of human groups and the relentless competitive struggle between them. History, the author maintained, was not so much the end result of the heroic acts of individuals but of "group struggles," that is, of clashes of interest between tribes, nations, classes, parties, coteries, cliques, and so on. Sociologically conceived history, aiming at the exposition of natural societal laws, could therefore be written in an entirely "impersonal" vein. Such was the accomplishment of the scientific spirit of the age.

One of the readers of *Die Zukunft* was Theodor Herzl. He did not wait for the second article to appear. Immediately after he had read the first one, he sat down and, with the passionate impatience that was his part, penned the following letter to Gumplowicz:[13]

Wien-Waehering, 11 December 1899

Highly esteemed Herr Professor;

Your article in *Die Zukunft* of this week has aroused in me all sorts of thoughts and among them the desire to know your views about Zionism. I assume you have heard about this mad movement. I shall have a few publications sent to you; my own brochures and the stenographic protocols of the Third Basle Congress. It is a source of considerable amusement to me that universities and other serious circles do not seem to have observed or comprehended this movement up to now. A pretty detail: In my first pamphlet about a Jewish State, with which publication the Zionist movement, now worldwide in scope, began, I devoted a chapter to the legal foundation of government. In the place of the miserably opportunistic theory of *Naturnotwendigkeit*—not to talk any more about the *contrat social*—I put the theory of *negotiorum gestio* which, I believe, can stand up to your sociological interpretation. This theory, which at the very least could be made the object of scholarly discussion, has not been deemed worthy of so much as a glance by any one up to this moment. Obviously, I am not employing the proper scientific jargon. Kindly read the things that I am forwarding to you, if you can spare some time to observe a movement which doesn't belong to history yet, but quite probably will.

With the expression of high esteem, yours devotedly,

Th. Herzl

Obviously, this tersely styled letter attempts to arouse Gumplowicz's professional interest in Zionism; but it is hard to agree with Paul J. Diamant that the letter should be considered "a psychological masterpiece."[14] Particularly, it is not clear why Herzl stresses the theory of *negotiorum gestio*, which is juridical rather than sociological in nature. In "The Jewish State," Herzl describes this theory as follows:[15]

The marvellous legal sense of the Romans has created in the *negotiorum gestio* a noble master-piece. If a property whose owner is prevented from taking care of it is endangered, everybody can intervene to save it. This is the *gestor*. . . . The state is the product of a people's struggle for existence. In this struggle it is often impossible to produce a legal title by means of the usual cumbersome procedures. Indeed, any enterprise aiming at the common good would be condemned to failure, if one had to wait for a regular majority decision. . . . What does all this mean in our case? The Jewish people in the diaspora are prevented from taking care of their political interests and yet they are threatened in many ways.

Herzl concludes that the Jewish people need a *gestor* and that this *gestor* should not be an individual person but the legal instrument which he had devised for this purpose, namely, the Society of Jews. The theory of *nego-tiorum gestio*, even if transposed from private law to public law, contains at best a justification for the exercise of power but does not explain how power originates and how it is maintained. Sociologically speaking, Herzl would have been on firmer ground if he had referred to the introduction of "The Jewish State" where both antisemitism and the Jewish reaction to it are derived from the drive for self-preservation. In vain, so ran the argument there, do Jews try to be good patriots in the countries in which they live; who is the stranger in the land is "a question of power, like everything in the community of nations." It was decided by "the majority." This line of approach would have been difficult to assail from the point of view of Gumplo-wicz's theory; it would have touched the core of the professor's personal equation.

The reply to Herzl's letter was prompt and sharp.[16]

Graz, 12 December 1899

Very esteemed Herr Doctor:

You are mistaken in believing that I do not know your Congress speeches and your writings (also those of Dr. Nordau!)—I have read them *all* and I have them here. *Read*—with a great deal of *self-restraint* because I was very mad about *both of you*—repeatedly, in a rage, I threw these writings under the table—only to read on most attentively—and with increasing rage. I could well *condemn* you both, if I were not a determinist and therefore unable to condemn a crim-inal. I am an old penal lawyer and as such I would enter a warm *plaidoyer* even for you and Nordau: because I understand your motivation. I understand the *natural necessity* for this sad, senseless movement—and last but not least—I believe that the movement, all the nonsense that is in it notwithstanding, will bring about something good, namely a self-examination of the Jewish people and an initiation of moral regeneration.

You ask, why then did I sit still and why did I not stand up *against* Zionism? Because it would be in vain—because Zionism is much *too natural* a phenom-enon, but in spite of all that—a miscarriage of a movement! (There are many miscarriages of movements, currents that finally do bring about something good. They don't reach the *proclaimed* goal, but they force into being some respectable *byproducts*, things that nobody had thought about. Socialism, too, is such a movement.) By the way, what do I need standing up against Zionism, when I have developed for 25 years and in numerous writings a *theory funda-mentally refuting* it!

Your theoretical, historically-*meant* foundations of Zionism are all *wrong*! You Zionists are caught in a terrible historical misconception and you are endowed with a *political naiveté*, such as one can pardon only *poets*. You don't know that the Jews have been guilty twice of great historically wrong pronunciamento's— once, when they announced in Palestine that they came directly from Egypt and the second time, when they announced in eastern Europe that they came directly from Palestine! *Both* statements are wrong! Just as wrong as that our "Aryans" come from India! As one concludes here wrongly from language the descent, so one concludes there wrongly from *religion* to descent.

In the literary documents left by my son Max, I find a treatise about the "Origins of the Jewish *Religion* in Poland" which I hesitate to publish, lest I provide the antisemites with a couple of new cusswords — but which confirms the truth as to who these millions of Polish and Russian Jews really are! In *Palestine* were their ancestors as little as the Palestinians in Egypt!

This is your *historical* foundation! And now your *political naïveté*! You want to create a state without bloodshed? Where have you ever seen such a thing? Without force and without cunning? So very openly and honestly — on shares?

Go and write poems and feuilletons, you and your Nordau — but leave me alone with your politics! Or do you count on gondola-Willy [Wilhelm II, German Emperor] and Abdul-Hamed [Turkish Sultan]? You believe that these two fat meatclumps are capable of creating a state for the Jews — even if they were not "achbroishim" (rats) that they are! My dear Herr Doctor! Pardon my *damned* frankness, but these are my *opinions* on the matter. Since I don't think I'm infallible, *I don't talk anyone* out of Zionism who adheres to it. To me come enthusiastic Zionists and ask my advice (e.g. Dr. Moses Schorr of Lemberg). I told him I don't share these views, but I don't make anti-Zionist propaganda, — I don't take anyone away from it!

I don't know what good purpose this *nonsense* may eventually serve that has come about with such *natural necessity*. Since I don't know it, I remain remote and passive. I feel pity for this movement, just as I feel pity for a poor, sick man who writhes in pain and *whom I cannot help!*

With kindest regards, yours most devotedly,

Gumplowicz

This letter, the loose language to which it occasionally stoops notwithstanding, is a remarkable document. It reveals that Ludwig Gumplowicz was indeed more deeply touched by Zionism than he liked to admit. Why, one may ask, was he "mad" at the Zionist argument? A comparison with the letter to Philipp Mansch will provide the clue. There, he considered Judaism "still" a nationality, and the "still" indicated that he looked upon it as a fossilized remnant of the past. Now, he was compelled to look at Judaism as "again" a nationality, a vital part of the general movement of nationalities, a thing of the future. In his *Rassenkampf* he had said that the Jews "in their unnatural stubbornness preferred to keep alive an eternal race struggle against themselves rather than sacrifice their outlived and mummified nationality to the rejuvenated and vital culture of other countries and ages."[17] Now, he must have felt that Zionism's plea for a rejuvenated Jewish nationality was either a terrible historical mistake or else a deadly challenge. Or could it have been both? As a sociologist, Gumplowicz could hardly have failed to recognize the "natural necessity," as he called it, of the Zionist movement as an expression of the drive for self-preservation of an embattled group, as the antibody, as it were, to the virus of antisemitism; he even admitted that it may serve the purpose of "moral regeneration." As a reaction to antisemitism, then, Zionism appeared only "too natural," and yet it spelled "nonsense," because the Jewish people, not being rooted in their native soil and not occupying a clearly definable territory, could not meaningfully strive for political independence. The idea of a Jewish state, so Gumplowicz persuaded himself, was still running counter to the mainstream of history; but the undercurrent of anxiety in his persuasion is unmistakable.

Indeed, Gumplowicz is not all sure of his ground. After having thundered away at Herzl's "madness," he emphasizes that he does not look upon himself as infallible and that he does not wish to be considered an anti-Zionist.[18] Why? The reason is that, on the basis of his own theoretical premises, he could not deny that there was a chance for the ultimate success of the movement for Jewish statehood, if and when the stage was set for the application of superior force. To be sure, he did not believe that the chance was real, and he poked fun at the idea that the German emperor or, for that matter, any of the great powers, would exert themselves on behalf of the Jews; and a Jewish army was a laughing matter in those days. Gumplowicz's attack on the utopian, the pacifist, the universal dreamer in Herzl, his bitter mockery of "the state without bloodshed," which he believed was conjured up in the writings of Herzl and Nordau, must be understood in the light of his contention that states and nations are conceived in conflict. He surely had a point there. Considering the events of 1948 and 1956, are we not compelled to admit that he was quite right, even if we may be inclined to add that he was unfortunately right? The interpretation which has been offered, that his was "a shrieking voice from the camp of the opponents of Herzl and the enemies of Zion," must be rescinded.[19] If Ludwig Gumplowicz had lived to witness the events of our days, he would have been like Balaam who went out to curse and found himself a blessing. He would have admitted that if the improbable came true, and if the desperation of a people that found itself dragged to the edge of the abyss became a force of overwhelming momentum, the Jewish state, the mockery of the centuries, was bound to be rasied to the light of day.

Nevertheless, the triumph of the visionary who takes the future on faith is more profound than the grudging admission of the scholar. Theodor Herzl has written a postscript to his encounter with Ludwig Gumplowicz, which we must mention before we bring these deliberations to a close because it reveals the prophetic luminosity of his mind. In an article in *Die Welt*, called "Unterwegs" (On the Way), which was written one year after his lively exchange with the renowned sociologist, he could not help noting that "if professors at the universities were not such terribly absent-minded people who always leave their umbrellas somewhere in gray antiquity, they really should be most attentive to the problem as to whether our contemporary doings have been wisely or foolishly enacted. Even our mistakes might be utilized for drawing a lesson. But the *Herren Professoren*, who don't comprehend a thing when it's being born, arrive at the scene much later; after the event, of course, they know everything better than we do and they explain to us precisely how matters have come to pass."[20] He went on to reminisce on his experience aboard ship to Palestine and to say that the day will surely come when the floating caravan of Zion will reach its goal. The people who were on the first boat—he observed their devotion and their spirit of sacrifice—will then offer the best guarantees for the future of the Jewish state. "But once the beachhead is secured, there will be many ships to follow."

1958

Notes

1. Bernhard Zebrowski, *Ludwig Gumplowicz—Eine Bio-Bibliographie* (Bio-Bographische Beitrage zur Geschichte der Rechts- und Staatswissenschaften, Heft 7; Berlin, 1926).
2. *Os'm Listow z Wiednia* (Krakow, 1866); quoted by Zebrowski.
3. The letter, written in German, is in the collection of Abraham Sharon (Schwadron), now at the Hebrew University in Jerusalem.
4. Italicized passages indicate underlining in the original letter.
5. See Zebrowski, note 2. (Summary from Z's book).
6. The original designation of Gumplowicz's academic position was *"Dozent für Verwaltungswissenschaften und Verwaltungsrecht."*
7. Ludwig Gumplowicz, *Ausgewählte Werke*, edited by Prof. Franz Oppenheimer (Frankfurt), Prof. F. Savorgnan (Rome) und Prof. M. Adler (Wien) vonProf. G. Salomon (Frankfurt), Innsbruck, 1926, vol. IV, Foreword by Franco Savorgnan.
8. The most penetrating analysis of Gumplowicz's thought is contained in G. Salomon's introduction to Ludwig Gumplowicz, ibid., vol. I. of *Ausgewählte Werke*.
9. Gumplowicz himself was aware of this point and emphasized it. Compare: ibid., vol. I, p. 433.
10. Ludwig Gumplowicz, *Der Rassenkampf—Soziologische Untersuchungen* (Innsbruck, 1883), p. 323.
11. The following statements, originally published in an article by Gumplowicz which appeared in the *Politisch-Anthropologische Revue*, are quoted here from a report about this article in *Jüdisches Volkblatt*, Wien (31 March 1905). Interestingly, Gumplowicz's ideas are quoted in this periodical in support of the position of Jewish nationalists and autonomists in Austria.
12. Otto Bauer, "Die Nationalitätenfrage und die Sozialdemokratie," in *Marx Studien*, vol. 2, Max Adler und Rudolf Hilferding editors (Wien, 1924), pp. 361–81
13. The original German version of Herzl's letter to Gumplowicz, as well as excerpts from Gumplowicz's article in *Die Zukunft*, were published by Moses Schorr in *Fetschrift zu Simon Dubnow's Siebzigstem Geburtstag*, edited by Ismar Elbogen, Josef Meisl, Mark Wischnitzer (Berlin, 1930), pp. 262–65. Moses Schorr, later chief rabbi of Warsaw, was a pupil of Ludwig Gumplowicz and had received the original of Herzl's letter directly from his teacher.
14. Paul J. Diamant, *Theodor Herzl als Staatsrechtstheoretiker* (mimeo). Unpublished—mimeographed copy.
15. Theodor Herzl, *Der Judenstaat* (Wien, 1896), pp. 67–70.

16. Ludwig Gumplowicz's reply to Herzl, the German original of which is in the Zionist Archives in Jerusalem, has never been published. It has been circulated in mimeographed form, however, in Paul J. Diamant, op. cit. In the present rendering, underlined passages are retained from the original. I am using this opportunity to express my thanks to Alex Bein and Paul Alsberg of the Zionist Archives as well as to Paul J. Diamant for giving me access to this important document.
17. Ludwig Gumplowicz, *Der Rassenkampf*, p. 334.
18. It should be noted here that one of Gumplowicz's most renowned pupils, the sociologist Franz Oppenheimer, was among the earliest adherents of Herzl in Germany. The similarities and dissimilarities between the theoretical positions of teacher and pupil cannot be pointed out here. See Franz Oppenheimer, *Der Staat* (Frankfurt am Main, 1919).
19. Diamant.
20. (H.), "Unterwegs" in: *Die Welt*, vol. 4, No. 1, (Jan. 5, 1900).

10

The Life of Clementine Kraemer

Clementine Kraemer was my father's only sister, and her marriage to a brother of my maternal grandmother, the banker Max Kraemer, made her doubly related to her nephews and nieces. In addition, the facts that her marriage was childless and that my father adored her and followed her advice whenever he could made her feel motherly towards me and my five brothers and sisters, and her influence on our upbringing was considerable. But Tante Clem, as we called her, was also a public figure. She was among the initiators of Jewish social work, as well as of general welfare activities in Munich, a friend of many interesting people, and a successful author of short stories and children's books. I think her life and work is worthy of recording.

My recollection of Tante Clem is vivid, but I was fortunate enough, in preparing the following account, to have the assistance of her best friend, Erna Rheinstrom-Feuchtwanger, the widow of the late, unforgettable Dr. Ludwig Feuchtwanger—manager of the publishing house of Duncker & Humblot and editor of the *Bayerische Israelitische Gemeindezeitung*—and a sister of the well-known expert in commercial and financial law, Professor Heinrich Rheinstrom. Erna Feuchtwanger lives in Winchester, England, but on the occasion of her visit to her brother in New York in 1959, I compared notes with her, and I must say that the exchange was rather one-sided and that I came out the richer for it. Furthermore, while I am writing these lines, I have beside me what appears to be Clementine Sophie Kraemer's entire literary production, stories and articles from newspapers and periodicals, books, unpublished manuscripts, even reviews. They were diligently preserved by my father and came to this country in my parents' luggage.[1]

Clementine Sophie Kraemer, née Cahnmann, was born in 1873 in Rheinbischofsheim, Baden, as the second child of Gustav Cahnmann (originally: Kahnmann) and Auguste, née Levi, of Mühringen in Württemberg. When the little girl was about seven years old and her brother Sigwart eight, her parents moved to Karlsruhe, where my grandfather opened a dry goods store on the

Kaiser Strasse, which used to be the main thoroughfare and business street of the town, the capital of the Grand Duchy of Baden. Tante Clem went to school and lived there until her marriage in 1891, but she, as well as her older brother, our father, spent all her vacations either in Rheinbischofsheim or in Mühringen with paternal or maternal grandparents and other relatives. Hence, it may be said that her childhood was spent in rural surroundings and that the people she knew best were the Jewish traders and peddlers of the southwest German villages and the peasants among whom they gained their livelihood.

Tante Clem has sketched a few episodes of this world, which is now gone forever, in a sequence of five stories called "Erinnerungen" (*Jüdisch-Liberale Zeitung*, 1924), one of which, entitled "Der Grossvater und der Hofbauer," had already been published separately a few years earlier (*Ethische Kultur*, 1915). Reminiscences and flashbacks also occur elsewhere, especially in "Der Weg des jungen Hermann Kahn" (*Allgemeine Zeitung des Judentums*, 1918), in a burlesque anecdote, "Das Kofferle," and in an unpublished story, "Esther."[2] Life with both grandparents is described as simple, full of fun, and affectionate. Above all, on Friday evenings in Rheinbischofsheim, says a passage in "Erinnerungen," "when one sits at the table, praises the Lord, who has made wine and bread grow for us, eats noodle soup, fish and boiled beef in a parsley sauce; and grandfather tells stories about the world outside and has grandmother tell him about all that had happened at home while he was away during the week—one imagines one is in high heaven . . ."

But there are shadows as well as lights. Tante Clem's "Erinnerungen" also call to mind the figures of the sick and the poor, of beggars, village idiots and sex fiends, and the message of sympathy with those who are marked by fate and of helpfulness for those who are afflicted with illness and poverty is unmistakable. The grandparents, especially those in Rheinbischofsheim, who lived among a more outgoing population and consequently were more outgoing themselves, are shown as the friends of everybody in the village, especially of the needy and the despised. The contrast to the thoughtless treatment meted out to unfortunates by the majority of villagers, Jews and Gentiles alike, is driven home. Even business relations would seem to have retained a human touch. The story of the delegation of peasants from a neighboring village, who visited old Moses Kahnmann on the occasion of his seventieth birthday to offer him a free plot in the cemetery because he had always been "such an exceptionally Christian Jew," is charmingly told. And it is said in addition that, contrary to the peasants, the Jews did not cherish the thought of death.

In many respects, the two villages and the two grandparental families were quite different. Rheinbischofsheim is a large, sprawling place, situated in the most fertile plain in southern Germany, which stretches from Mainz down to

Basle in Switzerland. The rich soil bears an abundant harvest of grain, vegetables and tobacco. At half an hour's distance from the village flows the broad Rhine, marking the frontier between Baden and Alsace and, on clear days, one can see from a rooftop the tower of the famous Münster in Strassburg on the glimmering horizon. Indeed, part of the Cahnmann family had come from Alsace; some cousins lived there. Mühringen is narrowly built on a stony hillside in the Württemberg Black Forest, and the place is dominated by the castle of the Barons von Münch, but the surrounding country shows greater variety than the level country along the Rhine, with silvery brooks and green meadows and darkly wooded hillsides. Accordingly, the Cahnmann family was rustic, emotional, given to practical jokes and sudden fits of temper, and fond of eating, drinking, and making merry, while people in the Levi family were temperamentally more steady and economically more thrifty, of a kindly disposition, sensitive and reflective.

Grandfather Cahnmann (Tante Clem's father) was successful in his business, which he had started on a shoestring. He was always in action, restless, even to the point of impatience, but friendly and sociable in his private life. I remember him playing the mouth organ and reciting from the *Alemannische Gedichte* by Johann Peter Hebel. Grandmother Cahnmann, more equiliberated and refined in temper and manners than her husband, had a sunny disposition, a reflective mind, and a good literary taste. Both, with only an elementary school education, impressed people with their sincerity, their good humor, their open minds, and their readiness to help. They worked hard and never went on vacation until my grandfather retired from business. They associated with persons above their station and climbed the social ladder rapidly. A bit of this social-climber spirit stuck with Tante Clem all her life.

When Tante Clem, as a young married woman, came to Munich (about 1891), the scene changed radically. Her-parents-in-law, Bernhard Kraemer and Regina (née Marx), were very wealthy people but quite clannish. Bernhard Kraemer, son of the Parnas of Ichenhausen, in the Bavarian district of Schwaben, had moved to Munich as early as 1860 and had made a considerable fortune in real estate. His wife came from a family of respectable merchants and court Jews, was proud of her *yichus*, and had a domineering character. Bernhard Kraemer was by far the most successful man in his family, but the Marx family were all of them well-to-do people, of intellectual inclinations, individualistic in attitude, and at times rather overbearing. Uncle Max Kraemer, Tante Clem's husband, who had learned banking in London, partook of these traits. He was highly intelligent, loftily idealistic, contemptuous of philistines, a mathematical genius, widely read in the philosophical literature from Plato to Nietzsche, but without a sense of reality. As a businessman he was a failure. His younger sister, Sophie, had married a younger brother of my maternal grandmother, Louis Levi, who had become his partner in the banking business. His older sister, Johanna, was already widowed when Tante Clem joined the family circle in Munich. Her husband, Jakob Schülein, had passed away a few years earlier, but her husband's family was very much in evidence. The Schüleins had come to Munich as poor, orphaned country boys, had started in the real estate business and small-scale banking, but had then taken over a bankrupt brewery and gone into the brewery business themselves. Thanks to the commercial acumen and the forceful personality of Uncle Joseph Schülein, the Unionsbrauerei, as the enterprise was called, grew from a modest start to be the second largest brewery in Bavaria until it was merged with the largest enterprise in the brewery industry, the Löwenbrauerei, in 1921. The name Schülein became a household word in Munich, but in the 1890s this was still far afield. In those days, the Marx family looked down on the Schülein family. I mention all this chiefly because Hedwig, the daughter of Johanna Schülein, née Kraemer, was to become my father's bride and beloved wife and the mother of six healthy Cahnmann children. Her older brother, Julius Wolfgang, in the 1890s the "miracle boy" of the family, afterwards a student of law, finally became a landscape artist. At eighty, he is still keenly alive to all intellectual problems and painting as vigorously and beautifully as ever.[3]

The city of Munich in the 1890s and the early 1900s was a far cry from Karlsruhe. The latter, fanning from the grand ducal palace, was a quiet residential town, but Munich was second in rank only to Berlin in Bismarck's new German Reich. Munich had no ambition to contest Berlin's position as a political and financial centre, but it was a focal point of cultural stimulation and in this respect in every way Berlin's counterpart. Berlin was simultaneously stiffly militaristic and intellectually alert, narrowly class-ridden and ambitiously progressive, but Munich was politically conservative and socially democratic, moving at a leisurely pace, yet agitated by all the cross-currents of the period. The lower classes were the children of peasants, refreshingly unsophisticated, and good Catholics, even if they voted Social Democratic candidates at election time. Upon this background, liberals and clericals, symbolists and naturalists, Wagnerians and anti-Wagnerians, even the adherents of one or the other would-be artistic genius formed informal conventicles. There was the university, one of the foremost academic institutions in Germany, and splendid art collections and exhibitions of European significance. The city was pleasing, even beautiful: a medieval core overgrown with baroque additions, expanding into broad, neo-classical avenues, the gift of the munificence of the Wittelsbach kings. The class structure was acknowledged and overlooked at the same time. Everybody mingled with everybody else in the *Bierkellers* and at carnival time in the world-famous and carefree Munich *Fasching*.[4]

The Jewish community was less homogeneous than the Jewish communities of Karlsruhe, Stuttgart, Nuremberg, and other cities in south Germany. As the study of Professor Arthur Cohen—as well as a minor one, written by myself—has shown, the Munich Jewish community had originated as a settlement of privileged court Jews;[5] the right to found a family remained rigidly restricted until 1861. From then on, the sons of village and small-town Jews from the Swabian and Franconian districts of Bavaria had moved in, followed by migrants from farther-away places in Württemberg, Baden, the Rhine Palatinate, and Silesia. In the 1870s and 1880s, radical reformers created dissension in the community, while at the same time the rumblings of popular antisemitism were heard, represented, among others, by Dr. Leopold Sigl's biting paper, *Das Bayerische Vaterland*. But in 1887, the magnificent *Hauptsynagogue* was dedicated, a building worthy of the city's skyline and a symbol of the respectability of the top-hatted worshippers.[6] Theodor Herzl's stillborn attempt to call the First Zionist Congress to Munich caused no more than a ripple.[7]

There remained two strange elements in the picture. One was a group of baptized or otherwise estranged Jews, small in number but socially prominent. Some of them were academic and artistic leaders of the greatest impact on the cultural life of the city, such as the literary historian Michael Bernays— son of the famous Haham Bernays of Hamburg—who made Goethe the centre of an esoteric cult, and the conductors Hermann Levi and Felix Mottl, who elevated Richard Wagner to a high pedestal around which frantic admirers gathered.[8] Some of these found their way into Tante Clem's social circle. I remember from later years the author Richard Riess, a north-German Jew who had married a Catholic Munich girl, for years Tante Clem's literary mentor, and Professor Paul Joachimsen, another north-German Jew, an incisive historical analyst and a thoroughly baptised fundamentalist Lutheran. But there was another element, more numerous and in many ways more foreign. In the 1890s, Jews from Galicia, Rumania, and Russia began to trickle into the city. Some of them were intellectuals who mingled easily with other intellectuals, but the majority started at the bottom of the social ladder, as miserable "old clo'es Jews," tailors, egg dealers, peddlers, fur and tobacco workers, and outright *Schnorrers*. The trickle became a minor flood in 1904–05, after the pogroms in Kischinev. Here was a new problem of Jewish, as well as of humanitarian, impact, which had to be met.

I do not want to be accused of the "organistic fallacy," so ill-reputed among sociologists, but I believe that as a healthy human body forms antibodies to cope with the onrush of illness, so does a healthy society in the face of challenge. In the case of the Jewish community of Munich, the antibody against assimilation and divisiveness was the München Loge UOBB, an offshoot of the B'nai B'rith movement which had orignated in the United States of America. The München Loge had been founded in 1897 by a handful of courageous men who braved the stigma of "Ghettoizers." This emphasized what Jews have in common and intended thereby to bridge the gap between the liberal and orthodox wings of Judaism. Most of the members were men who had migrated to the city from small towns and country places; the indigenous Munich Jewish haute volée, apart from the Orthodox Fraenkel and Feuchtwanger families, remained aloof. I do not know whether Uncle Louis Levi was a founder member, but I do know that my grandfather and father, Gustav and Sigwart Cahnmann, were interested in the movement from the start and that they joined the lodge formally when they definitely moved to Munich in 1901.[9] My grandfather's son-in-law, uncle Max Kraemer, joined likewise, although, at the same time, he was an ardent adherent of the, Gesellschaft für Ethische Kultur.

My father served on many committees of the München Loge until he became vice president and, for two consecutive terms, president in the 1920s. He told me repeatedly in later years that the Kischinev pogroms had stirred him deeply and that he took time off from his business to undertake a speaking tour through some of the south German lodges to further the drive for funds which were designed to assist the victims and integrate them into the existing Jewish communities.[10] I also know that my grandfather in these years was the chairman of the lodge's welfare committee and that he had his whole heart in the work. I had a belated inkling of this when I visited Palestine in 1936. I had been told that, when coming to Haifa, I could get overnight accommodations in the boarding house of a woman who formerly had run the Restaurant Weiss in Munich. Upon entering the house, she hugged me enthusiastically, exclaiming that the Cahnmann family was bringing her luck. I could not understand what she had in mind until she explained that I was her first guest in the restaurant which she was about to establish in the boardinghouse, as my grandfather had been her first guest when she opened her little eating place in Munich. To this I replied that grandfather had not stepped into the situation unintentionally, as I had. In his official function, as it were, he had granted the woman the loan which enabled her to start her little enterprise, and he saw to it that he was there in person when the doors opened for the first time.

Why do I tell all this? Because grandfather and his friends in the München Loge helped Tante Clem and her friends to establish the Israelitische Jugendhilfe, the first agency for Jewish social work in Munich.[11] As Elizabeth Kitzinger tells in her article "*Jüdische Jugendfürsorge in München, 1904–1943*" (in: Hans Lamm, *Von Juden in München*, Munich, 1959, pp. 75–79), a great many needy Jewish children had come to Munich in the wake of the Russian pogroms. Two young girls, Elizabeth and Luise Merzbacher, began to take care of some of these children, first in their own apartment, then in rented rooms. In March of 1905, the München Loge became the main source of finance. School children whose parents could not supervise them, were taken care of in the afternoons. In the evenings, the rooms were occupied by a girl's club (*Mädchen Klub*), where working girls found recreation and the opportunity to learn new skills. The ladies who took charge of the institution were Ida Kohnstamm-Blumenstein (married to Dr. Carl Blumenstein, likewise a member of the München Loge), Hedwig Jacobi, Marta Reutlinger, Erna Rheinstrom-Feuchtwanger, and Clementine Kraemer. The three first-named devoted themselves chiefly to the care of children, Erna Rheinstrom and Clementine Kraemer chiefly to the care of the working girls.

Elizabeth Kitzinger reports that the number of children cared for grew from 8 in 1904 to 150 in 1914, but no figures are available as far as the working girls are concerned. It must suffice to say that Erna Rheinstrom, who was exceedingly clever with her hands, took over sewing and tailoring lessons while Tante Clem offered courses in elementary German and literature. There were also discussions on problems of education and hygiene. Further initiated were social evenings, with speakers and musical performances, and *Mütter-abende*, where mothers could participate in their daughters' achievements. Some of these social evenings blended with the activities of the Toynbee Halle, which were likewise supported by the München Loge. The Kinderheim (children's home), growing steadily, hit the jackpot only in 1920, when a client of Professor Heinrich Rheinstrom, Baronesse Rosa Benedicta von Neuschotz, was prevailed upon to contribute 50,000M. This generous gift made possible the acquisition of the house Albani Strasse 9 in Munich. Also, a *Lehrlingsheim* (home for apprentices), a home and vocational school for adolescent boys, was among the institutions created by the Israelitische Jugendhilfe, and supported by the München Loge, and so were other institutions. The Jugendhilfe, as a separate institution, continued until 1929, when it was taken over by the official Kultusgemeinde.

Returning to the aspect of the work for which Erna Rheinstrom and Clementine Kraemer took responsibility, it ought to be said that they encountered difficulties which are nowadays not easy to imagine. Many of the girls—and even more so their parents—were very primitive. They came from little out-of-the-way places in"Half-Asia." They knew nothing about elementary rules of hygiene, such as the use of flush toilets or the undesirability of eating one's food with one's fingers. Some of them did not know how to clean a room or to make beds or to use a sewing needle. And it was Tante Clem's despair that they pronounced German the Yiddish way, saying, for instance, *daitsch* instead of *deutsch*. But they learned quickly and eagerly and exhibited their newly won knowledge with great pride in achievement. However, I must add that in my opinion Tante Clem failed to understand the background of these girls. It is true that the education of girls had been neglected among the Jews of eastern Europe until about the first decade of the twentieth century. But I am sure they were not as naive as they appeared to be to Tante Clem.

The story in which Tante Clem relates her experience with some of these girls is among her weakest. She calls the Yiddish language jargon and neglects to take any notice at all of Yiddish literature. From our present vantage point in the social psychology of interpersonal relations, we are inclined to maintain that it would have strengthened the self-respect of the girls if they had met with a fuller understanding of their cultural background. When all this is said, however, it must be acknowledged that the girls were grateful for the simple sympathy which they found. They knew that their personal problems were taken seriously.

Through Israelitische Jugendhilfe, Clementine Kraemer became aware of the work of the Jüdischer Frauenbund in Deutschland. She was among the founder members of that organization in Munich, remained through many years the chairman of the Munich branch, and was a member of the executive board of the head organization of the Jüdischer Frauenbund, which had its office in Berlin. She helped initiate branches all over Germany and addressed gatherings on numerous occasions. She participated in the projects of the Frauenbund and was especially interested in the Heim des Jüdischen Frauenbundes in Neu-Isenburg, near Frankfurt am Main, and in the special creation of the Munich branch, the Jüdische Haushaltsschule (Jewish School for Home Economics) in Wolfratshausen, near Munich.[12] But there was also an employment service, poor relief, a *mensa*, and courses of various kinds.[13]

In the family circle, we nicknamed the Frauenbund the *Reisebund* because of the frequent business meetings to which the members of the national board were summoned. No doubt a great deal of useful work was done at these meetings, but, in telling the life of Tante Clem, I believe that even more important were the personal contacts which she made there. She met such excellent women as Ernestine Eschelbacher, Henriette May, Ottilie Schoenewald, Hannah Karminski, and, above all, Bertha Pappenheim. Bertha Pappenheim's crusade against the "white slave trade," in which nefarious activity both the traders and the girl-victims were mainly Jews, concerned her greatly.[14] When Tante Clem spoke about Bertha Pappenheim, one had the impression that she referred to a saint. Bertha Pappenheim's *Gebete*—prayer poems of which she was the author—and a photograph of Joseph Oppenheim's superb sketch of this remarkable woman were found among Tante Clem's papers when they arrived in New York. Whoever looks at Oppenheim's sketch must admit that the other wordly beauty of that face is striking.

The closest personal friendship, however, developed between Tante Clem and Paula Ollendorff of Breslau. We all came to know Paula Ollendorff's son, Friedrich Ollendorff, one of the leading Jewish social workers in Germany and later in Israel, and her daughters, Helene, now in New York, and Lizzie, the youngest, who languished for many dreary months in a Munich hospital. Like Clementine Kraemer, Paula Ollendorff was a representative of "liberal

Judaism,'' but Friedrich Ollendorff was an active Zionist, even an adherent of *Mizrachi*. Zionism was discussed a great deal in the family. Father's best friend in Karlsruhe, Wilhelm Baehr, was a Herzlian Zionist *della prima ora* and a participant at the First Zionist Congress in Basle. One of the best friends of Kraemer and our parents, the unforgettable Dr. Eli Straus, initiator and organizer of communal social work in Munich, was the chairman of the Zionist local branch in the city. On my shelves is still the volume of Dr. Herzl's *Zionistische Schriften*, which I received from Eli and Rachel Straus as a bar mizvah present. There were other ardent Zionist among the best friends of the family, for instance, Paula Meyer of Berlin. But father, uncle Max, uncle Louis, cousin Heiner Wolf in Stuttgart, and others were members of the Centralverein and active in the Fortschrittliche Volkspartei (later: Deutsche Demokratische Partei) besides. We younger people received the impression that all these positions were possible—and entitled to a respectful hearing—if they were embraced with sincerity.

Clementine Kraemer has left her *Confessio Judaica* in a story entitled ''Der Weg des jungen Hermann Kahn,'' which appeared in a number of sequences in the *Allgemeine Zeitung des Judentums*, February-April 1918. It is more a swan song than a forecast of the horrors to come. The hero is cast very much in the likeness of Tante Clem's brother, our father. She also may have thought of her cousins Max Cahnmann, of Rheinbischofsheim, a doctor of medicine, and Julius Levi, of Stuttgart, both of whom were among the victims of the First World War. The story starts with the description of the hero's background in a southwest German village, a *mixtum compositum* of Rheinbischofsheim and Mühringen. For quite a while, the situations change back and forth between the warmth and good humor of a rural Jewish family circle and the varied experiences during school years in the city, where Hermann enters into friendly relations with Gentile boys and girls, among them a young lady of aristocratic birth, Marie Louise von der Uhlenburg. Yet, accidental remarks indicating the persistence of anti-Jewish prejudice are interspersed, and there is a lot of reflection, stimulated by happenings during subsequent student years in Heidelberg and Munich, and even on the occasion of the funeral of Hermann's father, about the human values of the Christian and the Jewish way of life. Various arguments for making Jewish-Gentile relations ''intelligible'' are mentioned: for instance, that human nature is the same everywhere; that Jews are always on the defensive; but a ''solution'' by means of baptism and voluntary disappearance is rejected. Hermann's widowed mother even turns down a flattering proposal for a second marriage, coming from one of her deceased husband's Gentile business friends, because she fears that there could be no ultimate understanding.

In the meantime, Hermann meets a racy Jewish girl student from Berlin, but of eastern European descent, named Salomea Fingerhut, who succeeds in drawing him into deepening discussions about Zionism. She speaks about a Jewish "race," mocks Hermann as a would-be "Arminius," and pities him for his frustrated love affair with Germany. He, on the other hand, defends his German birthright, accepts Zionism as a philanthropic enterprise, but rejects it as *eine Art Trotzjudentum*, a mere reflex of antisemitism. His relationship with Salomea reaches a climax when he attends a Zionist gathering with her and, in the discussion period, attempts in a rather embarrassed way to lay bare his emotional ties with the environment from which he sprang. But the audience is hostile to his message. Nevertheless, he concludes with a plea for understanding. Some of us, he says, may turn eastwards to rebuild the ancient homeland, but those who want to keep the hearth fire burning in the country of their birth should not be turned down either. The atmosphere of Zionist gatherings at that time, with the poetic heights of their emotionalism on the one hand, and their fanatical intolerance on the other, is exceedingly well-depicted.

Disappointed, Hermann returns now to his affection for Marie Louise von der Uhlenburg. Significantly, he meets her not on the dance floor or in the meeting hall, but on outings in the Bavarian mountains. While the young people, half absentmindedly, lose their way on returning from such an outing, they exchange opinions about many things about which they find themselves in happy harmony, such as their love for nature and for literature, but they handle dangerous political problems, when they do come up, rather gingerly. The climax is reached here when Hermann accepts an invitation to visit the young lady in her home and gets involved in a discussion with her father, a retired officer of the imperial army. The meeting begins with good intentions all around but blows up when the major remarks, upon a hint by his daughter that Hermann had rejected an offer to become a political candidate for the Freisinnige Partei (a progressive liberal party), that Hermann's chances would not seem as bad as one might assume, because "this Jew-Party may well out-gyp all the others." As a result, the relation with Marie Louise goes to pieces, as had the one with Salomea, and Hermann tells the progressive politicians, when they visit him again, that he has made up his mind to run for the contested seat in Parliament, "as a German Jew." The story ends when he receives a written apology from Marie Louise. He comments: "The time had not yet come. Let's help bring it about. Perhaps for ourselves. Or only for others: who knows . . . "

I am not certain whether I am competent to judge the artistic value of "Der Weg des jungen Hermann Kahn." It would seem to me that the story merely marks off the expanse of the problem, but does not fill the canvas. But I do know that the documentary value of this confession will be recognized as the years go by. The tension between ethnic attachment and universal goal, between the integrated south-German Jew and the independent east-European

Jew, between the Jewish academician and his Gentile schoolmates are vividly described. However, no serious tension is reported between the generations, only the stages of development from country to city, from relative isolation to situations of contact. This is not so in an unpublished companion piece, entitled "Esther," which retraces Hermann's way in a female variant. Here the breakaway of the hero, who is a dancer, from the subservient role in which a girl used to be cast in the Jewish tradition, is sharply accentuated. To the tension between Jew and Gentile is added the lack of comprehension between mother and daughter and even the violent inner contradiction between occupational goal and emotional urge. By way of contrast, Hermann and Marie Louise appear as the representatives of their respective family traditions, and the internal tension which plagues them is the reflection of an external conflict. But one element in that conflict situation is overlooked. The frustrated desire to be "accepted" by the academic and aristocratic elite is feelingly depicted, but what is not seen is the revolt of the masses, the destruction of values, the rejection by demagogy. When that came to pass, the elite, if ever so reluctantly, sacrificed the Jews in order to save their own skins. In Heinrich Heine's words: "*Es ist eine alte Geschichte, Doch bleibt sie immer neu, Und wem sie just passieret, Dem bricht das Herz entzwei.*"

"*Der Weg des jungen Hermann Kahn*" leads the hero into political action. This was the way my father had chosen when he was a young man, opposing Bismarck and what Bismarck stood for, Rektor Kemnator, who urges Hermann to accept the candidacy for political office, stands for Rektor Heimburger in Karlsruhe, a democrat in the 1848 tradition, who had been my father's political mentor. Tante Clem's contribution to political action is connected with the history of the women's suffrage movement. Erna Rheinstrom-Feuchtwanger tells me that the Munich branch of the Verein für Frauenstimmrecht was launched (in either 1909 or 1910) at a meeting in the Café Luitpold in which representatives of the British suffragette movement, who had come over from London, spoke. They had been invited by the wife of ex-professor of history and president of the Deutsche Friedensgesellschaft, Ludwig Quidde, who was later a member of the Weimar parliament and a Nobel Prize winner for peace. Quidde, a rosy-cheeked, white-goateed scholar, and politically more far-sighted than many others—although a miserable practical politician—was one of the most frequently quoted men when it came to political discussions in our family circle. The meeting in the Café Luitpold was called by Mrs. Quidde, Dr. Sutor, a child psychologist, and three Jewish women, namely Erna Rheinstrom, Nettie Gerstle-Katzenstein, and Tante Clem. As a result, Erna Rheinstrom and Tante Clem organized a tea party in the Regina Palast Hotel, and on that occasion the Munich branch of the "Verein" was formally inaugurated. Subsequent propaganda activities were so organized as to appeal primarily to working women, ranging from academically trained women and volunteer social workers to members of the trade unions and domestic servants. Success came in 1918, when women's suffrage became a law. In that year, the secretary of the Verein für Frauenstimmrecht, Dr. Rosa Kempf, was elected as a democratic member of the Bavarian Diet.

During World War I, the *Jüdische Frauenbund* stepped into the general arena. As war broke out, it appeared that an organizational set-up was needed to administer the contributions which the federal government and as the city of Munich were ready to pay to the families of soldiers who had lost their breadwinners and become needy. To meet the challenge, the Fraueninteressen-verein, the Katolische Lehrerinnenverein, the Katolishe Frauenbund, the Evangelische Frauenbund and the Jüdische Frauenbund combined forces; representatives of the city and of the Hausbesitzerverein (Association of Real Estate Owners) were added. Twenty-six welfare districts were created throughout the city, and for each of these districts representatives of the participating organizations were named to supervise the operations. Tante Clem's office was on the Kohleninsel in the Isar (later Museumsinsel), now the site of the Deutsches Museum. The Museumsinsel marks a geographical break. North of it, on both banks of the river, are fashionable residential neighborhoods, but to the south stretch poor and even slum districts. I remember the office well, as my parents sent me there repeatedly to help with the distribution of food and cash, carry packages, and so forth. In the diary which I kept during those teenage years, I mention that I fainted once in the narrow corridor which was filled with sweaty women and their children, waiting for their turn. Certainly, the contrast between the comfortable spaciousness of our suburban home and the squalor in which the welfare clients lived impressed itself on my mind in those days—and I assume that my parents considered the impression a wholesome educational influence. There was a soup kitchen, where either food or food stamps, entitling the recipient to get milk, soup, bread, and so on, were distributed; also, provision was made for infant care. Needs were ascertained by periodic visits to the homes. Tante Clem and Erna Rheinstrom succeeded in supplementing the official rations by soliciting support from Jewish businessmen, for instance, when the firm Carl Bach & Company donated suits and coats at Christmas time.

Shortcomings and setbacks were inevitable in a pioneering enterprise of this sort. Psychiatric care was in its infancy. On one occasion, Erna Rheinstrom had to rescue a girl from the mental hospital in Eglfing where she had been sent without her consent and without proper diagnosis. Miss Helene Sumper, the gentle, grey-haired president of the Katolischer Frauenverein, was threatened with a revolver by a man who had been called to the colors, and at another time an army recruit simply placed an infant on her office desk and vanished from the scene. In addition there were administrative frictions. Tante Clem, who suffered from frequent migraines, was at times unable to appear at her desk during office hours. During one of these absences, her office was occupied by representatives of the Hausbesitzerverein, who declared that they intended to take over. Offensive language was used, and it is possible that antisemitic sentiments were not absent. Erna Rheinstrom protested immediately to the city, asking for an apology; otherwise, she said, both Tante Clem and she would resign. A representative of the city asked the ladies "on his knees," (as the German expression goes,) to reconsider their resignations, but as no apology was forthcoming from the real-estate people, the resignations became effective. This occurred in the summer of 1918, shortly before the conclusion of the war and the absorption of voluntary welfare services in the official Hinterbliebenenfürsorge (Survivors' Benefits Administration).

World War I was a great divide and the end of the war ushered in a new world. It is therefore appropriate at this point to devote a few words to the role of the home of Max and Clementine Kraemer in the social life of Munich in both periods. In the prewar period, the people who assembled in the apartment at Georgen Strasse 22, in Munich's suburb of Schwabing, were relatives and friends from the Jewish community on the one hand, and literary figures on the other. The two groups were quite separate. Among the first group were the bankers Heinrich Marx, Hugo Marx, and Hugo Heilbronner, the industrialist Willy Marx, the lawyer Carl Blumenstein, and the painter Seym Hermann. The latter, a native of Poland, later residing in the United States, had become a member of the family because of his marriage to Anna, a Rumanian orphan girl who had been adopted by uncle Elias Marx. The wife of Heinrich Marx, Alice, née Scharff, of Landau in the Bavarian Palatinate, was a lady of great charm and beauty, as was Anna Hermann. Other members of the circle at that time were Maurice and Hedwig Ettinghausen, whose eldest son, Walter Eytan, has for years been the Secretary General of the Israeli Foreign Office and then Ambassador of Israel in Paris. Hedwig Ettinghausen was a daughter of Rabbi Kahn of Heilbronn, a cousin of my paternal grandmother. In 1940, she gave me a chance to go to England and thus saved my life. Maurice Ettinghausen, a native of Frankfurt am Main and a strictly Orthodox man, was a British subject and a world-renowned antiquarian bookseller in Oxford.

The second group was more typically "Schwabing-like." In the pre-war years, Schwabing was an El Dorado of artists and writers from all parts of Germany as well as from the neighboring countries of eastern Europe. Also, many of the professors teaching at the university and the Technische Hochschule, as well as at the Academy of Arts, resided in Schwabing. The places where the artists and the Munich burghers met were certain restaurants, coffee houses, and cabarets, but especially the masked balls of the Munich carnival, the famous *Fasching*. Here the native girls, healthy, naive and easily carried away by an "interesting fellow," entered into liaisons, some of them lasting and some not so lasting, with real and imagined counts and with artists and would-be artists of all kinds. The complete abandonment of class distinctions—apart from anything else—was a remarkable feature of the Munich *Fasching*. Tante Clem loved to make her observations on these occasions and to describe the contrasting characters. An example is her short story "Bal paré," which appeared in a little volume called *Münchner Bilderbogen*, edited by Richard Riess.[15] She met writers such as Richard Riess, Gustav Horn, Hermann Reissiger, A. De Nora, and others on these occasions and was mentored by them in her own efforts at developing her abilities as an author. A letter of Hermann Reissiger's, offering literary advice, has been preserved among her clippings. Richard Riess, a Jew from Breslau, who had married a very pleasant and very simple Catholic girl, I remember personally. Another member of this group was Ferdinand Kahn, a sad-looking bachelor-lawyer and a good humorist.

More impressively in my recollection looms another group, with strongly philosophical and theological interests. As a member of the Gesellschaft für Ethische Kultur, Uncle Max became friendly with the preacher of the Frei-religiöse Gemeinde, Dr. Ernst Horneffer, his brother August Horneffer, and his eventual successor, Max Maurenbrecher. Another acquaintance was Wilhelm Ohr, one of the leaders of the politically progressive Freistudentische Bewegung, who died in World War I. Ernst Horneffer, a native of Pomerania and a tall, bearded, serious-minded man with a Dostoevsky-like face, was by training a Protestant theologian and by inclination—as well as through his marriage to the granddaughter of the philosopher Hermann Lotze—heir to the tradition of German idealistic philosophy, a follower of Plato, Kant, and Hegel. His philosophical discussions with Uncle Max, who was an enthusiastic *Nietzscheaner,* were interminable. Tante Clem enjoyed the situation although she understood little of these abstract topics. The Horneffers had six children. One of them, Wolfgang, became a sculptor, but died young.[16] Ernst Horneffer left Munich by the end of the war to accept a chair of philosophy at the University of Giessen. He combined theological liberalism with Prusso-German nationalism and a great deal of scepticism regarding the working of political democracy. The threat arising from the National Socialist movement he found difficult to comprehend, as it seemed to him to run counter to the best traditions of German idealism. He remained in correspondence with Uncle Max throughout the Hitler years and visited him as late as 1938, when Uncle Max was already a very sick man. The philosopher and the Jew continued to discuss metaphysical problems even in the teeth of the catastrophe.

After World War I, the scene changed. The relatives and the friends remained, but the writers and philosophers were replaced by Jewish intellectuals. The one man who remained as a link between the earlier and the later periods was Professor Paul Joachimsen, who taught history at a Munich Gymnasium, as well as at the university. A north-German Jew with a sharply

Semitic profile, he married a lively north-German Gentile and became a leading fundamentalist Lutheran layman, member of the Lutheran *Landessynode* for Bavaria. He remained conscious of his Jewish intellectuality, contemptuous of the muddle-headedness of the Nazis, and terrified by forebodings of the national disaster which he considered inevitable. Joachimsen was a most incisive thinker in the Rankean tradition and a forceful writer and teacher; his paper "Zur Historischen Psychologie des Deutschen Staatsgedankens," published in the *Dioskuren Year-Book,* is a masterpiece. Another link between the pre-war and the post-war periods was Dr. Carl Blumenstein, a dwarfish man who had married Ida Kohnstamm, daughter of a former executive secretary of the Jewish Kultusgemeinde. There was also kindly-faced Dr. Elise Dosenheimer, a literary historian and Hebbel specialist, who lectured in the winter months at the Jüdisches Lehrhaus in Munich and during the summer term at the University of Jena. She died in New York in 1959, ninety years old.

To these were added Rabbi Leo Baerwald and his wife Jenny, Dr. Eli Straus and his wife Rahel, and Erna Reinstrom's husband, Dr. Ludwig Feuchtwanger. In sharp contrast to his predecessor, Rabbi Cossman Werner, who had been a zealot of the prophetic message, Rabbi Baerwald primarily was a cultivated gentleman, urbane, reserved, sceptical, combining liberality in thought with traditionalism in practice. He was imbued with Kantian and neo-Kantian philosophy and, while his cool detachment aroused little enthusiasm, he succeeded in making Judaism intellectually respectable and, as it were, *salonfähig*. Eli Straus, on the other hand, was a man of action. He was the key personality in the Munich Jewish community in the 1920s. He came from Karlsruhe, like my father and Tante Clem, but from a strictly Orthodox and very learned family; one of his ancestors was the famous Baal-Shem of Michelstadt. He became the leader of the Munich Zionists, the indefatigable proponent of Volksgemeinde as against Kultusgemeinde, the initiator of the Jüdische Volksschule, of the Jüdisches Lehrhaus, and especially of the communal welfare services. Generally, he was the power behind the throne of the Neumeyer administration. He was a lawyer by profession, his wife a doctor of medicine; they raised six children. In addition to all this, they had time to spare for a most intensive social life; everybody who was or might possibly become somebody in the Zionist movement, from Shmarya Levin to a groping freshman student, could be encountered in the Straus home. Very different was Ludwig Feuchtwanger, brother of Lion Feuchtwanger, member of a remarkable dynasty that had produced bankers, lawyers, writers, scholars, Jewish community leaders, adherents of Agudas Jisroel and of socialism — and the philosopher Max Scheler. Ludwig Feuchtwanger, manager of the publishing house of Duncker & Humblot and later editor of the *Bayerische Israelitische Gemeindezeitung*, was a polyhistor. Originally a jurist and economist, he had become an expert in Semitics and Jewish history, philosophy, and theology. His critical faculties outranked his creative power. He left no magnum opus, but I believe it is safe to say that he considered the ancestral orthodoxy a respectable heirloom, yet a thing to stay away from; political and theological liberalism an ahistorical concoction, too weak to stand up in the vicissitudes of a turbulent world; political Zionism a bracing element in Jewish life, but an enterprise of dubious practicality; if he had permitted anyone to pin him down, he probably would have admitted that he was a cultural nationalist. Finally, it should be mentioned that Rabbi Leo Baeck of Berlin was an overnight guest in the Kraemer home on various occasions when he came to Munich.[17]

Tante Clem, although intellectually not the equal of these men, was nevertheless highly appreciated by them because of her originality and sincerity and because they knew that she admired intellectual clarity and witty discourse above everything else. However, in spite of Horneffer, Straus, and all the rest of them, she remained politically a pacifist and an adherent of religious liberalism in Jewish life. With the women in the circle she was connected in close friendship, above all with Erna Feuchtwanger, who had been with her from the early days and stayed until almost the very last. Among other close friends were Alice Marx, Sophie Heilbronner, Recha Stark, Clem Wolf of Stuttgart, my own mother (who was both her sister-in-law and her niece), and Suzanne Carvallo-Schuelein, the wife of my uncle, Julius W. Schuelein, and herself an eminent painter.

The 1920s and, even more so, the 1930s was the time when the old order of things had broken down but the new order had not yet arrived. We know in retrospect that the Weimar republic was only an interlude. As I look over Tante Clem's writings, most of which are from the period 1918–33, it strikes me that they neither reflect concern over the defeat of Germany exultation over the unexpected fruit of defeat, the breakthrough of democracy. The fate of collectivities, such as nations and peoples, seemed to be beyond Tante Clem's comprehension. The question which she asked herself was: What does this all mean for the individual human being, here, there, and everywhere? Hence, her reaction to the war was that to kill was a crime and her answer was a message of peace and goodwill among men. Her short story "Jugend," which mourns the death of a young soldier (she had in mind her cousin Julius Levi of Stuttgart), and also "Der Grossvater und der Hofbauer," (first published in *Ethische Kultur*, 1915) are examples. To the same category belongs *Die Rauferei*, which appeared as a book in 1928 (Gustav Kiepenheuer Verlag).[18] In a wry way, the same theme appears in the story "Besuch aus dem Schützengraben," where the occasion of a visit in my parents' home by our cousin Ferdinand Levi of Frankfurt is utilized to downgrade false heroic postures and to call instead for respect for the sick and wounded and crippled among the boys in uniform. Here, I must say a word in favor of education. I was then a teenage patriot, and I objected to some aspects of Tante Clem's attitude more than once, for instance, when she said, right in the middle of the war, that she thought Alsace should be returned to France. Her reason was that she knew from her cousin who lived first in Bischwiller and then Strassburg that the majority of Alsatians felt drawn to France and that they were indifferent to Germany. I objected to this as a testimony of moral weakness and a disregard for the collective dream of centuries. Today, I have swung around to Tante Clem's position that the opinions, even the whims, of individuals must never be taken lightly, and that the *plébiscit des tous les jours* reflects changing conditions and rewrites history.

So much about the war. But what about the breakthrough of democracy? The emergence of the new republic? No grounds for exultation offered themselves. The forced abdication of the good grand duke of Baden was a matter of regret. The Bavarian monarchy had been popular in gesture and benevolent in action and an object of envy for our friends from Berlin. Moreover, the transition from old to new in Munich had been violent. A north-German Jew, a writer and idealist dreamer, Kurt Eisner, had become premier of Bavaria. Women's suffrage, a cause dear to Tante Clem's heart, was about to be granted, and a delegation consisting of Tante Clem, Erna Rheinstrom, and Dr. Rosa Kempf waited to be received in audience by the premier in the building of the Bavarian Diet in the Pranner Strasse, when Eisner's private secretary, Hermann Fechenbach, appeared, pale and bewildered, and reported that Eisner, on his way to the Diet, had just been shot dead! Within minutes, everybody left and the streets took on the appearance of a graveyard. Forebodings of Hitler's terror! A concoction of clerical, separatist, nationalist, and racist sentiments combined in the years 1918-24 to make Munich more antisemitic than ever before—and after—in the city's history. In the late 1920s, namely, the Catholic Church and the large Catholic party, the Bayerische Volkspartei, recognized that Hitler's movement stood against Christian values, against popular government, and against Bavarian autonomy, but by that time fate was on its way and could no more be halted. These were exciting years, full of intellectual controversy, but it would seem that Tante Clem was quietly discouraged by the turn of public affairs. A great deal of resignation is adumbrated in " Der Weg des jungen Hermann Kahn," but still braced by the desire of the hero to join with others in political action. In the 1920s, political action was discarded as hopeless (a position with which I violently disagreed), and Jewish themes pure and simple came to the fore.

This matter of "Jewish themes" needs to be clarified, however. Generally, the 1920s saw a revival of Jewish consciousness. The Centralverein, a Jewish civic defense organization, gathered a large membership. The Jewish Lehrhaus Movement gained momentum. Books concerning the essence of Jewish ethics, the meaning of Jewish history, and the Jewish message to the nations appeared. Leo Baeck, then president of the B'nai B'rith, began to grow into the role of leadership, which he was to assume in a more definite manner in the 1930s. Martin Buber, the great thinker who fused East and West and carried both back to the word of the beginning, was eagerly read. Of these, Tante Clem was most attracted by Leo Baeck, whom she and her husband came to know intimately. The humanness and poetic simplicity of Baeck's interpretation of Judaism, as well as the quiet dignity of his personality, struck a chord in her. But her own interpretation was still simpler and more intimate. She returned to the mainspring of the strength of our people at all times, to the Jewish family. In the 1920s she wrote her "Erinnerungen" and most of her children's stories. These stories stand for the past and for the future. Since her thinking was entirely concrete, totally female, the past was represented to her by grandparents, by relatives, and by the village characters who surrounded them. To think of them, to conjure up their images, was a consolation and a source of strength to her. Her memory was not always accurate, but she captured the spirit of the old times convincingly, in "Erinnerungen" as well as in the pertinent passages of "Der Weg des jungen Hermann Kahn." A number of strands are combined here. About the pity of the downtrodden and the despised, the cripples and the idiots, I spoke earlier. There is, of course, the theme of emotional warmth and of family cohesion. The family theme is intimately interwoven with the theme of the interconnectedness of Jew and Gentile, of grandfather and the peasants. Finally, overarching all of these, is the theme of forgiveness. That is the theme of *"Der Grossvater und der Hofbauer."*

This story, which I believe is Tante Clem's best, proves that a Jewish story which is worth its salt must have universal appeal. As far as I can see, the story was published in four places, namely in *Kinderland (Monatsbeilage* of the magazine Ethische Kultur), further in the *Hannoversche Kurier,* in an unidentifiable publication, and in the *Jüdisch-Liberale Zeitung.* It first appeared in general periodicals in 1915; the *Jüdisch-Liberale Zeitung* reprinted it in 1924. The story relates an episode from the childhood of Tante Clem's maternal grandfather, Julius Levi of Mühringen. The grandfather, an orphan taking over his father's customers at the age of thirteen, called on a rich farmer to claim an outstanding debt. The farmer denied the obligation and unchained his huge watchdog, so that the boy had to run for his life. Tante Clem comments: "A person like this peasant in my eyes is more than merely fraudulent. He must be put on a plane with a murderer because—how easily— could he have put to rout in the heart of this boy the faith in all men." This, however, did not come to pass as far as the grandfather was concerned. He succeeded in providing a dowry for each of his six sisters, and after that was done created a comfortable existence for himself. One day, when he was in the company of friends, a wretched beggar appeared at the door and the grandfather, recognizing the once-so-proud farmer, passed the hat around. The old beggar broke down, weeping, and related that he had been unlucky ever since he had chased the little boy away. This is the story, but while she is telling the tale Tante Clem asks herself why it is that one works for the improvement of the human kind, if it is to no avail, since there will always be good people and bad people. But she adds that it may be of use, after all, if one considers that the one hundred years which had passed since the story with the farmer had happened are much too short a time to make any impression. "If one goes through the entire history of mankind from the very beginning," so she continues, "then one comes to the conclusion that the direction is upwards. For instance, cannibals have almost disappeared and so have tortures, at least as a public institution, and quite a few other things of that kind. To be sure, the movement upwards is not a very rapid one. And the larger part of the way is still before us." Tante Clem refers to the war which was then raging. What would she have said about the big rascals who are praised sky-high and awarded citations in our time? And what must she have felt when she faced a mean death, worse than torture, in the camp at Theresienstadt? Must she not have despaired of man and all his works? I wish I could be certain that the story of the love of man for man, which is stronger than all the evil hatreds of this world, has accompanied her to the judgment throne.

The children's stories stand for the future. In children, there is hope. In children one may study human nature; children are sincere, they call things by their right names, where grown-ups obscure matters with a lot of big words. Tante Clem was childless, and to observe and describe children obviously meant consolation to her. She describes "Schwälbchen," one of the daughters of Ernst Horneffer, and Heinz, a son of the sculptor Hugo Kaufmann. But all the other children appearing in her sketches and short stories, and also in her children's book *Fritzchen in Traumland* (Charlottenburg, 1919), as well as in drafts for unpublished children's books, are the six Cahnmann children, her nephews and nieces, and the scene is our home in the Sophie-Stehle-Strasse, in the suburb of Nymphenburg.[19] The series starts in 1912, with the description of our reaction to the funeral of our grandfather Gustav Cahnmann. One or two stories are from the war years, but the majority are from the period between the end of the First World War and the advent of Hitler. The stories do not convey a philosophy, as does "Der Weg des jungen Hermann Kahn" or "Erinnerungen." They are documentaries, preliminary drafts, and notes towards a study of human nature in the raw.

I believe I am justified in calling the stories Jewish stories. First of all, the children described are Jewish children. Not, to be sure, Jewish children with *Käpple* and earlocks, as Moritz Oppenheim had painted them a hundred years

earlier; rather, little patriots and rascals, hungry for love and eager for prestige, like everybody else; Jewish children, nevertheless. Secondly, and beyond all that, the Jewish quality derives from the fact that in them Tante Clem
tried to rediscover the Jewish past in her fashion, life-like, through children's
eyes. There is a Purim story wherein Esther and "Uncle" Mordecai are
family figures and a very funny Pesach story, as told by a young child. The
Israelites are depicted very realistically, eager to eat a lot before the exodus
and terribly afraid of the pursuing Egyptian hosts. But Moses's trust in the
Lord comes out quite forcefully.

The children's stories are vividly told, but whether the motivations are
always captured in vivo, as it were, is another problem. Tante Clem herself
relates at one point that my father chided her for being "not psychological."
In case my testimony should be permitted where my own case is concerned,
I might say that Tante Clem occasionally misjudged the nature of my emotions. During World War I, I was with all my heart with the armies in the
field, and I trembled for the fate of the country. Tante Clem, somehow, did
not bring herself to believe that the sentiment was genuine. It must be admitted, of course, that a great deal of love of self is contained in a teenager's
dreams of heroic deeds, but the preparation of the boy for the responsibilities
of the man is also there. In one of her earliest stories, Tante Clem says: "And
Werner weeps when he learns that grandfather has passed away . . . In stark
reality, he weeps because that very thing is going to give him some measure
of prestige with his brothers and sisters for a long time to come . . ." How
is it that she knows that so well? Perhaps I wept because I was older than the
rest of them and had a notion that the loss was irretrievable.

It is true that Tante Clem, being childless and emotionally so very close to
our father, was like a second mother to us. She wanted us to be our own true
selves, but she also wanted to make of us perfect ladies and gentlemen, in
speech, in manners, in everything, whether we liked it or not. We were fond,
and even proud, of her, but we felt her kind of concernedness as an intrusion.
She must have been aware of these mixed emotions. It saddened her to think
that her gift-offerings were not accepted and her affectionate feelings not
reciprocated. But that was not so. Much later, when I bade her farewell,
shortly before my emigration, she said to me: "And, of course, you will
forget your old aunt as soon as you'll step out of the country." It was certainly
not a very good observation. Have I really forgotten her?

Tante Clem's writings are an expression of her personality. They do not
belong to the category of great art, but they are frank and honest, almost shyly
afraid of big words and persistently intent upon reducing the so-called "issues"
to the simplicity of elementary human passions. One of Tante Clem's literary
mentors, Hans Reissiger, acknowledges this much in a letter, referring to an
unpublished short story, "Die Gauklerin," and dated Partenkirchen, 27 Feb-

ruary 1928. He says that the story shows a wealth of images and of emotional and intellectual excitement, and that tension and sympathetic participation are maintained throughout. He also praises the naturalness of the dialogue, but he adds that the danger of "chatting away," as he puts it, is not entirely avoided and that a more distinguished stylistic level, aiming at greater severity and distance, might have been desirable.

I believe that this judgment is much to the point generally, not merely with regard to the "Gauklerin" and a likewise unpublished companion piece, "Der arme Balthasar." The anguish of simple working people and servant girls who find themselves involved in situations beyond their intellectual grasp, even to the point of crime, is powerfully expressed there. But even in these stories, and certainly in others, a forced chattiness of style creeps in occasionally which mingles intimacy and remoteness in such a way as to create an uneasy feeling of artificiality. For instance, the dialogue in such pieces as "Die Rauferei," "Bal Pare," "Frauenfreundschaft," " Die Rosenwirtin"[20] and others does not always ring true, and the words put into the mouth of peasants, aristocrats, and bohemians sound at times a bit clichéd. Significantly, this weakness disappears entirely in the stories which deal with autobiographical and family themes. They do ring true to life because they cover home ground. Their value rests with the fact that they keep alive the memory of a generation which otherwise is past and gone, but whose lives and strivings deserve our earnest study in the future. They are documentaries of great value. As a melancholy record of frustration, "Der Weg des jungen Hermann Kahn" will be quoted by historians of German Jewry in days to come, but artistically, the crown belongs to "Der Grossvater und der Hofbauer." Here, the particular and the universal, Jewish fate and German atmosphere, personal reminiscence and moral conclusion are splendidly fused. In style and content, the touching simplicity of the great German master, Johann Peter Hebel, is reached. This story is a classic.[21]

The remainder of Tante Clem's life history can be told briefly. In 1929, the banking house Max Kraemer & Company went into bankruptcy. Actually, the substance had been lost during the period of the great German inflation. What remained in 1924 were the crumbs from the real estate holdings of my great-grandfather Bernhard Kraemer, that is, those tenements and lots which had been unsellable. To retrieve the grievous losses, Uncle Max ingeniously, but unrealistically, financed the activities of the firm by means of credits with other banks. Some investments, like the Bremer Presse (which produced beautiful books, among them Hugo von Hoffmansthal's *Deutsches Lesebuch*), were white elephants. Others, like the electrification of Styria, were chimeras. My father's firm, Chemische Fabrik Isaria, was precariously financed with drafts on the Bayerische Staatsbank. When the Bayerische Staatsbank finally decided that a check bearing the endorsement of Max Kraemer &

Company could no longer be honored, the house of cards collapsed. Tante Clem was utterly surprised and sorely disappointed. She had admired her husband's keen intellect and had never suspected that his generosity towards his wife and friends was based on a stupendous inability to face facts.

Tante Clem now took her life in her own hands. On the very day the bankruptcy was declared, she went to the owner of one of the most successful Munich textile houses, the firm S. Eichengruen & Company, and offered her services as a saleslady. She said that she had grown up among cottons and wools and silks and linens in her father's retail store in Karlsruhe, that she knew materials, that she knew how to sell, and that she liked people. She added that her only shortcomings were her frequent attacks of migraine but she was resolved to disregard them. She was engaged and advanced quickly to the position of first saleslady. S. Eichengruen & Company was an immensely popular place of business and there was always a throng of customers flowing through the aisles. Tante Clem was saddened by her experience, but proud of her achievement. She gained in respect among her friends.

Hitler's seizure of power horrified Tante Clem, as it horrified all of us, but her personal life was hardly affected. So little did the people of Munich heed the Nazi boycott of Jewish business establishments that S. Eichengruen gained, rather than lost, customers in the first years of Nazi rule. Indeed, buying in Jewish stores became an act of defiance; but the noose of official restrictions was tightened from year to year and from month to month, until it was clear that Jewish economic existence was to be throttled entirely. After 1939, hardly a trace of it remained. More and more friends emigrated and loneliness deepened. After some frustrated efforts she finally secured an affidavit to come to the United States from relatives in Chicago, Albert and Helen Heller. Mrs. Heller was a granddaughter of Mark Cahnmann, the youngest brother of Tante Clem's grandfather, Moses Kahnmann of Rheinbischofsheim. Mark Cahnmann, had emigrated to the United States in 1849. The Hellers had visited the Kraemers and my parents on a European tour in the early 1920s, and the contact had been maintained. However, the United States "waiting number" was too high to permit emigration before America entered the war.

Also, the efforts of the Danish author Karin Michaelis, who was a friend of Tante Clem, came to naught because of the slowness of bureaucratic procedures. Everything was almost ready for Tante Clem's departure for Copenhagen, when the German troops marched into Denmark.

I will not recount here the futile attempts of my brothers and myself, aided by our cousin, Max Levi, and one of the uncles of my mother, Julius Schülein, to bring our parents and Tante Clem to Shanghai, to Cuba, to the United States, to any place, if only it was out of the reach of Hitler's murderous designs. It must suffice to say that we were not successful. Pathetically, only the meager belongings of my parents and Tante Clem arrived in New York via Basle.

Among them were two remaining books, out of the more than five thousand items which once had been on Uncle Max's and Tante Clem's library shelves. One was Abraham Tendlau's *Sprichwörter und Redensarten deutschjüdischer Vorzeit*, edition 1860, a folkloristic work which faithfully mirrors activities and sentiments of the old south-German village Jews; the other was *Dichtergrüsse*, selected by Elise Polko, an anthology of what in the middle of the nineteenth century had been "new" German lyrical poetry. The poetic volume is inscribed to Fräulein Auguste Levi, Tante Clem's mother, and dedicated to her "in friendly memory of the 9th and 10th of August 1869 in Baisingen" by a youthful admirer who merely signed himself with his initials, "L.H." The selection of these two books is most telling. It shows that Tante Clem, at the end of her days, returned to the roots of her existence, the simple Jewish life along the banks of the broadly flowing Rhine and in the shadow of Black Forest firs, and to the lofty heights of German poetry, hallowed, as they were, by her dear mother's memory. The *avoth avotejnu* were calling her home. Buried among her papers was a slim third volume: Bertha Pappenheim's *Gebete*. Underlined therein are the words: "*Kraft, Kraft, verlass mich nicht, Recht und Unrecht haarscharf zu unterscheiden!*" (Strength, strength, do not forsake me, that I may discern clearly and sharply between right and wrong!). This is the last cry of a lost soul.

After Pearl Harbor, all hope was indeed lost. Father died of a stomach operation on 13 January 1942, three weeks before his seventieth birthday. His touching farewell letter to his family and friends, which mentions Tante Clem, was published in English, in *The Reconstructionist* (Vol. 9 no. 10, 25 June) as a classical *tzava-ah*, or "ethical will." Mother and Tante Clem were separated, mother living in the Judensiedlung in Berg am Laim and Tante Clem in the barrack at Knörr Strasse 148 in Milbertshofen. Both are suburbs of Munich, Berg am Laim to the east, Milbertshofen to the north of the city. From there, in the spring of 1942, mother was deported to Camp Piaski, near Lublin, in Poland, where she and her companions were murdered immediately. Tante Clem was brought to Theresienstadt a few weeks later, already weakened and gravely ill. Her body was frail, her pride humiliated, and the will to live had deserted her. I do not know the nature of her illness, but a cousin of hers and of our father, Ferdinand Levi, formerly of Frankfurt am Main, now of Buenos Aires, who miraculously survived the unspeakable horrors of life in the camp, told us that she suffered from a debilitating and demeaning dysentery and that she was left lying helplessly in a dark corner until death redeemed her. That was on 4 November 1942, according to volume 19 folio 166, item 664 of the *Sterbematrik* of Ghetto Theresienstadt. However, her nephews and nieces have had her name, as well as the name of our mother, inscribed on the tombstone of Sigwart Cahnmann and Max Kraemer in the Alten Israelitischen Friedhof, (cemetery) on the Thalkirchener

Strasse in Munich, and her cousin Ferdinand Levi has planted a tree in her honor in the land of Israel.

1964

Notes

1. The documents are deposited with the Leo Baeck Institute in New York. A full account of ''The Life of Clementine Kraemer'' is deposited at the same place; the essay in this volume is a slightly abridged version.
2. From the point of view of the family historian, the information contained in these stories is not always accurate. For instance, Uncle Leo, later an editorial writer for the *Chicago Tribune,* had not been a teacher prior to his emigration but a tailor's apprentice in Karlsruhe. Or, my grandfather's grandmother, Dina Kahnmann, née Netter, might have come to Rheinbischofsheim via Strassburg, but she was a native of Oberbergheim near Rappoltsweiler, in Upper Alsace. She emigrated to the United States in 1849 and died in St. Louis, Missouri in 1869. She had eight sons—not twelve, as Tante Clem says. Five of them emigrated to the United States; three—among them my great-grandfather Moses K.—stayed in the old village. From the point of view of the artist, of course, it makes little difference whether there were eight or twelve boys in the family.
3. The Munich family, then including my parental grandparents, is described with good humor in a poem which Tante Clem wrote and recited on the occasion of the betrothal of my parents. The poem, preserved by my father among Tante Clem's papers, bears the date of 1 June 1900. It describes the atmosphere of the extended Jewish family of this period very vividly. It characterizes numerous members of the Marx, Schülein, and Levi families. The only pure ''Cahnmann'' presented in the poem is my grandfather Gustav Cahnmann, the only pure ''Kraemer,'' my great-grandfather Bernhard Kraemer. Of interest are the allusions to my father's youthful political ''radicalism'' and, even more so, to the then-revolutionary manner of my parents' engagement, without any prearrangement by members of the family!
4. Many of the academicians and artists of varied origin had married Munich girls of humble families.
5. Arthur Cohen, ''Die Münchener Judenschaft 1750-1861,'' *Zeitschrift für die Geschichte der Juden in Deutschland* [ZGJD] 2 (1931); Werner Cahnman, ''Die Münchener Judenbeschreibung von 1804,'' *ZGJD*, 7 (1937).
6. *Festgabe 50 Jahre Hauptsynagoge München 1887–1937* (München, 1937).
7. Werner J. Cahnman, ''Munich and the First Zionist Congress,'' *Historia Judaica*, 3 (1941).
8. Michael Bernays and Felix Mottl were baptized. So was the physicist Leo Graetz, son of the Jewish historian Heinrich Graetz. I do not know whether Max Bernstein, the literary critic of the *Münchener Neueste Nachrichten,* was baptized, but he stood entirely outside the Jewish community. Herman Levi was formally Jewish, but I have it from my father that he once said to Rabbi Cossman Werner: ''How unjust is this world! You are a rabbi and if you had the name 'Levi,' it would do you no harm whatever. But, in my position, I would be much better off with a name like 'Werner.' *Se non e vero, e ben trovato.*''
9. My father came to Munich frequently after 1895. He and my mother became privately engaged in 1897. The formal engagement took place in 1900, the wed-

ding in 1901. From stories told by my father, I know that he was well informed about the preliminaries surrounding the launching of the München Lodge. The foundation day of the lodge was 21 April 1897, according to information received from Rabbi Leo Baerwald.

10. As might be assumed, the immigration of *Ostjuden* was hotly contested in the community. Emil Fraenkel, Rabbi Cossman Werner, and others furthered the influx, while such men as Lehman Bernheimer and Sigmund Raff stood in opposition. The line of division ran right through the membership of the München Loge.

11. The importance of *B'nai B'rith* for the revival of a positive Jewish consciousness, expressed in social action, can hardly be overestimated. It is perhaps symbolic that the last president of the Munich Jewish community, Ing. Karl Stahl, was an active B'nai B'rith man. He died in Theresienstadt.

12. Lotte Pick, "Die jüdische Haushaltsschule zu Wolfratshausen" in Hans Lamm, *Von Juden in München* (München, 1959).

13. An undated sheet containing an invitation to join the Jüdischen Frauenbund in Munich is among Clementine Kraemer's papers. It enumerates the activities of the organization.

14. Rahel Straus, "Bertha Pappenheim und ihr Werk—Ein Erinnerungsblatt zum 100. Geburtstag," *AJR Information* (May 1959).

15. Volume was published by Reuss & Itta Verlag, Konstanz am Bodensee, 1916. Other writings by Richard Riess are mentioned on the back pages of *Münchner Bilderbogen*.

16. Later, Tante Clem and Uncle Max had objections regarding Wolfgang H., whom they found lacking in depth and not free of prejudice regarding Jews (letter of 17 April 1928). Possibly they were right—I never felt that way about him.

17. In a letter dated 15 December 1923 which I received as a student in Berlin, Tante Clem writes: "Dass Du bei Baeck angenehme Stunden hattest, freut mich, ich verehre ihn auch sehr, mir scheint, dass er an reiner Menschlichkeit unübertroffen bleiben muss. Wir haben schon schöpferischere Menschen bei uns in Hause gehabt oder feurigere Geister, aber er ist in seiner Art vollkommen."

18. A review in English of *Die Rauferei* appeared in *B'nai B'rith Magazine—The National Jewish Monthly,* 42, no. 8 (May 1928). The reviewer emphasizes that "the author demands a literal interpretation of the commandment: 'Thou shalt not kill.'"

19. The unpublished manuscripts are "Liselotte auf dem Lande" and "Allerlei Kinder." Tante Clem had in mind to have these illustrated by our youngest sister, Lilo, now Rachel Dotan of Quiryat T'ivon in Israel, whom she considered (in a letter to S. Eichengruen, dated 26 December 1929) "a very gifted child." In fact, sketches by Lilo, then twelve years old, are attached.

20. The story, "Die Rosenwirtin," was published in: Bibliothek der Unterhaltung und des Wissens, Vol. I (1922).

21. I told Tante Clem once that the story reminded me of Johann Peter Hebel, and she smiled. Hebel, who was born at the three-countries-corner where Baden, Alsace, and Switzerland meet, was one of Tante Clem's earliest literary impressions. Her father knew many of his calendar stories and allemanic dialect poems by heart. In "Erinnerungen," Tante Clem relates how she stood, as a child, before the Hebel monument in the *Schlossgarten* in Karlsruhe, reading the moving inscription from one of Hebel's poems that "it must be lovely back home."

11

Martin Buber: A Reminiscence

More than two thousand persons jammed all available space in the Park Avenue Synagogue on 13 June last, at a meeting which had been called by the American Friends of the Hebrew University in memory of Martin Buber. Very little publicity had preceded the memorial convocation. This puts to rest, more effectively than words can do, the whispering campaign that had been carried on for years, that Martin Buber was an esoteric philosopher whom hardly anybody could understand and whose quality as a genuine interpreter of Jewish values was dubious. Possibly, quite a few of those present at the meeting, if asked, might not have been able to state what Buber stood for; but they testified by their presence to their awareness of the towering significance of that little man with the big beard and the twinkling eyes. They knew that one of the great sages of all times had passed away.

The Essence of the Message

Those who thought that way were quite right. Martin Buber himself did not intend to establish a philosophical system, nor did he care for his life and thought to be analyzed as a system. Indeed, to approach Buber analytically would mean to consider him as an "It"—to speak in his own language—that is, to use him as a conceptual device, a lifeless thing. What he had in mind was to restore to a position of effectiveness the concrete essence and presence of a human being in the midst of other human beings, to speak not from system to system but from man to man. This, he was sure, was the Jewish way, coming down to us from ages past, the response to Him who had said: *I am who I am.*

Therefore I will not attempt some kind of systematic analysis and critical evaluation. I shall leave this to those who think it can be done. I shall try instead to testify to the influence which Buber exerted upon my thinking and the thinking of my generation, in the belief that what I have to say will stand for a truth which, while it becomes manifest only in personal experience, nevertheless surpasses it.

What first attracted me to Buber when I was a young man in my late teens and early twenties, immediately after the conclusion of World War I, was a new interpretation not so much of Judaism as of Jewish existence, and not of Jewish existence of and by itself, but as a call to all men. The Victorian world of our fathers and grandfathers had fallen apart: On the one hand, we were confronted with the striving for material success and social respectability, while on the other hand we were introduced to Judaism as an "idea," hovering, as it were, over the vastness of a bustling world, without ever coming to grips with it, without uttering the word of creation. At the same time, the enemy, the eternal Amalek, was at the gates. In the world-at-large, there was, on the one hand, the escapist individualism of the poets and the youth movements and, on the other hand, the mighty socialist movement, already victorious in Russia, with its fixation on the improvement of "conditions" and its disregard for the hearts of men. At this moment in history, Martin Buber spoke to us about the renewal of Jewish existence and about the need for a new approach to human existence as two aspects of one and the same thing. What was postulated was no pantheism, merging God and Man into Nature, but openness to the world; confrontation, not dissolution; activity, responsibility, mutuality, a life lived not in the isolation of contemplation, but in the togetherness of a common task.

The Paradigm of Hassidism

This was the message of Judaism—"*von je und je*,"—to use Buber's favorite expression—but he presented it in the shape of its last embodiment, Hassidism. From his youth, which he spent with his paternal grandparents in Galicia and Bukovina, he was fully acquainted with the degeneration of the later phase of Hassidism as it was meant to be, in the very words of the founders, yet in a way that touched the hearts of his contemporaries. Through Buber's labor of love, such humble preachers and teachers as Nahman of Brtazlav, Sussia of Hanipol, Levi Yitzhak of Berditshev, Jacob Yitzhak of Pzysha, Schneur Zalman of Ladi, and others were resurrected to a luminous afterlife. The immediacy of experience, the genuineness of intention, the attachment to the here and now in action had to be conveyed. All this was presented not as something new, but as a renewal of the call from Sinai. In these years, Buber was the magician who fused East and West and carried both of them back to the Word of the Beginning.

The Hebrew Bible

The impact of the Hassidic books has stood in the way of the appreciation of Buber as a biblical scholar. Buber was a superb Hebraist; the root of a

Hebrew word was alive in him, and he explained the meaning of the word philologically, as it were, from the root up! The translation of the Bible into German, which he started in collaboration with Franz Rosenzweig and completed only in the last decade of his life, is masterly in the way it faithfully renews the original meaning of the Hebrew word in the words of another language. Truly, there is a meeting of minds contained in the meeting of words. The Hebrew word is not profaned by reduction to everyday language so that it may sound familiar even to the most mediocre of the mediocrities who walk the earth with us (as in some of the usual "modern" translations); it is literally translated into a German word which sounds forth as clear and demanding as the original. It seems remarkable that the history of the Jews of Germany in recent centuries, which began with Moses Mendelssohn's translation of the Hebrew Bible, ended with the translation of the same Bible by Buber and Rosenzweig. But while Mendelssohn intended to introduce the Jews of the Ghetto to the idiom of German culture, the aim of Buber and Rosenzweig was to lead the heirs of the Emancipation back to the recognition of their Hebrew origin. Ironically, however, because of the elimination of German-speaking Jewries in the Hitler period, the Buber-Rosenzweig Bible has become a farewell gift to the German people, a *monumentum aere perennius* of the German-Jewish symbiosis.

Yet, in the trying days after 1933, when the hand of the killer was at our throats, the word of the Bible, as interpreted by Buber, spoke to us. It was then, in the glorious work of the *Mittelstelle Für Jüdische Erwachsenenbildung*, that Buber, the teacher and comforter, was at the height of his career. No longer in Munich, in the rococo elegance of the Museumsaal and before the intelligentsia of the city, did the intense man with the flowing black beard appear, but in the modest, Stiese-like Gemeindesaal, before the agitated boys and girls of the Jewish youth associations and their friends and relatives; and not as an interpreter did he come, but as a guide. On one particular weekend he "learned" with us the Book of Jonah. He took up root for root and word for word, with all their analogies, most thoroughly. Whether one knew much Hebrew or little, one had to go along and understand. Then he proceeded to explain the scene, the essence of a *navi*, the nature of the task of the *navi* was called upon to perform among his people, and the concatenation of power in the larger world of the ancient East. Finally, he told us that the book before us was not literature but live speech, a force of the present, a here and now; and he started to read. When he spoke about "Nineveh, the great city" and its people for whom the Lord cares, if and when their minds turn from their evil ways, we knew that the prophet had addressed himself to us. It was in moments like these that we felt we had become "strong and of good courage."

I and Thou

We were so intensely Jewish in these years that I do not remember whether I knew *I and Thou*, the work in which Buber's thought is condensed, and which has carried his fame around the globe, already in these earlier years; but I am certain that I *have* become fully aware of it only much later. Probably, in the 1920s and 1930s I felt I was not in need of listening to the larger call which is sounded forth in *I and Thou* because I was so very conscious of the origin of the call. Written after the books about the Hassidic teachers and their teachings had been brought out, and prior to the publication of Buber's later works of biblical interpretation, *I and Thou* is indeed a summation of the Hassidic experience and an introduction to the meaning of the biblical message. Through Israel, the "I" and the Eternal "Thou" have entered into a covenant which is to be ever confirmed in a very personal encounter. This, to Buber, has been the essence of the Jewish faith at all times. As Abraham pleaded with the Lord for the sake of justice, so did Levi Yitzhak of Berditshev. As Jacob refused to release the angel of the Lord unless he were blessed by him, so do we decline to go without answer in moments of great impact. As God spoke to Moses in the burning bush and to Elijah on Horeb and to Daniel in the lion's den, so will He speak to us, if the time is ripe. The Bible is a record of dialogue. The Lord-on-High demands, and man below should be ready for the service, so that, through man, the work of Creation can be renewed each day.

Sociology of Personal Relations

In addition, as I see it, *I and Thou* contains the elements of an inspired sociology. It is little known that Buber was as fully aware of the great sociologists who were his contemporaries as he was aware of the currents and cross-currents of socialism that agitated public opinion in his time. He was a sociologist, in his own way, as he was a socialist. With nobody, except perhaps later with Franz Rosenzweig, was Buber connected with more intimate ties of friendship than with the saintly, Tolstoy-like socialist, Gustav Landauer (who became a martyr at the hands of German proto-fascists in 1919), and with the subtly associative philosopher-sociologist, Georg Simmel. Buber was the editor of forty small volumes called *Die Gesellschaft*, in which, in Simmelian fashion, institutional forms and social movements were described and analyzed as manifestations of psychic relationships. Perhaps one can say that Buber viewed the personal relation between man and man in the way of a Simmelian triad, with the Eternal Thou as an ever-present partner. Certainly, Buber's "I-It" and

"I-Thou" relationships are kin to Ferdinand Toennies's "arbitrary will" and "essential will" and to their institutional counterparts, *Gesellschaft* and *Gemeinschaft*, that is, a segmental association based on interest as against a total communion of all aspects of life.

We will return to Buber's view of *Gemeinschaft* in a general, as well as in a Jewish, context further on. At this point, I merely wish to note that the vision of a total communion made Buber argue against the notion of a charismatic democracy, as conceptualized by Max Weber but exemplified most vividly by Theodor Herzl's impassioned claim to leadership. Buber admitted that all the evidence of history confirmed Weber's view about the ways by which the forms of domination are maintained, but he expressed the hope that a more dialogic relationship between leaders and followers would be confirmed in the future. He based this hope upon his understanding of the fundamental nature of man.

As a sociologist, it seems to me of interest to observe in this connection that Buber's view of the potentialities of the human condition—although in its existentialist formulation very different from the prevailing pragmatist inclinations of American thought—in its practical workings-out has considerable affinity to the conclusions of the symbolic interactionist school in social psychology, as represented by the writings of Charles H. Cooley, John Dewey, and George Herbert Mead.

A Zionist Credo

Buber was opposed to both the extremes of individualism and collectivism, that is, to the monologic sin of "separating oneself from the community," as well as to the prospect of a totalitarian domination. But he cautioned against the illusion that idyllic forms of family life and work relations could ever be restored. As to the Jewish situation in particular, he warned that the breakdown of the ancient unity of fate and faith was a serious matter, and that it could not be counteracted by pious wishes. New forms of human relations, especially work relations, as well as new modes of Jewish living, would have to be sought and explored. It was under this aspect that he supported Gustav Landauer's and Franz Oppenheimer's kinds of socialism, that he joined Hapoel Hatzair and sympathized with A. D. Gordon and his concept of *amadam*, that he promoted Jewish art, founded the Jüdischer Verlag and helped initiate the drive for the Hebrew University. He did not emphasize the political goal of Zionism, but he believed fervently in Zionism's redeeming power, through the twin factors of the settlement on the land and the renewal of the Hebrew language. He trusted in the creative potentialities of a new confrontation.

Encounters with Arabs and Germans

I did not have the good fortune of meeting Martin Buber again in the last decade of his life, but I know that the problems of Jewish-German relations, and of Jewish-Arab relations, agitated him deeply in those years. Small minds disapproved his advocacy of Arab causes, as well as his reappearance in Germany after 1945, where he was eagerly awaited by large audiences. As far as the Arabs are concerned, he opposed the military government in the Arab areas of Israel, protested against the expropriation of Arab landowners in the Galil, and warned against inflexibility in the question of the Arab refugees, because he was convinced that Zion was either to be redeemed by justice or doomed to failure. He was certain that there was no future for either Jew or Arab in the Middle East if the two peoples could not accustom themselves to living with each other. He was equally certain that they would have to make a start by talking to each other earnestly, and with the goal of union in mind. Ben-Gurion thought differently, but the future is yet to reveal who was the greater realist in this vital matter.

With Germany Buber was intimately connected, not only spiritually, through Kant and Bach, but also physically, through his wife and his daughter-in-law, both of whom were converts of German derivation. He explained to his German listeners after the war that, as far as the monstrosity of the mass murder that had been committed was concerned, he failed to have the faintest glimmer of comprehension and, consequently, that he found common emotions such as "hatred" or "forgiveness" totally inapplicable to the case. But he added that this lack of comprehension did not apply to the German people. He said that he realized that there had been the most varied reactions: there had been those who were weak, those who were afraid of facing the truth, and those who resisted the evil in one way or another. He concluded by expressing his conviction that the final battle between homo humanus and homo inhumanus had barely started, and that the accent was therefore on youth. I believe I acted from the same conviction when I had my own encounter with German youth in Munich last year. I take this coincidence as an assurance that the generations of Israel will continue to be linked to each other, and through Israel the generations of man.

1965

PART IV

Reflections on the German-Jewish Symbiosis

12

Friedrich Wilhelm Schelling and
The New Thinking of Judaism

The Jewish community in the German-speaking areas of Central Europe during the eighteenth century showed signs of disintegration, which must be attributed to the collapse of the Sabbatian movement. The leading scholar of this period, Jonathan Eybeschuetz (1690/95–1764), was accused of Sabbatian inclinations, and although he knew how to defend himself publicly against the accusation, the embittered controversy left in its wake an atmosphere of consternation and exhaustion. The Frankist movement, which derived from Sabbatianism and led unambiguously away from traditional Judaism, was carried on after Jakob Frank's death in Offenbach (1791) under scandalous circumstances by his daughter Eva, until the remnants of the Frankist enterprise collapsed in the year 1817.[1] In these circumstances, even the pious rabbi Nathan Ha-Kohen Adler (1741-1800) in neighboring Frankfurt abstained from an open confession of kabbalistic beliefs.[2] He avoided quoting the Zohar, but he privately introduced his favorite students to theoretical and practical Kabbala. He conducted services according to the Sefardic rite and followed the prayerbook of Yizhak Luria. Besides the study of Hebrew and Aramaic, he engaged in studies of philosophy and the natural sciences—fields of which he attempted to make use in the pursuit of the theoretical and practical Kabbala. These tendencies continued also later. Therefore, Gershom Scholem's statement that the kabbalistic tradition in Germany breaks off "rather abruptly" after Nathan Ha-Kohen Adler had passed away (1800)[3] is only conditionally correct. It was modified by Scholem himself and stands in need of further modification. It is true that Kabbala in its conventional form was only sporadically continued after 1800, and, at any rate, more secretively than publicly. But one can recognize from an enumeration of the students, and the students of the students, of Nathan Ha-Kohen Adler, and from a review of their activities, that the continuation and transformation of the kind of thought that derives from Adler's Yeshiva tends to assume central significance in the unfolding of a second Emancipation, by which we mean a movement to be placed alongside and after the first Emancipation which emanates from Moses Mendelssohn and the Berlin circle.

To Adler's students belonged Rabbi Mendel Kargau, later in Fürth, Rabbi Joseph Schnaittach, later in Freudental, Rabbi Moshe Sofer (1762–1839), later in Pressburg (Bratislava), Rabbi Seckel Loeb Wormser, the popular Baal-Shem of Michelstadt, and Rabbi Abraham Bing (1752–1841), later Chief Rabbi in Wuerzburg (1798–1841), who, in turn, exerted considerable influence through his students.[4] The most remarkable personalities among the students and adherents of Bing were: Seligmann Baer Bamberger, the "Würzburger Rav" (educated in Fürth, but Abraham Bing's assistant and successor), the leader of the Gemeindeorthodoxie, in contradistinction to Samson Hirsch's Trennungsorthodoxie; Rabbi Nathan Marcus Adler (1803–90) of the Frankfurt family, later Chief Rabbi of the British Empire and the initiator of Anglo-Orthodoxy; Rabbi Jakob Ettlinger (1798-1871), later in Altona and Mannheim; and Chacham (he refused the title "rabbi") Isaac Bernays (1792-1849), later in Hamburg; and it should be added that Bernays and Ettlinger, again, were the teachers of Samson Raphael Hirsch and Esriel Hildesheimer. Although Abraham Bing never openly adhered to Kabbala, one can see from the book of Berthold Strauss, *Die Rosenbaums of Zell,* published in London in 1962, that kabbalistically tinged piety was widely disseminated among his pupils.[5] This book has contributed decisively to the revision of the initial opinion of Gershom Scholem that kabbalism in Germany had come to an end with the death of Nathan Adler. We now know from the publication of Berthold Strauss that Mendel Rosenbaum of Theilheim in Lower Franconia, a descendant of a Chmielnicky refugee of 1648, founded a Yeshiva in Zell near Würzburg where he was assisted by Abraham Bing's student, Eliezer Bergmann. Eliezer Bergmann, who became Mendel Rosenbaum's son-in-law, emigrated in 1835 to Palestine. A grandson of Mendel Rosenbaum, Reb Hile Wechsler, published in 1881 a book which is signed with the pen-name "Jaschar Milo Davar" (pointing to Pinchas Moshe of Hoechberg-Hile Wechsler). This book predicts, on the basis of dreams and signs and under the impression of the Stoecker movement, the demise of German Jewry, and calls for the return to Zion.[6] One passage in the book runs as follows: "One intends to make us into strangers in these regions where we have lived so long and which are dear to us just because we turn our eyes toward Jerusalem and the promised land." A son of Hile Wechsler, Rabbi Salomon Wechsler, emigrated, as had done Eliezer Bergmann, to Jerusalem, where he joined the Bratzlawer Hassidim. According to the testimony of Rabbi Pinchas Kohn, a number of kabbalists were found among the rabbis in Franconia by the middle of the nineteenth century. However, what is significant about the students, and the students of the students, of Abraham Bing is not the subterraneous continuation of the kabbalistic tradition, but the combination of that tradition with national-cultural ideas that came to the fore in the garb of romantic philosophy. Abraham Bartura, a descendant of Eliezer Bergmann, told me in Jerusalem that Abraham Bing, according to a family tradition, animated several of his students to attend universities, presumably for the purpose of enabling them to effectively confront the spokesmen of the religious-liberal persuasion in Judaism. For instance, Joseph Schwarz of Floss in the Upper Palatinate studied geography; after his emigration to Palestine (1833), he authored a book, *Tevuoth Ha-Arez*, which deals with the geography of the Holy Land.[7] A son of Abraham Bing, Beer Abraham Bing, published in 1820 a book, *Obed und Thuerza oder eine Kunde aus der Vergangenheit, erzählt in hebräischer und deutscher Sprache*, a sentimental story of a romantically transformed Israel of antiquity, which would deserve to be rescued from oblivion.[8] In the preface, Beer Bing speaks about the need to counteract "the decay of our sacred father-language" and to lift the veil from that golden period "when we formed our own government and where our nation was among the participants in power." That sentence contains germs of cultural as well as political Zionism.

Although the old Kabbala was not disappearing, it nevertheless was pushed into an anonymous existence, so that even a man like Abraham Bing could assert without further qualification that it was not obligatory[9]; yet, in its place ideas emerged which continued the old tradition in a new language. The catalyst of the new trend in Jewish thought was Schelling. Friedrich Wilhelm Joseph Schelling (1775-1854) was then at the height of his creativity. A youthful genius, he received a call to the University of Jena at the age of twenty-two, on the basis of his first published writings. From there he went in 1803 to Wüerzburg and in 1806 to Munich, where he taught at the Bayerische Akademie der Wissenschaften, becoming its president. Franz von Baader and Heinrich Jacobi taught in Munich simultaneously with Schelling. After 1826, until he was called to Berlin in 1841, Schelling taught at the University of Munich, which had been transferred there from Landshut, and also taught for short periods in Erlangen and Stuttgart. Schelling's writings on the philosophy of identity appeared 1801–06, his writings on the philosophy of liberty 1804–15. Schelling's most inspired document, the fragment "Die Weltalter," was printed for the first time in 1811. The edition of 1814 (or 1815) is considered the most complete elaboration of that piece. The earliest lecture on the philosophy of mythology and the philosophy of revelation are from the same time. Schelling lectured about these topics after the opening of the university, but the groundwork for the philosophy of mythology reaches back to the period when the treatise about "Die Gottheiten von Samothrake" had appeared, which was read at the public meeting of the Bavarian Academy of Sciences on 12 October 1815.[10] As can be seen from these data, the usual distinction between the younger and the older Schelling can hardly be maintained. Schelling's philosophy, in the main, was completed in the first decades of the century. To be sure, the programmatic world view contained in his writings was never formulated in a systematic way, but it was precisely that circumstance which contributed to its strength at a time of change. The listeners were fascinated by the element of expectation.

The man who introduced the new language of Schelling in Jewish thinking was Isaac Bernays of Mainz, a pupil of Abraham Bing. Young Bernays came to Munich at the moment when the main features of Schelling's thought had been conceived and were delivered for the first time as his reputation was growing. Bernays, who had studied at the University of Würzburg, was a tutor and secretary in the house of the Bavarian court agents, Jakob and Salomon Hirsch. Jakob Hirsch was raised to the peerage in 1818 under the name Hirsch auf Gereuth.[11] The family Hirsch granted Bernays a half-year furlough to enable him to attend the lectures of Schelling and Jacobi in Munich. The rabbinical permission came from Abraham Bing. Nothing is known about Bing's extra-rabbinical reading, but the fact that he delegated his student to Munich permits conclusions. One must assume that the study of Schelling's philosophy, and possibly the conclusions which Bernays drew from that philosophy, conformed to the thinking of Abraham Bing. Familiarity with Schelling's philosophy is reported about Bing's Frankfurt fellow student, Seckel Loeb Wormser of Michelstadt.[12] At any rate, Schelling's influence on Bernays became a historically effective factor.

The stay in Munich made it possible for the young Bernays to see the manuscripts of the "Philosophie der Mythologie" and the "Philosophie der Offenbarung," which were published more than three decades later from Schelling's literary estate. Schelling's lectures made a deep impression on Bernays, as his son Jakob Bernays later indicated.[13] Isaac Bernays has formulated his own thoughts in two thin volumes, Der Bibel'sche Orient—Eine Zeitschrift in zwanglosen Heften, which appeared in 1820 and 1821.[14] Bernays's authorship was widely asumed during Bernays's lifetime. We do not intend to enter here into the controversy as to whether Bernays actually authored or coauthored the Bibel'sche Orient or not. Hans Bach, who has investigated the Zeitschrift as well as the literature about it most intensively, has arrived at a positive result.[15] Others have expressed doubts. I agree in this regard with Heinrich Graetz who says in a footnote to the eleventh volume of his history that Bernays, to be sure, has disowned paternity of the Bibel'sche Orient, but that these small volumes "nevertheless project his spirit faithfully."[16]

The spirit of the Bibels'sche Orient is the spirit of Herder and Schelling. The Bibel'sche Orient explicitly refers to Herder's "The Spirit of Hebrew Poetry". The basic idea of Schelling's philosophy, which finds its expression in the Bibel'sche Orient, is as follows: God and world cannot be grasped conceptually but must be recognized as a reality.[17] From this basic deliberation derive consequences of such a kind that God and world, time and becoming, promise and fulfillment are interwoven in widely extended and splendidly lucid formulations. A conceptual, or negative, philosophy of causal explanations precedes a positive philosophy of comprehensive reality. But the negative, or intellectual, philosophy cannot promote a relationship to existential reality. The God of positive philosophy is prior to time and within time, time's point of departure, and time's destination—he is, according to the word emanating from the burning bush, the one "who was and is and will be." Also, the gods of mythology, who are corporeally conceived, are not a distortion or an allegory, but a reality in their own right which, to be sure, has not advanced to the recognition of the All-and-One. The content of mythology is not to be conceived as a product of thought, but as a necessary process, a historical fact. Peoples come into being *pari passu* with mythology, and along with peoplehood arises polytheism as their mode of expression and languages as their spiritual potentiality. With languages, again, unarticulated existence is elevated to perceptive vision, by means of which and beyond which revelation is carried back to its origin and the cleavage overcome. Revealed religion, like mythology, is concrete and real, not, as one might assume, merely doctrinal. Revelation has its pinnacle in Christ, but is contained already in the Old Testament. The Hebrews are constituted as a people because they differ, if only in a comparative understanding, from other peoples—in reality and literally they are, as the meaning of the word indicates, transients (*ivrim*) whose attachment is to the principle of unity. In the seventh lecture of the "Philosophy of Mythology," Schelling pleads in a grandiose manner the cause of the unity of the Torah. According to Schelling, *Elohim* means the generally accepted and immediately experienced God who even contains the potentiality of polytheism; *Jehova* is the God who is called by name and recognized as unique.[18] The idea of the becoming of the concept of God, who nevertheless represents a unity, is expressed in various passages by Schelling. So, Elohim speaks to Abraham and tells him to sacrifice Isaac, while the angel of Jehova (*malach adonai*) hinders him to lay his hand on the boy. When Moses inquires about the name of God, so that he might be enabled to reply to the children of Israel, he receives the answer: "Thus shalt thou say: Jehova, Elohim of your fathers, he sent me unto you, this is my name for ever."[19] Schelling's philosophy of time and eternity is grounded on the foundation of philology. One receives the impression that Schelling was a master of the Hebrew language from the word-roots. Thus, he designates eternity as the overcoming of time, because victory and eternity are expressed in one single root, *nezach-nizachon,* in "the meaningful Hebrew language," as he puts it. *El olam* is the God who existed in time and eternity and who is convincing on account of his continued existence (*nizeach*).[20] What Schelling recognized in the Torah was mythology along with revelation, partiality along with universality, the beginning along with the goal.

Bernays (or whoever the author of *Bibel'sche Orient* may be) drew Jewish-philosophical consequences from the basic principles of Schelling's deliberations.[21] Schelling's argument provided an opportunity for Bernays to confront the Jewish representatives of enlightenment, or, as he called them, "our Friedlaenderianer," with the actuality of history. Rather than contrast an ethically conceived Bible to a superannuated ceremonial law, as the propagators of enlightenment did, Bernays traced the ceremonial law back to its biblical source. At the same time, it was his intention to argue against the conventional overgrowing of the biblical foundation by what he called the "stifling decree" of talmudic interpretation. Looked upon that way, the *Bibel'sche Orient* holds middle ground between congealment and shallowness. As for Herder and Schelling, so was for Bernays the Bible the *Nationalbuch* of an old people; the Hebrew language the manifestation of the *Volksgeist,* that is, the spiritual existence of the people; ritual law, which regulates conduct, the symbolic expression of the incomprehensible; and cultus the body of Judaism, representing esoteric truth in a way in which it can be grasped. Particularly instructive is what Bernays has to say about the Hebrew language. The Hebrew language is presented as a genuinely human "remembrance of the oldest world-ideas" whose verbal designations, to be sure, have been transmuted into monotheistic meanings. For Bernays, the Bible was, and is, beyond its particular aspect, the testimony to the initial condition of the world, an image of what is eternally valid, and an exemplary model of the future of humanity.

Hence, as "the body of the creative word is transformed into the world of externality," the temporal term of eternity is interpreted as unfolding in history and as guided by providence. What was shown in the Bible was "a world-historical document of the dominion of providence and its divine efficacy upon the human mind, demonstrated in an exemplary way in *one* people", and "this people, as long as its law reigns over it," as standing for all humankind. Bernays recognizes that the Lord simultaneously is "our God" (*elohenu*) and the "one God of the whole world" (*echad*). The usual translation: "The Lord, our God, the Lord is One" blurs this coincidence of opposites. While the essence of what is pagan is expressed in the plastic image, the Jewish way is the "symbolic act," whose task it is to concretize (*versinnlichen*) the idea, not, as in the religion of reason, to spiritualize (*vergeistigen*) the concrete.[22] Moreover, the author of the *Bibel'sche Orient* meets in one point with the liberal spirit of the time. He makes the Bible, rather than the Talmud, the focal center of Jewish thought. The Kabbala—by no means condemned to a subterraneous existence—is recognized as "the national treatment of Essenic ideas" and as a "spiritual organ" as far as its numerical system is concerned, but is not accepted as subjective phantasies and arbitrary speculation of theosophers or as an "ascetically inspired twisting of the meaning of the law by Yizhak Luria—but the spell is broken. The *Bibel'sche Orient,* as also Max Wiener emphasizes,[23] is conceived in Schelling's image. It is an enthusiastic document which embraces everything, yet grasps nothing. However, one must not forget that the *Bibel'sche Orient* is merely a fragment and that elaboration and conclusion are missing. Nevertheless, what remains is a document in which what is specifically Jewish is expressed in the language of the philosophy of the time.

The regional element must not be disregarded at this point.[24] Briefly put: while the Mendelssohnian Emancipation is a manifestation of the Enlightenment, and through the Mendelssohn circle, Friedlaender, Jakobson, and the Hamburg Reform Temple, centered in Berlin, Koenigsberg, and Hamburg, that is, in the large north-German communities, the second Emancipation is part of the romantic movement and south German in derivation and tendency. Frankfurt, through Nathan Ha-Kohen Adler and his students, is the point of departure. Wuerzburg, through Abraham Bing, Mendel Rosenbaum, Seligmann Baer Bamberger, and others, is the point of collection, with Bernays included in the Wuerzburg group. Munich, through Schelling and possibly Baader, is the locality from where the philosophical stimulations emanated which introduced Jewish traditionalism into the spiritual world of Europe. The combination of the traditional and the philosophical is first marked by Bernays, later confirmed by Loewengaard. At the same time, the tie to village and small town in preserved, as in Michelstadt near Frankfurt (Wormser), Zell near Wuerzburg (Rosenbaum), Freudenthal near Stuttgart (Schnaittach), and in Muehringen-Hechingen and other places in Wuerttemberg, again through Loewengaard. However, combinations and entanglements are associated with that basic theme: Bernays transferred the second Emancipation to Hamburg, where a vigorous Orthodox community maintained itself until the Hitler time— somewhat as a reaction to the reformist Hamburg Temple. That outcome shows that Bernays cannot have been as ineffective a teacher as is commonly assumed. It ought to be recognized, on the other hand, that Bernays's pupil, Samson Raphael Hirsch, a native of Hamburg, transferred the stimulation he had received from Bernays to Frankfurt in a rationalistic-didactic reformulation which would have been foreign to Bernays. Finally, with Franz Rosenzweig, the movement was reversed, inasmuch as he returned the neo-Kantianism of Hermann Cohen to a revised Schellingian existentialism. These interrelationships will be further clarified in the course of our study.

We must now turn our attention to an author who hitherto has remained unknown, Hirsch Maier Loewengaard (1813-1886) of Rexingen, Wuerttemberg.[25] Loewengaard, Rabbinatsverweser and rabbi in Berlichingen, Jebenhausen near Goeppingen, and Lehrensteinfeld (all in Württemberg), later left the rabbinate, worked, apparently only for a short while, in the editorial offices of the *Israelit* in Mainz as a colleague of Rabbi Markus Lehmann, and in 1859 finally moved to Basel. He lived there as a private scholar (Dayyan and Shi'ur Rabbi). He died in Basel 1886, at the age of seventy-three. Loewengaard was a student of Rabbi Gabriel Adler in Muehringen, then studied at the yeshiva in Hechingen and at the Universities of Tuebingen, Heidelberg, and Munich. Through Gabriel Adler, like Bernays through Bing, Loewengaard was connected with the yeshiva of Nathan Ha-Kohen Adler in Frankfurt. Gabriel Adler, educated in Frankfurt, was the son of the Landesrabbiner Marcus Adler in Hanover and a brother of Nathan Marcus Adler of London, chief rabbi of the British Empire and founder of Anglo-Orthodoxy.[26] Nathan Marcus Adler was a student of Abraham Bing; the father was a student and near-relative of Nathan Ha-Kohen Adler.[27] As the Yeshiva in Hechingen soon declined, numerous students assembled around Gabriel Adler. One must assume that Gabriel Adler transmitted the Kabbalistic tradition of the Adler family to Löwengard, who acknowledged the fact openly, as may be concluded from his pen-name "Juda Leon." "Juda" stands for Löwengard (the Lion of Juda!) and "Leon" for the Spanish kabbalist Moses de Leon, who was the author of the *Zohar*, according to Gershom Scholem.[28] In his writings, Löwengard quotes, apart from Moses Maimonides, also Moses Nachmanides, one of the small number of Spanish kabbalists who have contributed remarkably to rabbinic literature. Three publications of Löwengard have been preserved, two under his proper name, one under the name of Juda Leon. In these three publications, Löwengard advocates a reform of conventional Judaism, but a reform which continues, not destroys, tradition. Löwengard thus stands for a third solution which is not identical either with Orthodoxy or with liberalism. We are going to follow Löwengard's argument through his three publications.

The first publication, published in 1841 by the author under the name Juda Leon, bears the title *Beiträge zur Kritik der Reformsbestrebungen in der Synagoge* (Contributions to a Critique of the Reform Movement in the Synagogue). It is prefaced by a motto from Lessing: "If Catholic and Protestant insists on Catholic and Protestant, why should only the Jew not be permitted to show the Jew?" An even more significant motto is offered in the text: "Le roi est mort, vive le roi."[29] The young author admits in the foreword that he had composed his words "in the first excitement about the nonchalance and distinguished coolness with which some pronounce en passant judgment of death over large parts of the Jewish religious system." Löwengard's commentary, as he calls it, is directed against the sermons of Dr. Maier (Stuttgart) and Rabbis Mannheimer (Vienna) and Salomon (Hamburg). Löwengard expresses the opinion that all revealed religions had arrived "at the point of desperation"; yet, contrary to the paganism of antiquity which could "throw itself in the arms of a newly blossomed lively creed,'' our contemporaries merely "faced an empty abyss.'' The Jews particularly had progressed in the fifty years since Mendelssohn "from modest doubt to a complete lack of faith and to total indifference.'' It is Löwengard's thesis that what exists deserves consideration, but that, on the other hand, institutions are subject to change. The old-time rabbis had been in the possession of moral power, that is, of the confidence of the community, but had neglected to make concessions to the educated public, while the modern theologians, without enjoying universal confidence, overemphasize "prophetic Judaism,'' disquieting the conscience without achieving a pacification of reason. The question was now: rupture or accommodation? The educated members of the community should find it possible to show "patience with the traditional shape of religion'' without making those less educated feel insecure on "the dizzying heights'' of abstraction. Tolerance needs to be combined with rabbinic scholarship. Löwengard concludes with the comment that he was not the servant of any party in Judaism.

Löwengard is impartial also in his subsequent remarks. Yet, while he blames the "cocooned rabbis'' who never had taken notice of "the whistling loom of the time,'' he is much more outspoken vis-à-vis the newfangled "preachers.'' The sermons of the reformers, he feels, could neither touch the authority of the Talmud nor replace the belief of redemption of Zion by the expectation of "universal enlightenment.'' The doctrine of the Messiah was not thought through to its end by those who incessantly talk about it, because the Messiah was supposed to be "king and teacher''; "teacher'' alone was not enough. It was not possible to draw a line of division between the Talmud that incorporates "pure tradition'' and those parts of it that are less obligatory; nor could one counterpose Bible and Talmud, or Prophets and Law. It was a superficial understanding of the spirit of the prophets to believe that "one could forge weapons against religion itself by availing oneself of the magnificent prophetic lectures against the abuse of the ceremonial aspects of religion for the purpose of a justification by work or in the service of hypocrisy.'' Prophetic Judaism was not a "partial concept'' but the "whole Judaism.'' Torah derived from Moses and Moses was the greatest prophet. "Freedom of discussion'' was necessary, but not "those victory bulletins before the battle had actually started.'' One could not help asking oneself what the "final goal'' of all the radically negative efforts was supposed to be? And what was the lever of change? Was apologetics helpful in the battle for emancipation? "Just try,'' Löwengard asserts, "and eliminate everything from our religious life and confession that might lend itself to misjudgment—prejudice against us, rather than vanish, would stand out even more glaringly.''

The fronts are changed in Löwengard's publication of 1842, *Auch einige Worte über das neue Gebetbuch im Hamburger Tempel* (A Few Words about

the New Prayerbook in the Hamburg Temple).[30] While Löwengard is a traditionalist in the question of the retention and justification of the ceremonial
law, he favors more freedom in reforming the synagogue service, provided
such a reform would not violate the spirit of tradition. According to Löwengard, there are three possible areas of reform in Judaism: reform of dogma, of
casuistry, and of cultus. In the area of dogma, changes are excluded; in
casuistry, that is, in the decision of single legal cases, the question was about
the limits of reform; but radical reforms are called for in the cultus. Bernays
and Ettlinger, Löwengard believes, had made a mistake in their declaration
against the Hamburg Temple, because their condemnation was directed precisely against those efforts of reform that had the greatest justification, namely,
those in the area of cultus. One must appreciate, he continues, these two
rabbis in their "peculiar ways": Ettlinger should continue with investigations
about "willows and watercress" (meaning minutiae rather than essentials),
while Bernays was best advised if "he persisted in his contemplative inclination." He surely was not meant to be a reformer. One could not accuse the
Hamburg prayerbook of a "sin against the positive content of the Jewish
religion." However, Löwengard argues not so much against Bernays and
Ettlinger but against the great mass of Orthodox "coreligionists," meaning
that he turns "against the veto of inertia, against the organization of a dignified divine service," against the overloading of the service with "too great
a quantity of prayers"; he is in favor of the introduction of instrumental music
and community singing, provided, however, that what is "characteristic of
the synagogue" be preserved and, he adds, preferably without the organ and
Protestant chorals. The use of the Hebrew language in prayer was to be
preserved, but not in the case of a worshipper who does not understand the
wording of the prayer. He wishes to shorten prayers and to omit passages
which contain hostility against other peoples. However, with all conceded
freedom of choice and interpretation, Löwengard turns against the overem-
phasis on the individualistic point of view that is inherent in the efforts of
reform. For instance, he says, we express in the Mussaf prayer the expectation
that the whole of Israel, not the isolated worshipper, may be led up in joy into
"our land"; the "messianic hopes" of the synagogue remained in force even
if the messianic belief, from the point of view of the individual, may be
considered "logically untenable." "The right of the individual" had to take
second place to "public service," if held against the principle that "the faith
of all fortifies the faith." No matter whether one considered the newer religious conditions "progress" or a "misfortune," the fact remained that "the
sincere teacher of religion" was no more in a position, as previously, to
demand obedience "as something which goes without saying." Just as little,
however, should the teacher feel justified "to throw away this plentiful and
productive stuff en bloc, as if there were no more validity to it." What the

people mean by religion has "a tough life" and would give "a lot of trouble" to the radicals. On the other hand, faith, as with Maimonides, is not to exclude philosophical justification. It is obvious that Löwengard is a conservative who wants to change only where change serves preservation.

The picture of Löwengard may be complemented by the protocols of the second and third German rabbinical assemblies in Frankfurt am Main (1845) and Breslau (1846), in which he participated.[31] The protocols show that Löwengard, not always in agreement with the majority of participants, must be considered an adherent of a reform which preserves tradition. He speaks for the maintenance of the Hebrew language in the service, especially regarding the reading from the Torah, while he is inclined to permit the vernacular regarding reading from the Prophets (*neviim*) and Writings (*ketubim*). Similarly, he is for the idea of the Messiah, but against a political Jewish state; for the admission of the organ in the synagogue service and the abolition of conventional modes of mourning, such as rending the garments, growing of the beard, and the like. On the other hand, Löwengard votes against the motion of Wechsler to reduce the period of mourning from seven days to three; against the motion of Hess, to leave mourning habits to the "religious-moral sentiments of the mourners"; and against the motion of Holdheim which opposes any kind of new casuistry, with the reason that one had "abolished already enough," meaning more than enough. In addition, he is of the opinion that one should not "initiate" new reforms. Reforms should be considered admissible only "where the cleavage has already entered the consciousness."

With his third publication, *Jehova, nicht Moloch, war der Gott der alten Hebräer* (Jehova, not Moloch, was the God of the Ancient Hebrews), which was published in 1843 in Berlin, Löwengard makes his entry into the political arena. More importantly, this writing is an outstanding source for our knowledge of the powerful influence which Schelling exerted upon his Jewish listeners.

The Moloch story belongs to the history of antisemitism in Germany, especially in Nürnberg. F.W. Ghillany, professor and city librarian in Nürnberg, against whom Löwengard polemicizes, was the author of a book which appeared in Nürnberg in 1842 with the title, *Die Menschenopfer der alten Hebräer, eine geschichtliche Untersuchung* (The Human Sacrifices of the Ancient Hebrews, a Historical Investigation). The book reads like a prelude to the propaganda of Julius Streicher. Ghillany quotes verbatim passages from the books of the Bible, in order to prove that the ancient Hebrews had sacrificed human beings and that Moloch, not Jehova, was the original God of the Hebrews. Toward the end of the book, he observes that remnants of the sacrificial cult had continued surreptitiously: even after the Persians had abolished it. Ghillany alludes to the possibility of the continuation of "human sacrifices on the occasion of the Pessach festival.'' In the style of the later nazistic assertions, he continues: "The accusation which arose among Christians and Mohammedans is consequence of such a possibility, that even the Hebrews, who presently are dispersed among the nations, occasionally indulged in human sacrifice, does not belong to the area which I have staked out in writing the present book.'' Thus Ghillany dispatches the poisoned arrow which in the Hitler period had such a deadly effect all over Germany. The slogan "*Franken voran*" must be remembered in that context.

Löwengard says in the foreword to his polemical publication that he is speaking out because no Jewish scholar had attempted a refutation of Ghillany's book, possibly because it had not yet aroused the attention of Jewish scholars. Following the Schellingian argument, Löwengard admits that the biblical narration demonstrated that the majority of the people of Israel had adhered to "mythology" and that only a small band had stood for pure monotheism. As examples, he mentions Jephta, Samson, and the golden calf. On the other hand, he indicates that Prophets, Talmud, and Midrash had combatted the powerful impact of paganism in Judaism, had branded the worship of idols as a crime, and had elevated the service of the one and only God to a legitimate principle. We will return later to the mythological connection; at this point, it may suffice to refer to Löwengard's admission that even "some features in the biblical-talmudic ceremonial prescriptions were of intrinsically pagan origin" and that a division of the laws of Moses "in those that emanate from the principle of pure monotheism and those which do not rise above the level of paganism," as advocated by "men of progress among Jewish theologians," failed to correspond to the reality of ancient history. Among these "men of progress," to mention but one example, one would have to count S.L. Steinheim, who had attacked Isaac Bernays's "antibiblical" *Bibel' sche Orient*,[32] possibly, but not demonstrably, under the impression gained from reading Ghillany's book. "This abominable piece of writing," says Steinheim about Bernays, "has no other goal but the total negation of the revelation of the living God by fusing and equating the Holy One of Israel with the damnable idols of Canaan." In contradistinction, Löwengard's argument reads like a defense of Bernays and Schelling. Löwengard agrees with Maimonides that "the obligatory power of the ceremonial law must remain untouched by the results of rational research"; on the other hand, he asserts, however, that "even the most attractive motives which may be found regarding this or other ceremonial laws had only homiletic value, no imperative weight." The first-named argument is directed against Spinoza and his adherents and successors, including the "men of progress"; the latter argument is directed against Samson Raphael Hirsch's conception of "Israel's duties." One surely must agree with Löwengard that Ghillany's book could hardly have found "a more lenient adversary among the Jews."[33]

All the more emphatic is Löwengard's refutation of Ghillany's inflammatory "phantasmagories" in the second part of his publication. Ghillany maintains that Jehova had been imposed on the ancient Hebrews and that in heart and deed they had remained Moloch worshippers. Abraham, Moses, Samuel, and David had been admirers of Moloch. To be sure, the "Moloch religion, Moloch constitution, and Moloch literature of the ancient Hebrews" had been "totally destroyed by the Jehovistic revolution," yet not so "totally" that they had not been "transmitted" (*fortgepflanzt*) by means of the "thirsting after Christian blood" of the latter-day Jews! We do not have to follow here in detail the low-level arguments of Ghillany and the sharp refutation by Löwengard. Yet, the controversy contains implications which ought to be mentioned. In the final sentences of the second part of his brochure, Löwengard points to the *causa efficiens occulta,* as he calls it, of the "shameful role" to which Dr. Ghillany has condemned scholarship.[34] He points to the "arrogance of many learned theologians, of predominantly flat-rationalistic or narrow-minded esthetic inclinations, by means of which they are ashamed of the connection between the Old and New Testaments." Another thought is added to this observation. Löwengard refers to the "higher criticism" of the biblical writings that was already proliferating at this time, from Eichhorn to Hengstenberg, to Ewald, to the "moderately negative" critique of Gesenius and the "immoderately negative" critique of Gramberg.[35] In referring to the negative criticism "which does not leave one stone upon the other in the writings of the Old Testament and has an eye only for what is disparate in these books," Löwengard combats the school of Wellhausen avant la lettre with an argument which can be compared to the opinions of Sampson Raphael Hirsch, Benno Jacob, and Franz Rosenzweig at a later time, but which turns more immediately against the demagogic distortion of the criticism of Ghillany.[36] Nevertheless, the theologians mentioned by Löwengard are also meant. The effect which was desired subconsciously, although not always consciously intended by these scholars, was to destroy the unity of the Torah and to replace that unity with a conglomerate of heterogeneous particles. The idea was that a continued historical existence was denied to these fragments and that Judaism was a lost cause. As a matter of fact, the real existence of the Torah does not depend on any critical analysis. Critique per se is justified. Yet, it remains true that the splintering of the Torah leads to the denial of the right of existence of the Jewish people which is founded upon the Torah, and true that the denial has become historically effective, as subsequent events have demonstrated. In that context, Löwengard's conclusion is prophetic in character. As a "lonely Jew" and all "reverence for the heights and depths of German scholarship" notwithstanding, he predicts: "Once upon a time, truth will demand a strict accounting from those who fondle a lie and from those who do not resist it as much as they can."

The conclusion, as well as some comments in the first chapter of Löwengard's publication, *Jehova, nicht Moloch, war der Gott der Alten Hebräer*, point to the core of the double thesis which we wish to present: first, that the influence of the personality and the philosophy of Schelling on the thinking of the spokesmen of the second Emancipation, which may be called a conservative emancipation, cannot be gainsaid; and second, that the thinking of these spokesmen, as well as of Schelling, had emanated from kabbalistic sources.[37] The interrelationship can be documented. We are informed about the personal contact between Schelling and Löwengard through a document which I have discovered in the Geheimes Hausarchiv in Munich. King Max II of Bavaria had asked Schelling, his former teacher, about his opinion and recommendation regarding the emancipation of the Jews, when that question had gained timeliness in the revolutionary year 1848. Schelling immediately sent a memorandum to the king, to which he attached a private letter. In the letter, Schelling points out that, in case emancipation should be granted, the Jews most likely would demand a Jewish consistory and a Jewish faculty, presumably side-by-side with the existing Catholic and Protestant theological faculties at Bavarian universitites. He continued:

> I believe that both institutions, properly introduced, could only lead to a good end. The main thing seems to be that the Jews should be turned away from the thoughtlessness of their presently practiced religion which, if not checked, can only terminate in unrestrained atheism. I would say that in Bavaria or nearby, people could be found who might be called to a chair at the Faculty of Theology. In my time, numerous candidates for the rabbinate studied in Munich; they even attended lectures by Catholic theologians, for instance, exegetic lectures by Allioli about books of the Old Testament. I had many Jewish listeners in my own lectures, especially in the philosophy of revelation, and there were many good minds ["*viele gute Köpfe*"] among them. If the occasion should arise, I could name a person who in the meantime has made a name for himself as a writer (Löwengard, Rabbi in Jebenhausen near Goeppingen, Wuerttemberg); he might be also useful as a consultant prior to any decisions to be made about a chair. I have seen him here (in Berlin) only two years ago; without the political changes that have occured, he might have been able to find a position in Prussia that would have been in line with his capability; I will hope that he has preserved himself mentally under the pressure of the miserable conditions in which he has had to make a living.[38]

One must conclude from that passage that Schelling has had a chance to read Löwengard's writings and that he has found himself in agreement with them. It appears that Löwengard has conferred with Schelling in Berlin in 1846, and it is fair to assume that he has asked Schelling to help him in finding a professorship; he did not feel comfortable in the rabbinate. Schelling made an effort to help, but without success. Not even the emancipation legislation was enacted at that time.

One can go a step further and say that Schelling was most attentive to his Jewish students, apart from Löwengard, and to the problem of Jewish-Christian relations in terms of theology, as well as to the problem of Jewish existence in the contemporary world. It must be kept in mind at the same time that Schelling was an intense Christian in faith and that he was holding fast to the belief that Judaism had "fulfilled" itself in Christianity. For further elaboration, let us turn to the twenty-ninth lecture of his "Philosophy of Revelation."[39] Here, Schelling finds that "the blood of bulls and goats" (Hebr. 9: 13) in biblical sacrifice had brought about "only purification," but failed to liberate "Man's innermost being, his conscience."[40] The sacrifices had to be repeated over and over again because they could not do away with "the real reason for the discord of man with God." The repeated sacrifices pointed toward the last great sacrifice which was to abolish paganism and Judaism at the same time. To be sure, Schelling adds that it must not be doubted that the sacrifices of the Old Testament had "real significance" in their time because otherwise "that of which they were paradigms would have lost significance"—the reconciliation through Christ. That passus is accompanied by a lengthy note which covers a whole page and which testifies to the intensive dialogue (*Gespräch*) which took place between Schelling and his Jewish listeners. Schelling says in the note:

> One of my listeners has written to me repeating what he had mentioned verbatim earlier, referring to my statement that the relation of man to God in Judaism was external, not personal, and that the external atonement with God had not done away with the discord of man and God; he considers this statement as not in accordance with the Old Testament. Regarding these statements, I would say:
>
> 1. The author of the letter cannot ask that I, from my point of view, should think differently about the external, servant-like behavior, than the apostle Paul who must be granted a deeper insight into Judaism than I or he can ever have. Paul speaks about the servant-like spirit of Judaism, e.g. when he says (Rom. 8: 15): 'For ye have not received the spirit of bondage again to fear, but you have received the spirit of adoption.' Or, Paul admonishes the Galatians (5:1): 'Stand fast therefore in the liberty wherewith Christ has made us free and be not entangled again with the yoke of bondage.' And what he means by the yoke of bondage, one may understand from what follows. He continues: 'Behold, I, Paul, say unto you, that if ye be circumcised, Christ shall profit you nothing. For I testify again to every man who is circumcised, that he is a debtor to do the whole law.' It is to be concluded that the yoke of bondage is nothing else but the totality of Mosaic law.
>
> 2. It is the teaching of the apostles that the atonement whereof the Old Testament speaks is only such that the inner disunion, the discord with God in man's mind, is not abolished thereby and that it follows that the sacrifices must be performed repeatedly. The entire epistle to the Hebrews, which reveals an author with a deep knowledge of Mosaic law, is written in this sense. However, I will admit to my esteemed listener that enough passages occur in the Old Testament which demand voluntary obedience, that is, a love of God. Surely,

isolated rays of a higher atonement break through, especially with the prophets or in passages in the prophetic writings. This must be explained from the contradiction which I have shown to exist in the constitution of the Old Testament, namely, the contradiction between what is contained in it independent of revelation and what is revelation itself. Revelation breaks through, primarily in the prophets, only in a veiled way in the law of Moses. Prophetism as a potentiality already was contradictory to the law—it was quasi the Dionysic element in the Old Testament. The Jew, when he performed the sacrifices which the law demanded of him, followed the same necessity, the same impulse as the pagan who was performing his sacrifices; what distinguished Jews from pagans was what was prophetic in them, that is, the future which was indicated in prophecy.

Schelling concedes to his Jewish listeners that Torah and Prophets, but especially the Prophets, have known the principle of love. But he holds fast to the idea that the "process," as he calls it, of mythology equally embraces Judaism and paganism and that revelation, although contained in Judaism and not in paganism, breaks through only in the "future," that is, in Christ. Moreover, Schelling makes a further concession, and one which transforms the adversary position into a dialogic encounter.[41] To be sure, the Jews had excluded themselves from the great movement of history because they rejected Christ, and one could only wish and pray that "the veil" be removed from their eyes, but he adds that it

certainly would be very wrong to alienate the Jews from their ancestral religion and to give them instead a general, absolutely ahistoric and purely theistic religion. As long as they hold fast to their ancestral religion, they retain a connection with true history, the divinely willed process, which is the true life. . . . Totally broken away and torn away from that connection, the Jews never again would find another connecting link and they would become in a different and even worse way than what they are now and what so many are in our time who have lost the connection with history, and who, like the Jews, are *extorres* and *exsules,* homeless and banished and never finding rest. However, a general conversion of the Jews to mere theism or to a so-called pure religion of reason is not to be expected.

Schelling contends that the Jews are a people held in reservation (*"das vorbehaltene Volk"*). The promises that were given to them will not have been in vain. "The day will come," he says, "when they will be readmitted in the divine economy from which they are now excluded and almost forgotten."[42] It remains a secret, when that day will come, but "in the meantime, the necessary civil rights should not be withheld from them." Schelling had used a similar argument in favor of the emancipation of the Jews in the memorandum to King Max II. In the quoted words from the "Philosophy of Revelation," Schelling's position is even clearer. He appears as a stimulator of a conservative emancipation in Judaism, from a decidedly Christian vantage point, to be sure, but nevertheless in recognition of the continued historical existence of Judaism.

Löwengard's comments on Schelling in *Jehova, nicht Moloch, war der Gott der alten Hebräer* must be appreciated in the light of such passages as the one just cited from the twenty-ninth lecture of the "Philosophy of Revelation." Löwengard speaks in the first pages of the *Moloch* brochure about the "unmatched" enthusiasm of the listeners for Schelling and about "the field of knowledge" (*Wissenschaft*) which he has reshaped and recreated.[43] He refers to Creuzer's *Symbolik*[44] and to Schelling's concept of the "mythological process" which he believes carries the student far beyond Creuzer.[45] However, the Jew stops if he hears symbolic expression and mythology mentioned in a biblical context. He suspects an impermissible contradiction. According to Löwengard, the novelty of the combination made "an extraordinary powerful impression on the entire auditorium," but in addition a tragic impression on the Jewish listeners, because they felt as if they had been robbed of the crown jewel of monotheism. Nevertheless, Löwengard concedes to Schelling's exposition the seductive spell which the mythological process cast over Israel, along with the entire world of antiquity. Israel frequently resorted to apostasy. Neither the "low folk" nor the "class of magnates," only a small group of the faithful, had adhered to Jehova in love. Löwengard quotes Judges 11 and 14, Midrash Rabba, Tractate Sanhedrin, and other passages which should confirm the thesis of the comprehensive mythological process. "A considerable part of the mosaic-talmudic ceremonial law," according to Löwengard, fails to rise above the level of paganism; neither could the ceremonial law be considered as "a mere staircase on which one might ascend to ordinary moral purposes." Nevertheless, one should emphasize "what remains significant in biblical-talmudical ceremonial matters, for instance, in the celebration of the Sabbath and the holidays and in the interdiction of the eating of unclean animals." With this argumentation, Löwengard intends to grant the pagan character of many biblical precepts, yet demonstrates the limits for the applicability of a hypothesis which indiscriminately intermingles biblical Judaism and Canaanite paganism. One might comment here that Löwengard appears to draw the contrasts too sharply. For Schelling, the God that is One, eternal, and can be spoken to was present already in the Burning Bush and the experience of Elijah on Horeb. In Schelling's own sight, therefore, one can comprehend mythology and monotheism as having risen simultaneously and without standing in need of the christological fulfillment which Schelling considered as the one and only consequence of his biblical faith.

The concluding paragraphs of the *Jehova* book start with a confession which permits a further clarification of Löwengard's and his friend's relation to the person and thought of Schelling. Here are Löwengard's words: "The old darkness has been stirring mightily in these last years. All evil passions, all superannuated errors, all mean insinuations are awakened to a life of terrible reality and set upon the Jews. Or is the aim only against the Jews? Is this possibly the beginning of a widely extended historical tragedy?" In view of this "widely extended historical tragedy" which Löwengard sees coming, he accuses both those who are conventionally pious and those who are new-fangled reformers of an inadequate comprehension of the truths of Judaism. The synagogue, he maintains, could not possibly occupy a dignified position in the eyes of outsiders as long as the internal confusion in religious matters absorbs the best parts of its strength. Löwengard uses the opportunity of a last, sad meeting he had with a terminally ill friend, whom he had known since his student years, to point to the significance which the philosophy of Schelling could have for a new orientation of Jewish thinking. Löwengard considers as "unthinkable and inefficient" a middle position between the parties—rather the need was for a bold new initiative. But what is the right path? In what manner should one direct the carriage of the synagogue weighed down, as it was, by an unnecessarily heavy load? One thing was certain to him: one should not "experiment with an organic structure as if it were dead matter." Instead of attempting a "formation from the inside out," one observes that bitter strife has arisen between those who argue about "measure and weight" and those who are ready to race ahead "with an entirely empty carriage." Löwengard interrupts the "melancholy discussion" with his ill friend in order to remind him of the "intellectually enjoyable days of our youthful friendship in Munich and our companionship as listeners to Schelling's lectures." The remark stirs the smouldering ashes to a fire of enthusiasm. The friend replies: "Oh, yes, I would like to hear Schelling once again, at least for one year— and then die." "But," I asked, "could you listen once again with the old undimmed delight to the exposition of the development whereby God, after he had said "yes" must not, following a well-known proverb, say b, but become b? How b, as the time was fulfilled, turns into $c-c$ meaning Christ, and so on? "Why not?" replies the friend. "For Christian listeners, the philosophy of revelation may appear disturbing because they are opposed and even hostile to the dogmatic content of their own religion. For what meets them in a delightful garb in a philosophical lecture, and offers itself with winning grace as a mere "remote possibility," presents itself to those in the Church as an unfriendly and tyrannical dogma. But to me, who is dogmatically free, these possible thoughts, this truly admirable combination of the facts of history, provide an unspeakable enchantment. . . . Yes, for one more year I would like to be able to listen to Schelling—then I shall gladly die."

The intensity of this confession indicates that Schelling must have been a master of dialogic communication, or, in other words, of a "narrating philosophy."[46] By a "narrating philosophy" we mean a philosophy which records and interprets what has actually happened, far away as it may have been, a philosophy which presents, in the words of the dying friend, a "combination of the facts of history." The sceptical attitude of the Jewish listener, who is confronted with the christological turn of Schelling's thoughts, is being overwhelmed, on the other hand, by the boldness of the communicated conception, by the surprising connection between, and joining together of, seemingly far-distant historical events, by the fire of indisputable conviction. Schelling speaks to the listeners, as Karl Jaspers puts it, "with the excitement of philosophical ardor, with the will to make understandable what is rapturous, with a solemn mode of expression, with the dignity of philosophy, with the effects of rhetoric splendor."[47] Jaspers attaches a negative connotation to this description, as if Schelling had been more a magician than a philosopher. This evaluation does not change the fact that few of the Jewish scholars of his time equalled Schelling in the philosophical analysis of the events recorded in the Bible, in the lucidity of the comprehension of what is meant by time and eternity and what is the essence of the religious experience. The Jewish listeners found that they were elevated above themselves, yet they felt that they remained within the bounds of their own being. They experienced an emancipation "from the inside out."

Our deliberations are not ended with that statement of Jaspers and the confirmation of it in the writings of Löwengard. It remains to be demonstrated that what the Jewish students listened to in Schelling's lectures was their own Jewish heritage in philosophical transformation. Schelling appeared to them as a master of the Hebrew language, which had been neglected by the Jews of his generation and, at any rate, as a challenging interpreter of biblical thought. In addition, he was a successor of the Christian Kabbala. We cannot deal extensively here with the stimulations which Schelling had received from the representatives of the Christian Kabbala and with the intellectual cross-currents which connected his philosophy with kabbalistic thought. Suffice it to indicate the following: Schelling was the son of a Protestant minister. He was a student of the famous *Tuebingen Stift,* along with Hegel and Hölderlin. Deliberations and speculations about the imminent spiritual redemption of the world were, no doubt, alive in the pietistic atmosphere of the *Stift.* One must give the word here to Schelling himself:

> The most glaringly one describes the lack of peace, the discord, the phenomena which threaten disintegration in our time, the more assuredly can the truly informed see in all these things but the omen of a new creation, of a great and lasting reconstitution which, to be sure, would not be possible without painful labors because the reckless destruction of whatever is rotten, fragile and faulty must precede everything else. Yet, there must be an end to this struggle because

no end—and purposeless progress, as imagined by some—is possible. Humanity does not proceed into the infinite; humanity has a goal."[48]

Lofty expectations of this kind could be disappointed, but not refuted. Schelling was an heir. The chief representative of theosophic ideas in Württemberg Protestantism in the generation preceeding Schelling was Friedrich Christian Oetinger; his thinking has influenced Schelling and Hegel.[49] Oetinger had been in contact with Jewish kabbalists in Frankfurt am Main and Halle, and he knew through them, as well as by means of other sources, such authors as Jakob Boehme, Christian Knorr von Rosenroth (the author of *Cabbala Denudata,* a Christian commentary on the *Zohar*), and Yizhak Luria; he was acquainted with the book *Ez Chaim* of Chaim Vital.[50] Schelling had some inkling of those connections. He refers to the Kabbala in various passages in his writings. Schelling asked his father, in letters dated from the years 1802 and 1806, to send him the works of Oetinger, both for himself and for the Catholic philosopher Franz von Baader, whom Schelling had met in Munich in 1806.[51] Baader was attracted by the mysticism of Jakob Boehme, and he stayed in contact with the theosophical author Franz Joseph Molitor in Frankfurt am Main. Apart from Baader, Molitor seems to have been influenced by Schelling himself and by the Jewish kabbalist Ephraim Joseph Hirschfeld. Later, he published a *Philosophy of History of Tradition,* which contained an intensive and sympathizing, though uncritical, description and explanation of Jewish mysticism.[52] It is noteworthy that Molitor is mentioned and his application supported in the very same letter of Schelling to King Max II of Bavaria, which also contains the suggestion of a possible professorship for Löwengard. Schelling says that he considers Molitor's book important "for the history of philosophy, especially of Christianity." This passus indicates the nature of Schelling's interest in the Kabbala as presumably supportive of Christianity. In contradistinction, Franz von Baader, according to David Baumgardt, belongs to the few German thinkers of the nineteenth century who were ready to recognize in Judaism a religious entity in its own right, not merely a precursor to Christianity.[53] Baader was in intimate contact with Schelling until Schelling broke relations with him.[54] It is not out of the question that Baader, besides Schelling, influenced Bernays during his stay in Munich. Baader considers Israel the contracted image of humanity and the Hebrew language akin to the "original language" of mankind (*"Ursprache"*)— ideas that recur in the *Bibel'sche Orient.*[55] The line of transmission from the Swabian pietists, especially Oetinger, and also from Boehme and Baader, to Schelling cannot be gainsaid.

The intellectual connections indicating Schelling's acquaintance with the Kabbala are not less compelling. One concept that is prevalent in kabbalistic thinking is the idea of the "breaking of the vessels" (*Shevirath-ha-Kelim*), meaning that the vessels which contained the splendor of eternity are broken and that the break, or fall, into isolation must be healed.[56] However, the fall, Schelling asserts, is the means of revelation, because there is no revelation without eclipse, as there is no consciousness without the unconscious, no return without previous departure, no becoming without being.[57] Now, in the political state, we have "free human beings, but separated from God."[58] In the way of counter-image, one may say that God conceals himself in order to become conscious of himself, because all consciousness is concentration, collection, bringing together. Many passages in Schelling deal with concentration and expansion, but one must discern between concentration upon oneself, wherefrom derives the freedom of action, and the retreat, or contraction, of God out of the created world (*tsimtsum*), which makes possible the action of man.[59] *Tsimtsum* means that God "hides himself" or that he "retreats," whereby according to the Lurianic Kabbala, the sphere of freedom comes into being.

With Schelling, as well as with the Kabbala, the creation of the world and what is in it is a conscious act, not a necessary process, as with Hegel, in whose system reason takes the place of freedom. In God is necessity, to be sure, but only as that which presupposes freedom, "because a being must first exist, so that it can act freely."[60]

It is significant in the present context, where we deal with the mutuality of influence, to indicate the existence in the Kabbala of a doctrine of the trinity of powers (*Potenzen*), but not of persons, as well as a trichotomic psychology. The trinitarian distinction is between "highest crown," "wisdom," and "understanding." The trichotomic psychology divides mind or soul into *Neshamah* (breath of soul), *Nefesh* (drive of soul), and *Ruach* (spirit of soul). Christian Kabbalists have interpreted these ideas along the line of the Christian doctrine of the holy trinity. A trichotomic psychology is contained in Schelling's "Stuttgarter Privatvorlesungen." The trichotomic point of view, which was derived from the Kabbala, was taken over from Boehme by Oetinger and has been transmitted through him to Baader and Schelling.[61] In such manner, Schelling and the Christian Kabbala move away from the concept of unity which is essential in Judaism—a concept which, on the other hand, stands in the very center of Schelling's thought. Even Schelling's reply to the Jewish listener can be put to question, if one refers to the following passus from "Die Weltalter": "The New Testament is built on the foundation of the Old and obviously presupposes it. The beginning, the first great points in the systems which are developed into the outermost parts of the New Testament, are to be found only in the Old. But the beginnings are the essential, and whoever is unaware of them can never arrive at the whole."[62] If the beginnings are the essential, revelation is contained in them. Here we get into the area of the self-contradictions of Schelling, into which we do not intend to enter. Analysts and commentators should not be requested to interpret unambiguousness and logical consequence into the enthusiastic thinking of Schelling. As we have seen, the christological interpretation was not accepted by Schelling's Jewish listeners in his own time. But his demand of unity in the process of becoming, which is founded on the words of the Torah, has awakened the imagination in the same Jewish listeners, as if it had been spoken from their "inside out."

In view of Schelling's contacts with his Jewish listeners, I cannot agree with Scholem's sweeping thesis that a *deutsch-jüdisches Gespräch* (a dialogue between Germans and Jews) has never occurred.[63] To be sure, there is ample evidence for the phenomenon of the Jewish "cry into the void," which calls for fraternization and remains without reply. But Schelling provides a counterexample. If one takes as a criterion Scholem's statement that a dialogue requires two participants "who listen to each other, who are ready to recognize the partner as what he is and intends to be and to reply to him," then Schelling's note in the "Philosophy of Revelation" and the following paragraphs in the text must be accepted as contributions to a *Gespräch*. To be added are Schelling's comments in his letter to King Max II of Bavaria, wherein the chances for the integration of Jews as Jews—through consistory and theological faculty—are considered, as well as his efforts in providing an academic position for Löwengard, and finally his friendly chats with the philologist Jacob Bernays, a son of Isaac Bernays, who once had been Schelling's student. The picture is complemented from the Jewish side by Löwengard's report in the *Jehova-nicht-Moloch* brochure. Nothing is detracted from the dialogue by the fact that Schelling speaks as a Christian and the Jewish partners are Jews. To be sure, Schelling hopes for the ultimate baptism of the Jews, but he does not wish to tear them away from their "ancestral religion" in the meantime. He considers the Hebrew language as a font of wisdom for Jews and Christians. All in all, the documents which we have point to the fact that nobody can enter into a more meaningful dialogue than the Christian who is a convinced Christian and the Jew who is a conscious Jew.[64]

At this point, a comparison of Löwengard and Bernays is called for. Löwengard differs from Bernays in that he relates to Schelling differently. Bernays takes from Schelling and Herder the emphasis on the sensual, the concrete and the individual, whereby the individual ought to be understood not only in terms of the human personality but also in terms of the collective individual, the group, and the nationality. Language is the expression of the collective individual, of peoplehood. Judaism, its universality notwithstanding, is a national religion, and the Jewish ritual is the garb in which the meaning of the religious message is symbolically manifested. Löwengard, like Bernays, refers to the Kabbala, but compared with Bernays, he holds to a middle line, philosophically as well as in practical application. Bernays is not politically attached or engaged, while Löwengard, belonging to the generation that comes after Bernays, recognizes more clearly than Bernays the danger that arises from the demagogic distortion of romantic philosophies and turns against them. Also regarding religion, Löwengard is more accessible to some of the aims of liberal reform than Bernays. While Löwengard holds the line on ritual and dogma, as Bernays does, he intends to render the divine services more flexible; he wishes to lighten the load of the "heavy carriage" of conventional religious practice, at least as far as public worship is concerned. Bernays was not ready for concessions precisely in the area of cultus. Löwengard is an adherent of Schelling's philosophy of mythology, which includes Judaism in the total history of the peoples of antiquity and retraces the history of humanity to biblical origins; he is, like Bernays, an adversary of the religion of reason, and wishes to preserve what is hallowed by tradition and made popular through usage. The difference in the area of language is that Bernays has enhanced Schelling's elevated speech into baroque extravagance, while Löwengard returns that speech to an occasionally ironic, even sarcastic, but commonly intelligible idiom. Although Samson Raphael Hirsch, as we shall see, hardly continues along the line of Bernays' philosophy, modern Orthodoxy, as inspired by Hirsch, nevertheless arises as a consequence of Bernays's thoughts. Löwengard, on the other hand, who combines in his thinking liberal and conservative elements, must be considered as a precursor of a "third solution."

Löwengard left Germany in 1859 for Basel, Switzerland. He has left no public record there. We do not know whether he terminated his activities in Germany because he was dissatisfied with the sterility of Jewish life, or because he considered the reactionary tendencies in German political thinking as threatening, or because he could find allies neither in the Jewish nor in the German camp. All these motives may have been present. It is certain, however, that Löwengard's writings, hardly ever read, soon were completely forgotten. Neither the liberal nor the Orthodox rabbinate could comprehend, let alone appreciate, his reformistic traditionalism. Löwengard's writings met with a fate similar to the dream-prophecy of Hile Wechsler, although for different reasons. Both aftereffects of the influences which had emanated from the yeshiva of Nathan Ha-Kohen Adler have died away. Even Bernays is mentioned only occasionally in the literature. But the influences which derive from Schelling, intertwined with those coming from Adler, have remained alive, although they required a reformulation in a changed situation. Two of these reformulations must be mentioned, the one of Samson Raphael Hirsch and the one which is connected with the name of Franz Rosenzweig. In the present context, the difference between these two is that Schelling lives on in Hirsch only in a derived and altered way, while Rosenzweig returns to Schelling in full strength.

Samson Raphael Hirsch (1808–88), a native of Hamburg and the founder of neo-Orthodoxy, was a student of Isaac Bernays, as well as of Jakob Ettlinger, both of whom were students of Abraham Bing. In that sense, Samson Raphael Hirsch is connected in a twofold way with the tradition which stems from the yeshiva of Nathan Ha-Kohen Adler. The same holds true for Hirsch's cofighter, Rabbi Esriel Hildesheimer (1820–99), the founder of the Orthodox Berlin Rabbinical Seminary, who studied Semitic languages at the University of Berlin, 1843–45, and who very likely attended lectures of the aging Schelling. We know of both Abraham Bing and Jakob Attlinger that they counselled their students to combine the study of Torah and Talmud with secular studies, especially with attendance at universities.[65] From this combination are derived both the Hildesheimer Seminar as well as Hirsch's thesis of "Torah-im-derech-erez," although Hirsch, in terms of practice, seems to have been satisfied with secular education on the *Mittelschule* level.[66] Ettlinger's ideas carried further; he advised candidates for the rabbinate to aspire to a doctoral degree.

University studies or not, Hirsch's attitude has nothing to do with philosophical penetration. On the one hand, he would not be satisfied, as Mendelssohn was—to whom he explicitly refers—with a mere side-by-side coexistence of the Torah-true observation of *mizvot* and philosophical humanitarianism.[67] Humanitarianism should emanate from the study of Jewish moral teachings and the observation of the commandments of the Torah. On the other hand, Jewish humanitarian teachings based on the Torah and secular knowledge should be taught simultaneously, but without philosophy and Judaism being united, as they were with Bernays. Hirsch says in the last letter of *The Nineteen Letters on Judaism* that he had written the book to provide teachers the opportunity of becoming true Jews so that they could rear young souls for Judaism.[68] In doing this, he followed Bernays's example, to start with thorough instruction in the Bible and the transmission of secular knowledge, to be followed by the study of Talmud only after the completion of the thirteenth year.[69] However, Bernays neglected the organizational aspects of instruction. He lacked the intention as well as the capability to popularize the Torah. That is what Heine referred to when he wrote to his friend Moses Moser: "I have heard Bernays preach . . . none of the Jews understood him, he wants nothing and will never play a different role; but he is nevertheless a highly intellectual person."[70] Hirsch played that different role which Heine had in mind, the role of the founder of neo-Orthodoxy, without being a "highly intellectual person."

Hirsch's pragmatic attitude, which differs from Bernays's philosophical orientation, is manifested in several of his writings, especially in the *Nineteen Letters*.[71] In the nineteenth letter, Hirsch says the present time requires that we serve the daily practice and that we present Jewish teachings "immediately for life,'' while the development of scientific principles may come later. In the second letter, he explains, supposedly with reference to Bernays, that one should not learn the Torah ''for the purpose of conducting philological and antiquarian investigations, or to find support and corroboration for antediluvian and geognostic hypotheses, or in the expectation of unveiling supermundane mysteries [but] as a book given us by God that we learn from it to know ourselves and what we are and should do in our earthly existence.'' We will return to the problem, which comes to the fore at this point, of the transformation of what is religious into the moral, of the knowledge of God and his ways into a knowledge of ourselves. Obviously, Pinchas E. Rosenblüth's opinion, that Hirsch had continued along the path mapped out by Bernays, needs to be complemented by the observation that he traveled in a different direction.[72] The lack of philosophical penetration with Hirsch means more than a turn from theory to practice. It means that he turns away from the Schellingian philosophy of mythology as a stage in the development and a precondition for the coming about of revelation. It had been this comparative science of religion of Schelling which Bernays had adopted into Judaism in the *Bibel'sche Orient* and which encountered a lack of understanding and a resistance both among conventional Orthodoxy and rationalistic reform. This general opposition may have prompted Bernays to deny the authorship of the *Bibel'sche Orient* without a concomitant alteration in attitude. An essential element in the opposition becomes translucent in the accusation of S.L. Steinheim, who could see in the thesis of the *Bibel'sche Orient* nothing but ''a veritable seduction to a base service of idols.''[73] Those who criticized Bernays disregarded what Löwengard had emphasized against Ghillany, namely, that ''pure monotheism'' had arisen on the ground and soil of paganism while at the same time outgrowing paganism.

Hirsch kept away from complex religious-philosophical deliberations. In a noncommittal way, Hirsch's view and approach have some affinity to some aspects of the philosophies of Kant and Hegel. He emphasizes repeatedly, especially in his lecture on the occasion of the Schiller celebration of 1859,[74] the relationship of Judaism and ''the morally ennobling spirit of Schiller.'' In this regard, he agrees with the majority of educated German Jews in the nineteenth century and also with the Russian Jewish intelligentsia in the same period. There is no trace of a romantic inclination, as in Bernays, especially regarding the philosophy of language and the emphasis on nationality. Isaak Heinemann, in his paper on Bernays and Hirsch, arrives at the statement that Judaism for Hirsch, in contradistinction to Bernays, was not an initially oriental phenomenon, not defined in terms of nationality, not subject to historical development, but divinely inspired and oriented toward universalism.[75] Hirsch combined religious orthodoxy, in the sense of doing one's Jewish duty, with political liberalism. In contradistinction to older representatives of

Torah-true Judaism, who had taken a skeptical attitude toward the ideas of the French Revolution and the Emancipation, Hirsch welcomed the beginning of a new time in which he believed he could see "the dawn of a reawakening human existence in the human kind."[76] Hirsch was an individualist; his ideal image of a Jew was the *Jissroelmensch,* someone who personally represents Judaism in all his acts. While Bernays wanted to concretize the spirit of Judaism, Hirsch was intent on spiritualizing Israel's national existence and her institutions. Folk and land and what was Orient-like in the Bible were for Hirsch at best stages of development, ultimately obstacles on the eternal way of Judaism. Schelling had been of the opinion (in the seventh lecture of the "Philosophy of Mythology") that the very fact that the Hebrews had not "partialized" themselves as a people had become their "particularity." Hirsch liberalizes this conception when he calls the Jewish state of antiquity a mere "means for the fulfillment of Israel's spiritual calling." Israel, he writes, has received the Torah in the desert, without a land, and nothing but the observation of the divine will could be the basis and purpose of Israel's existence.[77] In other words, land and state had never been ends in themselves but means for the fulfillment of the Torah. How much more was this the case in the light of the shining horizon of the awakening of the peoples in the new time, under which, as one may say, the *Golah* had been transmuted into free citizenship.[78] Now, the Jews are in a position where they can do justice to their task, to disseminate among the peoples the divine teaching which had been entrusted to them, for the redemption of mankind.

The impulse that comes from Schelling and that has been transmitted by Bernays lives on in Hirsch in the idea of the unity of the Torah as an expression of the unity of the divine essence, and also in the literal understanding of the world of the Torah. At first glance, it would seem that the same were true about Hirsch's understanding of symbolism.[79] Actually, Hirsch does not, as Rosenblueth thinks, go farther in symbolism than Bernays;[80] rather, he deviates from the understanding of the symbolic which is found with Bernays. Symbolics shall not, as defined by Hirsch, "teach rules for the understanding of symbols," and translate, as it were, what is symbolic into the language of reason.[81] Rather, what is symbolic is a concrete sign for a spiritual reality, which one recognizes in the symbol. So, for Bernays, cultus is "the concretization of the idea" of Judaism, hence the *Shema,* the symbol for the unification of the national, and the universal, the Torah scroll, which is shown and from which one reads, the symbol of the unity of God and Israel. What is symbolic connects us with the meaning of that which it represents. Hirsch, on the other hand, pursues in symbolics the didactic purpose of deducing a moral end from that which, as he believes, is hard to understand. So, circumcision, rather than to tame savagery—as with Schelling—is taken as a sign for the obligation of the *Jissroelmensch* to adhere to the covenant with God. The sprinkling of drops of wine on Seder eve serves not the defense against the powers of evil but represents the disengagement of man from sin.[82] Prayer does not mediate the encounter of man and God but means that man should judge himself and ascend to the highest degree of moral freedom. The holy is overlaid by the moral. Dayan I. Grunfeld is right, to be sure, in emphasizing that Kabbala and mysticism were never considered as separated from Halacha,[83] except perhaps in the *Salto Mortale* of Sabbatianism and Frankism, but what is decisive in the present context is that the transmutation of the religious into the moral is not in line with Schelling's thinking. One must add that the ecstatic element in the tradition of Judaism, which had been alive and combined with Halacha in the yeshiva of Nathan Ha-Kohen Adler, in Hirsch's generation had disappeared from consciousness. In that sense, Hirsch was a "prevented mystic," as Scholem points out,[84] with the addendum that it was the spirit of the time which provided the prevention. The demanding God had become a teacher of morals. Now, Torah-true Judaism attempts to penetrate once again to an appreciation of the holy, to a philosophy of revelation in a Jewish understanding, in the synthesis of Rabbi Abraham Kook. With all that, it remains true that the organizational construction, or the institutionalization, of modern orthodoxy is Hirsch's merit and that his discipleship with Bernays has been historically effective.

Franz Rosenzweig (1886–1929) belongs to a later generation. He had nothing to do with the problems of the *Bibel'sche Orient* and the applicability to Judaism of the "Philosophy of Mythology." On the other hand, Rosenzweig consciously referred to Schelling, even if he did so in a transmutation of Schelling's Christian revelation, meaning revelation as a historical event, to a Jewish revelation, meaning the personal experience of the encounter of God and man. Rosenzweig takes his departure from the "Aelteste Systemprogramm des deutschen Idealismus,"[85] which he had discovered and analyzed, as authored by Schelling. (The manuscript is from 1796.) He proceeds from this point of departure toward the fragment "Die Weltalter" of 1814, which he considered to be the prototype of a new philosophy, and to Schelling's lectures about "Die Philosophie der Mythologie" and "Die Philosophie der Offenbarung."[86] These lectures were published from Schelling's literary estate, but their conception goes back to the first decade of the century. The total work of Schelling, which is anticipated in the "Systemprogram," begins with idealism and ends with an existentialist realism. In addition, Schelling states in "Die Weltalter" that it is his intention to complete in a dynamic way the static realism contained in the philosophy of Spinoza.[87] As against the concept of absolute being of Spinoza, Schelling poses the concept of absolute action. God knows no necessity, or determination, because a God who "had" to do something, would cease to be a God. The God whom Schelling has in mind acts in liberty. He reveals himself in the universe which is nothing else but his "swelling heart." In the "Systemprogramm," Schelling derives philosophy from poetry and poetry from mythology. In this regard, he recalls Giambattista Vico whom, however, he fails to quote. At the same time, Schelling emphasizes that the beginning must point to the goal. A philosophy turned toward what is "concrete" ("*eine sinnlich gewordene Philosophie*") ultimately was bound to create a new religion. The new religion of Schelling, in Rosenzweig's hands, became a renewed Judaism. Rosenzweig repeatedly refers to Schelling in *The Star of Redemption,* as well as in the paper "Das Neue Denken" (The New Thinking), which paper he wishes to be understood as "additional comments" to *The Star of Redemption.*[88] In a letter to his mother of 15 April 1918, Rosenzweig says that he sees in Schelling "before everything else" his "patron saint." The fact that he, Rosenzweig, was the one to discover the "Systemprogramm," appears to him as an event due to the one "who was destined for it."[89] Guided by Schelling, then, Rosenzweig takes the decisive step which leads Jewish thinking in his generation away from idealism.

In the present context, it seems remarkable that Rosenzweig in the letter to his mother declares his agreement with the final result of the philosophy of Hermann Cohen. Cohen is considered an eminent representative of Kantian idealism. Yet, Rosenzweig, in the quoted letter to his mother, refers to his sure "feeling that Cohen's religious philosophy was no plain consequence of the rest of his system," but rather "something like a new phase." Rosenzweig was convinced that Cohen in the work of his old age, *Religion of Reason According to the Sources of Judaism,*[90] had left behind the Kantianism of the rest of his system. He had postulated the recognition of the one and only God as the central experience in Judaism. He had proceeded from the world of pure thought to the realistic conception of the correlation Man-God. It should be noted that Julius Guttmann and Alexander Altmann have expressed doubts about this interpretation of Rosenzweig.[91] Alexander Altmann is of the opinion that religion neither was superordinated to Cohen's three methodic directions of cultural consciousness, logic, ethic, and esthetic, nor that these are considered to be basic to religion; rather, religion is seen as merely "affiliated" (*angegliedert*) with them by means of the concept of correlation. In a similar vein, Guttman speaks of the "incorporation" (*Eingliederung*) of the idea of God into the system of ethics. Rosenzweig admits that Cohen shares this opinion and that nothing was further from his thought than the intention to "dislocate the pillars of the system."[92] Nevertheless, he maintains that Cohen had discovered a breakthrough of experience, "the lost paradise of humanity," the living God, and that he had endeavored to confront man with God, even if only in the way of an appendix to the idealistic system. In paraphrasing Rosenzweig, one can say that in his view that which is essentially existential in Cohen has broken through the methodic precepts of idealism. At any rate, the reference to Cohen as well as to Schelling indicates the two components of Rosenzweig's thinking, the philosophic and the Jewish, both of which have in common the relation to the words of the Bible. However, the proviso is necessary that Rosenzweig turns to Cohen only at the point where Cohen's philosophical thought flows into the bed of Jewish faith.

Rosenzweig differs from Samson Raphael Hirsch in that he does not combine his belief in the sacredness of the Torah with the assumption of the literalness of revelation.[93] He is in agreement with Martin Buber in this regard. Neither does Rosenzweig see in the oral tradition a "parallel stream" to the written tradition, as Hirsch does, but rather a Torah that is "read," as against a Torah that is "written," that is, a dynamic Torah as against a fixed Torah. What connects Rosenzweig with Hirsch, especially with Hirsch's translation of the Bible, is the belief in the unity of the Torah, as against the tendency of higher biblical criticism to philologize out of the biblical text the total view of world and creation which is contained in the Torah. Rosenzweig does not admit a contradiction between the cosmological creation of the first chapter of Genesis, which leads toward man, and the anthropological creation of the second chapter, which starts with man. Neither does he believe that a fictitious "Elohist" has composed the Bible interchangeably with an equally undemonstrable "Jahvist." Rosenzweig omits at this point any reference to Schelling, whose interpretation of the Bible would have made the higher criticism superfluous, if the representatives of higher criticism had known and appreciated Schelling. In the "Philosophie der Offenbarung," Schelling points out that what is meant with *Elohim* is the immediate content of consciousness, what is meant with *Jehova* or *Jahve*, however, is the God that is recognized as the true God and called by name.[94] The *Elohim* of Creation, to whom Schelling concedes a polytheistic plural, is called by his name *Jehova* whereby unity in plurality is postulated. However, Rosenzweig refers to Schelling's essay "Die Weltalter." In analogy to the "Philosophie der Offenbarung," Schelling contrasts in "Die Weltalter" creation (*Schöpfung*) as a subconscious "bringing forth in the beginning," to making (*Machen*) as a conscious act in which speech is indicated.[95] The Lord speaks to Moses, the "spoken word of God" pervades the Bible.[96] In speech, that is, in encounter, Cohen's Man-God correlation and Buber's I-Thou relationship are expressed, while none of these are present in initial Creation.[97] In other words, we are confronted in speech with a sequence of events, not with a separation in thought. In a formal way, Schelling, as well as Rosenzweig, are following biblical precedent in that they interpret from the meaning of words and from their roots. In words, meanings are contained which are revealed not by means of logic, but through philology.

Schelling puts the following guiding sentences at the beginning of the fragment "Die Weltalter": "We know the past, we recognize the present, we divine the future. What we know is narrated, what we recognize is described, what we divine is prophesied."[98] It was Schelling's intention to narrate, that is, to render as a story "the beginnings of life" and thereby to understand the present as well as to assay the direction which the present may take. It should be observed at this point that narration points toward mythology because *mythos* in Greek means narration—*vera narratio,* according to Vico—in the sense of a legend which carries us back to the events of the beginning and which illuminates from there the problems with which we are confronted. Schelling's intention remained unfulfilled. Schelling imagined "Die Weltalter" to be "some kind of preparation for the objective, descriptive science which was to come," because he did not believe that his own time was ready for the task.[99] Rosenzweig continued and complemented Schelling's theme in his own way in the second part of *The Star of Redemption.* "God spoke" is the fulfillment. "God created" is the beginning.[100] Rosenzweig explains that the initial words which cannot be heard will become audible as real words in living speech. "Real speech confronts us in the place of speech prior to speech." When Schelling predicts that all future philosophy will be "narrating," he intends to indicate, as Rosenzweig comments in a letter to Rudolf Ehrenberg, "the autobiographical confession" which implies an act of speech and an expected reply, that is, a dialogic encounter.[101] In a narrating philosophy— and consequently in a narrating sociology—we wish to know how everything really has come to pass, how events present themselves in time and place, not how that which has occurred is being organized in a system of concepts, either logically or dialectically. A "philosophy of experience" must start when a negative philosophy with its thought constructs grinds to a halt.[102] Accordingly, Judaism is a fact, Christianity an event, and none of these is exhausted in a construction of thought. Conceptual thinking, in Schelling's terms "negative philosophy," is necessary as a precondition, but does not reach up to existential being and to action which is realized in the state of being; and being and action are accessible only to *post festum* recognition. Consequently, thought and faith are two sides of one and the same thing, in Schelling's terms, an "identity"; however, it should be added that thought is overarched by faith. Rosenzweig replaced Schelling's twofold division of thought and faith with a threefold division of thought, faith, and faithful thought, as in a Hegelian sequence of thesis, antithesis and synthesis, Yet, the priority of being before thinking is preserved.[103] The result is a "philosophizing theology," as Buber has emphasized in a paper on Rosenzweig which also refers to Schelling.[104] In a comparative historical view, one can say that Schelling takes his departure from the Kabbala while Rosenzweig, by means of his encounter with Buber, is led on to Hassidism. Hassidism, to be sure, is a narrating theology. What is told by the Hassidic Rebbes and about the Rebbes is designed to concretize the holy and to guide devotion to the deeds of the Beginning.

Rosenzweig has reintroduced Schelling into Jewish thinking. As a student of the historian Friedrich Meinecke, he has done this from a liberal and Hegelian point of departure, from which he turned to an existentialist and traditionalist mode of expression. He has translated the rhapsodic language of the Siddur (daily prayerbook) in a hymnic philosophy of a Schellingian cast. One does not know what would have been if Rosenzweig's premature death and the destruction of the Jewish community in Germany had not rendered the reintroduction into a conclusion. But what once began, lives on. To be sure, Rosenzweig's philosophy, which to him was a perfected whole, cannot be the last word for posterity. Similarly, Hirsch's achievement as an organizer stands in need of revision. Indeed, Schelling's own thought requires a comment. Schelling was near to the sources of religious inspiration and the religious experience of reality. We have traveled far from there. We cannot share Schelling's motivation, nor can we speak his language, but we can permit ourselves to be guided by his language and by the way he gave expression to it. We can listen where experience is lacking. It is here that the present contribution finds its place. Our task is the redefinition of Jewish experience. If one contemplates at the end of our investigation both interpenetrating lines, the one from Nathan Ha-Kohen Adler, his students, and the students of his students, and their being influenced by Schelling, and the one leading from Schelling across the generations to Rosenzweig, one is driven to the conclusion that the "new thinking" has not yet caught on, that the "second Emancipation" has not been finished, that the "third solution," which would be traditionalistic and reformistic at the same time, has not been found. To formulate a faithful philosophy of Judaism, which might unite in a new combination the elements which are available, remains a task for us and for those who come after us.

1981

Notes

1. Eva Frank passed away suddenly during an investigation by the governor of Mainz, leaving behind debts in the amount of three million guilders. The Frankists believed in a kabbalistic trinity consisting of the highest cause (*der heilige Uralte*), the God Israel's (*der heilige König*) and the female complementation (*Shechina*). The last-named aspect provided an opportunity for sexual orgies. Compare Heinrich Graetz, "Frank und die Frankisten—eine Sektengeschichte aus der letzten Hälfte des vorigen Jahrhunderts" in *Jahresbericht des Jüdisch-*

theologischen Seminars (Breslau, 1868), pp. 1–90; compare further the more extended analytic study of Gershom G. Scholem, "Die Metamorphose des häretischen Messianismus der Sabbatianer in religiösen Nihilismus im 18. Jahrhundert" in *Judaica*, 3: 198-217.

2. Markus Horowitz, *Frankfurter Rabbinen—Ein Beitrag zur Geschichte der Israelitischen Kultusgemeinde in Frankfurt am Main* (Jerusalem, 1969), p. 213f.; J. Unna, *Guardians of our Heritage,* ed. L. Jung, (1958) pp. 167-85; *Encyclopaedia Judaica*, vol. 12, pp. 284-85.

3. Gershom G. Scholem, "Zur Literatur der letzten Kabbalisten in Deutschland" in *Zwei Welten—Siegfried Moses zum fünfundsiebzigsten Geburtstag* (Tel Aviv, 1962), pp. 359-76; "Die letzten Kabbalisten in Deutschland" in *Judaica*, pp. 218–46; also Gershom G. Scholem, *Kabbalah* (New York, 1974), p. 85f.

4. Stefan Löwengart, *Aus der Geschichte meiner Familie—Die Familie Bing—Der Familienname Löwengart*, 1973, manuscript with literature, Nationalbibliothek, Jerusalem; Seligmann Baer Bamberger, *Geschichte der Rabbiner der Stadt und des Bezirkes Würzburg* (Wansbeck, 1905). Seligmann Baer Bamberger, although not a student of Abraham Bing, was connected with the kabbalistic tradition through his brother-in-law, Rabbi Seckel Wormser, district rabbi in Fulda, who, in turn, was a cousin of Rabbi Seckel Loeb Wormser, the famous Baal-Shem of Michelstadt. S. Esh, ed., *The Bamberger Family, the Descendants of Rabbi Seligmann Baer Bamberger, the "Würzburger Rav"* (Jerusalem, 1979).

5. Berthold Strauss, *The Rosenbaums of Zell—A Study of a Family* (London, 1962).

6. Jaschar Milo Davar aka (Reb Hile Wechsler), title unknown (Würzburg, 5640–1880). For a derivation of the pseudonym, see Scholem, *Zwei Welten*, p. 367. An investigation according to the principles of the psychoanalysis of Jung is contained in James Kirsch, *The Reluctant Prophet* (Los Angeles, 1974).

7. Compare Abraham Bartura, *Jissu harim shalom—Mikhtevi Massa' Va-'Aliyah, 1834–36* (Jerusalem, n.d.) and "Die Heimkehr des Jerusalemiten Eliezer Bergmann," *Pessach Festschrift der Israelitischen Religionsgemeinschaft Württembergs* (April 1973): 4–10.

8. Beer A. Bing introduced comedy into Hebrew literature as well as a realistic style and a pastoral description, which may have had some influence on Mapu. Around the same time, Salomon Ha-Kohen (1772–1845) published a drama, *Amal-ve-Thuerza* (Roedelheim, 1812), wherein, somewhat farther-reaching than Bing, he propagated a life of moral purity and rural labor. See Chaim Shapira, *Toledot ha-Sifrut ha-Ivrith ha-Hadasha* (History of Modern Hebrew Literature), chap. 1: "Sifrut ha-Haskala be-Merkaz Germania 1784–1829" (Enlightenment Literature in Central Germany) (Reprint Massada, Tel Aviv), pp. 534–50.

9. According to a memorandum of Chief Rabbi Abraham Bing and a majority decision of the Israelitische Kreissynode in Würzburg (1836), reported in *Sulamit*, 1, no. 8, 372–81.

10. Compare forward of the editor of Schelling's works (Schelling's son) in the 4th and 6th vols. of Schelling's works in the Schroeter edition.

11. Joseph Prijs, *Die Familie Hirsch auf Gereuth* (Munich, 1931).

12. Michael Wormser, *Das Leben und Wirken des in Michelstadt verstorbenen Rabbiners Seckel Loeb Wormser* (Offenbach, 1953), p. 39. The Baal-Shem of Michelstadt was a renowned representative of "practical Kabbala." His advice and

help were sought by many poor, ill, depressed, and disturbed people, Jews as well as Christians. A fine characterization is found in the paper by Eli Straus, "Eine Ahnentafel unserer Familie" in *Bulletin des Leo Baeck Instituts*, 21, 6. Jahrg., 1963, 52-66.

13. Hans Bach, "Bernays und Schelling—Eine unbekannte Tagebuchaufzeichnung," *Zeitschrift für Religions-und Geistesgeschichte*, 25; no. 4 (1973): 336–40.

14. *Der Bibel'sche Orient—Eine Zeitschrift in zwanglosen Heften*, vols. 1, 2 (Munich, 1821). The first announcement bears the date of 20 May 1820.

15. Hans Bach, "Der Bibel'sche Orient und sein Verfasser," *Zeitschrift für die Geschichte der Juden in Deutschland* [ZGJD], 7 (1937): 14-45. See also by same author, "Isaac Bernays," *Monatschrift für Geschichte und Wissenschaft des Judentums* [MGWJ], 83 (1939): 541–47.

16. Heinrich Graetz, *Geschichte der Juden, vom Beginn der Mendelssohnschen Zeit (1730) bis in die neueste Zeit*, vol. 11, chap. 9, 2d ed. (Leipzig, 1900; 1st ed. 1870), pp. 399-404.

17. The earliest lectures of Schelling about the philosophy of mythology go back to the time when the fragment "Die Weltalter" was written, that is, to the years 1811–15, as may be concluded from the foreword of the editor to vols. 4 and 6 of Schelling's collected works. See *Friedrich Wilhelm Joseph von Schellings Samtliche Werke*, ed. Manfred Schroeter (Munich, 1954–60). I refer chiefly to lectures 1–10 of the "Philosophy of Mythology" (in vol. 6), especially to the grandiose seventh lecture; and to the fragment "Die Weltalter" (in vol. 4, *Schriften zur Philosophie der Freiheit*, pp. 571–720); finally, to the "Philosophy of Revelation" (vol. 6, pt. 1, ninth lecture, pp. 176–97, and pt. 2, twenty-ninth lecture, pp. 511–43) and to the *Stuttgarter Privatvorlesungen*. As a rule I am quoting Schroeter, except where the Schroeter volume was not available.

18. Schelling, "Philosophy of Mythology," vol. 6, lecture 7, pp. 146–76.

19. Schelling, "Philosophy of Revelation," vol. 6, lecture 29, p. 514; "Die Weltalter," vol. 4, p. 278. The school of higher biblical criticism could have learned from Schelling.

20. "Die Weltalter," vol. 4, p. 636.

21. Literal quotations from the *Bibel'sche Orient* are documented in the text.

22. In another passage, Bernays turns against the "fashionably cool waters" of a religion of reason which, as he says, rests "on the dogmatic soil of isolated statements." In contradistinction, he wishes to present the "historically concrete and lively way in which the acting revelation unfolds."

23. Max Wiener, *Jüdische Religion im Zeitalter der Emanzipation* (Berlin, 1933), pp. 111–18.

24. I have emphasized in a number of papers that no unified German Jewish community existed prior to 1871. Instead, one must differentiate between southwest-German, northeast-German and southeast-German (Bohemian-Austrian) Jewries. "A Regional Approach to German-Jewish History," *Jewish Social Studies*, 5, no. 3, (1943): 211–24; "Two Maps on German-Jewish History," *Chicago Jewish Forum*, 2, no. 1 (Fall 1943): 58-65; "The Three Regions of German-Jewish History," *Chicago Jewish Forum, Jubilee Volume dedicated to Curt C. Silberman*, eds. Herbert A. Strauss and Hanns G. Reissner (New York, 1969) pp. 1-14.

25. The documentation of the life of Hirsch Maier Löwengard contains question marks. The best information is contained in A. Taenzer, *Die Geschichte der*

Juden in Jebenhausen und Göppingen (Stuttgart, 1927), pp. 163-64 and in S. Winniger, *Grosse Jüdische Nationalbibliographie,* vol. 4 (Czernowitz, 1925– 26), pp. 166–67. Löwengard, who also used the pen names "Salem" and "Juda Leon," was born on 3 March 1813 in Rexingen, Neckarkreis (Württemberg), as son of the peddler Raphael Hirsch Löwengard and Judith, née Levi. He passed away on 12 May 1886 in Basel. It is reported that he was buried in the Israel- itischer Zentralfriedhof in Hegenheim, Alsace, but neither his tombstone nor entries with the city of Basel or the Jewish community in Basel could be found. Two sisters were married in Bischheim aux Saum near Strassburg. Taenzer and Winniger comment on Löwengard's stay in Mainz and Basel, but there is no trace of it in the *Israelit.* It is reported that Löwengard had worked in the editorial office of the *Israelit.* It is worthy of note, moreover, that Rabbi Markus Leh- mann, the editor of the *Israelit,* designates himself as a student of Kabbala, although, as Scholem (*Judaica,* 3, pp. 218–46) comments, nothing points to- ward the Kabbala in Lehman's writings.

26. Alexander Elsaesser, *Gabriel Adler, weiland Bezirksrabbiner in Oberdorf, ein Lichtbild* (Esslingen, 1860). Gabriel Adler was rabbi in Mühringen, 1811–35, then rabbi in Oberdorf, 1835–60. Adler was related to the family of Gabriel Riesser through his wife, who was the daughter of Rabbi Pinchas Katzenellen- bogen in Oettingen. Many young students of Judaism assembled around Gabriel Adler in Mühringen when the Yeshiva in Hechingen began to decline after the death of Rabbi Loeb Aach (1820). Among these students were Berthold Auer- bach and Hirsch Maier Löwengard, who studied at the same time. My great- grandfather, Julius Levi (Mühringen), was a friend of Berthold Auerbach and likewise a student of Gabriel Adler. About Gabriel Adler's Talmud school, in which he may have cooperated with the Rabbinatsverweser David Dispeker in Hechingen, see also the "Historisch topographische Beschreibung de Rabbin- atsbezirks Mühringen" by the district rabbi, Dr. M. Silberstein, 22 December 1875, manuscript, Hessisches Hauptstaatsarchiv, Abt. No. 1040/4. Scarce in- formation is contained in *Zur Geschichte der Juden in Hechingen* (Nach den Urkunden und Mitteilungen des Gemeindevorstehers Isaac Levi und des Rab- biners Fr. Samuel Mayer dargestellt, katalog vol. 1; New York: Leo Baeck Institute, n.d.). The Yeshiva in Hechingen was dissolved 1850, after the spon- soring family Kaulla had moved away.

27. Nathan Marcus Adler, after 1831 Landesrabbiner in Hannover, was called to London, 1845, as chief rabbi of the British Empire. The father, Marcus (Mor- decai) Adler, was Rabbinatsverweser (*Stiftsrabbiner*) for the "Land Hannover," 1802–29.

28. Gershom G. Scholem, *Major Trends in Jewish Mysticism* (New York, 1961), pp. 186–204 et passim.

29. Juda Leon, aka Löwengard *Beiträge zur Kritik der Reformbestrebungen in der Synagoge* (Stuttgart, 1841), p. 7.

30. Tübingen, 1842.

31. *Protokolle und Aktenstuecke der zweiten Rabbinerversammlung,* abgehalten in Frankfurt am Main vom 15. bis 28. Juli 1845 (Frankfurt am Main, 1845), pp. 16, 54, 106, 133, 147. *Protokolle der dritten Versammlung deutscher Rabbiner,* abgehalten zu Breslau vom 13. bis 24. Juli 1846 (Breslau, 1847), 279–285.

32. *Allgemeine Zeitung des Judentums,* No. 15v. 9.4.1842.

33. Löwengard, *Jehova,* p. 25.

34. Ibid., p. 38.

35. The authors quoted by Löwengard are Protestant theologians and orientalists. Johann Gottfried Eichhorn (1752-1827), professor of Oriental languages and biblical exegesis in Goettingen, is considered the initiator of biblical criticism. Georg Heinrich August von Ewald (1803–75), Eichhorn's successor in Goettingen, was the author of a Hebrew grammar and of a critical *History of the People of Israel*. Ernst Wilhelm Hengstenberg (1802–69), professor of theology in Basel and Berlin, represents a different opinion about the topic. Karl Peter Wilhelm Gramberg (1797–1830) was the author of a *Critical History of the Religious Ideas of the Old Testament*. Heinrich Friedrich Wilhelm Gesenius (1786–1842), professor of Orientalistic studies and Old Testament in Halle, known as the author Gesenius-Buhl, (*Hebrew and Aramaic Dictionary of the Old Testament*), is considered only "moderately" critical by Löwengard. Contrary to Löwengard, Franz Rosenzweig (*Kleinere Schriften*, p. 135) has recognized Gesenius's achievement, which has not been matched by any Jewish scholar.

36. Löwengard, p. 29.

37. Ibid., pp. 39–43.

38. The memorandum, as well as the letter of Schelling to King Max II, are published in my paper, "Friedrich Wilhelm Schelling und die Judenemanzipation," *Zeitschrift für Bayerische Landesgeschichte*, vol. 37, no. 2, (1974): 614–25. Regrettably, the names of the inscribed listeners at Schelling's lectures are no more to be found in the files of the University of Munich.

39. Schelling, "Philosophy of Revelation," *Werke*, vol. 6, lecture 29, pp. 511–43.

40. Ibid., p. 538.

41. Ibid., p. 540f.

42. Ibid., p. 543.

43. Löwengard, p. 7f.

44. Georg Friedrich Creuzer (1771-1858), German philologist and anthropologist. His chief work is *Symbolik und Mythologie der alten Völker, besonders der Griechen* (1810–12).

45. Schellling, "Philosophy of Revelation," *Werke*, vol. 6, pp. 135–40, about "Das Heidnische in der mosaischen Gesetzgebung"; also concerning the "Inclination toward Idolatry in Israel" (p. 535).

46. Schelling postulated a "narrating philosophy" in the foreword to the fragment "Die Weltalter."

47. Karl Jaspers, *Schelling—Grösse und Verhängnis* (Munich, 1955), p. 265.

48. Schelling's "Philosophy of Revelation," *Werke*, vol. 6, lecture 1, pp. 3–17.

49. Ernst Benz, *Die christliche Kabbala—Ein Stiefkind der Theologie* (Zürich and Stuttgart, 1958); Gershom G. Scholem, "Die Entstehung der Kabbala von Reuchlin bis zur Gegenwart," *Judaica*, III (Frankfurt, 1973), 247-263. Among newer writers, Scholem mentions Brucker, Knorr von Rosenroth, and Molitor, but not Oetinger. For Oetinger refer to Rainer Heinze, *Bengel und Oetinger als Vorlaeufer des deutschen Idealismus* (Diss. Münster, 1969). Heinze emphasizes that Bengel, Oetinger, and even Schelling disclaim a system of knowledge and rely rather on the course of history. Only in the end of time, which all three thinkers believe to be near, will knowledge be completed and a true system become possible. One receives information concerning the inclusion of Schelling within such a frame of the history of thought by Wilhelm August Schulze, "Schelling und die Kabbala," *Judaica*, 13 (Zürich, 1957), 65-99, 143-170, 210-232 and Ernst Benz, *Schellings schwäbisches Geistesahnen* (Zürich, 1960). One does not need to identify with the details of Schulze's and Benz's line of

thinking to recognize that Schelling belongs among those influenced by the Christian Kabbala; and perhaps his inability to complete his philosophical system combines with a high expectation of a coming end-of-time of wisdom and understanding and possibly with his disappointment that it had not come to pass.

50. Concerning Oetinger's contact with the Frankfurt Jewish Kabbalist, Koppel Hecht, see note 58. It appears that Oetinger was acquainted with the kabbalistic concepts of *Tsimtsum* and *Shevirath-ha-Kelim*; Heinze, p. 59f.; Benz, *Schellings schwäbische Geistesahnen*, p. 278. Christian Knorr von Rosenroth's *Cabbala Denudata*, 2 vols., appeared in Solzbach, 1677 and in Frankfurt am Main, 1684.

51. G. L. Plitt, *Aus Schellings Leben. In Briefen*, 3 vols. (Leipzig, 1869-70); vol. 1, p. 373; vol. 2, pp. 101, 179.

52. Franz Joseph Molitor, *Philosophie der Geschichte oder über die Tradition*, 4 vols. (Münster, 1827–55). In the dedication of the second volume to King Ludwig i of Bavaria, Molitor expresses the expectation that his work should direct "the attention of noble minds to the treasures of Judaism." Compare Gershom G. Scholem, "Die letzten Kabbalisten in Deutschland," *Judaica*, 3, p. 219. About E. J. Hirschfeld, see Gershom G. Scholem, "Ein verschollener Jüdischer Mystiker der Aufklärungszeit," *Leo Baeck Year Book*, vol 7, (1962), pp. 247–68.

53. David Baumgardt, *Franz von Baader und die philosophische Romantik* (Halle, 1927), pp. 34-37 et passim.

54. Baumgardt, pp. 41, 200; Plitt, vol. 2 pp. 122, 134, 160f., 251f.

55. Baumgardt, pp. 37, 351.

56. Gershom G. Scholem's *Major Trends in Jewish Mysticism* (New York, 1961), p. 265f.; for the theory of contraction (*Tsimtsum*), see ibid., 260f; for the trichotomic psychology (*neshamah-nefeshruach*), see ibid., 240f. Schelling's knowledge of kabbalistic thinking is in all likelihood mediated by the Christian Kabbala and is not grounded in his knowledge of rabbinic literature.

57. Schelling, "Philosophy of Revelation," *Werke*, vol. 6, lecture 9, p. 176f.; "Die Weltalter," pp. 592, 594, 597f.; "Stuttgarter Privatvorlesungen," vol. 4, p. 324f.; Joseph A. Bracken, *Freiheit und Kausalität bei Schelling* (Freiburg and Munich, 1972), p. 28f.

58. Schelling, "Stuttgarter Privatvorlesungen" (1810), *Werke*, vol. 4, p. 453f. Jürgen Habermas, in an analytic and informative essay, draws attention to Schelling's contention that the liberation of man through the state was an illusion because the idea of a perfectly just order could result in nothing else but the worst kind of despotism. The state which attempted to treat spiritual phenomena with physical means was the image of a "fallen humanity." Jürgen Habermas, "Dialektischer Idealismus im Übergang zum Materialismus—Geschichtsphilosophische Folgerungen aus Schellings Idee einer Contraction Gottes," in his *Theorie und Praxis* (Frankfurt Sahrkanys, 1972), pp. 172–227. Compare Schelling, "Philosophical Introduction to the Philosophy of Mythology, *Werke* vol. 5, lecture 23, pp. 716–34. However, although Schelling contrasts state and religion, he nevertheless considers the state to be a precondition of spiritual life, differing in this regard from Marx.

59. Schelling, "Stuttgarter Privatvorlesungen," *Werke*, vol. 4, p. 321f. Compare Schelling, vol. 8, p. 74. More directly corresponding to the concept of *Tsimtsum*

is the passus in "Die Weltalter," p. 692, according to which God has the power "to retreat, to return for a while to the state of involution." *Tsimtsum* refers both to God's freedom to retreat and to the freedom of man, which becomes possible through God's contraction. Compare note 56.

60. The principle of freedom comes to the fore at various passages with Schelling, e.g., in "Weltalter," pp. 585-86, 679, 682 and in lecture 24 of the "Philosophy of Revelation." About the difference between Hegel and Schelling in the evaluation of the principle of freedom, compare Ernst Benz, *Schellings schwäbische Geistesahnen*, p. 282.

61. These interrelationships are pointed out by Wilhelm August Schulze, "Schelling und die Kabbala," *Judaica*, vol 13, pp. 82, 87, 158, especially concerning the teaching of the threefold life of the spirit and the theory of contraction. The Frankfurt kabbalist Koppel Hecht explained to Oetinger that one could sooner learn kabbalistic thinking from Boehme than from the Zohar, as reported by Oetinger in his autobiography. Compare Friedrich Christian Oetinger, *Selbstbiographie*, ed. by Hamberger (1846). p. 46 and the reference to it in Ernst Benz, *Die christliche Kabbala* and in Gershom G. Scholem, *Major Trends in Jewish Mysticism*, pp. 238, 405.

62. "Die Weltalter," Schelling, *Werke*, vol. 4, p. 647, about "The Disregard and neglect of the Old Testament."

63. Gershom G. Scholem, "Wider den Mythos vom deutsch-jüdischen Gespräch," "Noch einmal: das deutsch-juedische Gespraech," "Juden und Deutsche," *Judaica* 2 (Frankfurt am Main., 1970), pp. 7-11, 12-19, 20–46.

64. See note 13.

65. We are obliged for this important information to verbatim transmission. Concerning Ettlinger, to Rabbi Dr. M. Auerbach (Halberstadt and Tel Aviv); concerning Bing, to Abraham Bartura (Jerusalem), a descendant of Eliezer Bergmann. Bing's comment that it was of no use for candidates for the rabbinate—as in the case of candidates for the ministry—"to have regularly attended high schools and to have mastered the Latin and Greek languages," as reported in H. and S. Bamberger, *Geschichte der Rabbiner der Stadt und Bezirks Würzburg* (Würzburg, 1906), p. 86f., does not stand against Bartura's report. Latin and Greek seemed superfluous, but not philosophy and geography, as in the cases of Bernays and Schwarz. It is also possible that Bing wanted to avoid dependence on conditions imposed by the government, as far as the rabbinical office was concerned. It is certain that Bernays studied at the University of Würzburg, with Bing's approval. The position of Ettlinger is reported in Pinchas E. Rosenblueth's paper, "Samson Raphael Hirsch—Sein Denken und Wirken," in *Das Judentum in der deutschen Umwelt 1800-1850*, eds. Hans Liebeschuetz and Arnold Paucker (Tuebingen, 1977), pp. 203–25, note 27. Concerning Hildesheimer, compare David Ellenson, "Response by Modern Orthodoxy to Jewish Religious Pluralism: The Case of Esriel Hildesheimer," *Tradition*, 17, no. 4 (Spring 1979): 74–89. About the controversy Hirsch-Hildesheimer, on the one hand, and Seligmann Baer Bamberger, on the other hand, compare Herman Schwab, *The History of Orthodox Jewry in Germany*, trans. Irene Birnbaum (London, 1950), chap. 9. Ettlinger as well as Bernays, both students of Abraham Bing, combined talmudic scholarship with a wide knowledge of secular literature.

66. Rosenblueth, p. 317. It seems irrelevant at this point that Hirsch spoke about a course of education which combines the study of the Torah with general knowledge only after the formation of the Separatgemeinde in Frankfurt am Main 1853. Earlier or later formuated, Hirsch's educational philosophy was directed toward general rather than scholarly knowledge. Moreover, according to Hirsch, Jewish and secular knowledge should be cultivated simultaneously, which means that they were to remain separate entities, while with Bernays Judaism and philosophy interpenetrate. Hirsch's position is to be found in *Gesammelte Schriften* (Frankfurt am Main, 1925), vol. 1, p. 278f.; vol. 2, p. 449f.

67. Samson Raphael Hirsch, *Neunzehn Briefe über Judentum* (Frankfurt am Main, 1911), 18th letter, pp. 101–02. I am quoting according to the German original, but compare Samson Raphael Hirsch, *The Nineteen Letters* ed. Jacob Breuer (Jerusalem and New York, 5729–1969).

68. Samson Raphael Hirsch, *Neunzehn Briefe,* 19th letter, p. 137. Compare I. Grunfeld, *Choreb* (London, 1962), introduction.

69. Hans Bach, *Jacob Bernays—Ein Beitrag zur Emanzipationsgeschichte der Juden und zur Geschichte des deutschen Geistes im neunzehnten Jahrhundert* (Tübingen, 1974), p. 22; Isaac Heinemann, "The Relationship between S. R. Hirsch and his Teacher, Isaak Bernays" (in Hebrew), *Zion* (1951), p. 56; Rosenblueth, p. 300.

70. *Heinrich Heines Briefwechsel,* ed. Friedrich Hirt, vol. 1. (Mainz, 1950), p. 103; Letter to Moses Moser of 23.8.1823.

71. Heinmann's assertion (*Zion,* 1951, pp. 26–27) that Bernays's scholarly interests deviate in content and spirit from the *Bibel'sche Orient* and, consequently, that one could not ascribe to him the authorship of the *Bibel'sche Orient,* is erroneous. Moses Mendelssohn reports in his paper "Etwas über des sel. Bernays Synagogalvorträge" (*Orient,* 1849, no. 50, p. 218f.) that Bernays had occupied himself with Talmud, exegesis and Kabbala, without, however, any further reference to philosophy, and that he had lectured "with firmly closed eyes," that is, in total absorption and "with a candor that delighted the expert and aroused fear in the blind orthodox." Bernays's combination of strict ritual, mystic belief, and free interpretation had stayed with him throughout life. Hans Bach (*ZGJD,* pp. 44–45) arrives at the same judgment. Hirsch maintained the ritual, but gave faith and interpretation a didactic turn.

72. Rosenblueth, pp. 300–01.

73. See *Allgemeine Zeitung des Judentums,* no. 38f. 17 September and 24 September 1842, pp. 562–69. Compare Steinheim at a different note (note 32) as well as Abraham Geiger's related critique, quoted by Hans Bach, *ZGJD,* p. 30.

74. Samson Raphael Hirsch, "Worte, gesprochen bei der Schillerfeier 1859," *Gesammelte Schriften,* vol. 6 (Frankfurt am Main, 1912), pp. 309–321.

75. Heinemann, *Zion* (1951), p. 11.

76. *Neunzehn Briefe,* letter 16, pp. 87, 89.

77. *Neunzehn Briefe,* letter 8, p. 59; *Gesammelte Schriften,* vol. 3, p. 503.

78. Rosenblueth, p. 319; also Max Wiener is of the opinion that Hirsch "theoretically in no way remains behind the notions of radical liberalism" and that nothing in his symbolism carries beyond the moral. Max Wiener, *Jüdische Religion im Zeitalter der Emanzipation* (Berlin, 1933), pp. 72, 75.

79. *Gesammelte Schriften,* vol. 3: 212–447; Compare *Timeless Torah—Anthology of the Writings of Samson Raphael Hirsch* (New York, 1957), pp. 303-420.

80. Rosenblueth, p. 311.

81. *Gesammelte Schriften,* vol. 3: 214.

82. Quoted according to *Die Pessach Haggada,* ed. E.D. Goldschmidt (Berlin, 1937), p. 23.

83. Samson Raphael Hirsch, *Horeb—A Philosophy of Jewish Law and Observances,* trans. and intro. by Dayan I. Grunfeld (London, 1962), introduction.

84. Gershom G. Scholem, *Judaica,* I, "Zur Neuaflage des Stern der Erlösung" (Frankfurt am Main, 1953), pp. 226–35.

85. Franz Rosenzweig, *Kleinere Schriften* (Berlin, 1957), pp. 230–77.

86. Schelling, vols. 4, 6 (see note 17).

87. Schelling, vol. 4, p. 716f.

88. Franz Rosenzweig, *Der Stern der Erlösung* (Frankfurt am Main, 1921); in English, *The Star of Redemption,* trans. William W. Hallo (New York, 1970). "Das Neue Denken," in Rosenzweig, pp. 273–393. The influence of Schelling's philosophy on the formation of Rosenzweig's "New Thinking" is described and explained in the analytic study of Else Freund, *Die Existenxphilosophie Franz Rosenzweigs* (Hamburg, 1959), pp. 12–42.

89. Franz Rosenzweig, *Briefe,* ed. Edith Rosenzweig (Berlin, 1935), p. 299.

90. Hermann Cohen, *Religion der Vernunft aus der Quellen des Judentums* (Frankfurt am Main, 1919); Rosenzweig, "Einleitung in die Akademieausgabe der jüdischen Schriften Herman Cohens," in *Kleinere Schriften,* p. 331f.

91. Julius Guttmann, *Die Philosophie des Judentums* (Munich, 1933), p. 354ff; Alexander Altmann, "Hermann Cohens Begriff der Korrelation," in *Zwei Welten—Siegfried Moses zum fünfundsiebzigsten Geburtstag* (Tel Aviv, 1962), pp. 377–99.

92. Rosenzweig, "Herman Cohens Nachlasswerk," in *Kleinere Schriften,* p. 295.

93. Rosenzweig's letter to Jakob Rosenheim, *Briefe,* p. 584; *Kleinere Schriften,* p. 128f.

94. Schelling, "Philosophie der Offenbarung," vol. 2, lecture, 29, p. 514f.

95. Schelling, "Die Weltalter," *Werke,* vol. 4, pp. 688f., 707f.

96. Schelling, vol. 3, "Philosophie der Kunst" (1802), p. 503.

97. Martin Buber, *Ich und Du* (Leipzig, 1923), especially p. 25ff. The baseword *I—Thou,* in contradistinction to the isolated *I,* is manifested in the life of the child to whom consciousness of Self is brought from the outside. The human relation, shown in the child, mirrors the relation Man-God.

98. Schelling, "Die Weltalter," *Werke,* vol. 4, p. 571.

99. Schelling, *Werke,* vol. 8, p. 206.

100. Rosenzweig, *Der Stern der Erlösung,* pp. 139–42, 143–44, 185, 301 et passim.

101. Rosenzweig, *Briefe* (letter of 28 May 1917), p. 208. Paul Tillich emphasizes that Schelling has discovered "the category of encounter long before the contemporary Jewish and Christian philosophers of encounter." Paul Tillich, "Schelling und die Anfänge des existentiellen Protestes," in *Zeitschrift für philosophische Forschung,* vol. 9 (1955), pp. 197–208.

102. Rosenzweig, "Das Neue Denken," *Kleinere Schriften,* pp. 373–99, especially pp. 379, 383, 386–87.

103. The development from the twofold thinking of Schelling to the threefold model of Rosenzweig is analyzed in Else Freund, *Die Existenzphilosophie Franz Rosenzweigs* (Hamburg, 1959), pp. 73–79.

104. Martin Buber, "Franz Rosenzweig," in *Hinweise* (Zürich, 1952), pp. 244–51. Buber's paper is from 1930. Buber mentions Schelling's fragment, "Die Weltalter," as a precondition for Rosenzweig's conception of a new direction in Ju-

daism, as contained in the paper "Das neue Denken," *Kleinere Schriften,* pp. 373–409. Buber has lectured on Jakob Boehme prior to 1900, as Hans Kohn— *Martin Buber—Sein Werk und seine Zeit* (Koeln, 1961), p. 23—reports, but he gained acquaintance with Schelling very probably much later. Rosenzweig's paper "Das älteste Systemprogram" was written in 1914.

Index